Professional

from 35mm to large format

Landscape and Environmental Photography

Professional from 35mm to large format

Landscape and Environmental Photography

Mark Lucock

Guild of Master Craftsman Publications

First published 2003 by
Guild of Master Craftsman Publications Ltd,
166 High Street, Lewes,
East Sussex, BN7 1XN

ISBN 1 86108 315 7

A catalogue record of this book is available from the British Library.

Cover and book design by Danny McBride

Typeface: Swiss, Berkeley and Futura

Colour origination by Universal Graphics in Singapore

Printed and bound by CT Printing in Hong Kong

Dedication

This book is dedicated to the memory of my mother, Anna Martha Marie Lucock, who passed away the week this project was commissioned.

Acknowledgments

Nature and landscape photography is an absorbing passion that has taken me to some of the world's most fascinating places. While such destinations have greatly enriched my experience and understanding of life, they would be nothing without someone to share the moment with. I would therefore like to acknowledge the important contribution made by my wife, Jill, who has shared most of my travel experiences, and who is always there to support me 100%. I would also like to acknowledge the expertise of James Evans and Kylie Johnston whose exacting editorial skills have bought this book to fruition, and to thank Mark, John and everybody at CC Imaging Ltd in Leeds for turning out fantastic Velvia transparencies every time.

Contents

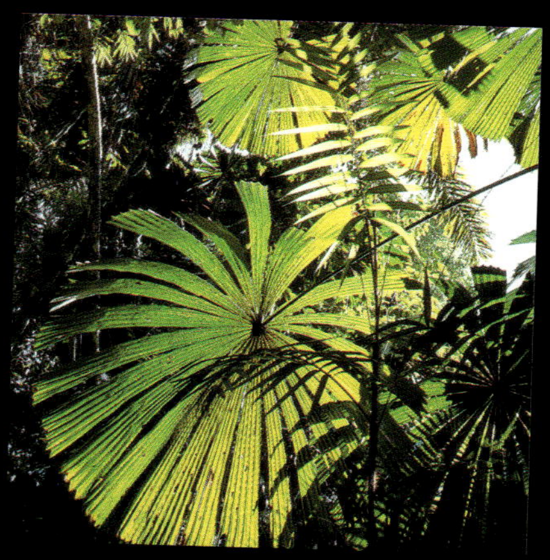

Part Two In the Field

Part Three Marketing Your Work

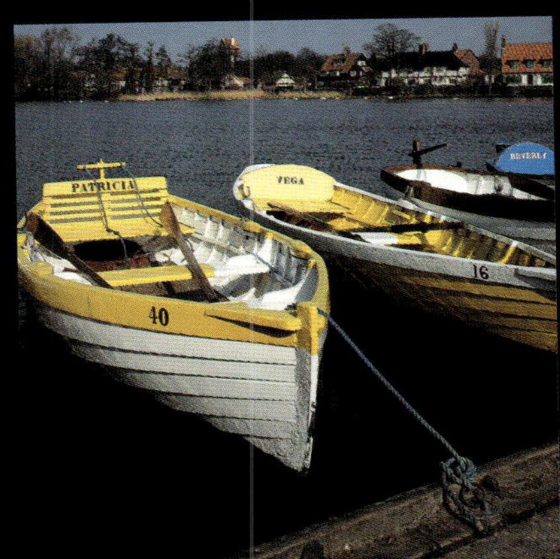

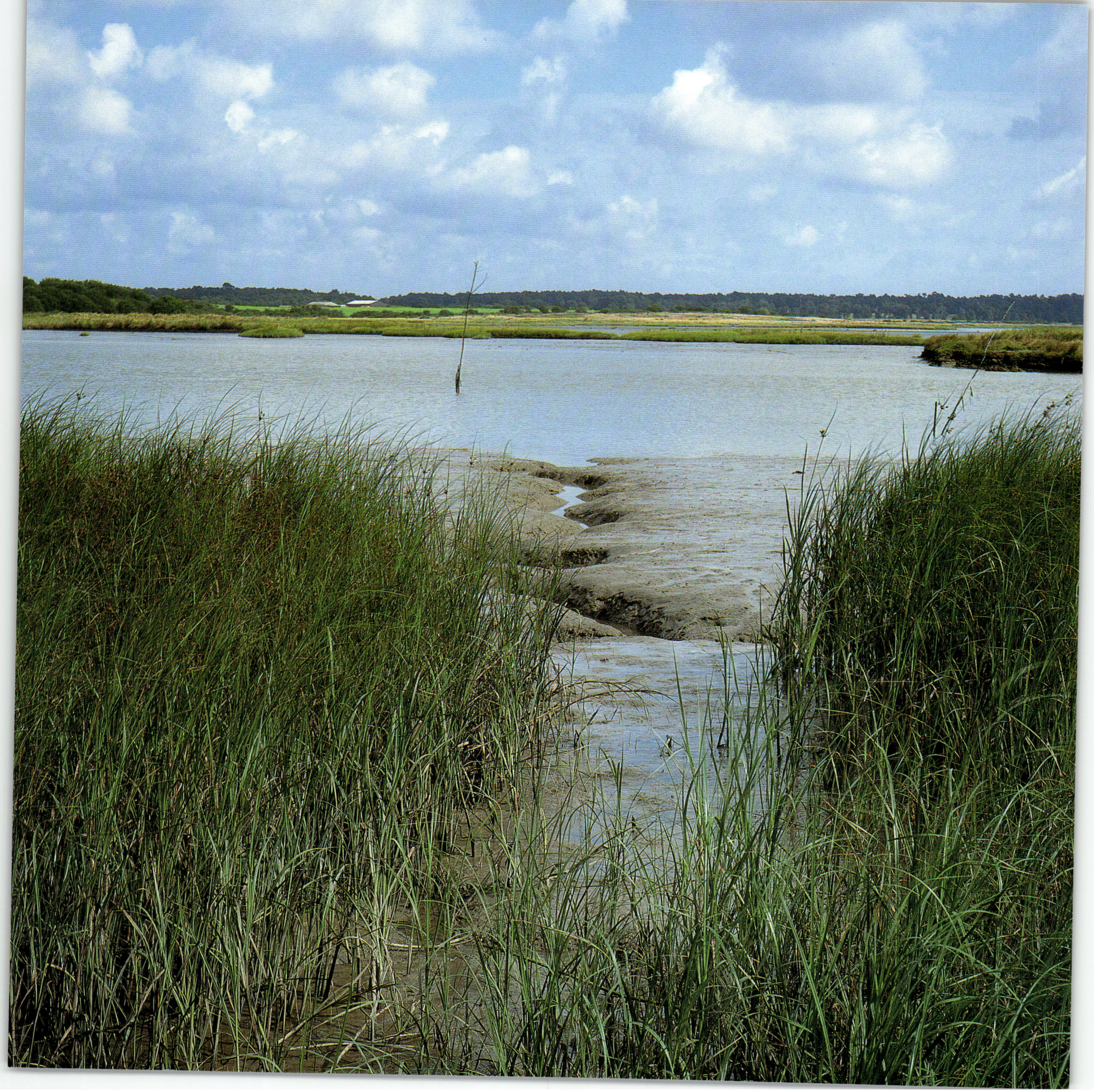

Introduction

For me, landscape and environmental photography is a passionate obsession that began when I first picked up a camera 20 years ago. It appeals to both the artistic and scientific sides of my nature. It should therefore come as no surprise that this book focuses on both the technical and the aesthetic aspects of the medium.

Starting with the technical, the book focuses on the full range of camera types from 35mm compacts to 5 x 4in view cameras. These two extremes are not mutually exclusive; many serious professionals use both 'auto-everything' 35mm compacts as well as large-format view cameras. I am one such example. It is no longer true that today's automatic 35mm compacts are exclusively the preserve of the snap-shooter. In the same section, I look at the myriad accompanying lenses, supports and accessories as well as film.

The book also deals with the fundamentals of the photographic process, from controlling exposure to using filters. And it explores the advantages and disadvantages of photography in different environments using a range of camera types.

But while camera gear is important, the hallmarks of every good landscape and environmental photographer are a creative spirit, and an appreciation that it is not a sexily advertised camera that defines the quality of a photograph, but an ability to recognize and work with light. The interplay of light can transform the ordinary into the extraordinary, producing a plethora of emotional connotations. Unfortunately, catching good lighting is very much a matter of chance. Most experienced landscape photographers know that good light usually means awful weather, although this rule is by no means hard and fast. Thus, the first lesson to learn is that a camera in itself cannot create the conditions for a great photograph. Neither can it find suitable subject material to record. These are down to you and luck. With landscape photography, if you do your job well, the type of 35mm camera you use is almost irrelevant; a 'point and shoot' compact camara can sometimes produce results that are indistinguishable from those taken on a single lens reflex (SLR) camera.

Of course, by using medium- and large-format equipment, the potential to take (and sell) quality landscape images can make a significant leap. Despite this accepted dogma, many photographers, myself included, still sell more 35mm than 120 roll film slides.

As your slide collection builds up, your photographic skills will develop. More importantly, you will learn how to critique your own work. Not only will you acquire an eye for a picture, but your technical expertise will help you to translate this vision onto film. In other words you will develop a sixth sense which helps you tailor exposures to achieve the optimum in composition and design. As your professionalism increases so your reward will be an increased sales potential for your images.

It is often said a good photographer is never without his or her camera. I'm not so sure. I regularly stroll through my local woodland without my photo gear. In this way I enjoy the broader, more spiritual

Mud flats on the tidal River Alde at Iken in Suffolk, England. This shot is of one of my favourite places. It was taken on the professional Fuji GA645Zi, which is like a zoom compact camera in concept, but yields large 6 x 4.5cm transparencies. It illustrates that operationally simple but functionally sophisticated compact cameras can produce excellent results.

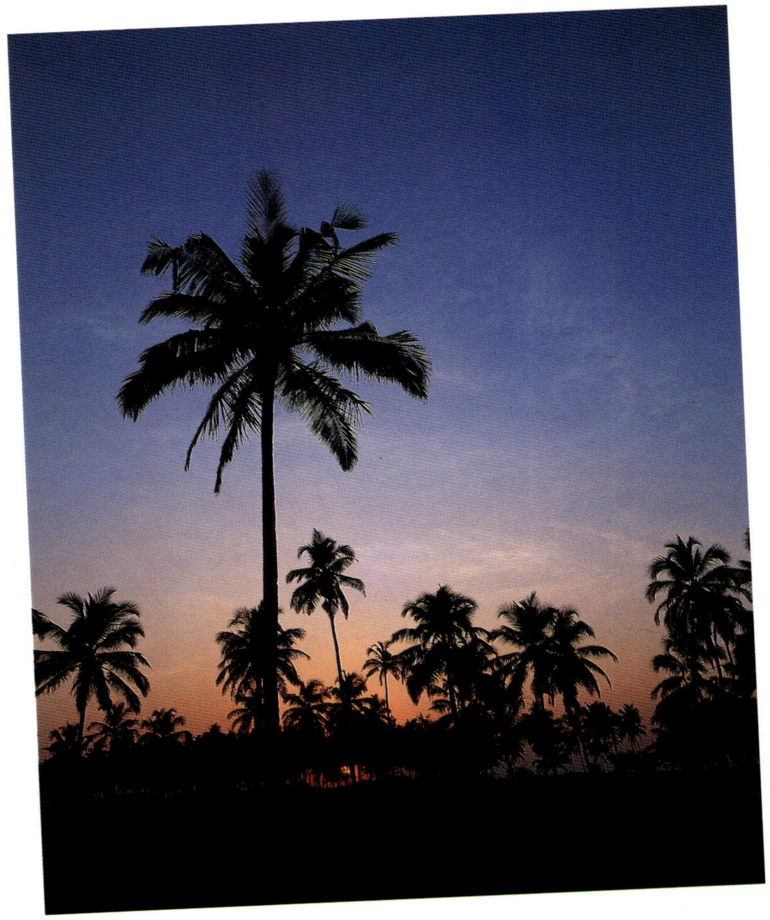

A group of palm trees silhouetted against the setting tropical sun in India.
Fuji GA645Wi, 1/8sec at f/22, Velvia, tripod.

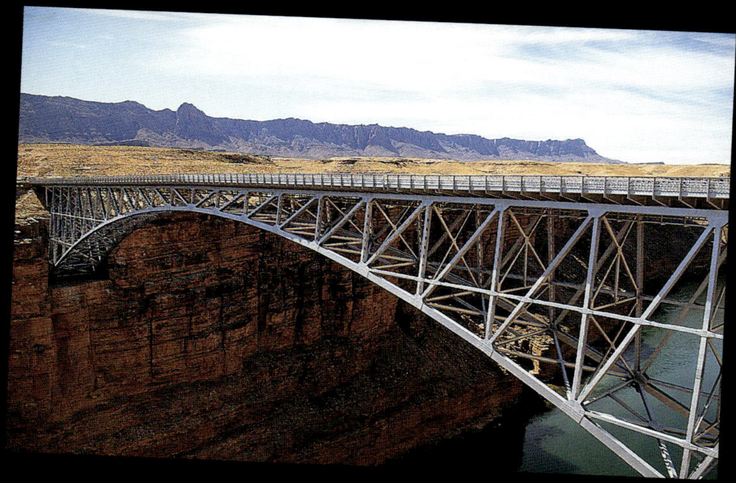

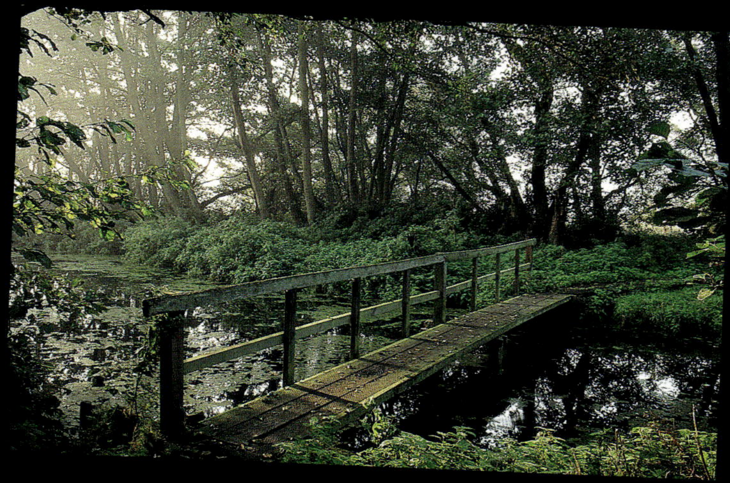

aspects of a woodland walk without feeling obliged to get at least one shot for the effort of lugging my kit along with me. If I see a particularly good scenic view, I can always return with photography in mind. It is tremendously exciting (not to mention financially rewarding) when you see your first landscape picture in a national magazine. However, no matter how successful you might become, you must never become blasé about nature. Photographing landscapes in the natural world is an enthralling pursuit. Don't nonchalantly shoot frame after frame without stopping for a moment to drink in the magical ambience of what it is that you are attempting to record on film. Nature can be many things – fragile or frightening – but it is always beautiful. Never let the thought of obtaining profit from your photography override the possibility of a spiritual experience with nature.

I hope my experiences offer you some new ideas, inspiration for your own travels and encourage your own pursuit of this magical craft.

Two very different types of bridge: one taken at the River Hundred, near Aldringham, Suffolk, England, is charmingly rustic; the other, the Navajo bridge that straddles the Colorado River in Northern Arizona, USA, an architectural modern marvel. Both make captivating images which will sell to the right market.
Both images Pentax MZ5n + 28–70mm zoom lens, Velvia.

A white-lipped tree frog. This tropical species is the largest tree frog in the world. These frogs can usually be found in Australian paperbark swamps, although in the dry season they are more commonly found in environments such as the suburban bathroom!
Pentax MZ5n + 100mm macro lens, 1/90sec at f/16, Velvia, off-camera TTL flash.

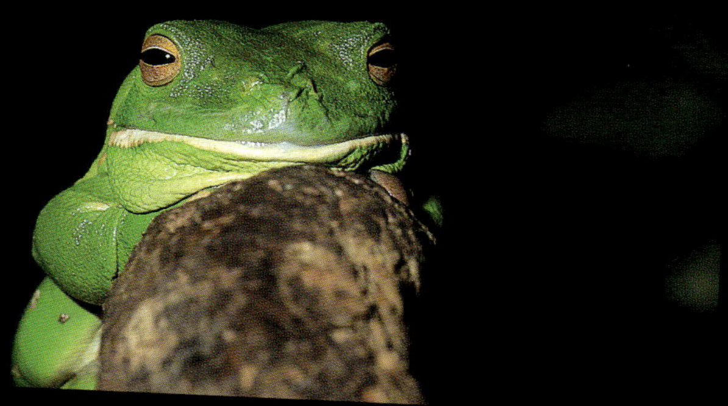

The Environmental Perspective

While this is a book on photography, let's start with something that's even more important and, for most of us, the *raison d'être* of why we expose metres of celluloid each year: the magnificence of our many special landscapes and wilderness areas.

Unfortunately, mankind's guardianship of Earth is likely to be very short-lived. Our small world has become so highly industrialized that our society is growing and metastasizing at a rate that traps the planet's decreasing biota into ever smaller, fragmented habitats. The consequence of our own meteoric success as a species contributes to the extinction of other species and to an increasing tapestry of concrete, steel and industrial bi-products – a poor substitute for virgin rainforest, ancient oak woodland or even that patch of rough scrubland that you walk your dog on. We live at a critical time in our planet's history. Never before has life in all its forms been in greater discord with human activity. It seems fitting that as the third millennium begins, we take stock of our unique place within life's elaborate, diverse milieu. We ignore at our peril the fact that this same milieu nurtures our very existence. Although the landscape and environmental pictures that I have taken for this book illustrate a variety of photographic techniques, I hope that they also reflect the intricacy and beauty of nature and remind us of the reasons for preserving them. I also hope that the pictures you take can one day do the same.

Many of my photographs show a view of life that remains unchanged from the beginning of the last millennium and, in many cases, a very long time before that. Others show a world dramatically changed from its primal state by human activity. Change is not always bad – some human elements in the landscape blend into the vista with absolute harmony. Sadly, at the turn of this new century, we create very few environmentally friendly elements. For myself, there are too many modern intrusions on our landscape (but, then again, I have never much liked change). However, over time, perceptions may alter. Perhaps one day we will view electricity pylons in the same aesthetic light as dry-stone walls or ancient pack-horse bridges. Photographer associates of mine are already drawing such parallels.

Many of the current global problems are best explained in the context of an evolutionary perspective. All organisms adapt to the

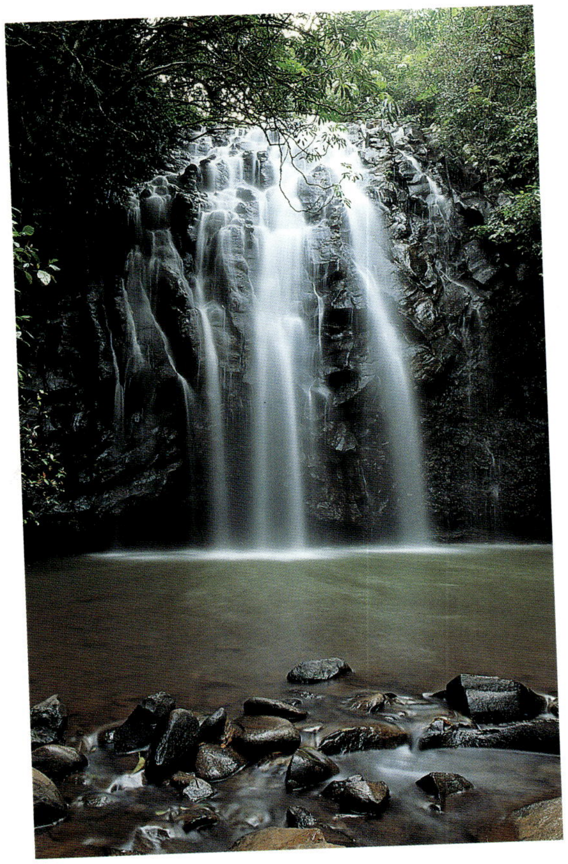

A steep muddy path takes you to Ellinjaa Waterfall on the Atherton Tablelands in Queensland, Australia. I took my turn in the queue in order to photograph this popular fairyland-like vista.
Pentax 35mm camera + 28–70mm zoom lens, on a sturdy tripod.

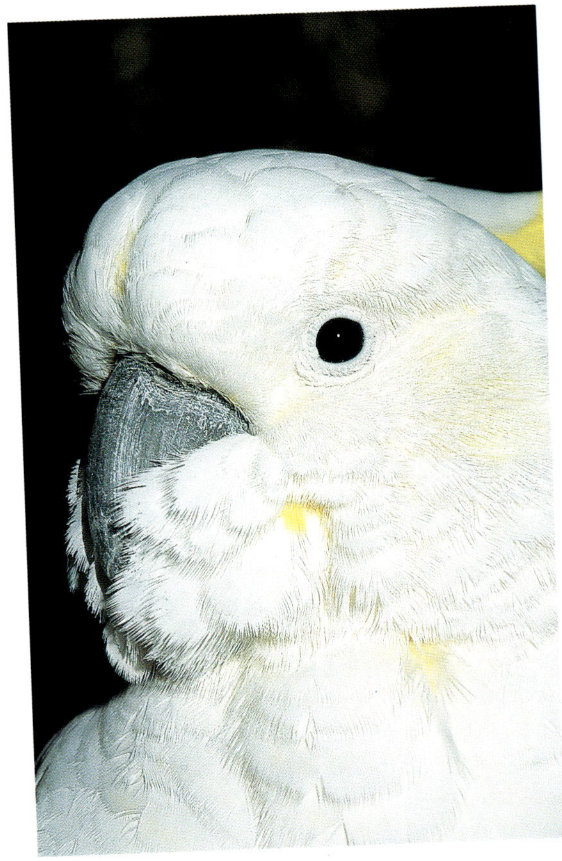

Even if you are predominantly a landscape photographer, you should strive to take a range of lenses with you when you travel so that you can record a variety of subjects. I took this cockatoo on 35mm equipment and will use it to supplement my medium-format landscapes of Australia for magazine submissions and photo essays.
Pentax MZ5n + 100mm macro lens, Velvia.

environment in which they find themselves but, by contrast, we humans adapt the environment to suit our needs. Our own genius at manipulating the world in which we live has spawned a dangerous arrogance that places us outside the normal rhythms of nature. We have attempted to play God, to understand and control life. As I write these words, I find myself leaning on an old copy of the science journal *Nature*. In this edition it is reported that mankind has successfully achieved the first phase of a task more fantastic and challenging than anything that goes before it. He has read the nucleotide sequence of the DNA which comprises chromosome 22. Today, the nucleotide sequence of the entire human genome is available. Information that can occupy approximately one gigabyte of a PC's hard drive, yet encode the template for the most advanced form of life on planet earth. This achievement makes landing on the moon pale into insignificance.

Molecular biological advances may well add to and, indeed, completely unravel our understanding of life processes but, unfortunately, it may also take a little something away. Ask a field naturalist, a nature, landscape or environmental photographer or any manner of hobbyist who regularly indulges a passion for nature why they are attracted to the living world and its landscape and, with few exceptions, the answer will be a derivative of some ill-defined spiritual desire to be at one with nature. Some people are very close to the 'spirit of nature', myself included. As a biologist who is also trying to explain the absolutes that define the mechanisms of life, I find myself torn between a spiritualism that I have no wish to explain – but simply enjoy experiencing and photographing – and a nature that constantly requires a detailed and meaningful interpretation.

Through many of the photographs in this book, I have attempted to convey the magic, mystery and magnificence of nature without sidelining its biological significance. I firmly believe that to marvel at nature is sometimes more important than understanding it. What could be more appealing than sitting on the edge of a canyon in Utah meditating on a fiery sunset as it lights up the surrounding rocks, rendering them a shade of vermillion that wouldn't look out of place on Mars? The answer is to have a camera and photograph such a vista – and further, to make the image look as if it was indeed taken in a place that is out of this world.

But our photography must be responsible. Unfortunately, mass pilgrimages to landscape icons by keen photographers sometimes lead to unacceptable behaviour. Recently, a photographer on a workshop decided to illuminate Delicate Arch in the Arches National Park in Utah for a night shot by employing synthetic fire logs in metal trays, which led to staining and discoloration of the base of the Arch: a serious mutilation of one of our planet's greatest natural landmarks. As landscape photographers, taking responsibility

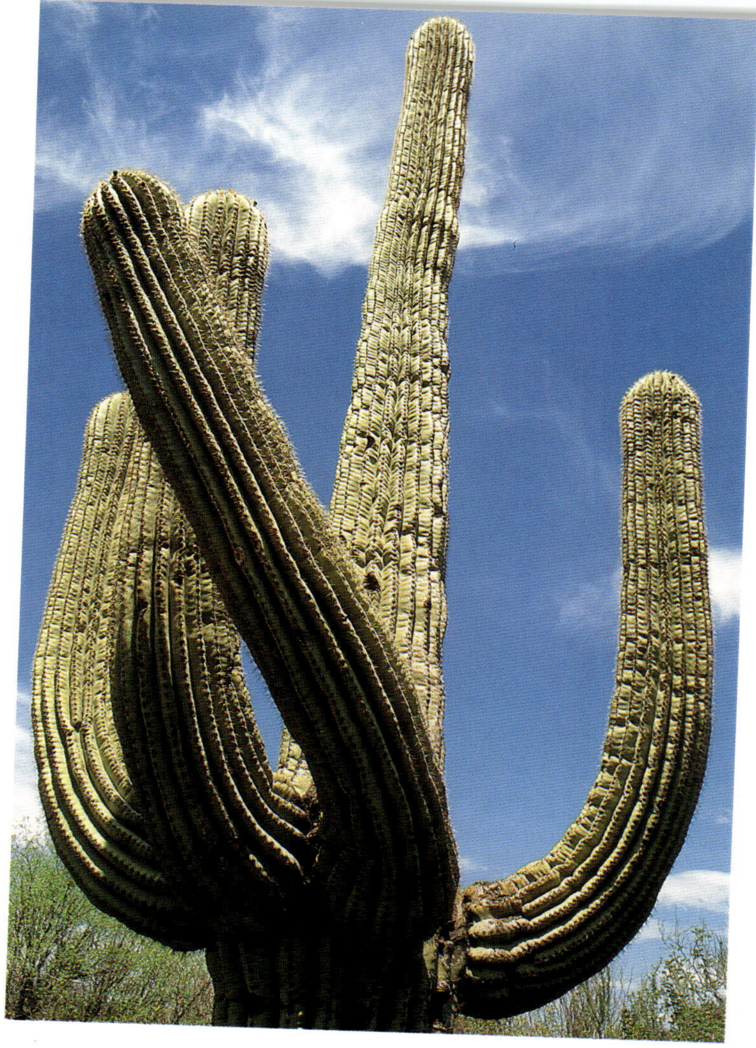

Always look for an unusual perspective, even in the most ordinary scene. This saguaro cactus was shot near Payson in Arizona. It seems to be pointing the way to water for any souls lost in the harsh desert environment. I was impaled by a nearby cholla cactus in my efforts to shoot this giant. The only practical way to remove a cholla cacti pad from your limbs (hand in my case) is to use a comb to lever it off. It was very nasty.
Pentax MZ5n + 28–70mm zoom lens, Velvia, tripod.

begins with assigning that little strip of blue paper on every roll of Velvia 120 to an appropriate place (not on the ground where we load our cameras), and ends by reducing our impact on the natural world wherever we tread. If we don't, access to such marvels may one day be restricted by the authorities.

Let us hope that we proceed into this third millennium with a renewed, vigorous empathy for the landscapes and nature that shape our planet. Who knows, your own photographs may in some small way help save the planet from our generally destructive

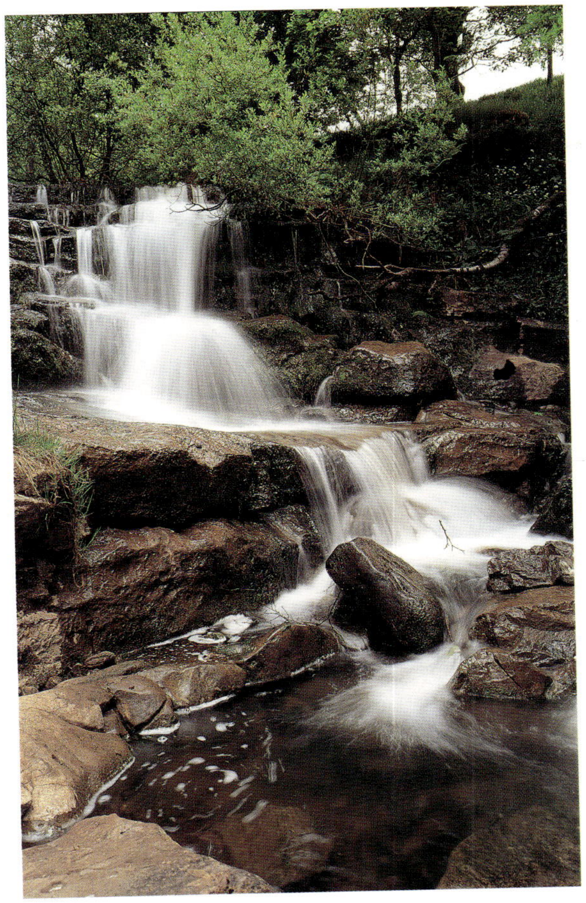

East Gill Force. This is a detailed rendering of one of my favourite waterfalls in the Yorkshire Dales, England.
Fuji GSW69III + 65mm lens, equivalent to 28mm on 35mm format + 81B filter to warm up the colours, Velvia.

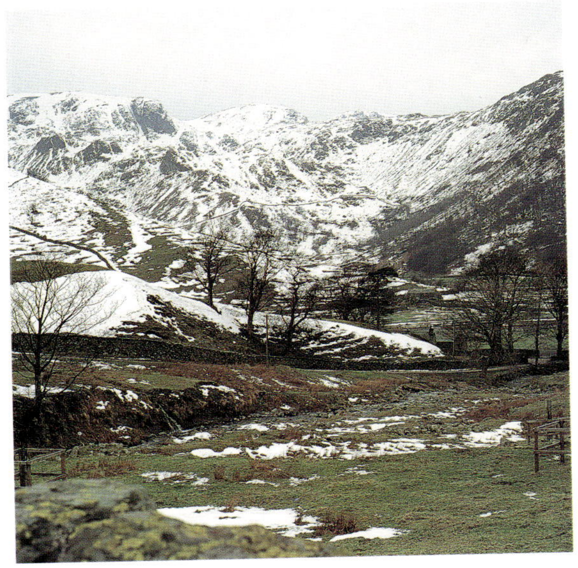

This picture of an isolated building viewed from the Kirkstone Pass in the English Lake District shows how – at least from a photographer's point of view – the built environment can sometimes blend into the natural world very well.
Hasselblad 500CM + 80mm lens.

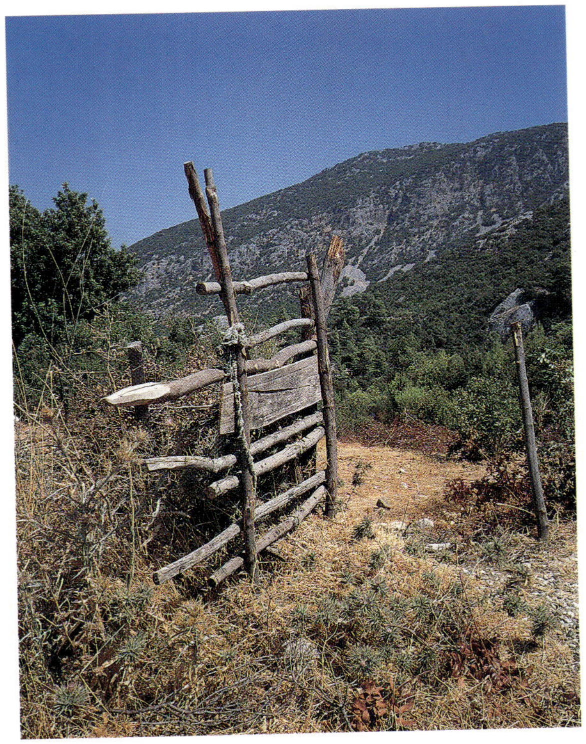

Like the isolated building above, this rustic gate taken in rural Turkey fits harmoniously with the mountainous backdrop.
Fuji GA645Wi, Velvia, tripod.

influence. If you need spiritual and photographic inspiration, seek out an image by Graham Osborne; it is my all-time favourite landscape image and appears in his book *Rainforest: Ancient Realm of the Pacific Northwest*. It is an extreme wide-angle view of a brightly coloured starfish in the foreground with 100% depth of field extending a couple of inches to infinity. It imparts the magnificence of Dolomite Narrows in Gwaii Haanas National Park, Queen Charlotte Islands, British Columbia. It shows that a single picture is worth a thousand words.

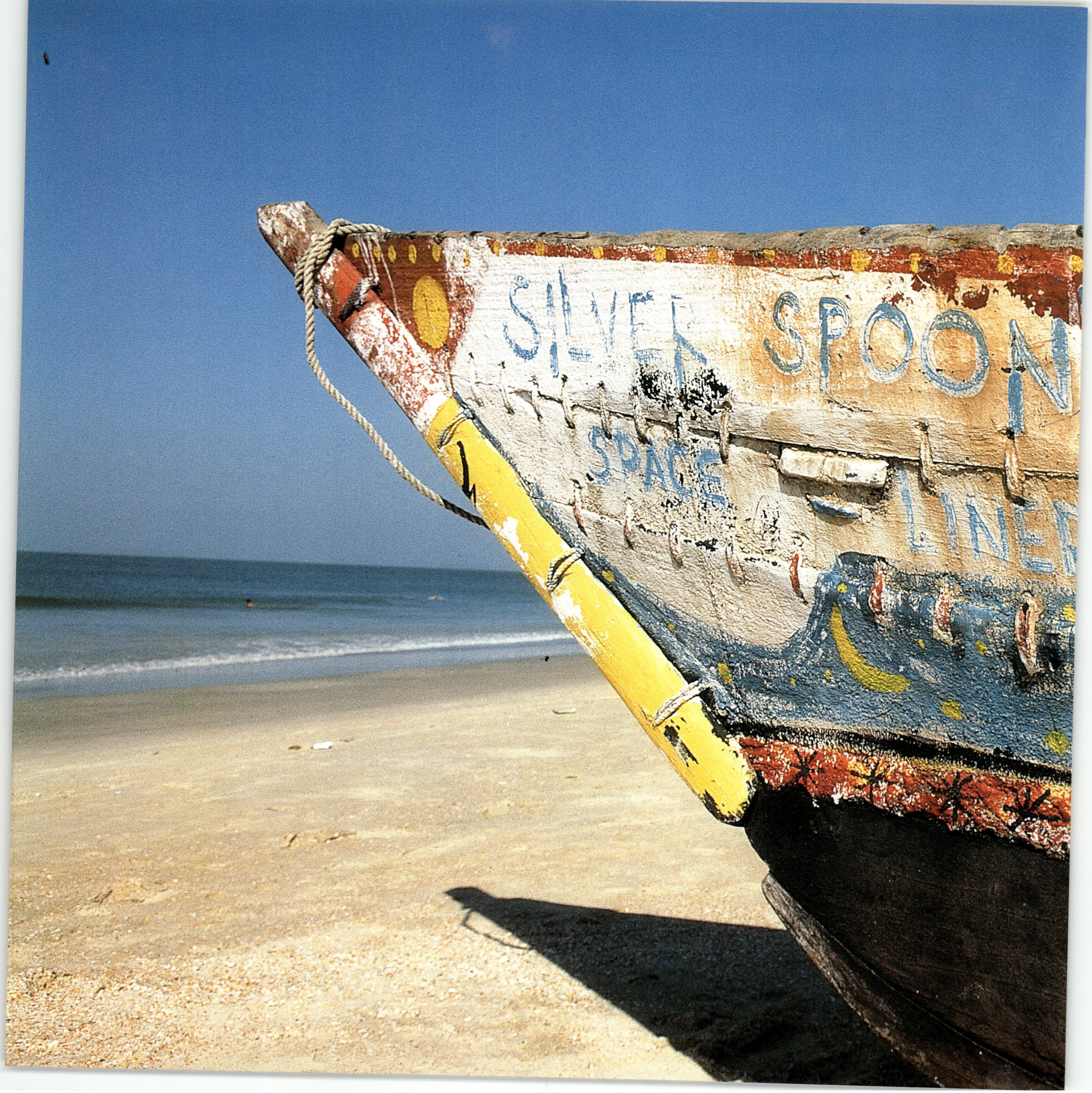
SILVER SPOON
SPACE LINER

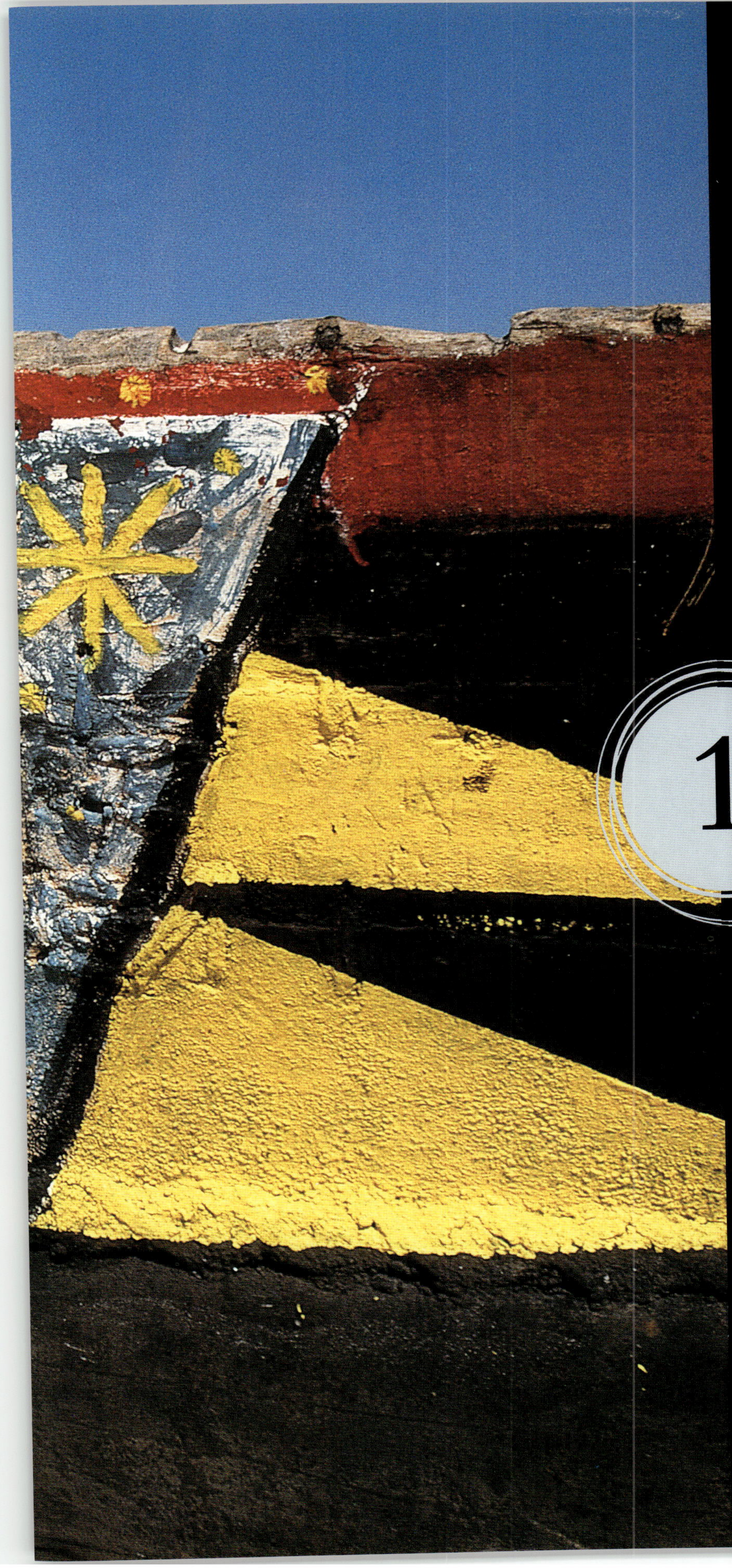

1 Technical Considerations

35mm cameras

Compacts

The 35mm compact camera comes in a variety of incarnations. However, despite the many levels of sophistication that have been incorporated into these popular cameras, they remain almost entirely 'point and shoot' devices. Therefore, this section is not the place to go into too much detail regarding the principles of exposure and other technical matters. Nevertheless, some – albeit limited – control over the appearance of the final picture is possible. Thus, careful technique can improve picture quality while attention to composition will provide results, at least for landscapes, that compare favourably to a 35mm SLR.

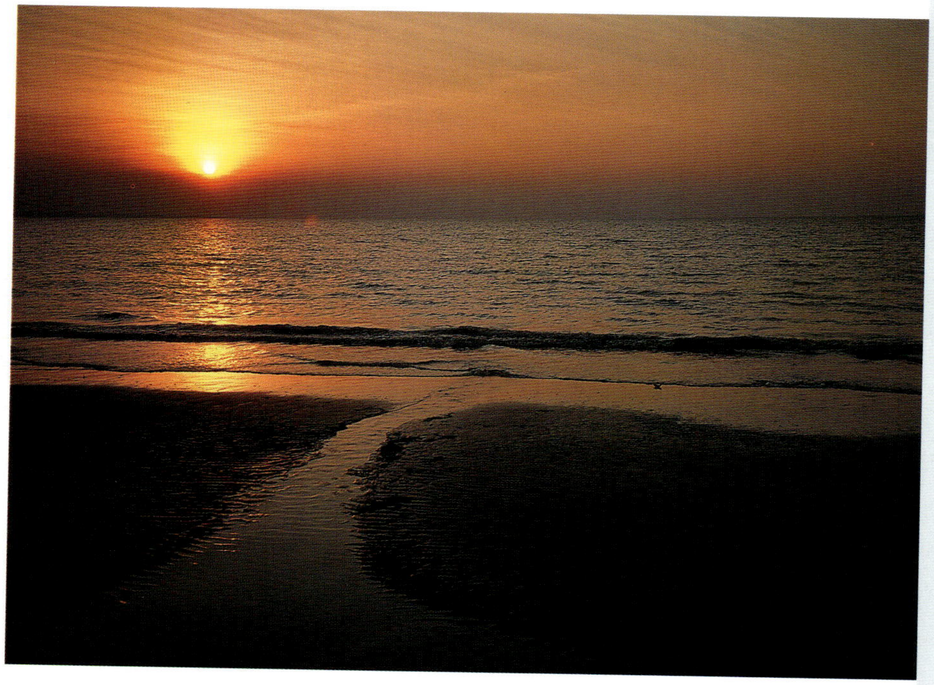

This beautiful and evocative sunset over the Timor Sea in Darwin, Australia, was taken on one of the cheapest compact cameras available. It was taken hand-held, all I did was turn off the flash and brace myself as best I could.
Pentax 738S, Velvia.

Advantages

Cheap.

Lightweight and portable.

Good for landscapes.

Some top-of-the-range compacts have sharp optics (Ricoh GR1v).

Flash is built-in for versatility.

Some models are weatherproof (e.g. Pentax 90WR and 105WR).

Models now have a good choice of zoom ranges to select from (e.g. Pentax 928).

Simplicity of use allows you to concentrate on the subject alone.

Disadvantages

Generally poor results for close-up and distant subjects (less of an issue in landscape work).

Difficult, if not impossible, to manipulate exposure.

Under rigorously controlled conditions results do not meet quite the same standard as those obtained with a 35mm SLR.

Compacts lack the versatility of SLRs; not only do they have little exposure control, few accessories are available for them.

You cannot change lenses on a compact, while the SLR has interchangeable lenses from ultra wide-angle fish eye lenses to super telephoto lenses with 20x magnification.

What you see is not what you get. With an SLR the subject is viewed through the lens, while a compact has a separate viewfinder and lens which creates a problem with parallax, particularly at close range.

35mm compacts: introducing a human element into the landscape

Adding people to a landscape scene can sometimes add a sense of scale and may augment the editorial sales potential of a slide. If you think about it, most magazines are about people doing things – rambling, biking or climbing. Equally, a good landscape image can be ruined by human intrusion. So, before pressing the shutter, think about whether you want to sell the image and who might be interested in buying it.

In this case study, the human element achieves different goals. In the first example, it provides a sense of scale and an off-centre focal point; a compositional trick that tends to produce more pleasing images. In the second, the two subjects are obviously keen walkers and therefore provide material for country-walking magazines. Aside from a reasonably careful composition, both images were taken without any other technical considerations; I simply braced my camera, pointed and shot.

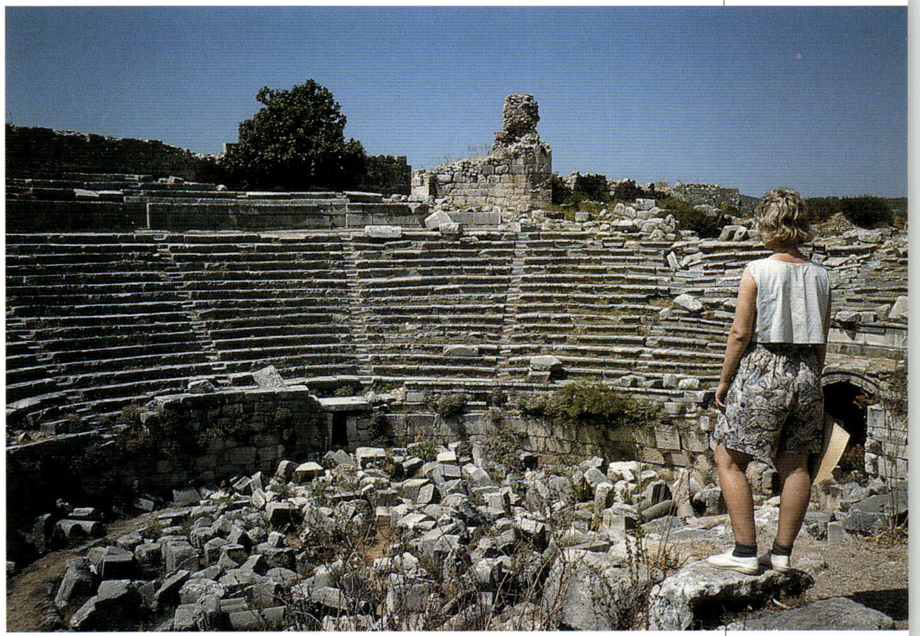

Tourist viewing amphitheatre at Xanthos in Turkey. The addition of a human element can augment sales. This tourist adds both scale and a focal point. *Yashica T3 + 35mm Carl Zeiss Tessar lens, Kodachrome 64.*

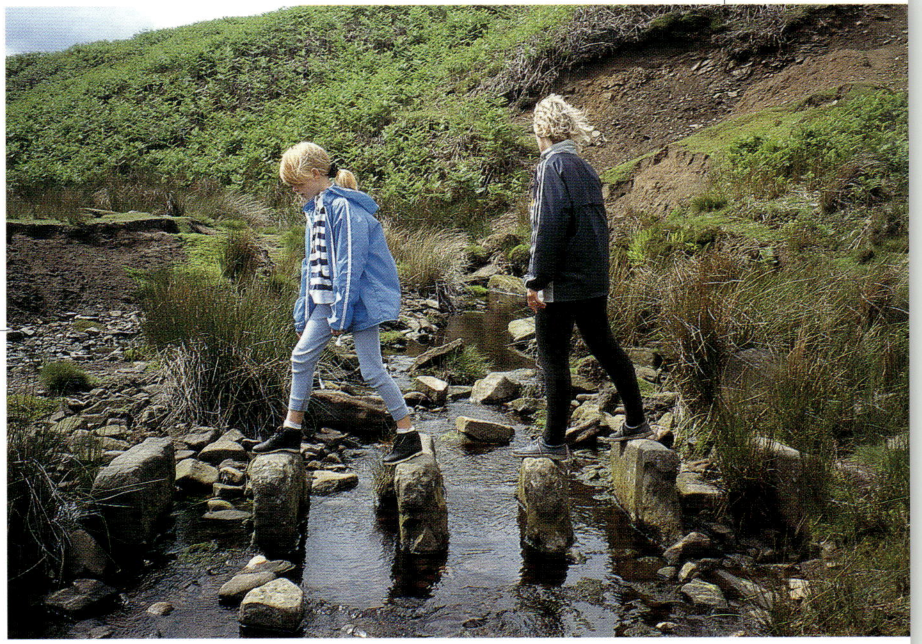

Walkers crossing a stream on Harden Moor, Yorkshire, England. Adding people can help sales, particularly if they are doing something relevant to the theme of a magazine title. *Pentax 90WR, Sensia 100.*

Most people have a compact, so the purpose of this section is to show you how to get the best from your camera. It really comes down to two things: a) holding the camera correctly and reducing any source of vibration, which means bracing the camera against a solid support or attaching it to a tripod, and b) composing the scene well. However, there are a few other tips worth knowing, and the following case studies deal with some of them. Of particular interest is a comparison in the quality of reproduction for these 35mm compact camera images with those from more professional cameras. I hope it helps you decide which camera best suits you, or which camera best suits a project or trip you may be undertaking in the near future.

Adding drama to a scene using a 35mm compact camera

There are many ways to add a sense of drama to the landscape. Not only does this make a slide stand out, it makes an editor take a second look. The three images are different examples of drama. One involves faithfully recording nature to demonstrate a dark menacing sky over the Bavarian alps. In this case I used a fence post for support but, other than applying my best eye for composition, it was a simple 'point and shoot' situation. While the camera's algorithms sorted all exposure details out here, the second image illustrates how to achieve impact by fooling the camera's 'auto-everything' exposure mechanism. The goat balancing on a rock was rendered as a silhouette by pointing the camera at clear blue sky and pressing down on the shutter sufficiently to lock exposure. This tells the camera that brightness levels are high. I then maintained pressure on the shutter release and re-aimed the camera at the goat, which was maybe two stops (exposure value units or EV) darker. Thus, when I took the picture, the camera was fooled into thinking the goat was brighter than it really was. Hence the goat was underexposed and turned into a more powerful composition.

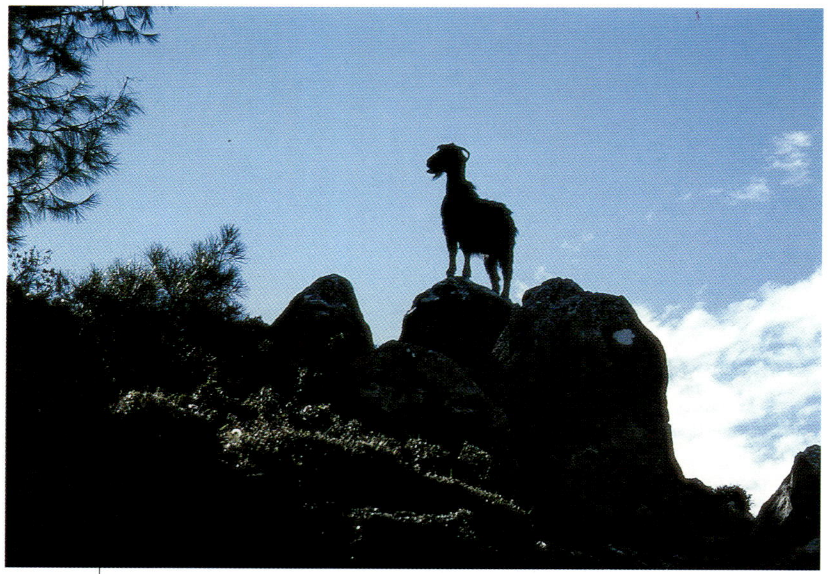

Taken near Fethiye, Turkey, this simple, dramatic silhouette of a goat shows how to fool an 'auto-everything' camera. Metering from a much brighter open sky underexposed the subsequent goat shot. This simple image has now sold twice. *Pentax 90WR, Sensia 100.*

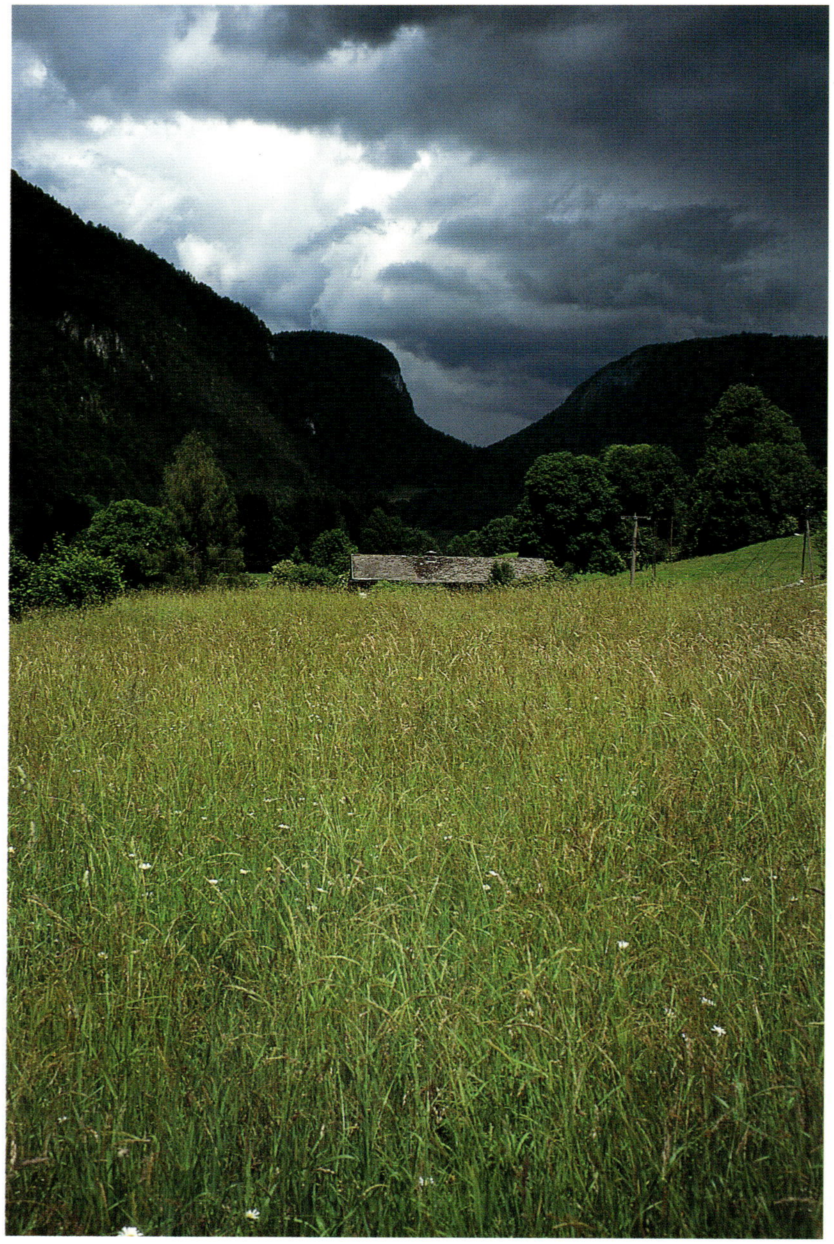

Brooding alpine sky, Berchtesgaden, Germany. A dark, menacing sky always adds drama. I used a fence post to stabilize my hand-held camera. *Pentax 90WR, Sensia 100.*

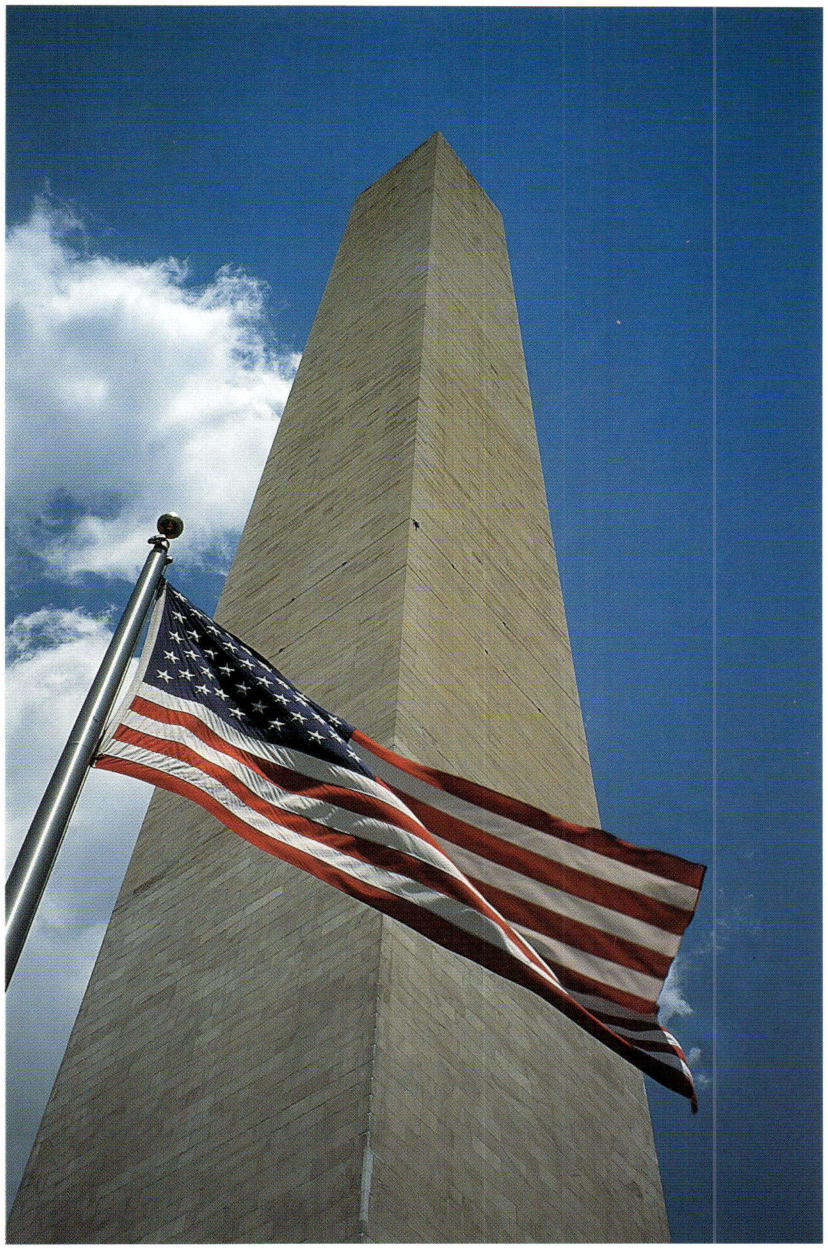

The juxtaposition of the Washington monument and the stars and stripes flag conveys a strong message that underscores the status of the United States in our world order.
Pentax 90WR, Velvia.

Maintaining a good depth of field using a compact camera

Depth of field is usually given no consideration in 'point and shoot' compact camera instruction. However, the success of a picture can be wholly dependent upon the depth of field. Depth of field refers to that part of the picture which is in focus. The greater the depth of focus, the more apparent sharpness in the image (see hyperfocal distance on page 67).This phenomenon is out of the photographer's control on compact cameras, but the two slides here illustrate ways in which one can improve the depth of sharpness.

A full discussion of apertures and field of focus will follow in subsequent chapters. But for readers who propose sticking with a 'point and shoot' camera, it is sufficient to know that for a given shutter speed, in order to maintain a standard level of exposure, the lens aperture closes down as the ambient brightness level increases. This produces increased picture sharpness. Compacts also often employ multi-point focus, which can automatically enhance sharpness through the camera's in-built algorithms.

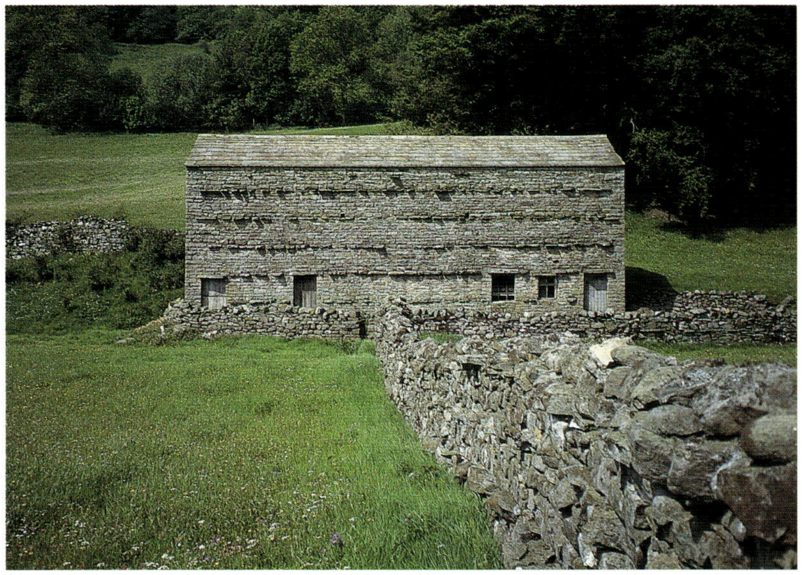

Striving for good depth of field with a compact camera. Shooting this on a bright day ensured a small lens aperture, while multi-point focus helped to keep everything sharp. Taken on the Corpse Way in the Yorkshire Dales.
Pentax 90WR, Sensia 100.

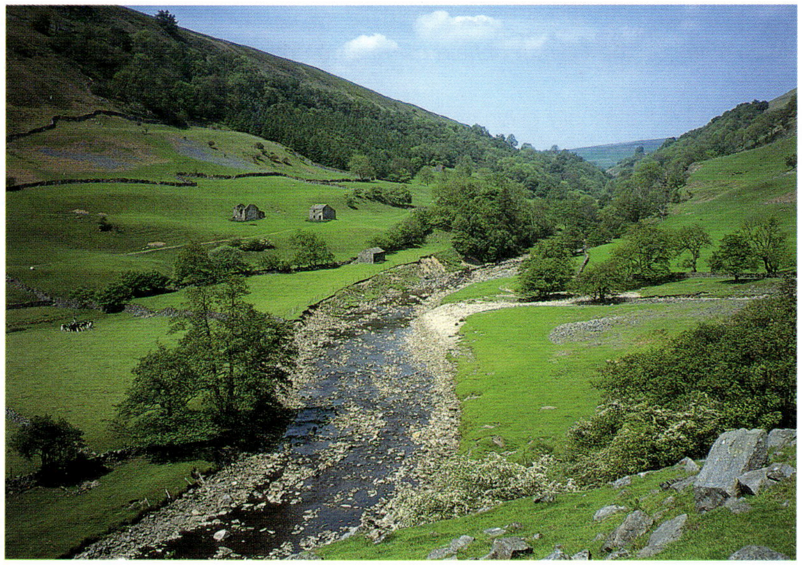

Another way to obtain good depth of field with a compact camera is to find a high vantage point, removing nearby subjects from view. For this shot of the River Swale in Yorkshire, England, I selected the widest lens angle, which improves depth of field. It was a bright day, so the lens aperture was, of necessity, small, and in addition, I selected infinity lock.
Pentax 90WR, Sensia 100.

Using a tripod to reduce camera shake with a 35mm compact camera

This case study shows the benefits of using a tripod to reduce camera shake. Tripods are generally bulky beasts, and remove any benefit of hiking with a portable, lightweight compact camera. However, for a small investment you can buy a mini-tripod that will fit in your pocket. These can be erected on any wall or large rock and ensure the optimum performance from your camera.

It is worth emphasizing that tripods are the simplest way to guarantee sharp transparencies. Editors and picture buyers always scrutinize transparencies using a quality 8x loupe over a light box. Any sign of blur or camera shake and your slides will fail the test and not be published.

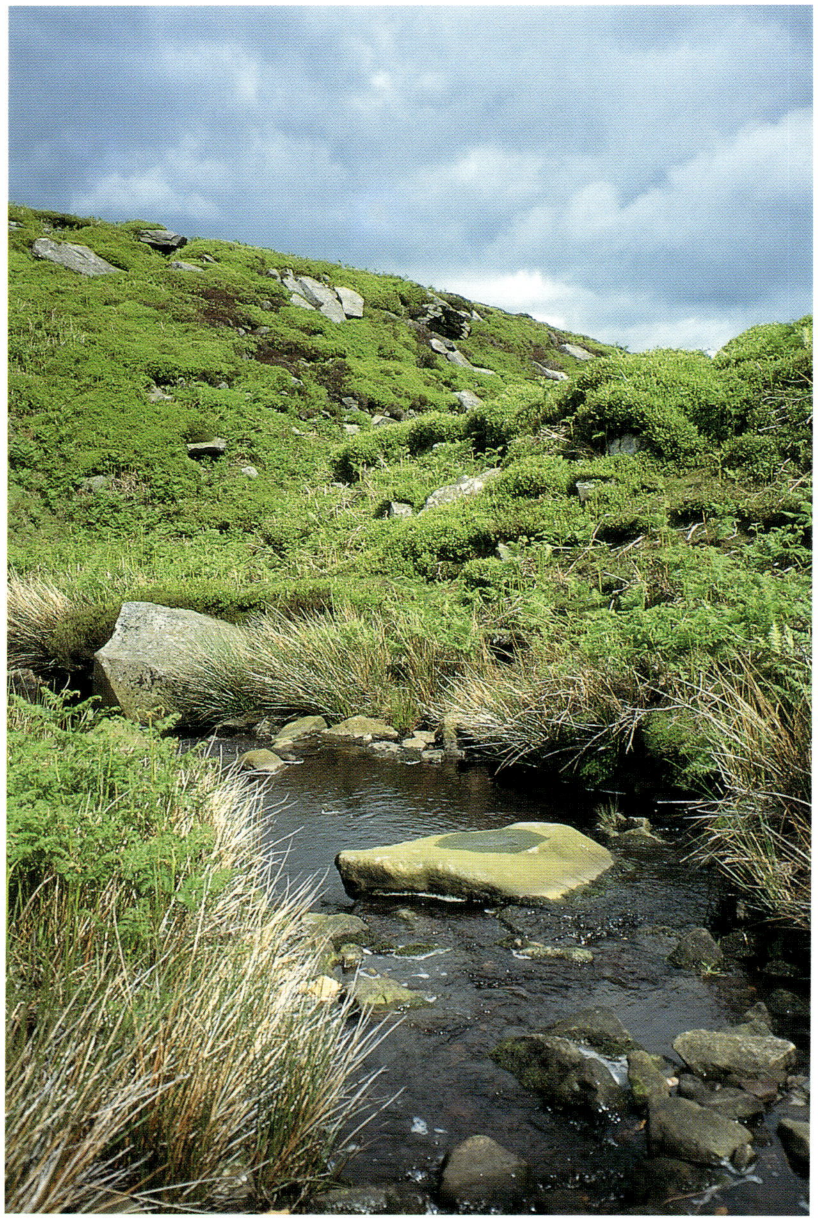

Moorland landscape taken with my compact camera fitted on a pocket-sized mini-tripod.
Pentax 90WR, Sensia 100.

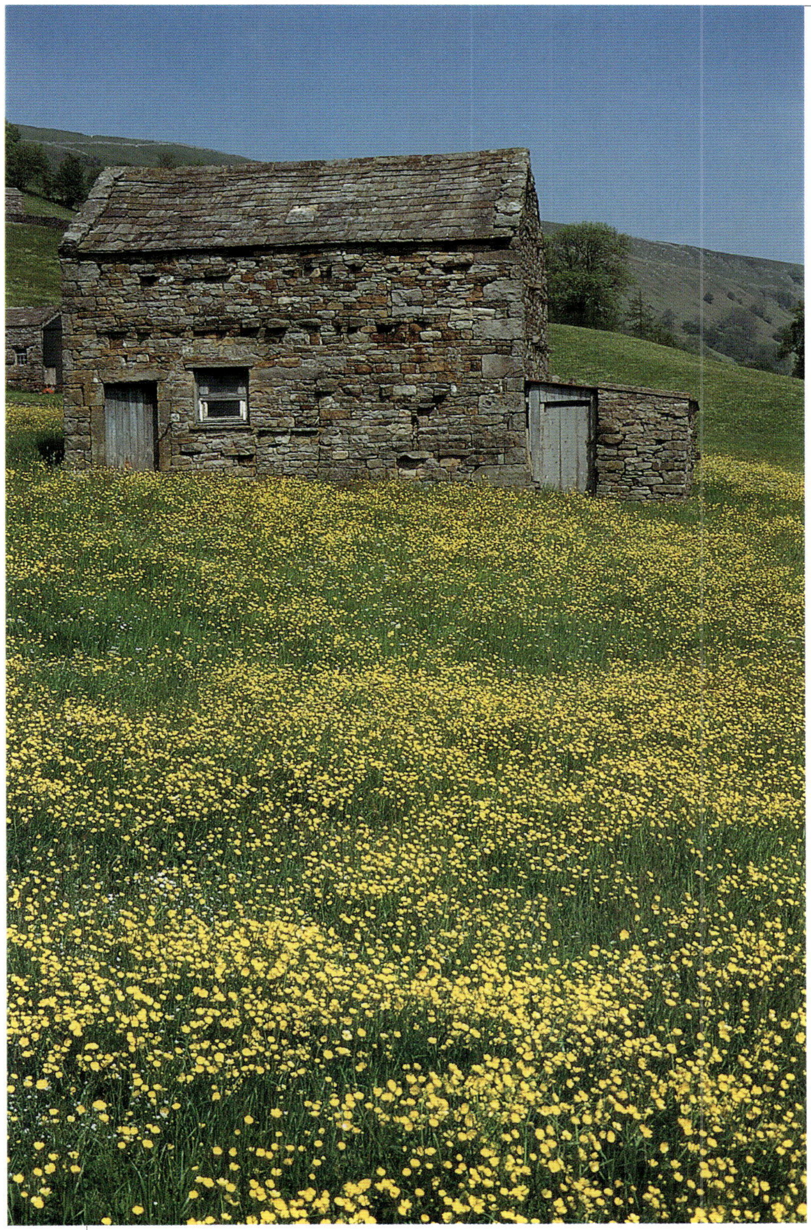

This image of Swaledale was taken on my compact camera and found an immediate market.
Pentax 90WR, Sensia 100.

35mm versus medium- and large-format cameras

A few years ago I went for a family drive out to the Yorkshire Dales in England; a 120-mile round trip from my home. When we arrived in Swaledale, the hay meadows were in full bloom – something I had not expected. The sight was absolutely stunning. I only had my Pentax 90WR 35mm compact with me, but, despite this, still managed to go through several rolls of Fuji Sensia. All the time I was there I was suppressing my anger at leaving my medium-format camera at home. I felt that, faced with an endless colourful mosaic of wild flowers, only my 6 x 9cm Fuji GSW69III medium-format rangefinder or larger-format camera could do justice to such a magnificent scene, so I returned the next day with my 6 x 9cm camera and took several carefully thought-out images. With hindsight, the lessons I learned are that: a) I couldn't have enjoyed the initial visit with my family if I had been carrying my medium-format gear the distance we walked that day, so my Pentax compact was perfect, and b) medium format does not guarantee sales.

Despite my irritation at only having a compact camera for a view that begged medium- or large-format treatment, I rapidly (within weeks) sold a 35mm slide of the meadows taken on the Pentax compact. However, I have only recently (three years after taking them) managed to sell some of the 6 x 9cm transparencies.

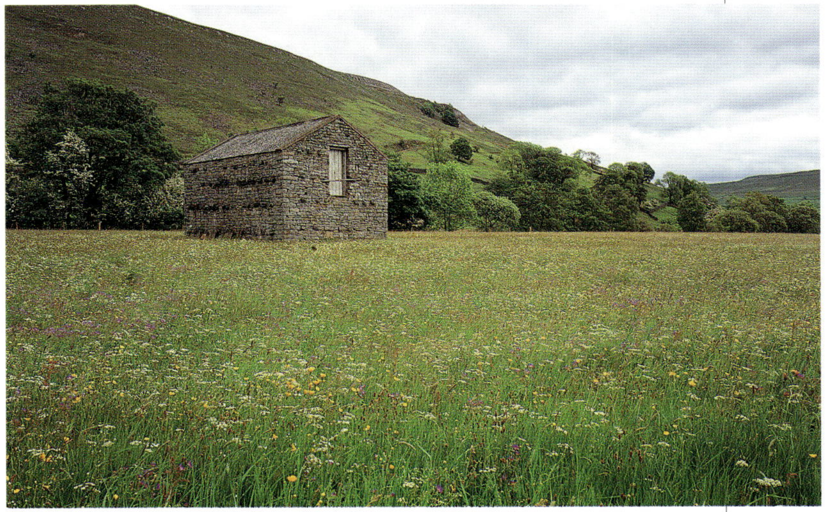

This 6 x 9cm shot of Swaledale is far superior, but its potential has yet to be appreciated by a picture buyer.
Fuji GSW69III + 81B warm-up filter, 1/8sec at f/22, Velvia, tripod.

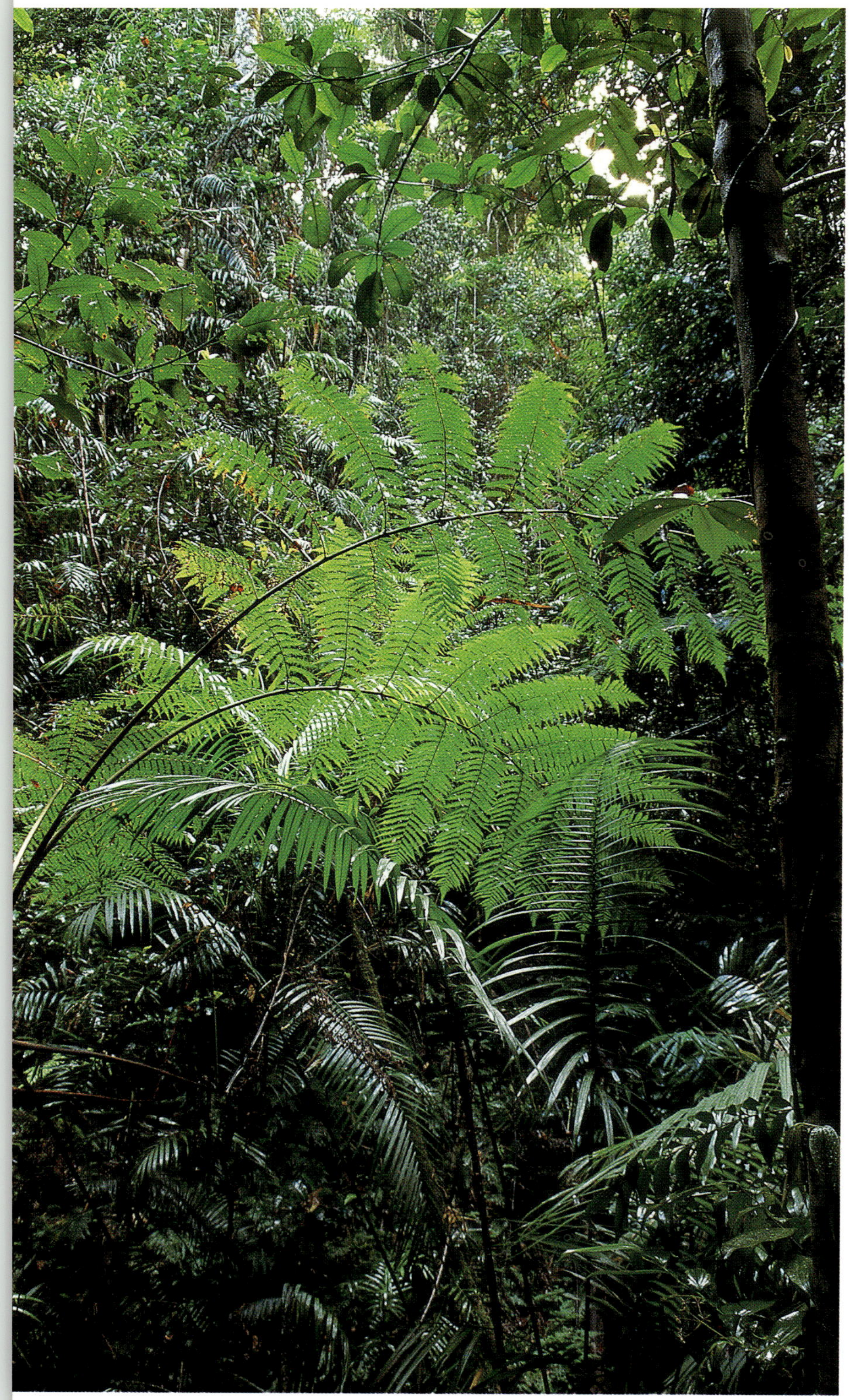

SLR cameras

In contrast to the compact 35mm camera, which *takes* pictures, with the SLR (single lens reflex) the landscape photographer *makes* pictures. The SLR provides the most convenient and adaptable mechanism for taking photographs of the entire spectrum of natural history subjects, and is particularly well suited to landscape and environmental photography. The budding landscape and environmental photographer should select a 35mm SLR camera from a manufacturer who can also supply a comprehensive range of quality lenses – Canon, Contax, Leica, Minolta, Nikon, Olympus, Pentax and, more recently, Sigma all supply suitable gear. Since a myriad of lenses is available, you can select the most appropriate and pleasing perspective for any given subject. To shoot a flowering plant and record as much information about its surrounding habitat as possible, you can use an ultra wide-angle lens in the range 17–24mm. For general landscape panoramas a 28mm lens is the accepted optic, while to compress distant landscapes, particularly mountains, you can employ anything from a 100–300mm lens.

In addition to a plethora of lenses, versatile flash technology, motor drives and advanced exposure systems make 35mm SLR cameras the nature photographer's panacea. However, before discussing the pros and cons of establishing a system based on a new or second-hand kit, it is important to understand the technical language of photography. The following sections deal with this in some detail. The basic principles of exposure hold true for all formats from 35mm and the various 120 roll film formats, right up to 5 x 4in sheet film cameras.

35mm SLRs are the most versatile of all cameras. One of my favourite features on modern SLRs is their ability to autoexpose film down to 30 seconds in low-light conditions. Although some compensation for reciprocity failure may be required (see page 22), results are often first class. Using a cable release and tripod, this long exposure was made of a tree fern in Wooroonooran National Park in Northern Queensland, Australia.
Pentax MZ5n + 28–70mm zoom lens, 15 seconds at f/11–16, Velvia.

This field of oil seed rape was shot on my Ebony 5 x 4in view camera, and shows how some movement in a scene can add interest to a picture. The blurred cow parsley contrasts nicely with the sharp buttercups in the foreground. Depth of field was extended by using front lens tilt (see page 53).
Ebony 5 x 4in view camera + Schneider 80mm Super-Symmar XL lens, 1/2sec at f/22, Fuji Velvia Quick Load sheet film.

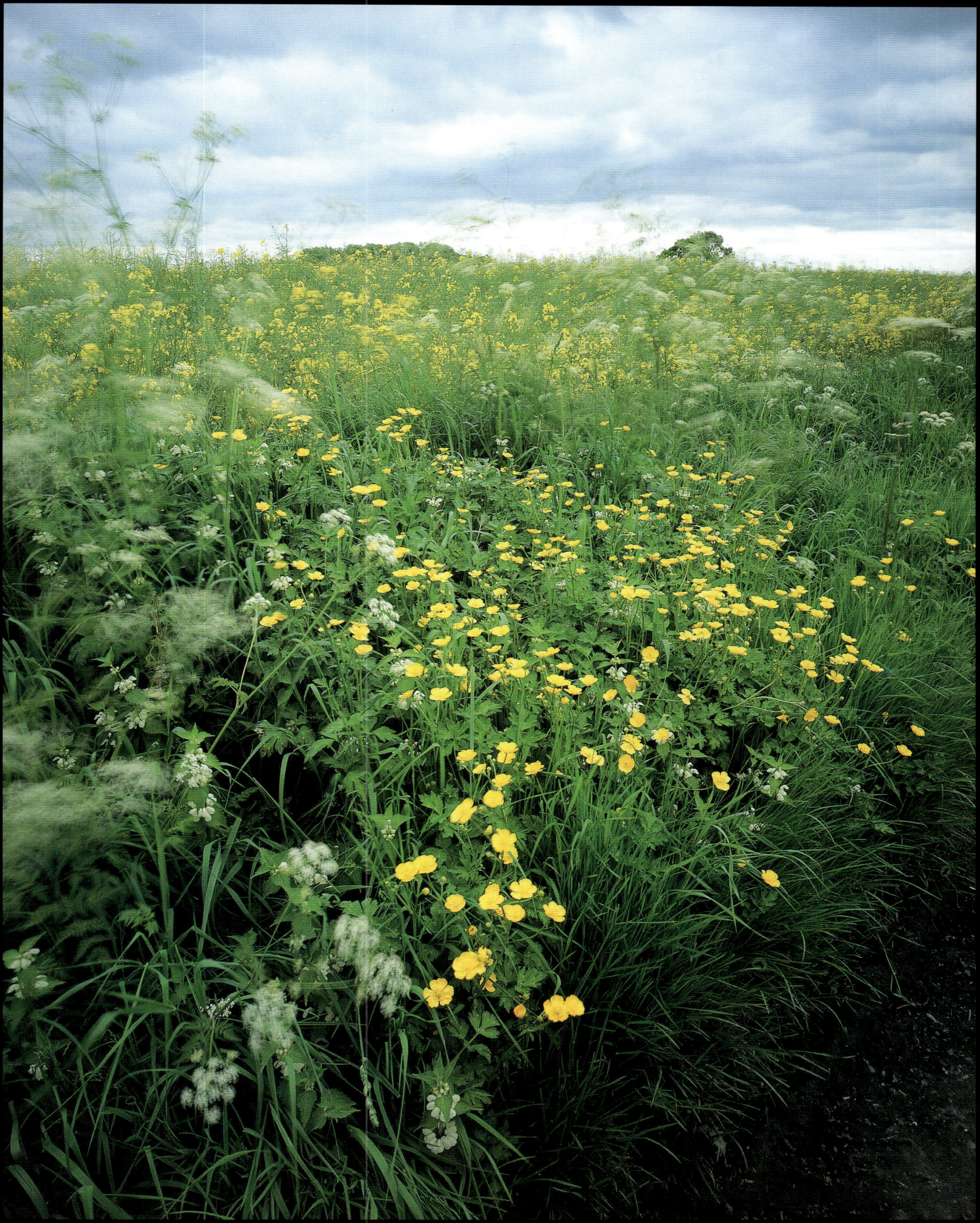

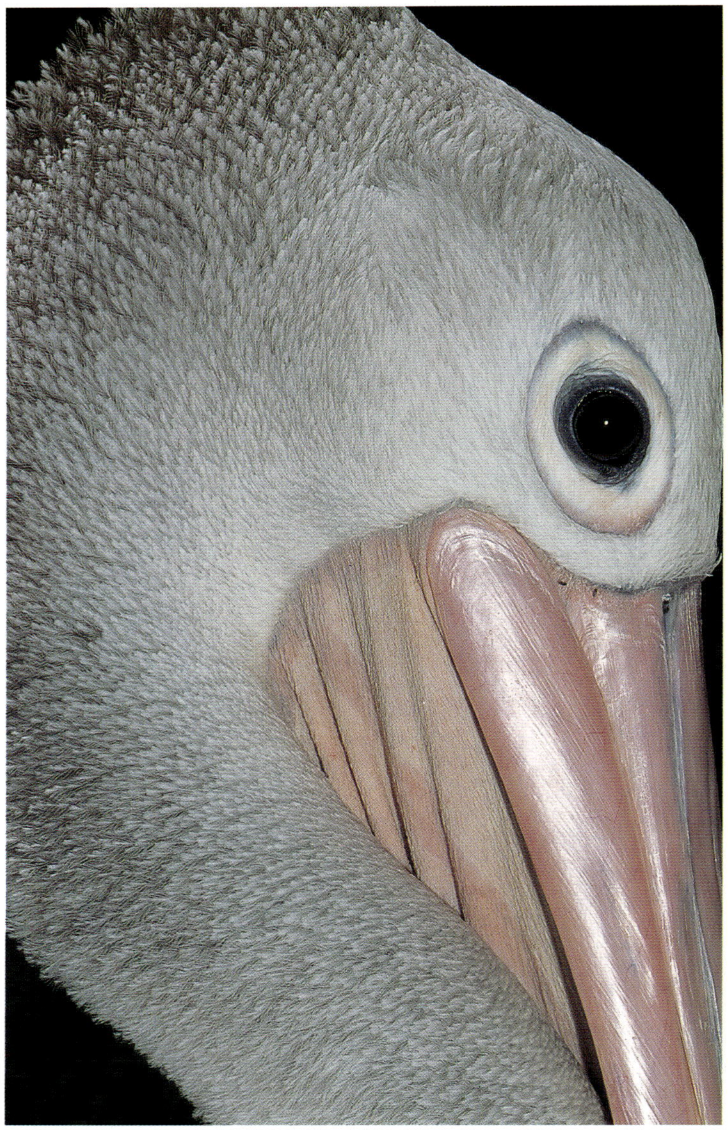

The good thing about 35mm SLR systems (new or second hand) is their versatility. One minute you can be shooting wildlife as in this abstract shot of a pelican and the next distant landscapes or diminutive close ups of butterflies. Furthermore, all three of these subjects can be shot with a single 100mm macro lens. Compacts and larger format cameras are generally not so versatile.
Pentax MZ5n + 100mm macro lens, 1/90sec at f/16, Velvia, off-camera TTL flash.

The principle of exposure

Comprehending exposure is central to the entire image-making process and its importance should not be undervalued. Basically, exposure is the balance between lens aperture, a camera's shutter speed and a film's sensitivity to light.

The aperture of a lens is defined in f-stops and refers to the size of the lens opening. Small f-stops, for example f/2, indicate large apertures while large f-stops, for example f/22 (up to f/64 on some large-format lenses), indicate small apertures. Thus, less light reaches the film emulsion as the f-number increases. Camera shutter speed is the duration that the camera's shutter mechanism remains open during the picture-recording process. Long periods of opening mean there is more exposure or, in other words, more light striking the film. Therefore, by regulating the balance between aperture and shutter speed one controls the amount of light reaching the film emulsion.

Films are rated according to their sensitivity to light. This is often referred to as film speed. Slow films require more light than fast ones in order to record a perfectly exposed image. Films are sold with an ISO number. A low ISO number means a slow, low sensitivity film and vice versa.

I have already mentioned 'stops'. Shutter speeds range from many seconds (in the case of recording traffic tail-light trails, maybe up to 30 seconds) down to 1/8000 of a second in modern cameras. A typical range is 4, 2, 1, 1/2, 1/4, 1/8, 1/15, 1/30, 1/60, 1/125, 1/250, 1/500, 1/1000 and 1/2000 (1/250 of a second is the maximum synchronization speed of flash on modern cameras, while older cameras typically sync at 1/60 of a second). This arithmetic sequence represents a series in which each shutter speed is half the preceding value and double the subsequent value. In fact, each doubling or halving of shutter speed represents a single stop; for example, 1/4–1/8 of a second represents a one-stop drop in exposure. Shutter speed is employed to: a) regulate the amount of light reaching the film emulsion and, b) to control the effect of a subject's movement; the slower the shutter speed the more likelihood of blur.

F-numbers defining aperture are also an arithmetic progression. This time the series reflects one stop changes in the amount of light admitted through the lens. Although each f-number is half the preceding value and double the subsequent value, the arithmetic change is not obviously reflected in numbers of the established f-stop series, for example f/1.4, f/2, f/2.8, f/4, f/5.6, f/8, f/11, f/16, f/22 and f/32. Nevertheless, f/8 lets in twice as much light as f/11 and represents a one-stop increase in exposure as does opening the aperture from f/2.8 to f/2. Thus, a one-stop

Natural Arch in Bryce Canyon, Utah is a fiery orange colour that begs to be photographed. Unfortunately, when I visited a fierce wind was blowing. In order to achieve f/22 on my Mamiya 7II plus 65mm lens, I needed a shutter speed fast enough to remain unaffected by the adverse wind conditions around my tripod. I needed f/22 for depth, and had just loaded a fresh roll of Velvia. On this occasion, rather than swap to ISO 100 film to gain a faster shutter speed, I opted to hang my camera bag from the tripod and pull down on the central column with all my weight. The result was a rock-steady assembly and a clean, crisp image.

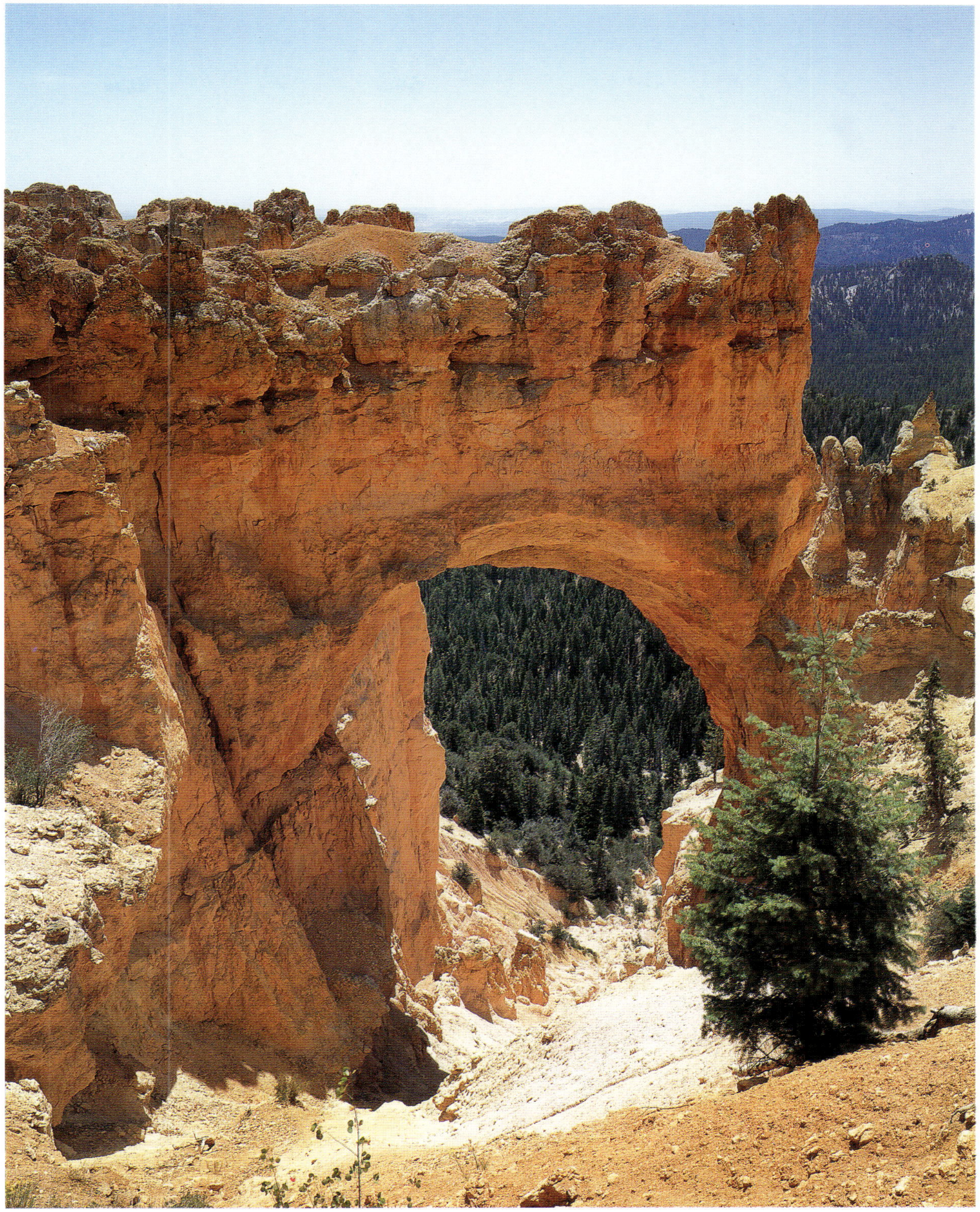

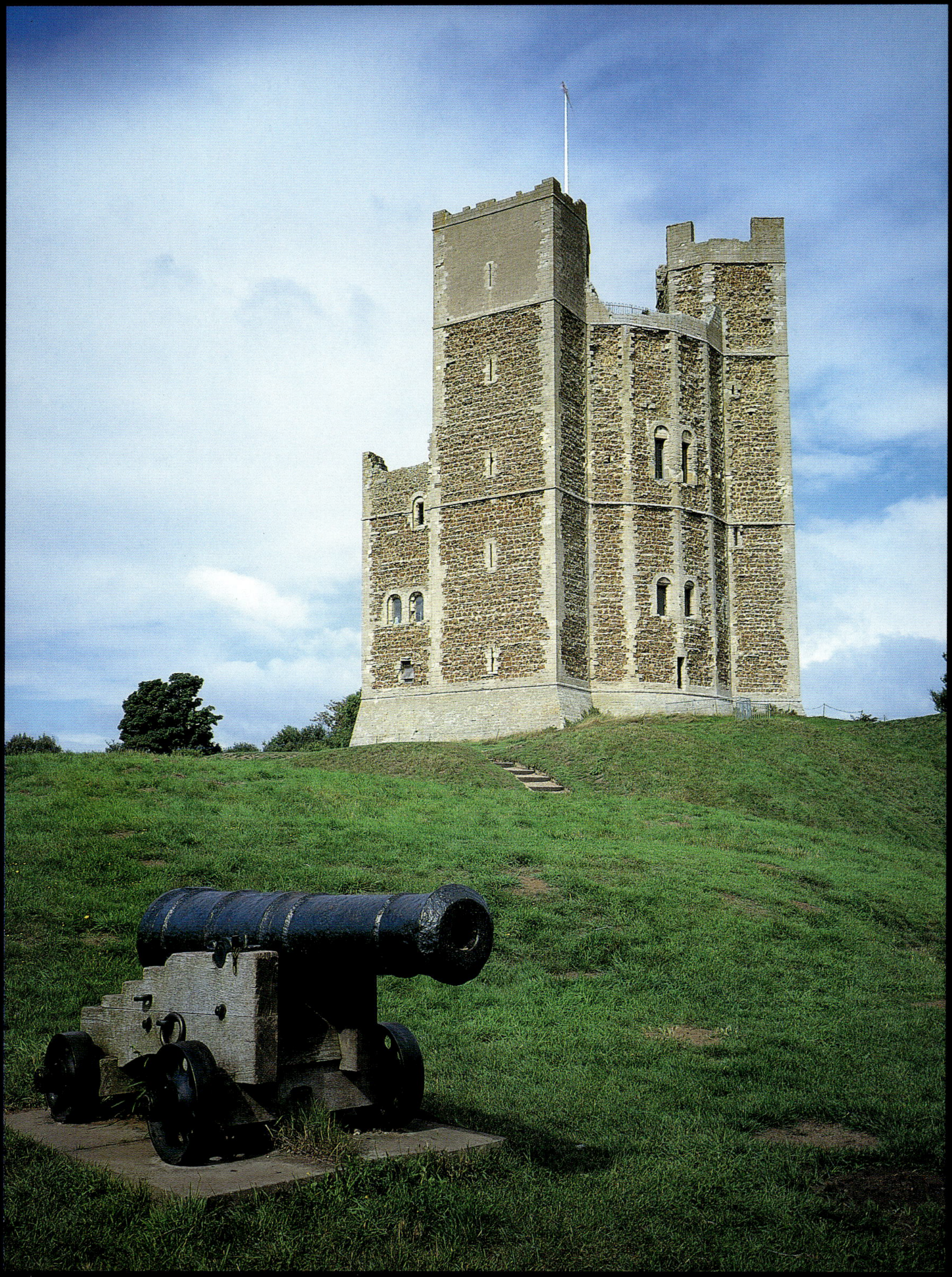

I have shot Orford Castle in Suffolk, England many times, but I had never considered placing a cannon in the foreground before. It certainly makes the shot more interesting and therefore more marketable. However, to obtain sufficient depth of field for this shot, I had to use a very small aperture indeed. The matching shutter speed was slow enough to mean that I needed a tripod, particularly as a strong easterly wind was blowing at the time.
Fuji GA645Zi, Velvia, tripod.

change in exposure represents either double or half of any given exposure value (EV).

As mentioned, the f-number dictates depth of field, or the zone of apparent sharpness. Shutter speed and aperture are linked by a reciprocal relationship. If you double the shutter opening time and close the aperture by one stop you are providing the film with the same amount (or quanta) of light as if you had halved the shutter speed and opened the aperture by one stop. Although in both cases the amount of light is equivalent, the effect in terms of zone of sharpness (depth of field) and motion-arresting potential will vary.

Throughout this book I refer to stops which should now begin gaining a quantitative meaning. For example, a photograph of scarlet poppies growing in a sea of white and yellow daisies requires 1/15 of a second at f/32 for correct exposure. Unfortunately, a steady breeze necessitates a faster shutter speed otherwise you risk getting a blurred image. While some landscape photographers may deliberately seek this effect, you might not. A two-stop increase of shutter speed to 1/60 of a second immobilizes the flowers that are dancing in the wind. However, to maintain the correct exposure we must also open the aperture by a corresponding two stops to f/16 – an aperture which still provides sufficient depth of field for this type of landscape subject.

Like f-numbers and shutter speeds, the speed or sensitivity of a film is also calibrated in stops. However, in this situation it is represented by a halving or doubling of the ISO rating. Examples of transparency film with a slow speed include neutral colour-balanced Kodachrome 64 and punchy, colour-rich Fuji Velvia ISO 50. The most popular medium-speed transparency films include Fuji Sensia 100 and Provia 100F, while moderately fast films include Kodachrome 200. Super-fast films are also available with a speed of up to ISO 1600. Faster films, however, are not particularly desirable, since with an increase in film speed comes an attendant increase in granularity. This level of film grain softens the image and creates a pointillist effect, and it is my opinion that landscapes should always be tack-sharp.

Halving the ISO number from ISO 400 to ISO 200, ISO 200 to ISO 100, ISO 100 to ISO 64/50, ISO 64/50 to ISO 25 increases the amount of light needed for a correct exposure by one stop in each case. Therefore, in the above example of poppies moving in the wind, it would be possible to retain the original f-number (f/32) for ultra-maximum depth of field, but use a faster film to facilitate a shutter speed which has greater motion-arresting potential. Assuming our original film was ISO 50, the shutter speed/aperture combination required for an ISO 200 film is simple to calculate. Kodachrome ISO 200 is two stops faster than Velvia ISO 50, so we need to change the camera's exposure by two stops to 1/60 of a second at f/32. This combination will prevent blur in the wind-blown flower, but is only one of several permutations in which an ISO 50 exposure of 1/15 of a second at f/32 could be changed by the two stops necessary to provide equivalent exposure on an ISO 200 film; for example 1/60 at f/32, 1/125 at f/16, 1/250 at f/8 and 1/500 at f/5.6 are all options. In windy conditions, freezing the action is important, but this particular subject also requires the best depth of field possible. Therefore, 1/60 of a second at f/32 is the only permutation that ideally suits this situation.

TTL metering

Why stretch the mind with all this theory? After all, both compact and SLR cameras can take pictures automatically without attention to details such as f-stops and shutter speeds, and film speed is taken into account automatically by DX coding. The amateur snapper can generally rely on through-the-lens (TTL) metering, which is accurate enough in most situations and provides results good enough for colour negative photography (prints). However, you have purchased this book because you want to gain expertize as a photographer.

Although TTL metering is probably the most significant technological asset in nature photography, you cannot absolutely rely on it in every situation. The message here is that you, and not the camera's auto meter, must have the final say in determining exposure. There are several established reasons for this:

- Not all scenic landscapes that you shoot are going to have average tonality. However, your camera's TTL meter has been calibrated to this.
- Certain subjects engender a creative need in the photographer to visualize the final image differently to how it was first perceived. Thus, at times, the camera must be forced to overexpose or underexpose an image.
- Films from the various manufacturers behave differently. Velvia has fine grain and a punchy impact, which is ideally suited to landscapes. However, its vibrant colours do not suit flesh tones. Kodachrome 64, which has a similar ISO rating, is neutral, so is fine for people shots as well as accurate (if less vibrant) landscapes. Many photographers consistently underexpose or overexpose a particular type of film. Velvia's colour saturation increases at one-third of a stop underexposure. Such treatment can modify the final image with a subjective quality that is often quite pleasing.
- Exposure compensation is critical for lighting conditions with heavy contrast that invariably fools the camera's TTL meter.

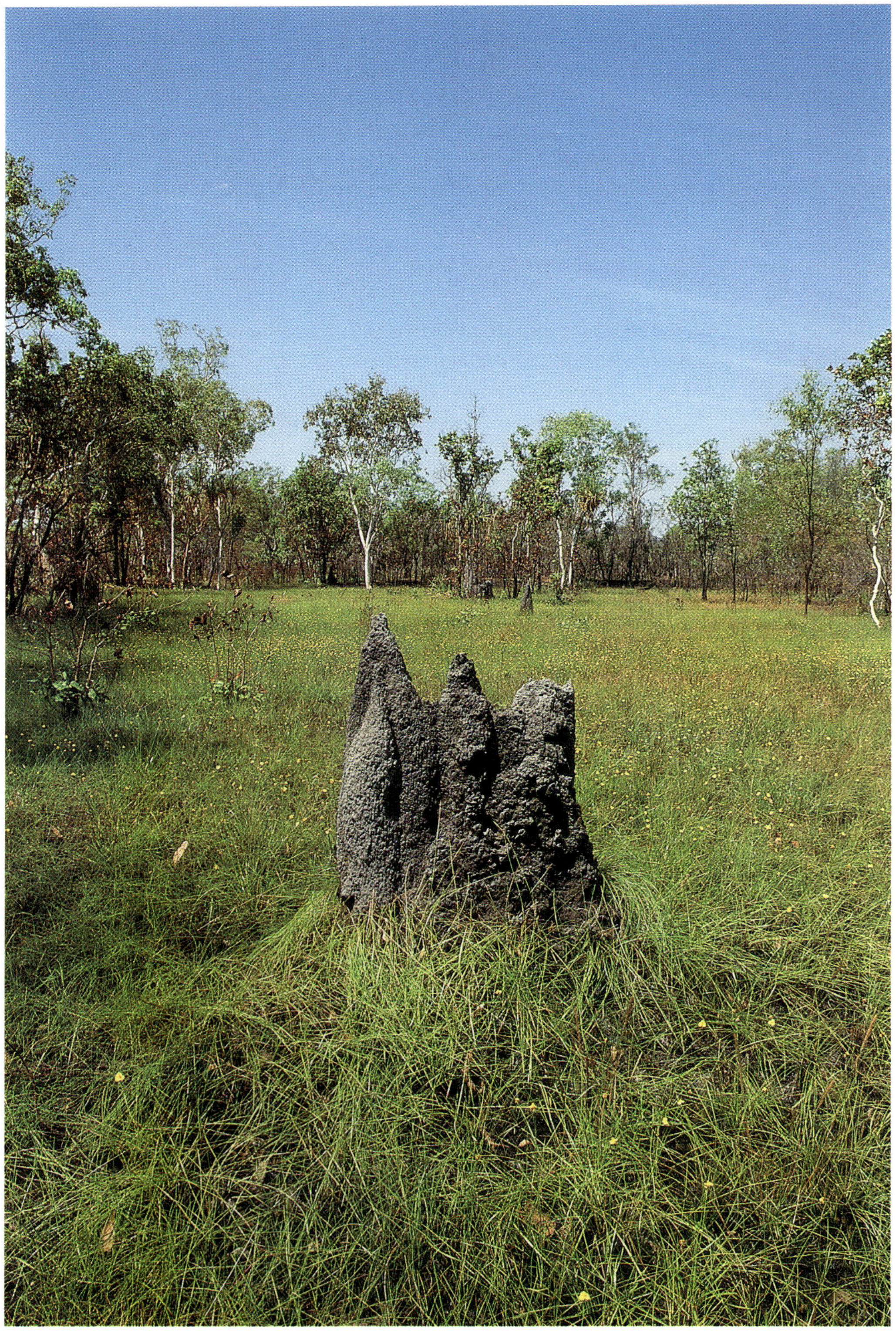

The camera's TTL meter provides an indication of light reflected off the subject. If the subject you are metering is mid-toned, your transparency will also be mid-toned. But if your subject is not mid-toned, you could meter an 18% reflectance grey card in the same ambient light as your subject and use this exposure to photograph your subject. Alternatively, you could employ a hand-held light meter in its incident mode. This measures light falling on the subject and not light reflected from it. If you don't have a grey card available when shooting a subject which is heavily contrasted against a dominant, light background, you can avoid underexposure by increasing the exposure by a half to one-and-a-half stops. Equally, a light subject contrasted against a dark background means the TTL meter overexposes a subject's detail leading to a blanched appearance. To compensate, the exposure should be reduced by a half to one-and-a-half stops. With experience the compensation factor becomes easier to judge.

A camera TTL meter works fine most of the time. However, this light-coloured termite mound required an extra half a stop to render correct exposure. This was hardly surprising, since the sun was so bright that even sunglasses proved ineffectual. We were miles from anywhere when we came across this: the only green grass we had seen with a termite mound in it throughout the Northern Territory. There was no chance to wait around for better light at the end of the day, nor could we return on another occasion, so I shot at midday and made the most of it. I used an 81B warm-up filter and bracketed extensively to compensate for the excess brightness. Taken in Kakadu National Park, Australia.
Pentax MZ5n + 28–70mm zoom lens, 1/30sec at f/22, Velvia, tripod.

Monument Valley from Redlands View, near the Arizona/Utah border. I needed to add extra exposure to compensate for the extreme brightness of this desert scene. Without this extra half stop the meter would have been fooled into a slight underexposure.
Mamiya 7II + 65mm lens, Velvia, tripod.

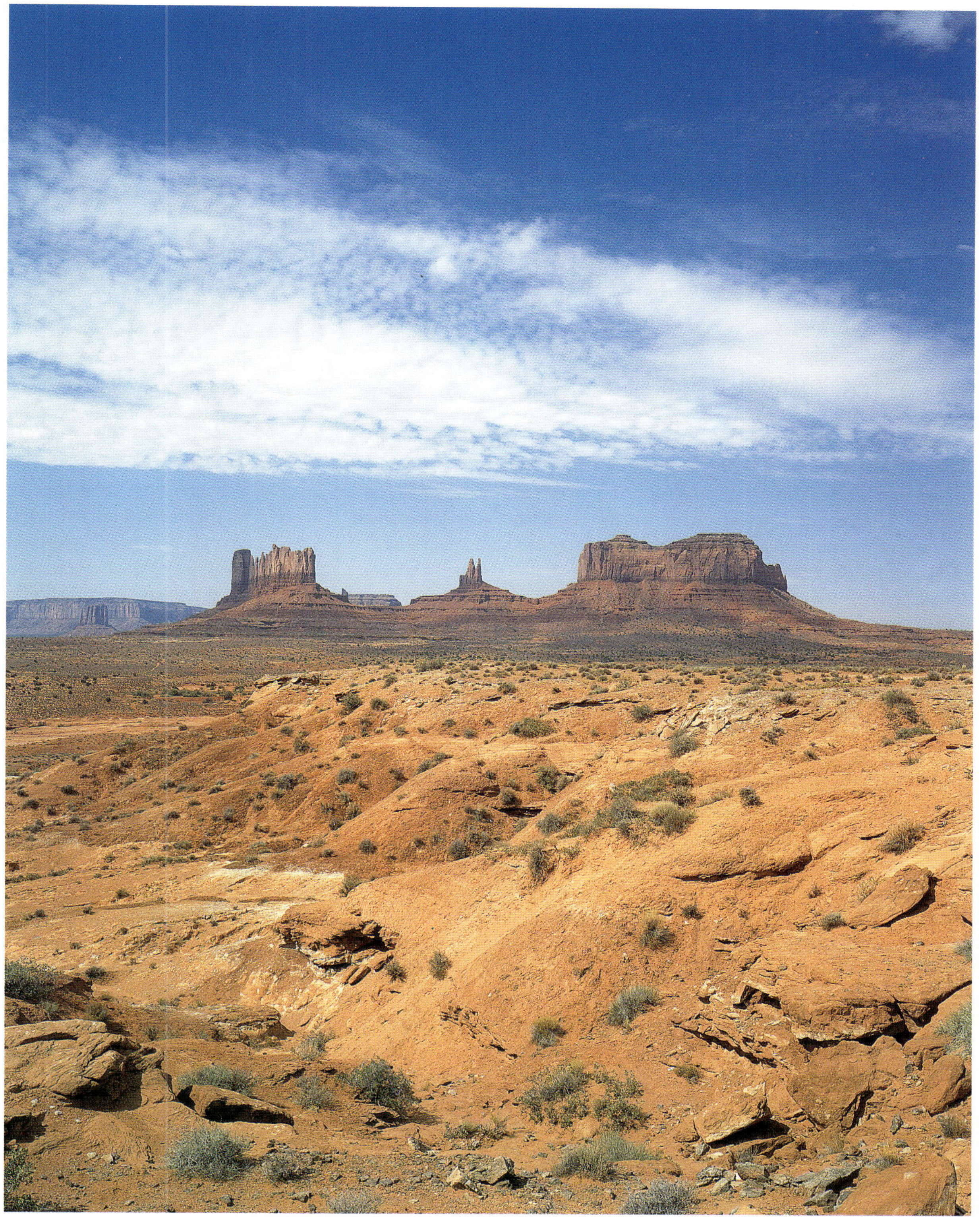

If using slide film, it has an exposure latitude approaching two-and-a-half stops either side of optimum; this means that –2.5 stops and you have a black cat in a coal cellar and +2.5 stops you end up with a white cat in a snow storm.

Modern cameras employ advanced TTL metering systems like matrix, spot, average, centre-weighted and multisegment metering, all of which can give excellent results. However, none of these can replace your ability to assess a subject tonality and make any appropriate adjustments. With regard to metering in tricky lighting conditions, you should also read the following sections on using neutral density graduate filters (see page 34) and reciprocity failure (see below).

Reciprocity failure

Reciprocity describes the inverse relationship between camera shutter speed and lens aperture (or f-stop). Thus, an aperture of f/16 at 1/60sec gives the same exposure as f/22 at 1/30sec or f/11 at 1/125sec. In other words, to maintain a constant level of exposure when you reduce the shutter speed, you must compensate by opening the aperture (i.e. setting a lower f-stop number) and vice versa. This established reciprocal relationship is what forms the basis of the algorithms which control our camera and hand-held exposure meters.

Under most normal conditions this relationship holds up, and one's meter can be trusted, provided that one bears in mind the well-known caveats about deviating from metered values for scenes which do not have average tonality based on an 18% grey scale. In other words, one must remember to overexpose for very bright scenes and underexpose for very dark ones, since such subjects can easily fool electronic meters.

Unfortunately, at very short and very long exposure times this reciprocal relationship breaks down. As far as landscape and environmental photographers are concerned, it is the effect of long exposure times that are most relevant. When shooting scenic views at the very beginning or end of the day, it is inevitable that you will have your camera on a tripod, combining a slow film like Velvia with the smallest aperture possible – no larger than f/16, and possibly f/32 or even f/45 if you are using a large-format camera. Under such conditions, your exposures will deviate from the normal reciprocal relationship between shutter and aperture. This phenomenon is more common than you might think. It not only occurs at either end of the day, but also in dense woodland – even when that woodland is under a tropical sun at midday. I hope the following case studies (see page 23) will be explanatory.

A word of caution: you can simply open the aperture until you get a sensible shutter speed that falls back on the normal reciprocal relationship between shutter and aperture. Unfortunately, you will rapidly lose depth of field, and what makes this sort of photography successful is achieving sharpness from near to far. In the example of the bluebell scene (in the following case study), I was using a very wide-angle 80mm Schneider Super-Symmar XL lens on my 5 x 4in Ebony view camera. This lens has little inherent depth of field, and cannot really be tilted for improving depth because of the three-dimensional structure of woodland. Because of this, I really did need the f/32 aperture to obtain every bit of depth possible in this marvellous scene.

Dealing with reciprocity failure is a lot easier with a fully automated camera that stretches to 30-second exposures. My Pentax MZ5n made light work of a small rainforest creek in Wooroonooran National Park. All I did was set f/22 and note that exposure was already 20 seconds in the mid-afternoon light. What I did was drop to f/16 and bracket until the shutter speed hit 30 seconds. I got some excellent shots with this approach.

Since most readers will probably be striving for the sharpest images possible, the following list gives some idea of what to expect from selected emulsions at or below ISO 100. The table is a mix of what the manufacturers suggest and what I have noted in the field through usage.

Fuji Velvia

At 10 seconds add +2⁄3, although as indicated above I have gone to +11⁄2 stops to correct reciprocity failure. A magenta filter (CC05) may help.

Kodak Kodachrome 64

At only 1 second an extra stop is required. This film is not recommended with anything above 10 seconds. A red CC10 filter may help.

Fuji Provia 100F, Sensia 100, Kodak Elite Chrome 100

These are fairly resistant to reciprocity failure up to 10 seconds and probably beyond.

Bluebell woods

I was shooting bluebells under a fairly transparent leaf canopy. It was about 7pm in early May. My Sekonic meter was reading about two seconds at f/32 in its incident mode. I guessed this was way under due to reciprocity failure, and this proved to be correct. My final 5 x 4in Velvia transparency was exposed for eight seconds at f/32, and was just about right (with hindsight, six seconds would have been spot on). As you can see, this represents in the region of a 1.5 stop increase in exposure to compensate for reciprocity failure.

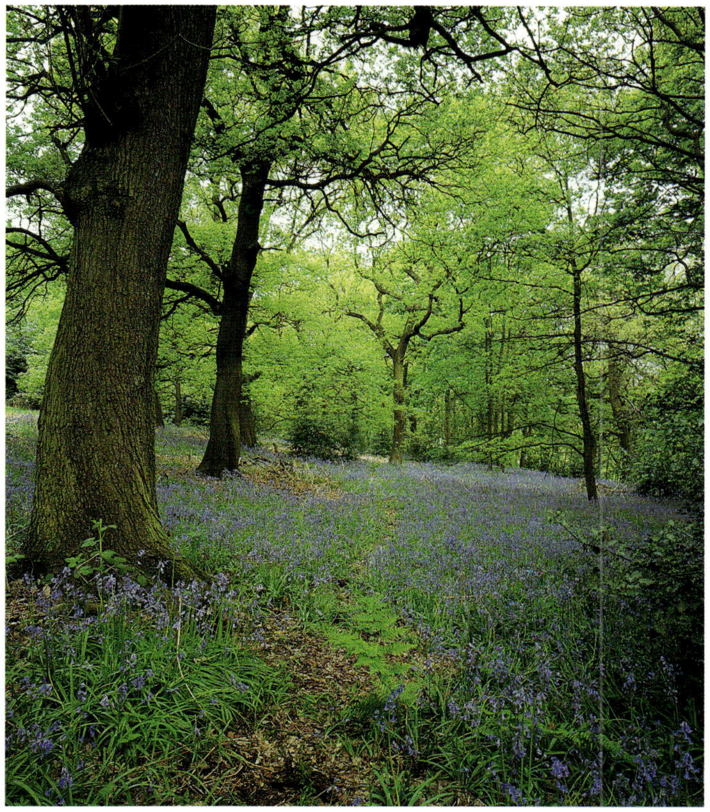

Taken at around 7pm in early May, this shot was taken in my local woods. Reciprocity failure meant that I ignored an incident reading of two seconds, and instead allowed eight seconds exposure. I had shot this scene many times on smaller formats and could predict the degree of extra exposure required with relative ease.
Ebony SV45TE + 80mm Schneider Super-Symmar XL, 8 seconds at f32, Velvia.

Tropical rainforest

A second example comes from shooting tropical rainforest at around noon on a bright, but overcast day. I set my Mamiya 7II on a tripod with its ultra-wide 43mm lens, and positioned it in 18in (45cm) of flowing water. I pointed the camera upstream to take in the marginal palms and foreground rocks and stones. The ISO 50 exposure was indicating four seconds at f/16. I bracketed up to 30 seconds to be sure of getting at least one perfect exposure of this magical scene. The best shots, however, were at eight seconds and f/16 – a full stop over that recommended. A similar story unfolded nearby where I shot the eerie buttress roots of the giant rainforest trees. Here 15 seconds at f/16 was required to get a good image.

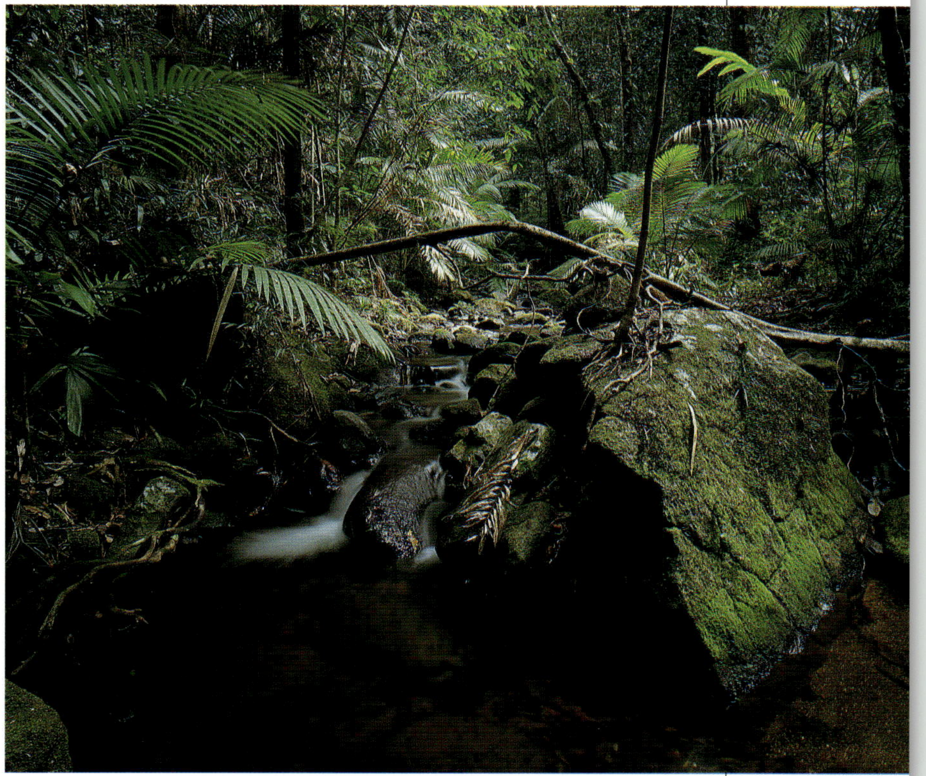

This stone was in a beautiful creek in the Mossman Gorge section of Daintree National Park. A few seconds of extra exposure was required to compensate for reciprocity failure.
Mamiya 7II + 43mm lends. Velvia, tripod.

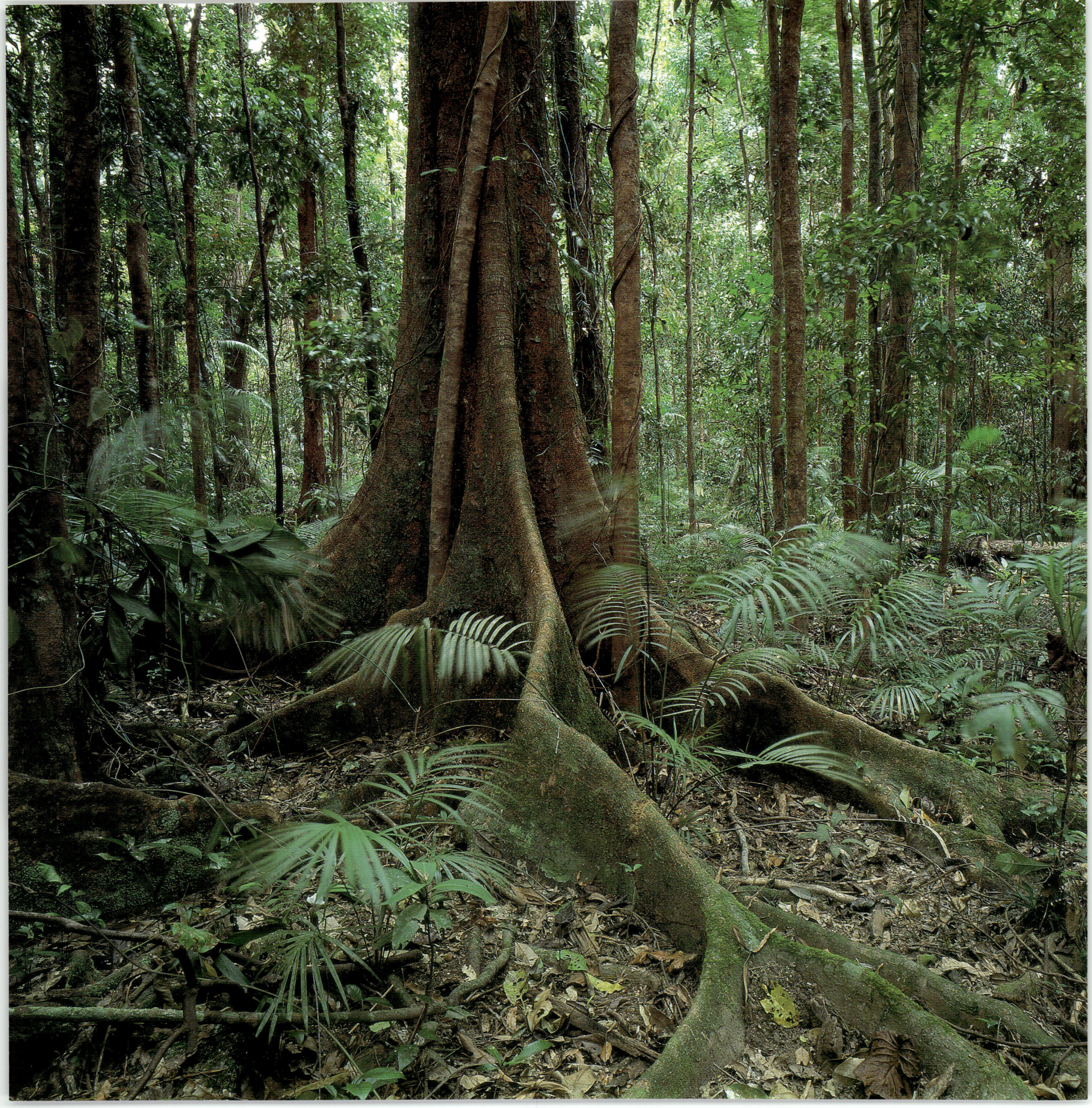

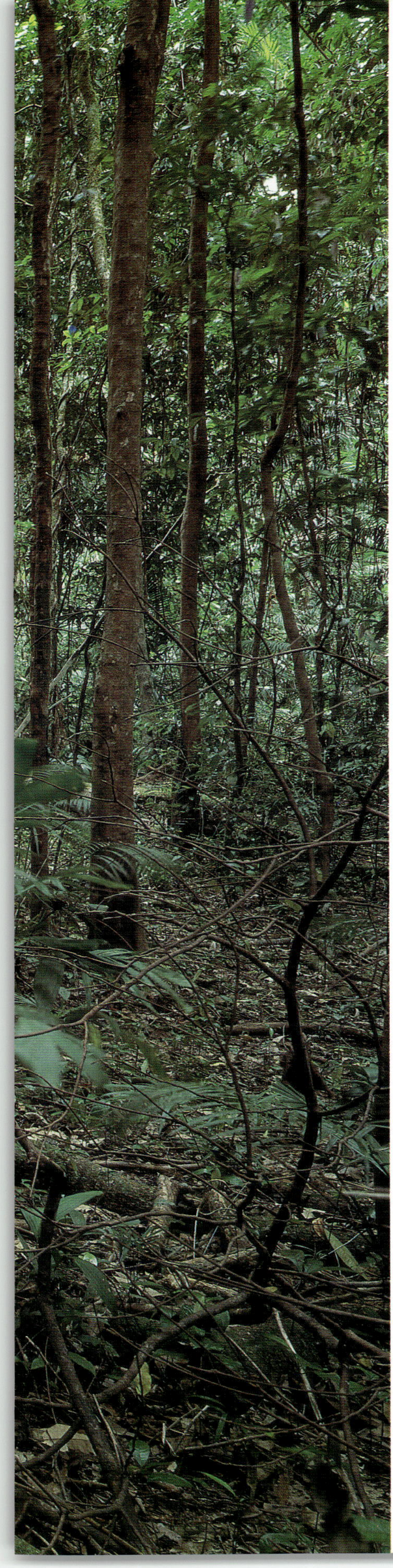

This tropical buttress root system was shot on full manual exposure control using the bulb setting. I added an extra 8 seconds to that indicated by my meter. To do this accurately I used a stopwatch. Taken at the Mossman Gorge section of Daintree National Park, Queensland, Australia. *Mamiya 7II + 43mm lens, tripod.*

Key 35mm camera features

Manual exposure control

This allows you to alter either the shutter speed, aperture or exposure compensation dial. Thus you can override the camera's 'auto' decision, for example for a tricky lighting situation or when you want to be creative. You can also exert full manual control with long exposures using the bulb (B) setting on your camera (this leaves the shutter open as long as the shutter release button is depressed).

Aperture priority exposure control

Aperture selection dictates depth of field and therefore the zone of apparent sharpness. For this reason it is extremely useful in landscape and habitat photography, where depth of field is particularly critical. Its automatic control of exposure makes it handy for use with a remote camera release. You should only consider buying a camera that provides a viewfinder read-out of the coupled shutter speed. This is crucial because at slow shutter speeds you need to employ a tripod – or firmly brace yourself in some way – in order to avoid camera shake.

Wide range of high-quality lenses

Your camera should be part of a system that offers high-quality optics in the 17–500mm range. If your budget is limited, rather than buy from the camera manufacturers, consider the independent lens makers, particularly Tamron, Sigma and Tokina. The cost of new optics from these manufacturers can be less than second-hand prices from the camera manufacturers. I regard my many Tamron lenses very highly.

Remote release

This facility is used with a tripod. Like a mirror lock-up, this feature helps prevent camera vibration when the shutter opens. It is particularly useful for shutter speeds below 1/30 of a second where unsteady or heavy hands could cause camera movement. There are two types of release cables: a simple cable which screws into the shutter release button and is mechanically operated, or the far more expensive electronic cable release which plugs into a dedicated socket (I bought mine second-hand for the price of a conventional release). On a recent visit to Arches National Park in Utah where the elements have hewed spectacular natural stone arches from the Colorado plateau, I was forced to rethink the use of cable releases. Delicate Arch is perhaps the most famous of the park's arches. It is nearly a two-mile uphill hike across steep, slick rock to reach Delicate Arch. On my last night in Moab where we were staying, I was determined to shoot the sunset at Delicate Arch. In 90-degree heat, I ran this hike in 15 minutes with a Benbo MK1 and rucksack stuffed with cameras and other paraphernalia. While I just made the sunset, my cable release exploded

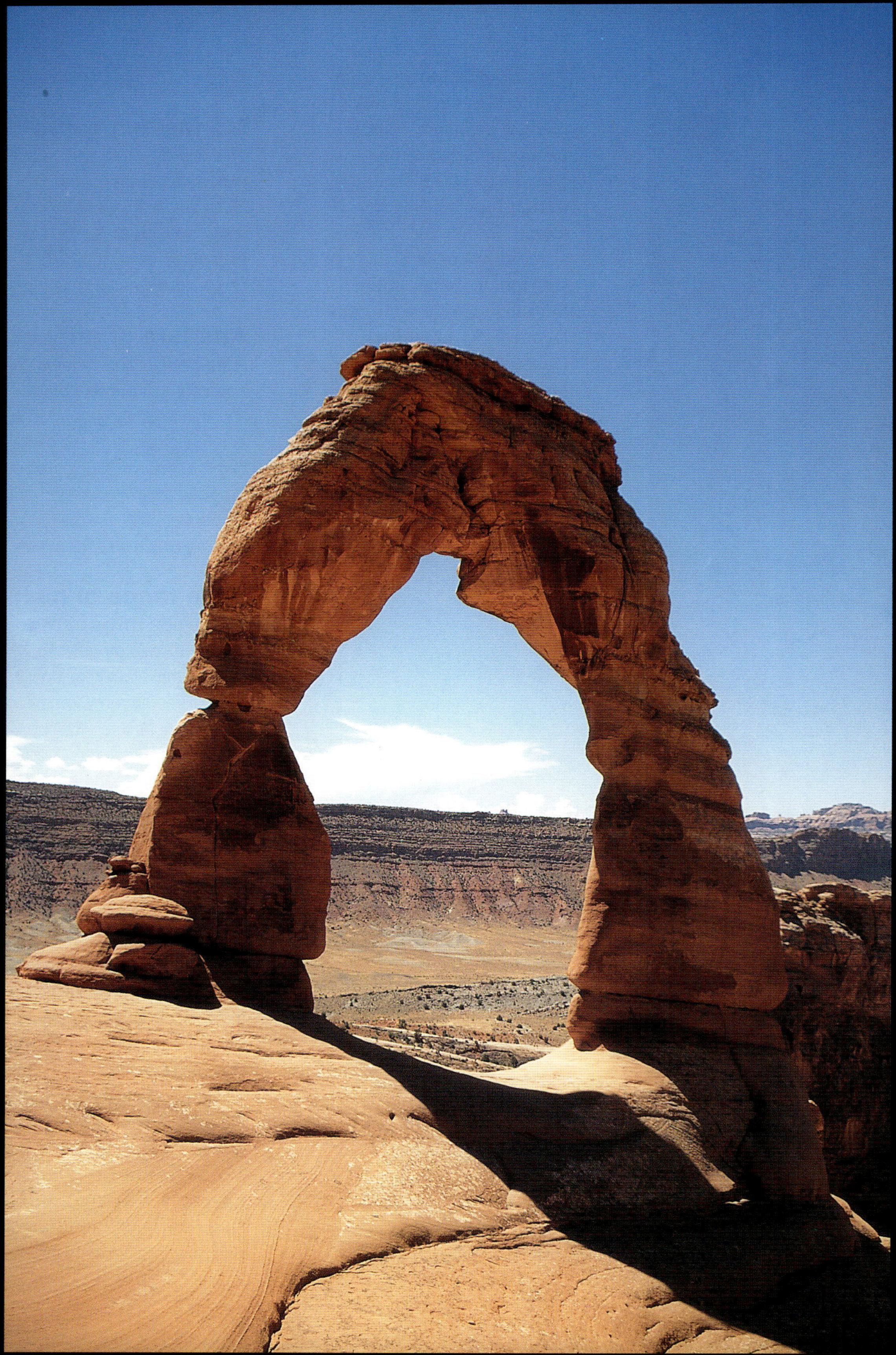

This entirely adequate view of Delicate Arch was taken midday on my 35mm kit. I added an 81B warm-up filter to tone down the blue cast, but contrast these results with the more pleasing, gentler hues which occur as dusk approaches. To compare, see the 6 x 9cm image of Delicate Arch shown on page 101.
Pentax MZ5n + 28–70mm zoom lens, Velvia.

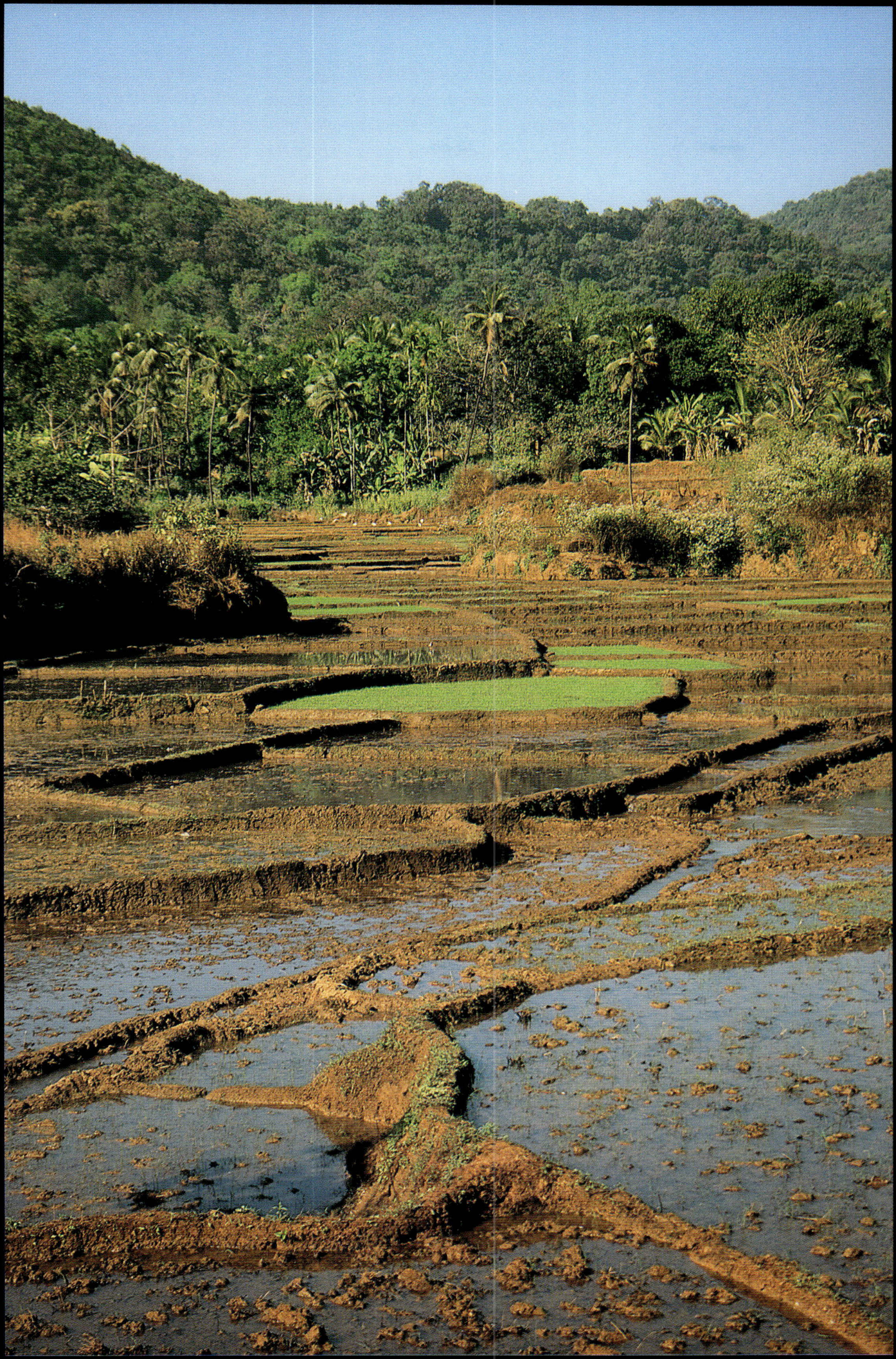

This view of terraced paddy fields in India was taken using aperture priority automation. As I didn't have a tripod with me, I needed to know whether the small aperture I had set for good depth of field would lead to slow shutter speeds and camera shake; most modern SLRs give you the matching shutter speed indication within the viewfinder.
Pentax MZ5n + 28–70mm zoom lens, 1/125sec at f/8, Velvia.

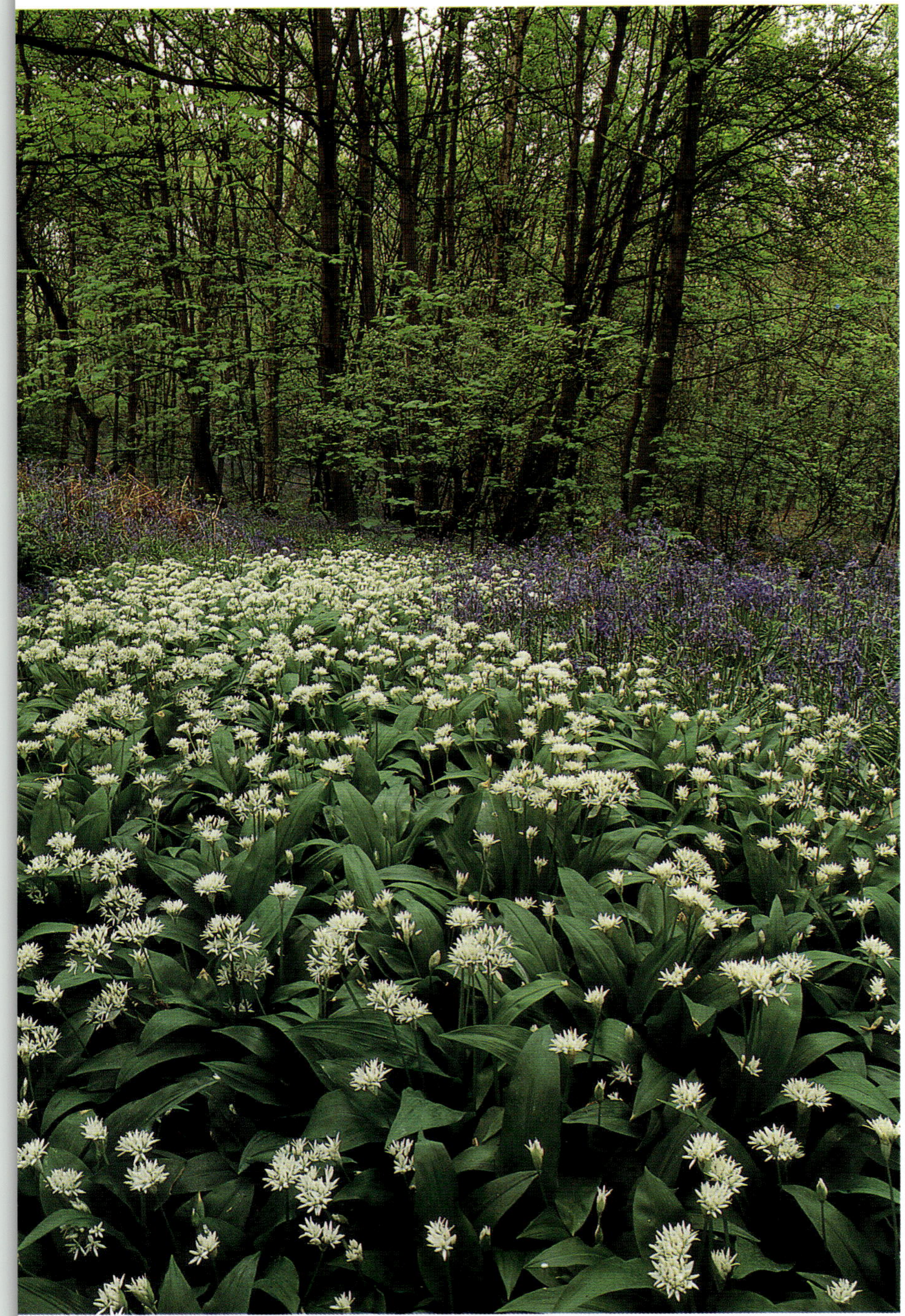

Understanding the extent of depth of field is important for scenes such as this woodland view where sharpness is required from very near to very far.
Pentax SLR + 28–70mm zoom lens set to f/22, Velvia, tripod.

into its component parts and died on the first frame, as indeed I nearly did. Interestingly, not one of my pictures suffered from finger release shake. As a result, I now question the wisdom of a cable release when using rangefinder cameras, especially if I'm using a sturdy tripod.

It is interesting what we are willing to do to record a great image. At sunset, the slick-rock amphitheatre around Delicate Arch is heaving with photographers. On my visit, there were probably 50 compact 35mm cameras and 20 SLRs clicking and whirring away. I counted two medium-format cameras and one 5 x 4in view camera. Of all these latter-day Ansel Adams prodigies, only myself and the owner of the view camera were using a cable release and tripod. While crowds like this may spoil the sense of wilderness that many seek at places like Delicate Arch, it is a price we must now pay, even if the odd frame is ruined by someone running into it as you push down on your cable release. This usually happens just as the fiery sky is at its most vibrant.

Depth of field preview lever

Depth of field refers to the zone of sharp focus which in most photography extends to two-thirds behind and one-third in front of the point of focus. The rules listed in the box below will help you control depth of field.

- The smaller the lens aperture, the greater the depth of field; an important consideration in landscape work.
- For a defined lens aperture, the depth of field will decrease as the distance to the point of focus decreases. Therefore, depth of field is a much bigger issue in macro photography than in landscape work.
- If the distance between film plane and point of focus is fixed, increasing the focal length of a lens will decrease the depth of field. This allows long lenses to isolate animals or plants from their surroundings making for more pleasing compositions. This, however, means the shallow depth of field one obtains with a 150mm telephoto lens in 35mm photography provides a similar depth of field as a 150mm-wide normal lens on a 5 x 4in view camera.
- For a given magnification and a fixed aperture, lenses with a different focal length (50mm or 100mm) will yield an image with the same depth of field.

Having a depth of field preview lever that stops the lens down to your pre-selected aperture provides an instant view of the plane over which sharpness extends. Thus you can control whether the peripheral content of a view is in or out of focus, or confirm that sharpness extends over the whole of your main subject.

Optional extras

If possible, your 35mm SLR should also have some means of automatic film transport, perhaps a built' in or separate autowinder or motor drive. Features like red-eye reduction and panoramic mode are more for the amateur market, so don't be misled by the glossy brochures. These features are rather gimmicky in my opinion. DX coding for film speed and autofocus are more useful, but should not be features that affect your decision whether to buy or not.

Second-hand 35mm kit

If you are thinking about purchasing second-hand kit, you should seek out reputable retail outlets that offer guarantees. Remember that many people off-load cameras because they are malfunctioning in some way. Don't be put off, though; buying second-hand is the most cost-effective way of building up a system and obtaining professional-quality results in landscape photography. Here are some rules for buying second-hand:

- Buy only from reputable suppliers.
- Smell the gear; a dank aroma could indicate mould which is the worst enemy of lenses.
- Check lens apertures (iris blades) open and close smoothly.
- Look for scratches on entry and particularly exit lenses.
- Check camera shutter speeds are coupled to apertures; establish the shutter stays open progressively longer as the aperture is closed down.
- Check film transport mechanisms work and that the camera back is not dented or distorted as this will leak light.
- If at all possible, the best test is to put a slide film through any prospective camera purchase. Slide film reflects exposure accuracy far better than print film.

When selecting a second-hand camera, you should be looking for a rugged and flexible tool. Buy into a system that has a good reputation for reliability. Compare any prospective camera to the following table, making sure that it has as many of the high scoring features as possible.

My now very old Pentax LX has many of these features, plus it has a sealed construction making it weatherproof – important in humid tropical or gritty desert conditions. Dust and water are your camera's worst enemies. When the batteries fail in my LX, its normally electronic shutter continues to operate as a mechanical-

Feature	Importance rating (1 = poor, 10 = good)
Wide range of high-quality lenses	10
Through the lens (TTL) exposure control (to include TTL flash)	10
Aperture priority exposure	10
Exposure compensation dial	10
Remote release facility	8
Manual exposure	7
Depth of field preview	6
Mirror lock-up (N/A to rangefinders)	5
Spot metering	5
Shutter priority exposure	4
Fully autoexposure	2

only shutter. While the exposure system is not as foolproof in tricky lighting conditions as the latest Pentax MZ series, this is still my personal all-time favourite camera.

I would say that about one-third of my 35mm lenses are second-hand. They all perform beautifully, some better than my new ones. I have several camera bodies that are now getting a bit old, but again these perform with the same style as my newer cameras. I have one camera which is a particular favourite. It is maybe 20 years old and I obtained it third-hand. Perhaps because of this I have no qualms about taking it to places that I would never dream of taking my more expensive kit – after all, dropping it into a cascading river or down a mountainside would not be the end of the world. Despite its age, it is capable of turning in high-quality images. I tend to keep a second-hand 28mm Tamron lens attached to it at all times. Together they make a neat little package for landscape photography which, with a mini-tripod, is highly portable. I use it particularly in adverse weather conditions so that I can concentrate on the subject and not the welfare of the equipment.

If you scrutinize the following waterfall image taken on an older second-hand 35mm SLR, I'm sure you will appreciate that they can be every bit as good as those taken on a modern all-singing, all-dancing 35mm autofocus camera worth three or four times the price. I think that results are also marginally superior to those obtained on a high-quality 35mm auto compact worth about twice the price of the second-hand SLR.

Buying second-hand kit is not just a way of entering the world of nature photography for the first time, it is a way of procuring highly desirable and otherwise prohibitively expensive optics. Some

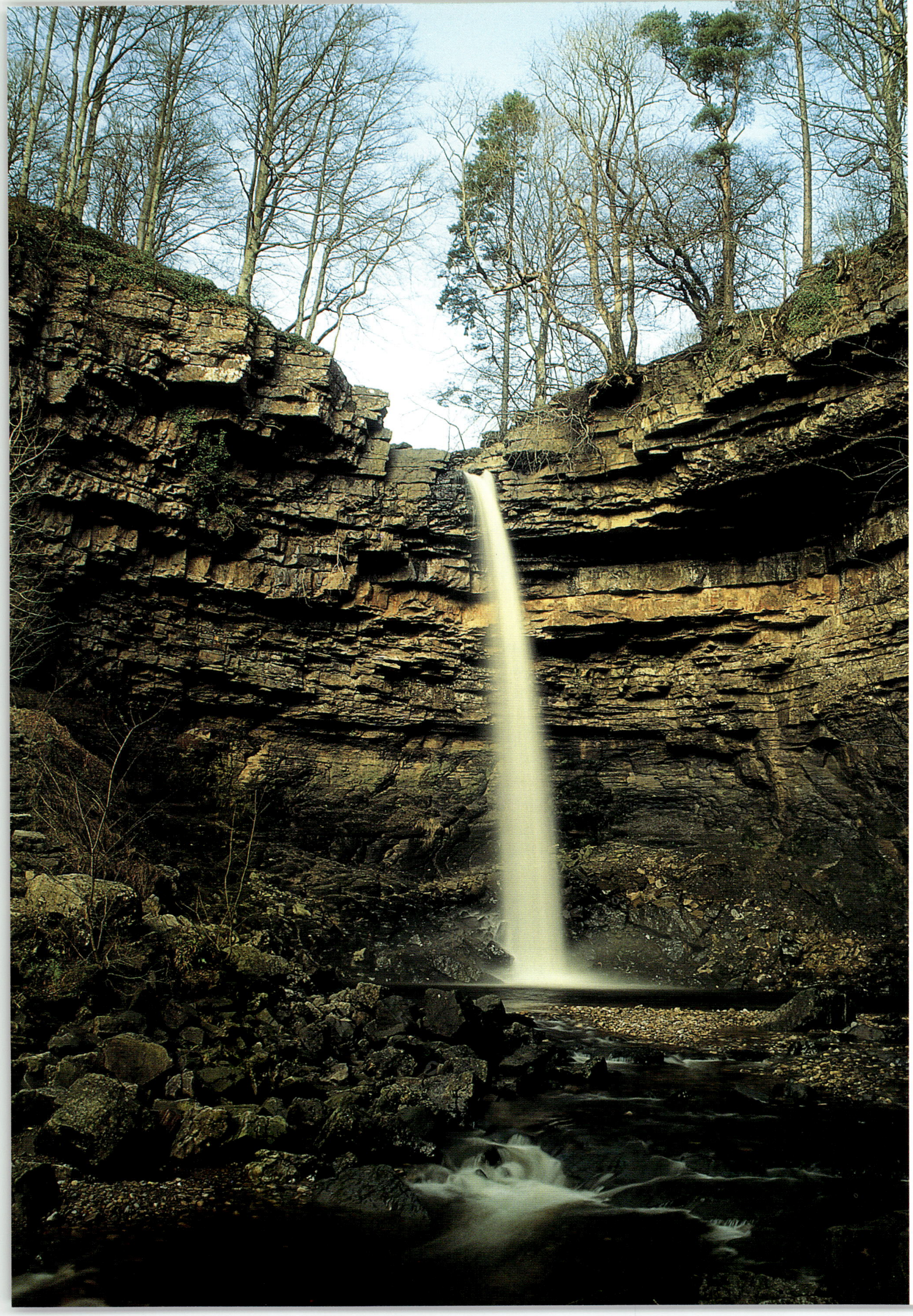

This 35mm transparency of Hardraw Force in North Yorkshire was taken on a second-hand Pentax ME Super with a second-hand 28mm Tamron lens. It shows how good results can be obtained on a budget. I use this camera and lens for all arduous, wet or generally nasty environments. At this price, if it breaks, it breaks; it is not the end of the world.
Pentax ME Super + 28mm Tamron lens, exposure between 1/2sec and 1 second, tripod.

aspects of nature photography are improved with long and fast lenses (having a large maximum aperture). For instance, a 300mm lens is most useful when it has a maximum aperture of f/2.8. This means that you can employ action-freezing shutter speeds. How much does such a lens cost? Approximately four months' salary at least, but buying one second-hand may only require starving yourself and your family for a month and a half. I bought my Pentax 300mm f/4 second-hand very cheaply. It was in pristine condition and works fine, proving that the second-hand market is important for everyone, whether beginner, keen amateur or professional.

If I was asked for my advice on what to buy as an initial 35mm start-up kit for nature and landscape work, I would select a second-hand camera body with TTL exposure control (including

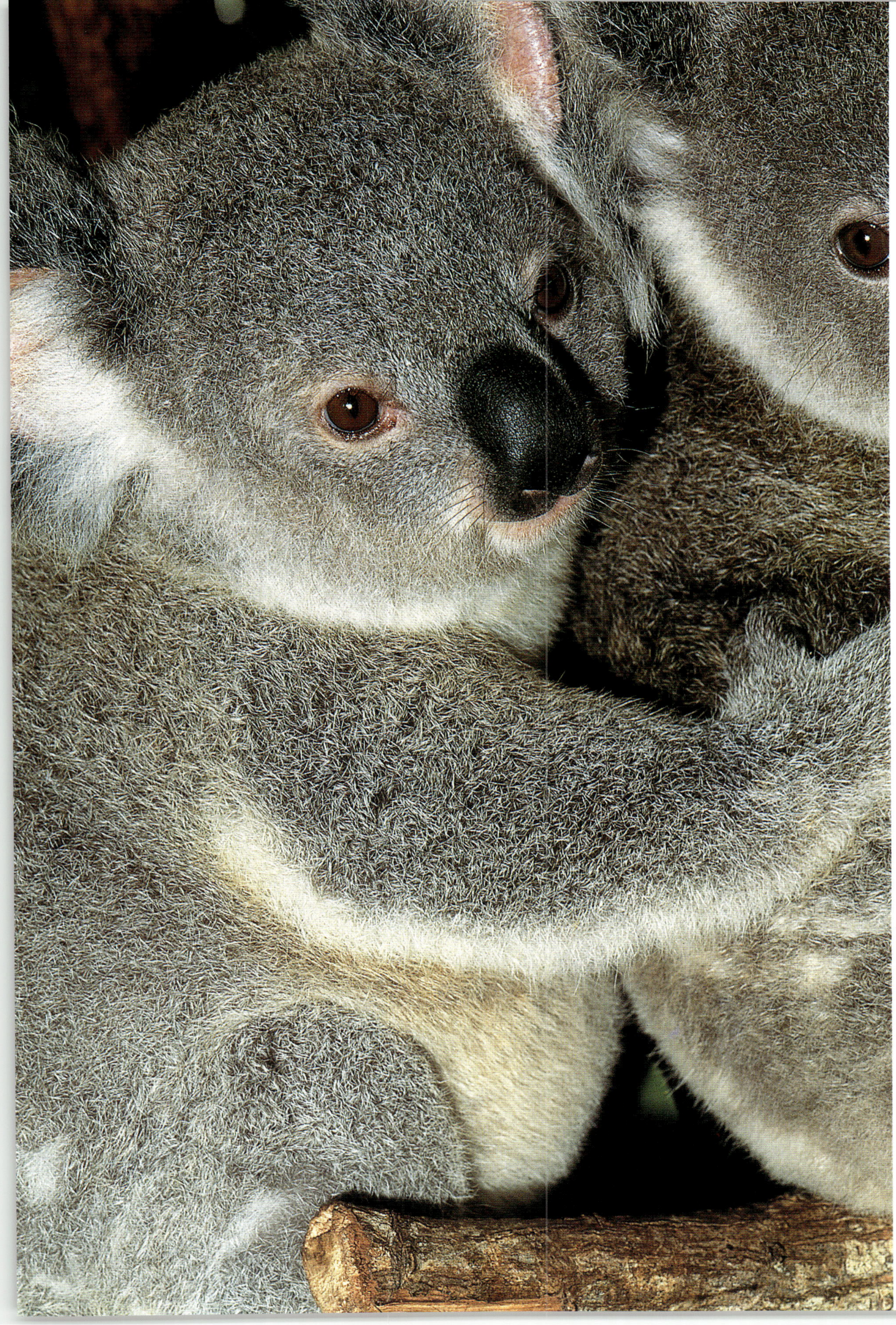

Highly marketable 'cute' images such as this koala can easily be taken with a typical beginner's 35mm set-up of camera plus standard zoom. ***Pentax MZ5n + 28–70mm zoom lens.***

flash) along with a 28–70mm wide-angle zoom, a 50mm macro lens capable of focusing from life-size magnification on film to infinity (good for landscapes and butterflies), and an 80–210mm zoom. This combination can be used for close-up, landscape and animal portrait studies, providing a good all-round combination.

It is sometimes possible to buy new and still get a bargain. All manufacturers today offer good value cameras. Often the specification of these models is extremely high. In addition, from time to time retailers offer special deals on equipment. Some people must have the latest version of a camera almost as a fashion statement but, if you are sensible, you can see through the marketing façade and aim to buy a tool, the best one you can afford to do the job.

I have remained faithful to Pentax over the years and one of the reasons is that, like Nikon, they supply autofocus lenses that have back compatibility with non-autofocus camera bodies, and vice versa. This is a very important point for people who have older, manual-focus bodies, whether they are new or second-hand. If you build up a manual-focus system, chances are that at

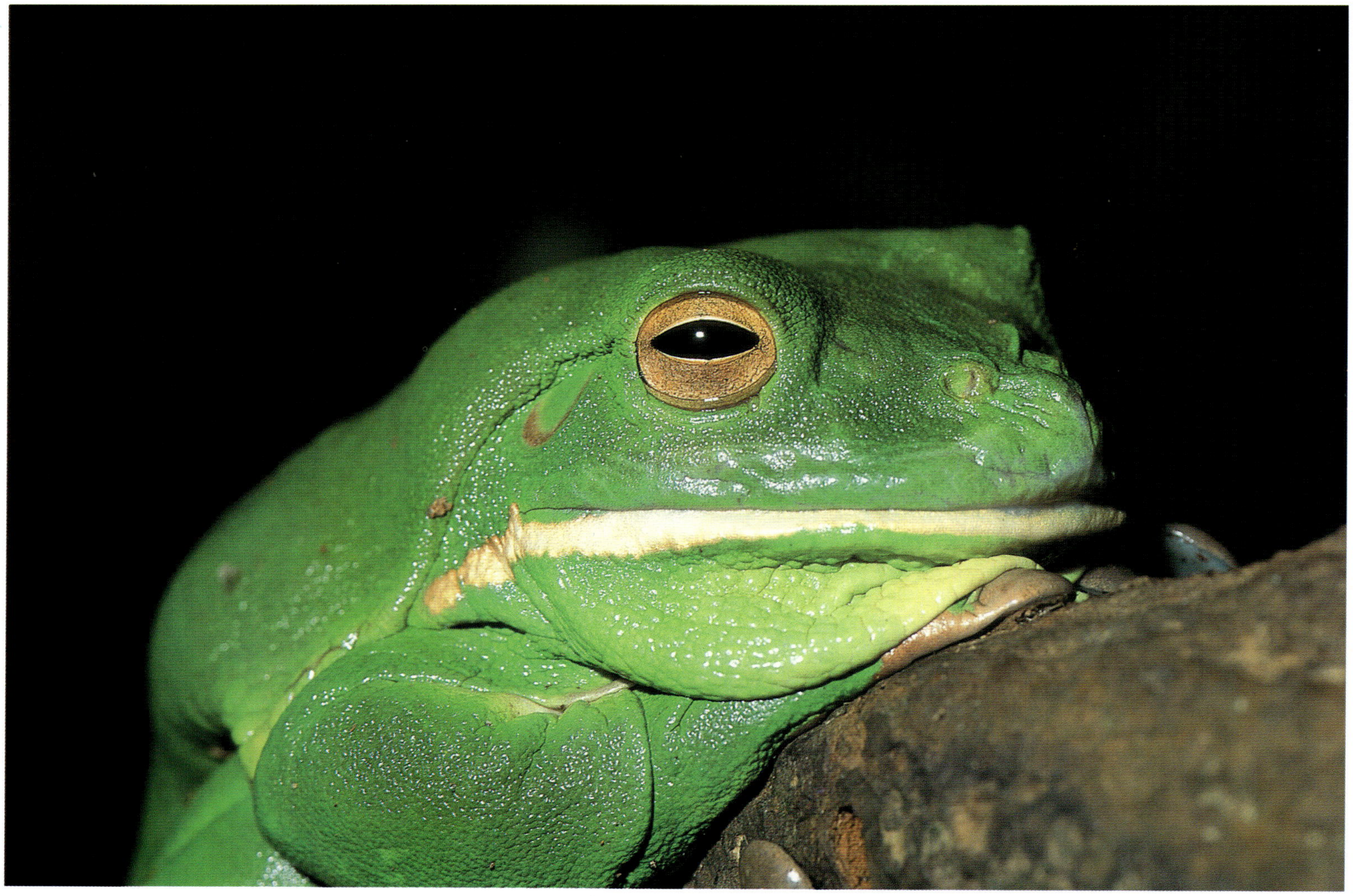

some point in the future you will want to buy a new camera which will most likely be autofocus. What a waste it would be to discard your old lenses if they can't be used on your new body. Also, if you have a new or second-hand autofocus camera body and it accepts both auto- and manual- focus lenses, you have access to a vast range of second-hand lenses to go with it.

While older cameras represent good starting points for budding photographers, one of the benefits of buying a new camera is owning an advanced metering system which can cope with difficult lighting better than older average or centre-weighted metering modes. These matrix/multisegment metering modes offer a distinct advantage in troublesome environments, woodland, for example, where light forms a patchwork mosaic of differing intensities. You can read more about metering in this environment on page 57.

Camera supports

Do you need a tripod? Quite frankly, yes. Look for heavy-duty construction to absorb the punishment dished out by extreme conditions. Look for a tripod which extends from very low to a good maximum working height without extending the centre column, which inevitably compromises stability. All the better if it has sealed legs so the tripod can be set up in water, sand or mud. Buy a strap to carry your tripod over your shoulder; it will make all the difference between taking your tripod with you on a long hike or leaving it at home. The camera should attach to the tripod by means of a quick-release plate which forms an integral part of a large ball and socket head. While with good lighting conditions excellent landscape pictures can be taken on 35mm SLRs hand-held, the golden rule is

This image was taken near the village of Goathland in the North Yorkshire Moors National Park. It was made possible with a very sturdy tripod, which was set up in 6in (15cm) of water.
Mamiya 7II and 65mm lens, Velvia, tripod.

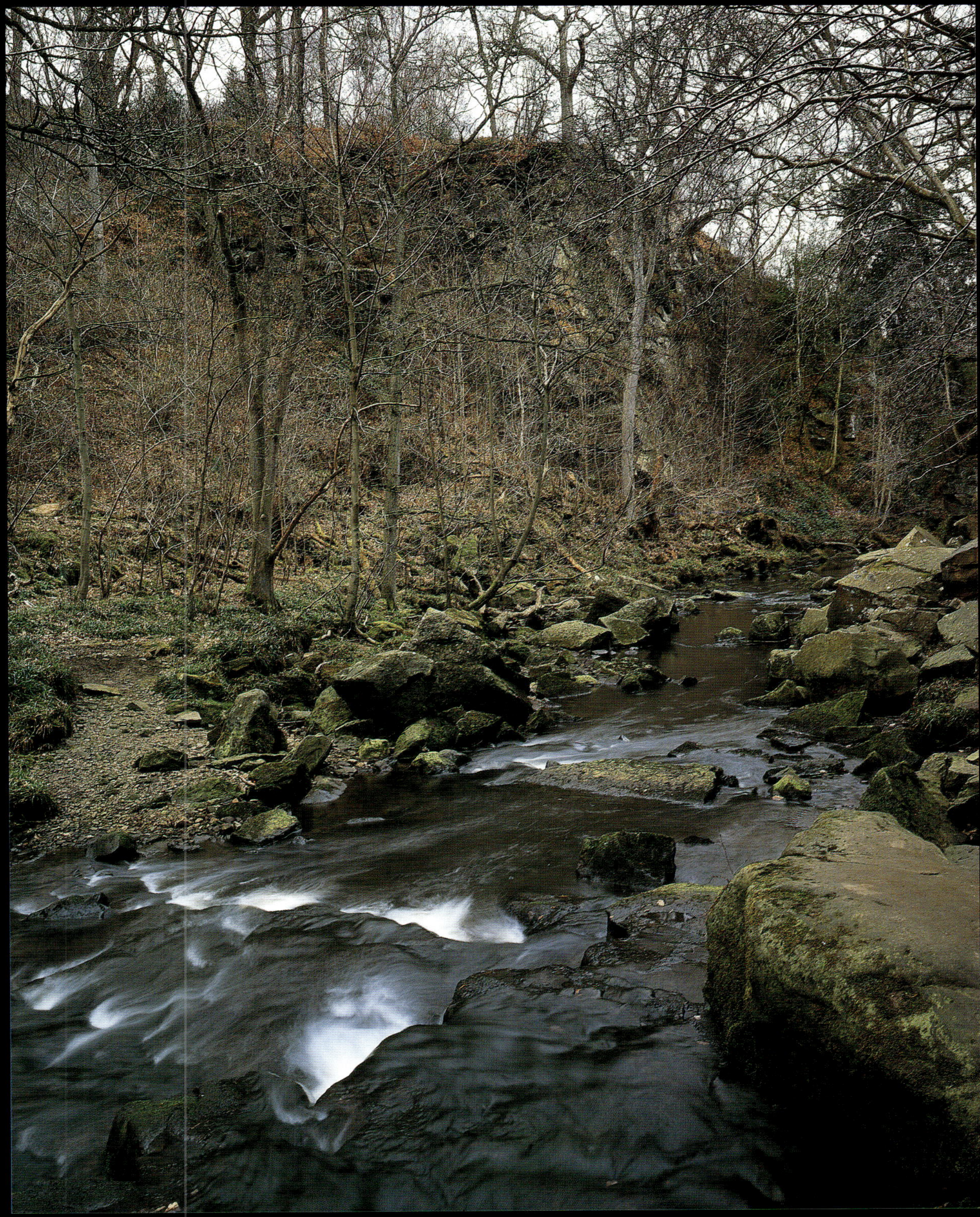

To illustrate the quality that it is possible to obtain with a fairly cheap medium-range SLR, examine the detail in this white-lipped tree frog. The Pentax MZ5n has everything one needs in a camera body and is compatible with a dazzling array of quality lenses such as the 100mm macro lens used to take this picture. Taken in Queensland, Australia.
Pentax MZ5n and 100mm macro lens, 1/90sec at f/16, off-camera TTL flash.

that at shutter speeds below 1/60, 1/125 and 1/250 of a second for 50, 100 and 200mm lenses respectively, you need to use a tripod to avoid camera shake. And with larger formats you really need a tripod on absolutely every occasion.

I use the Benbo Mark I and Unilock Model 1600 tripods. Both of these tripods meet all of the above criteria. They extend to about 5ft, (1.5m) and are based on a simple design in which the three legs are connected by a bent bolt. Along with the centre column, the legs can be locked into place by twisting a single lever. This means the legs move independant of one another and can be placed in any position imaginable on any terrain. The design allows the centre column to be twisted around from vertical to the horizontal for convenient low-level work.

Increasingly, tripods are being made from advanced materials such as carbon fibre, which provide a lightweight but strong construction ideal for hiking on difficult terrain. Manufacturers like Gitzo and Manfrotto make excellent carbon-fibre tripods. Unfortunately, the prices of these are two to three times that of conventional alloy tripods.

Filters

For me, filters are not an essential item of kit and should be used judiciously. However, every lens I possess has either an 81B subtle warm-up filter, UV or skylight filter attached to either protect the front element or to imbue a mild warmth to the scene. I also use a system holder by Lee for my large-format work. This allows me to use a range of warm-up filters (81A–81D plus a couple of 85 series filters), three hard neutral density graduated (or ND grad) filters (0.3, 0.6 and 0.9) and a single soft neutral density graduated filter (0.45). The Lee system allows me to pick-and-mix the combination and orientation of these particularly useful filters. The table below lists some of the filters that I use and represents a good starting point for landscape enthusiasts.

I must confess that since I began using Velvia, I no longer use a polarizer. This film is so vibrant and full of punch that I don't think one is really necessary. Additionally, I am currently experimenting with an enhancer and a set of magenta filters. Enhancers are quite expensive; they augment red/brown elements in a scene without affecting other colours. I bought it for my next trip to the canyons of the American West, but I am hoping it might enliven my autumn woodland scenes as well.

Many people put a lot of store in ND grads. They are particularly useful in compensating for the inability of film to handle extreme contrast in a scene. If you have a sky that is much brighter than the ground, you have two choices: a) to meter for the ground and overexpose the sky, or b) to meter for the sky or average the two (sky and ground) – in either event, underexposing the ground. To get around this problem you fit an ND grad to darken the sky and meter for the ground. In the final image, the grad should bridge the tonal gradient between sky and ground so as to look natural. Despite this, one could add a greater neutral density, and provide an evil, menacing sky. Personally, I have a problem with images that alter or

Purpose/Description	Filter Designation	Required increase in exposure	Colour temperature conversion
Warm up	81	1⁄3 EV	3300 K–3200 K
Warm up	81 B	1⁄3 EV	3300 K–3200 K
Warm up	81 D	2⁄3 EV	3700 K–3200 K
Warm up	85 C	2⁄3 EV	5500 K–3800 K
Pale blue cooling	82	1⁄3 EV	3000 K–3200 K
Pale blue cooling	82 A	1⁄3 EV	3100 K–3200 K
Neutral density graduated*	0.3 ND	1 EV**	N/A
Neutral density graduated*	0.6 ND	2 EV**	N/A
Neutral density graduated*	0.9 ND	3 EV**	N/A
Polarizer	Polarizer	Variable	N/A

*Note: *Available as hard or soft graduation. Hard is the best option for general work.*
***Damps down light transmission intentionally, therefore no increase in exposure required.*

distort reality too much. For this reason I avoid coloured grads such as tobacco, orange, blue or magenta. I particularly dislike sunset grads; I suppose I think of it as cheating and, in some cases, the results can look quite nauseating.

The ND grads and warm-up filters are by far the most useful filters around. A 0.3, 0.6 and 0.9 ND grad represent a one, two and three-stop loss of light respectively. Remember, grads used in system holders can be rotated, inverted and combined with other filters.

I only really started using filters when I began using large-format cameras. Until then, and even now, I have been a rangefinder fan, and this is the least filter-friendly type of camera available, as they do not permit TTL viewing. This means grads in particular are difficult to position correctly.

A final word of advice:

- Check camera compatibility with your filter system. My Lee system does not fit easily to my Fuji 617 90mm lens, for example, although I can hold filters in front of this lens if it becomes necessary.
- Never buy cheap ND grads; they often have a colour cast that tends towards magenta.
- Learn to recognize a tacky filter effect from a useful one.
- A filter is most certainly not always desirable. It is as likely to ruin a shot as it is to enhance one. Always try to subtly enhance rather than radically alter a view and you won't go far wrong.

Film

For the sharpest and therefore most marketable images you will need to select the slowest film speed. A slow film like Kodachrome 25 is virtually grain-free (although as I write this, Kodachrome 25 is unfortunately about to be discontinued). The latest version of Fuji Provia (Provia 100F) is also very fine-grained and, therefore, a sharp emulsion. As ISO number increases, so a compromise arises between film speed, grain size and, hence, sharpness. Even at ISO 200 and certainly at ISO 400 you lose any hope of a sharp, crisp image. Therefore, unless you are after a grainy, atmospheric image, fast film simply compromises the potential quality of images rendered by modern optical glass.

For compact cameras where little exposure control is possible, I recommend ISO 100–200 film since this offers a good compromise between fine grain and the shutter speeds required to handhold the camera in moderately bright conditions. When conditions are very bright apertures will be small enough to ensure a good depth of focus. I also regularly use ISO 50 Velvia in my compact cameras and in reasonably bright conditions this produces excellent results which are indistinguishable from SLR shots.

Colour negative film is for the snap shooter and, without exception, 35mm to 120 roll film transparencies are the preferred medium for colour reproduction in magazines and books, with a few publishers still favouring 5 x 4in transparencies. Since transparencies are often cheaper and easier to store in clear, easy-to-view filing systems, they are advantageous to you, too.

Films are often available as professional and more robust amateur versions. I always use amateur versions since these films have a longer shelf life – besides, I am limited as to how much film I can store in the fridge, and professional film must be stored cool.

Pin-sharp photography requires the fine grain of Kodachrome 64 or Fuji Velvia. However, as discussed before, if natural light is limited and you resort to a tripod and long exposure times, 'reciprocity failure' may occur. This is because the normal reciprocal relationship between aperture and shutter speed falls apart at exposure times of one second or more. The amount of extra light necessary to compensate for reciprocity failure varies from film to film. The table on page 22 gives the recommended exposure compensation for some commonly used slow- to medium-speed transparency films and this section discusses reciprocity failure at length.

Although film manufacturers recommend it, I don't take any notice of colour correction during long exposures. In fact, I often think that reciprocity-induced colour casts on long exposures of evening landscapes enhance an image.

Remember, process films immediately; don't leave them lying around after exposure. In extremely cold conditions film becomes brittle and sprocket holes tear very easily. In humid, tropical environments store fast and exposed film in sealed containers containing activated silica gel crystals. Avoid contact with mothballs, paints, solvent-based products, certain anti-fungal agents and foam insulation all of which is deleterious to film. At airports don't pack film in luggage that you plan to check in; a new generation of 'intelligent' X-ray machines can damage them. Instead, transport film as hand luggage. I recently bought an outdoor waistcoat that doubles as a photographer's vest. It is full of pockets, and on major trips I use this to get my 120 roll film and sheet film through airport security without subjecting it to X-rays. I ask you, what keen photographer can easily get his cameras and film to fit into a holdall that complies with the 5kg or so cabin luggage limit? (See also Travelling with camera gear, page 57.)

Medium-format cameras

Many of the camera features discussed in the context of 35mm SLRs are also common to medium-format cameras. Medium-format cameras form a more heterogeneous family of cameras than those of the 35mm genre. Although all medium-format cameras use 120/220 roll film, the amount of roll film format that can be exposed varies from 6 x 4.5cm to 6 x 9cm and beyond, depending on the particular type of medium-format camera being used. The choice therefore really comes down to which of the many roll film aspect ratios you prefer.

While 35mm is the most widespread film format in use today, and is ideal for quick as well as more considered landscape photography, it rapidly loses quality when blown up to large print sizes or projected on a screen. And while it is fine for editorial use, medium-format quality is even better.

In general, I guess that photographers using 35mm for landscape work adopt a more photojournalistic style. Those that use medium format for their landscapes are probably working to a stricter discipline that will ultimately see their work being pigeon-holed under either travel or fine art photography. I suppose this is a polite way of saying that medium-format landscapes have better potential for sales in advertising and up-market publications while those produced on 35mm have less potential in these markets. Of course, there is considerable overlap and flexibility between medium format and 35mm; some serious professionals exclusively use 35mm for landscape photography for every conceivable market. For my part, I often shoot scenics from the hip in a photojournalistic style using 35mm SLRs. While I sometimes also resort to a tripod for 35mm slides, I always resort to a tripod on medium format. What this means is that although medium format engenders a slower, more considered approach to landscape photography, you also lose some of the spontaneity and fun that shooting from the hip with a diminutive 35mm SLR provides. However, there can be little doubt that the larger medium-format transparencies translate into more sales when viewed on a light box. Indeed, on a side-by-side comparison, 35mm looks positively hypotrophic compared to a vivid 6 x 7cm or 6 x 9cm Velvia transparency.

At the end of the day, the larger the negative or transparency, the more the image can be enlarged without losing sharpness or colour. This means that any defects, grain and bleached colours, for instance, are less magnified on larger formats. So, in addition to reproducing larger and sharper images and having more impact on a light box, they are also more forgiving of their weaknesses than smaller formats.

Interestingly, the nominal size of medium-format transparencies indicated by the different camera systems and film backs that are available is in fact slightly larger than that actually produced. The following table illustrates the actual exposed area for a nominal film format size:

Format	Actual exposed area
35mm	36 x 24mm
6 x 4.5cm	56 x 42mm
6 x 6cm	56 x 56mm
6 x 7cm	56 x 69.5mm
6 x 8cm	56 x 76mm
6 x 9cm	56 x 84mm

I have seen many estimates of the increased size of the various medium-format aspect ratios over 35mm. Often they vary, so here is the true increase in size based on the actual exposed film area:

Format	Exposed area relative to 35mm
35mm	1
6 x 4.5cm	2.72
6 x 6cm	3.63
6 x 7cm	4.50
6 x 8cm	4.93
6 x 9cm	5.44

This is not the end of the story, since one must also take into account the amount that an image is cropped. For a standard 8 x 10in sheet of paper one would routinely crop 16.7% of a 35mm slide, 5.9% of a 6 x 4.5cm slide and nothing from a 6 x 7cm slide. This is why one of the major criticisms of the 6 x 6cm format is that a large area of the square format necessarily needs cropping away. It is also the reason why 6 x 7cm is referred to as the 'golden' format; it requires virtually no cropping. Personally, I have used many of the available larger formats, both in cameras that have SLR-type reflex viewing and in rangefinders. I can unequivocally say that I now take more 6 x 7cm images than any other aspect ratio. But you should judge for yourself what roll film format best suits you. Fortunately, they do not come and go like their 35mm counterparts which seem to last a couple of years to be replaced by another, not necessarily better model.

Which format is best for you? The following five slides of my local wood represent the main medium-format aspect ratios, and are reproduced at actual size: (from left to right) 35mm, 6 x 4.5cm, 6 x 6cm, 6 x 7cm, 6 x 9cm.

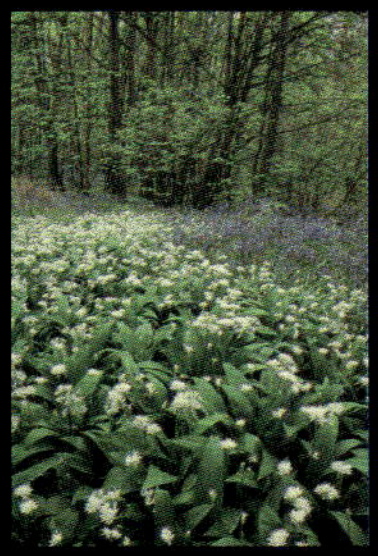

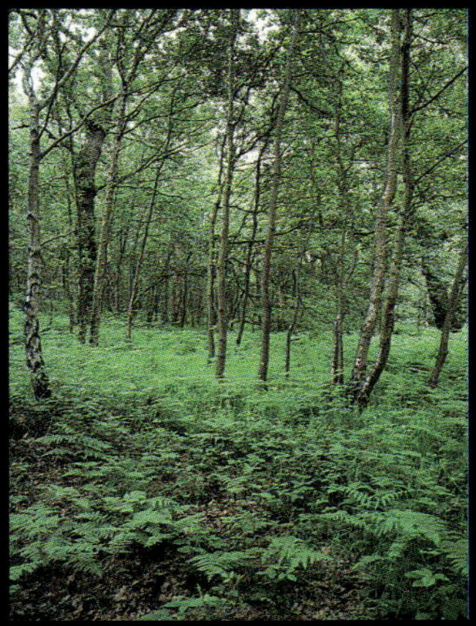

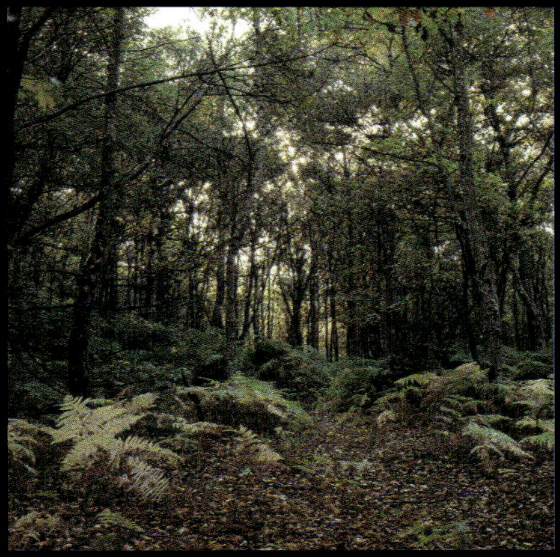

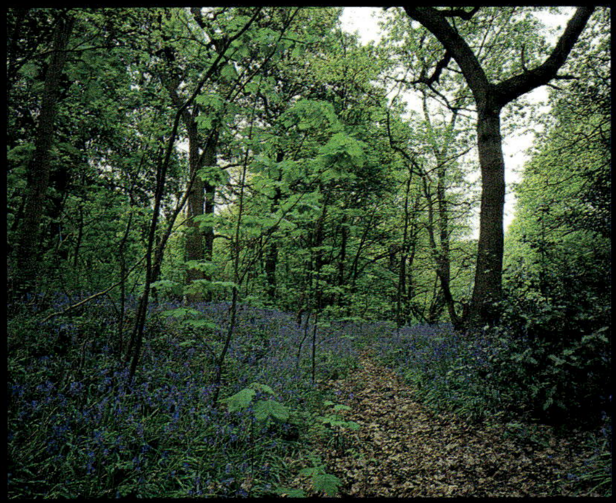

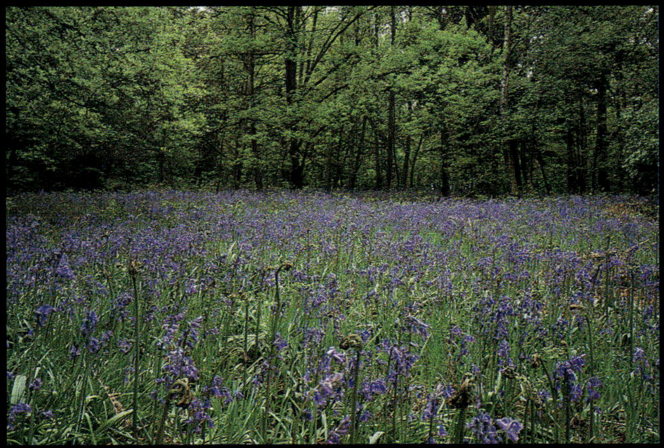

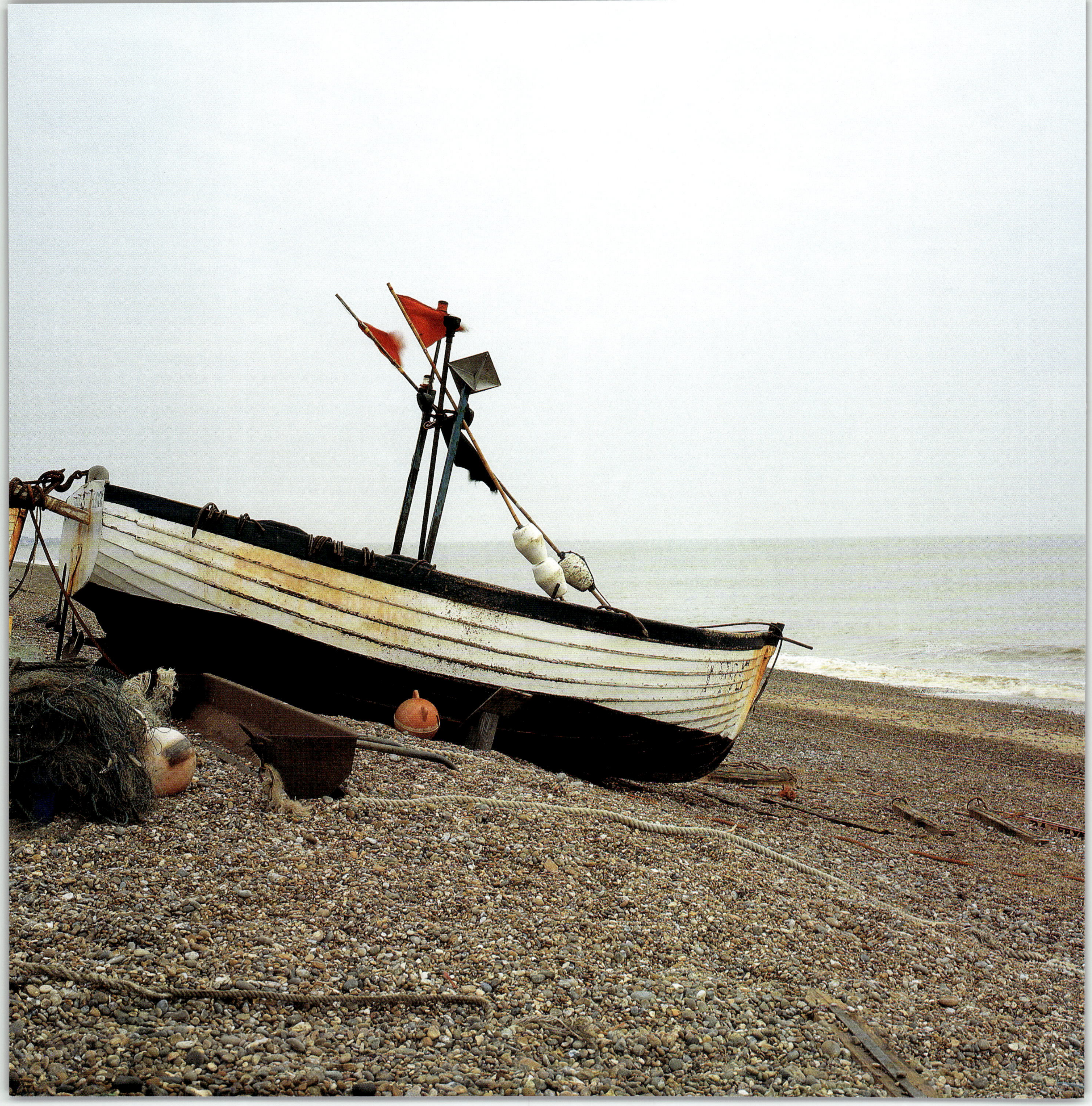

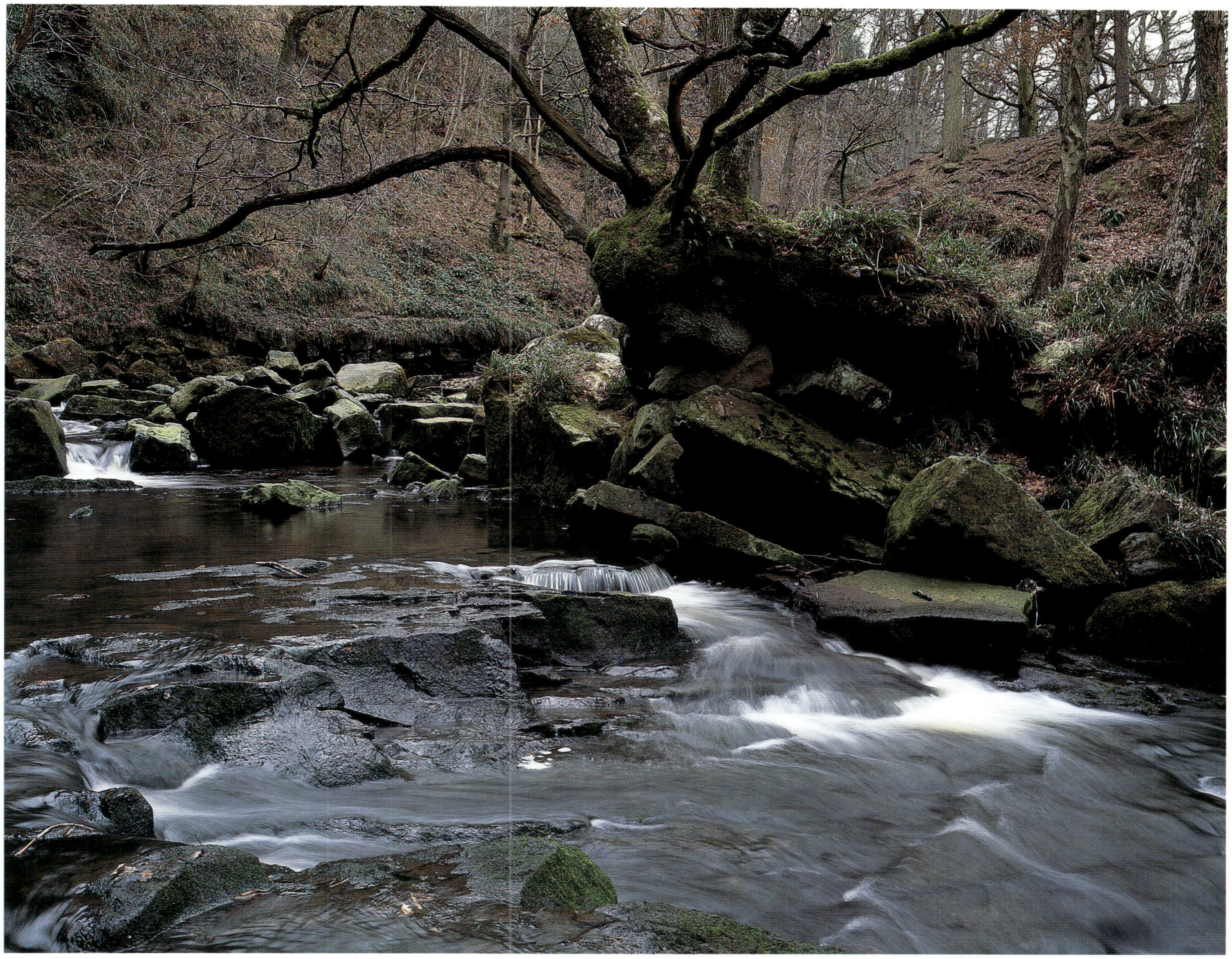

This shot of a woodland stream in winter is one of my favourite pictures. For editorial usage, the 6 x 7cm format requires less cropping. My main bread-and-butter medium-format camera these days is the Mamiya 7II.

The 6 x 6cm format can be adapted to many landscape subjects. It works well with this inshore fishing boat at Aldeburgh in Suffolk, England.
Hasselblad 500CM + 80mm lens.

Where do you begin selecting a medium-format camera for your landscape work? There is no simple answer. When I made the jump up from 35mm to medium format, I selected Hasselblad, the doyen of the format. This was a true system camera, which used Carl Zeiss lenses, the optical comparators for all other lenses. All photography magazines and many professionals revere these cameras. I undoubtedly took many a good landscape with my 500CM with standard 80mm Carl Zeiss Planar lens, selling several transparencies for editorial use. However, I soon felt limited by the square 6 x 6cm aspect ratio. You can usually search around and get a subject to fit this film size, but it isn't always easy to do so. In addition, for editorial use, the frame is likely to be heavily cropped, probably back down to the 6 x 4.5cm aspect ratio – and indeed Hasselblad do make a 6 x 4.5cm roll film back for their cameras. However, although my 500CM is an incredibly well-made tool, this is also reflected in the astronomical price. More significantly, it is reflected in the price of Zeiss lenses, which are not cheap.

For these reasons I moved across to rangefinders for my medium-format landscapes. Initially, I used the Fuji GSW690 III, a fixed lens, wide-angle camera costing less than half of the Hasselblad, but with an image size half as big again. I found the huge 6 x 9cm slides perfect for my landscape work. Unfortunately, while I liked the optical quality of the lens (equivalent to 28mm on the 35mm format), I soon yearned for the different perspective that a good selection of lenses can offer. I looked around and opted for a Mamiya 7II 6 x 7cm rangefinder with a 43mm lens (21mm in 35mm format), 65mm lens (32mm in 35mm format), and a 150mm lens (71mm in 35mm format). Unlike the Hasselblad and the Fuji, the Mamiya has a built-in meter giving automated exposure control that speeds up the picture-taking process enormously. (My wife is particularly grateful for this facility.)

Reading articles and reviews in the press inspired my first choice of medium-format camera. Today, you can use the Internet to make a better-informed decision by reading the experiences of amateur and professional photographers, as well as to view the kit used by professionals that have an internet presence. Use the Internet chat rooms to get the opinions of others. Americans in particular love to help and offer advice, which can often be more useful and technical in nature than you are likely to be offered at your local photo store. Part of the reason I opted for the full Mamiya 7II system was that other landscape photographers reviewed the camera so well in the photo press. Also, on the Internet, I read that in an independent test, the Mamiya 6 lenses were the finest optics available (excellent lpm [lines per mm] values). Whether this is true or not, the pictures I had seen published taken with these lenses did seem outstanding, and I rationalized that the Mamiya 7 lenses could not be so different, so why not opt for the camera? As a traveller, I find the Mamiya 7II extremely lightweight, optically perfect, and capable of delivering 6 x 7cm golden format transparencies demanded by picture buyers. As I understand it, part of the reason Mamiya 7 lenses are so good is that they are not part of a reflex system, which compromises lens design. Because no reflex system mirror box is present, the rangefinder lenses can be placed closer to the film plane, consequently yielding a sharper image.

At the time of selecting the Mamiya 7II rangefinder system, I really only had one other contender in mind: the Pentax 67II. This camera is bulkier than the Mamiya, but offers through-the-lens viewing, TTL flash control, a longer autoexposure range (to 30 seconds) and a wider selection of lenses. My choice was made on the basis of weight, the option of hand-held photography, and the reviews I had read.

The smallest medium-format cameras are the 6 x 4.5cm genre. This is the next step up from 35mm and is a format that has conserved many of the automatic functions of the smaller format, including autofocus. In this category are the Bronica ETRSi, Contax 645, three Mamiya 645 cameras (645 Pro TL, 645AF and 645E), Pentax 645NII, Bronica RF645, Fuji GA645Wi, Fuji GA645 and Fuji GA645Zi. If I was to buy a 645 system camera my choice would probably be the Pentax, however my only 645 cameras are in fact the highly portable 'point and shoot' Fuji GA645Wi and Zi. I think these sophisticated oversized compacts are simply brilliant for quick travel shots. The lens on the Wi is a 45mm wide-angle equivalent to a 28mm in the 35mm format.

The next roll film format is 6 x 6cm. Here we have the Bronica SQ-Ai and SQ-B, Exakta 66 III, Hasselblad cameras (555ELD, 503CW, 501C, 205FCC, 903SWC and 203FE) and two Rolleiflex cameras, the 6003 and 6008. Many famous landscape photographers have produced outstanding work with this format, one of the most talented and well-known being Charlie Waite.

The next format is 6 x 7cm and is the one I recommend. Cameras include the Bronica GS-1, two Mamiya reflex designs, the RB67 Pro-SD and the more advanced RZ67 Pro II. Also in this category is the brilliant Pentax 67II and two rangefinders: the Fuji GW670III and my choice: the Mamiya 7II. Most travel photographers who want to enter the world of 6 x 7cm usually opt for either the Mamiya 7II or Pentax. The Mamiya RB and RZ models are more the tools of studio photographers, although this is not always the case. Professionals like Jim Zuckerman have produced excellent landscape images using these cameras.

Beyond 6 x 7cm there is less choice. Fuji do the GX680 III and IIIS which are all-singing, all-dancing 6 x 8cm SLRs. These have many features in common with larger view cameras. They offer rise, fall, swing, shift and tilt. These movements are what make view cameras so appealing and are discussed in detail on page 53. The last to be classified as medium format is the 6 x 9cm aspect ratio, and includes the Fuji GSW690 III discussed above and the standard Fuji GW690 III with its less wide 90mm lens (equivalent to 39mm in 35mm format). Several 6 x 9cm view camera designs are also available by Linhof and Cambo. These are essentially baby brothers to a series of larger 5 x 4in view cameras.

Looking again at this list, if I had to make my choices again I would still pick either the Pentax 67II or Mamiya 7II which, for my type of travel/landscape photography, are probably the best choices for editorial and stock sales.

This image was taken in July in my local woodland. The 6 x 4.5cm format offers a substantial advantage over 35mm in terms of quality.
Fuji GA645Wi, Velvia, tripod.

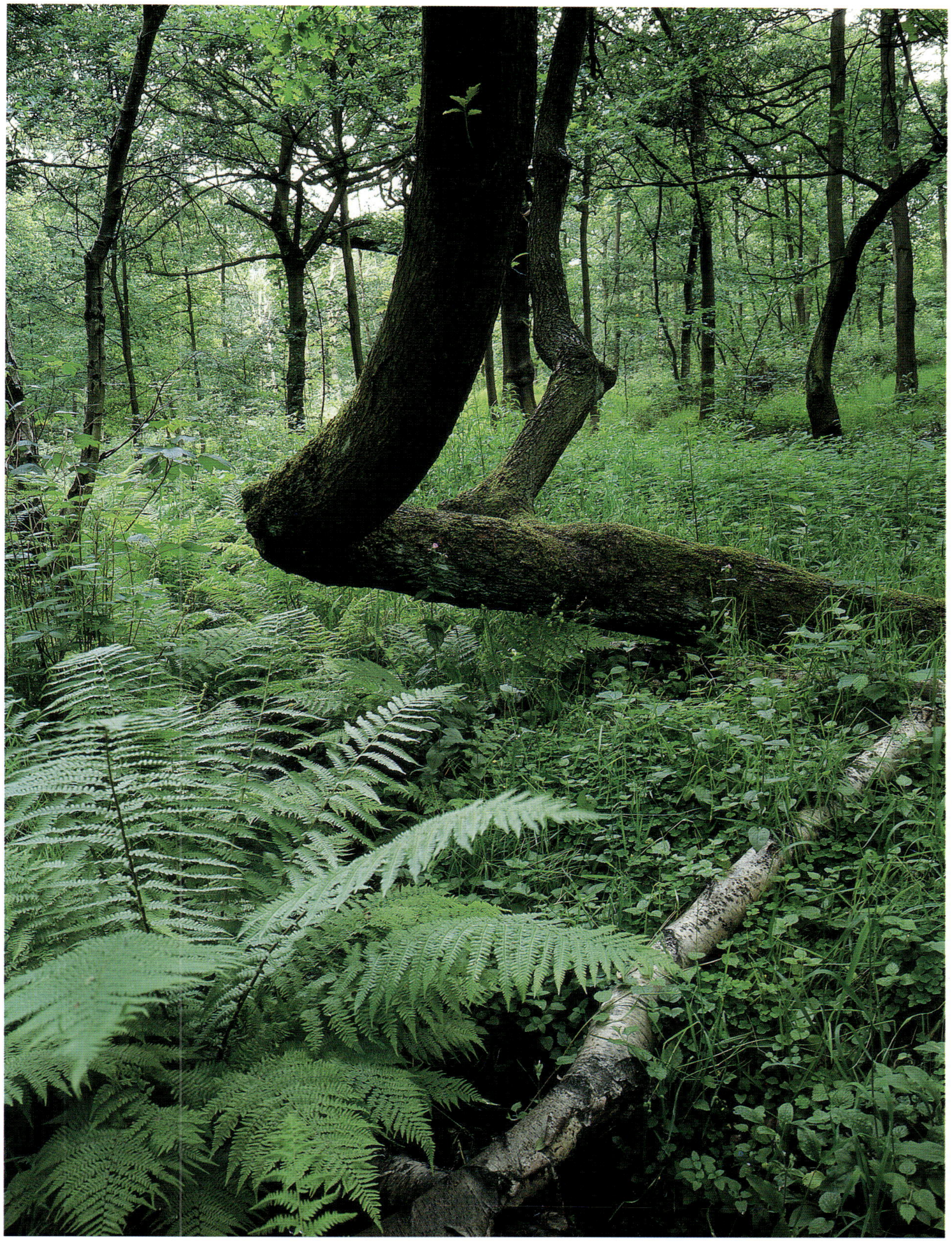

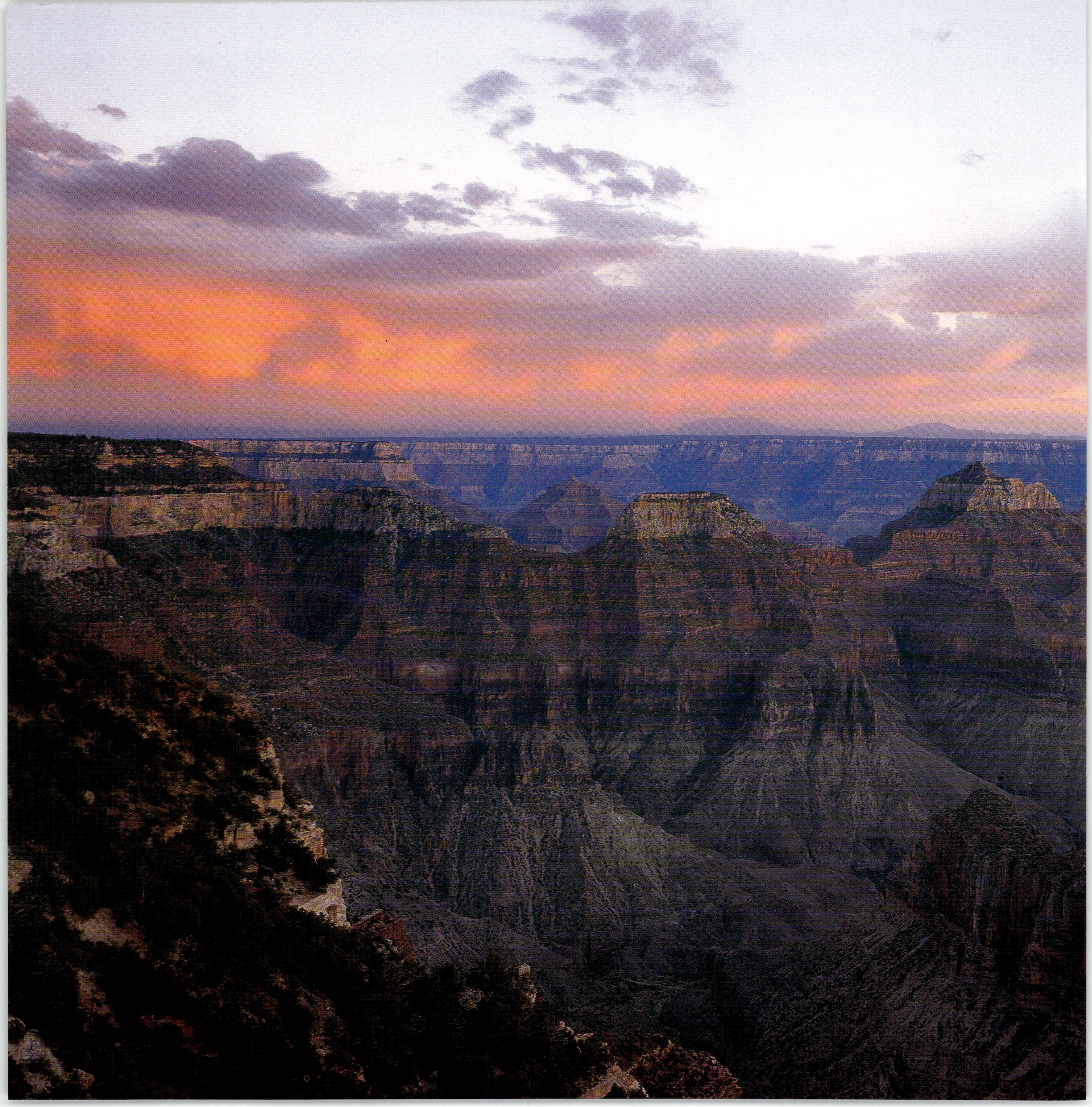

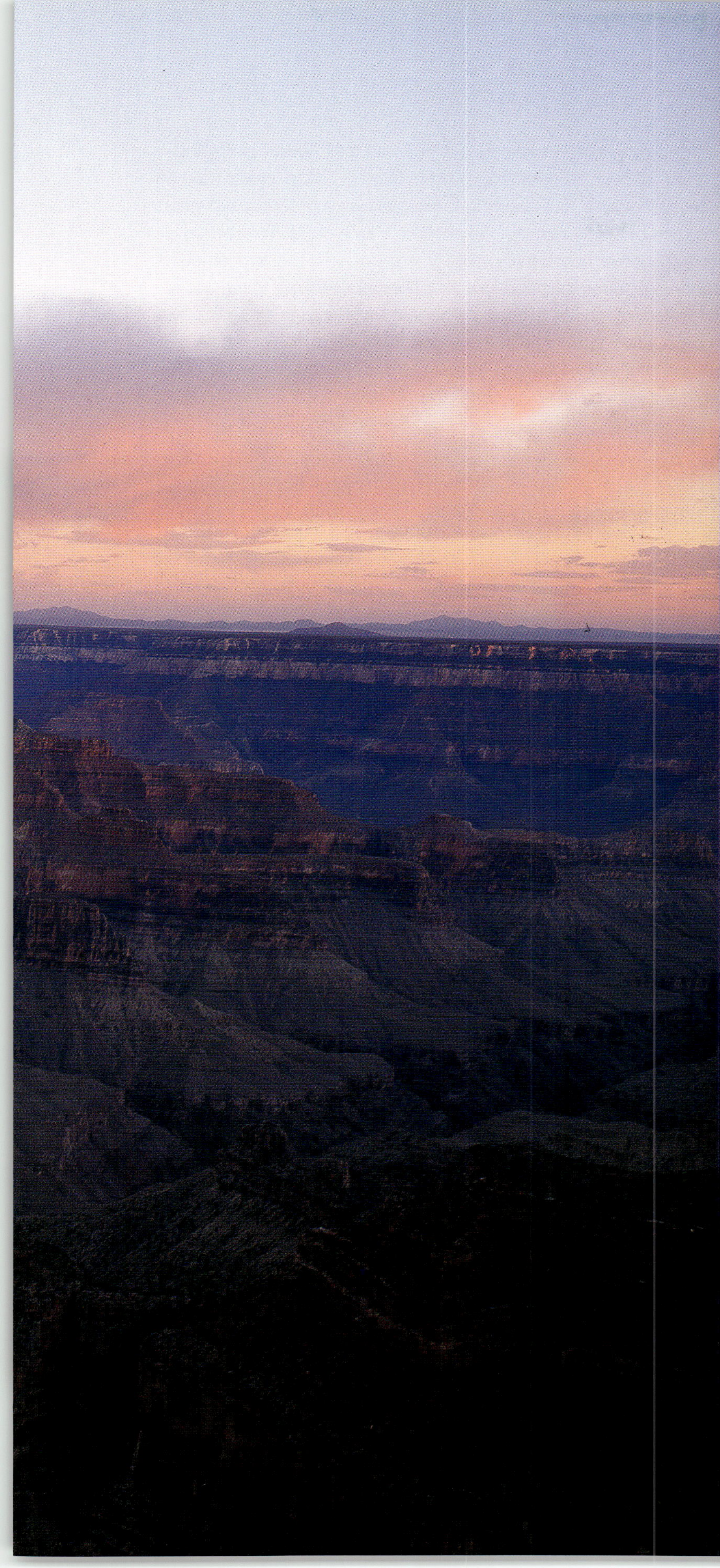

The beauty of the 6 x 9cm format is easy to see in this image of the Grand Canyon at sunset.
Fuji GSW69III, 1 second at f/8, Velvia, tripod.

Panoramic formats

In recent years there has been a real surge of interest in these roll film formats. One of the first books to be published featuring landscapes taken on the 6 x 17cm format was Colin Prior's book *Scotland: The Wild Places*. At the time few people dabbled in this format. Today, everybody who is anybody seems to use it. Stock libraries seem particularly keen, with the advertising market a lucrative client base for those who have the money to invest thousands in a 6 x 17cm body plus three lenses.

The main player in the field is Fuji with their GX617 body and 90mm, 105mm, 180mm and 300mm lenses. These lenses may be interchangeable, but accurate focusing is via a ground glass screen in place of the film, making exposures a time-consuming process. The only other non-rotating 6 x 17cm panoramic system camera is made by Linhof: the Technorama 617s III. Essentially these use large-format lenses that have a large enough image circle to cover the 6 x 17cm aspect ratio. The result is, in effect, the same as masking off a 5 x 7in large-format camera to produce a letterbox-style exposure frame.

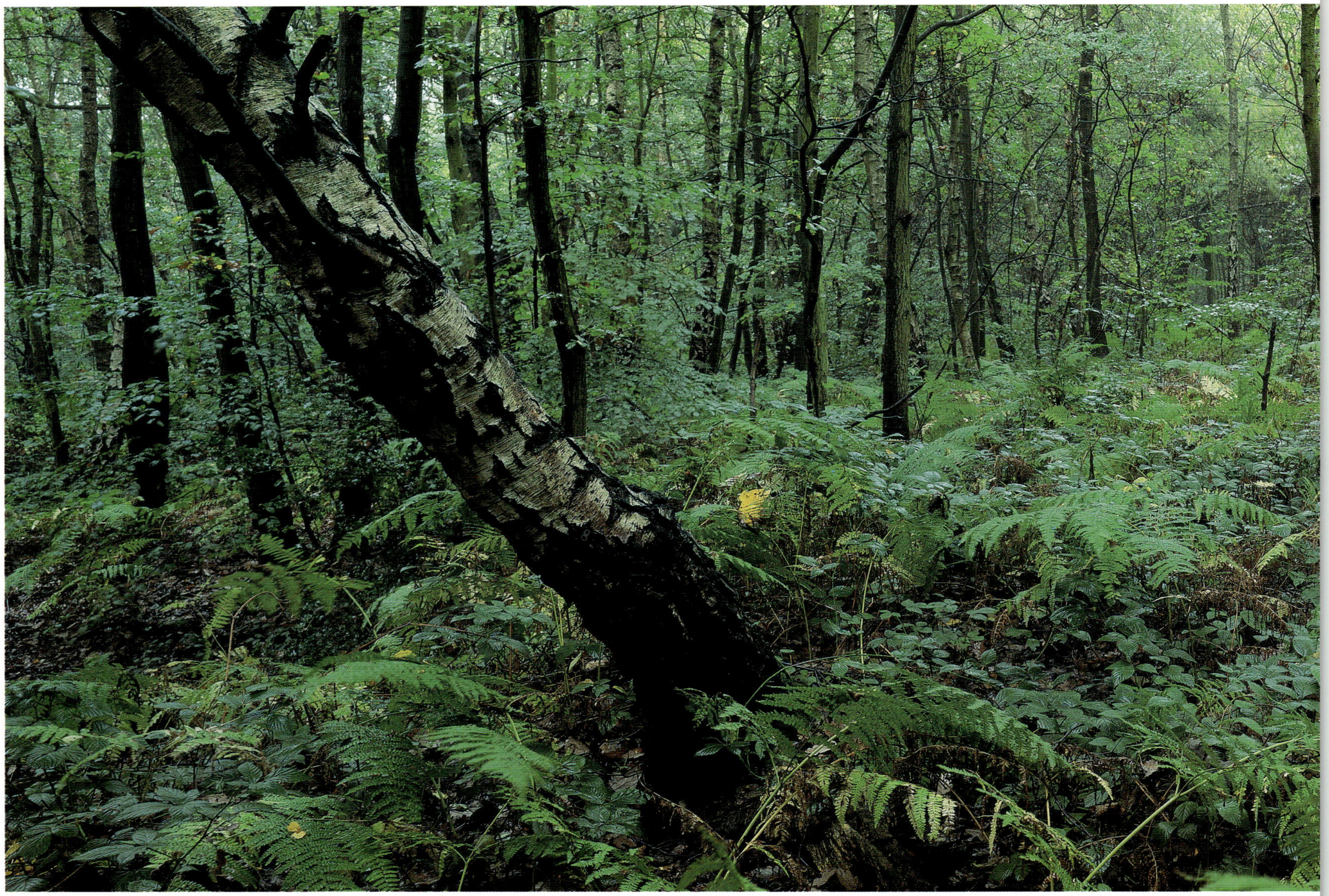

This shot of Yorkshire woodland was taken on a Fuji GX617 with its widest 90mm lens, a focal length equivalent to around 20mm on the 35mm format. However, one should remember that 6 x 17cm is essentially a letterbox view masked off from a 5 x 7in large-format camera. The lens, although wide for this format, has the same shallow depth of field as a 90mm lens on the 35mm format. What this means is that for scenes such as woodland you might be better off using a fairly high viewpoint and excluding quite a bit of immediate foreground interest. A tripod is not really optional with this camera, it is essential.
Fuji GX617 + 90mm lens, 6 seconds at f/22.5, Velvia, tripod.

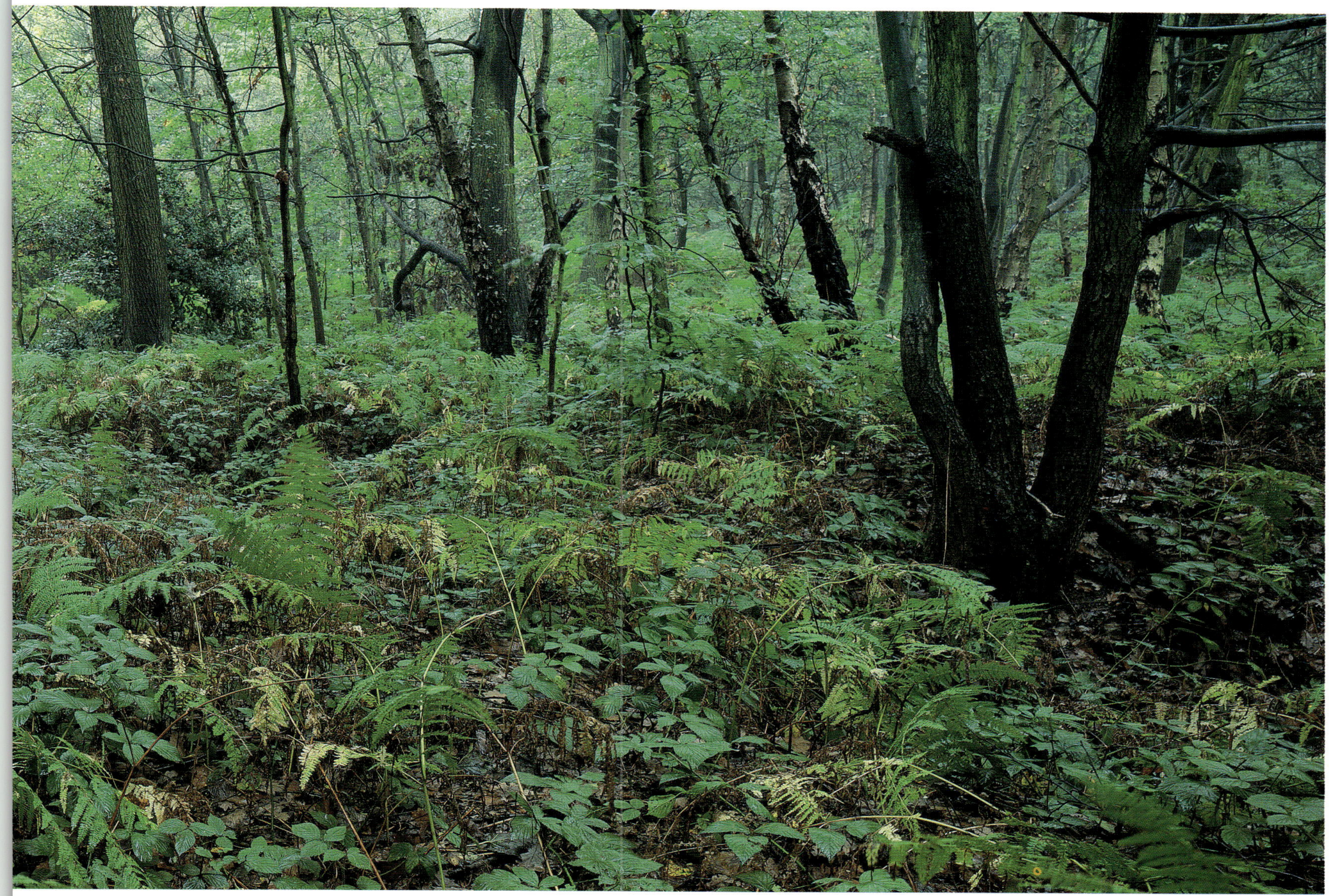

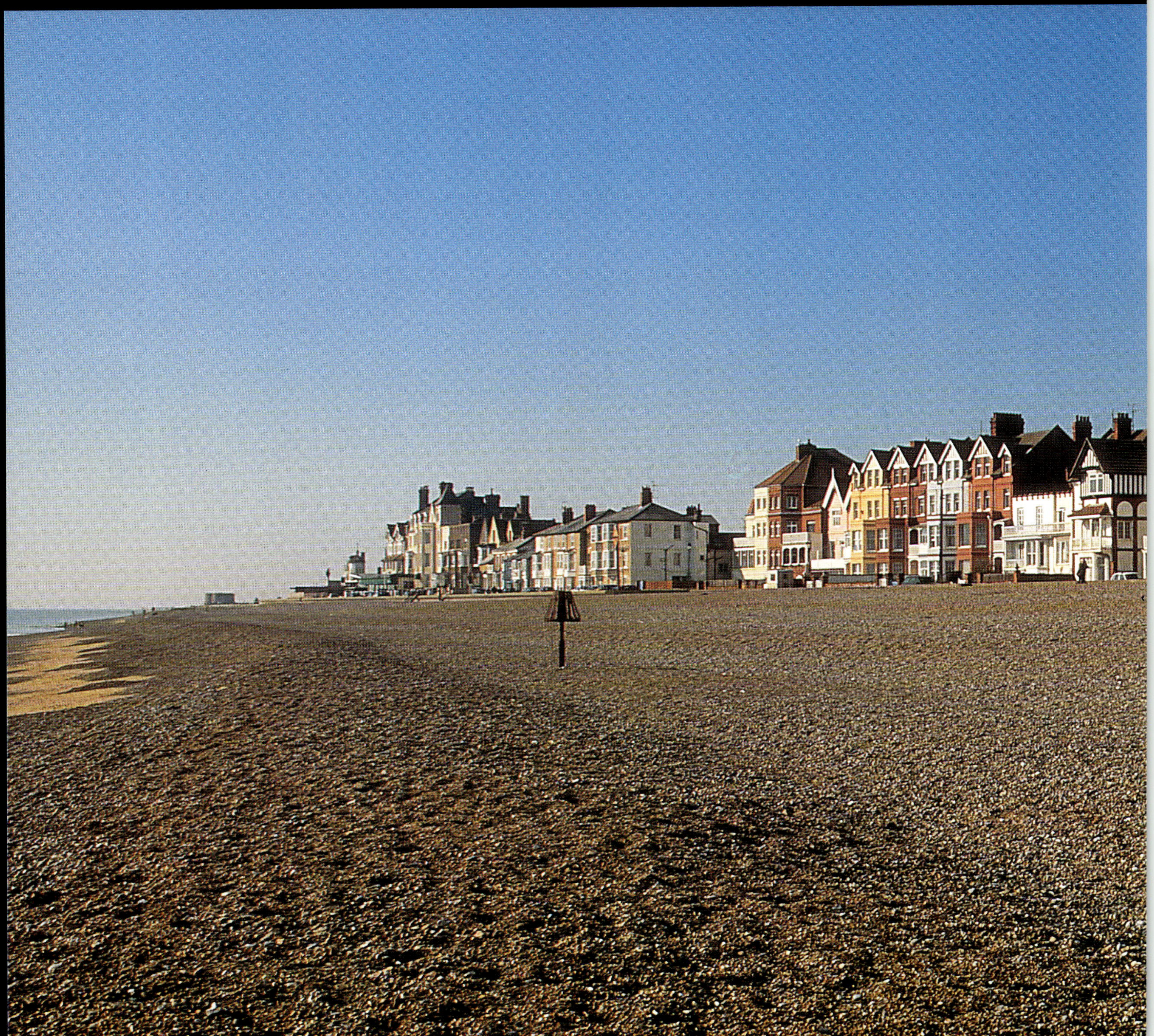

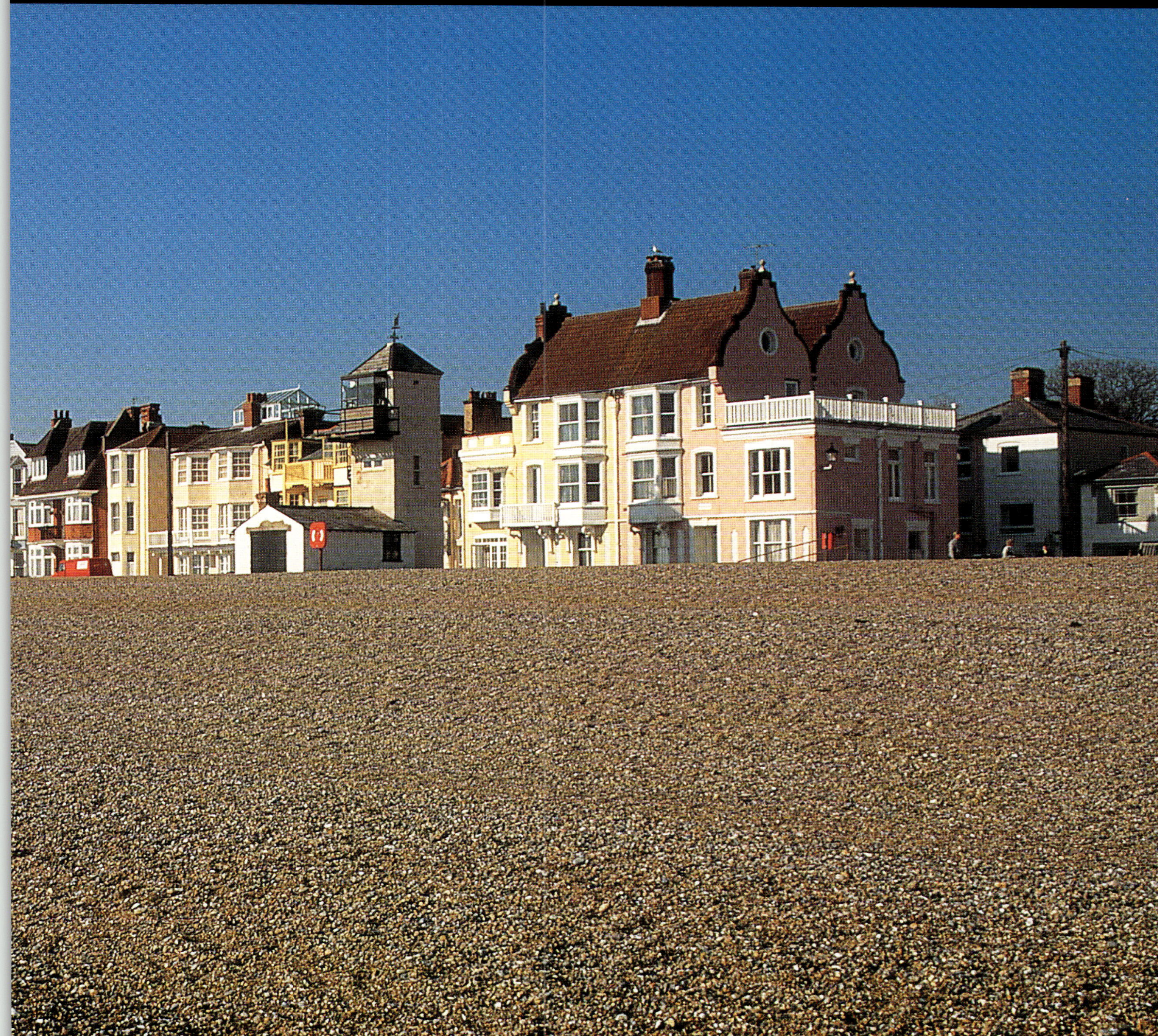

Previous page: Not all panoramic pictures require expensive kit. This view of a shingle seafront was taken in Aldeburgh, Suffolk, on my Pentax MZ5 in its masked-off panoramic mode.
Pentax MZ5 + 28mm lens, Velvia, tripod.

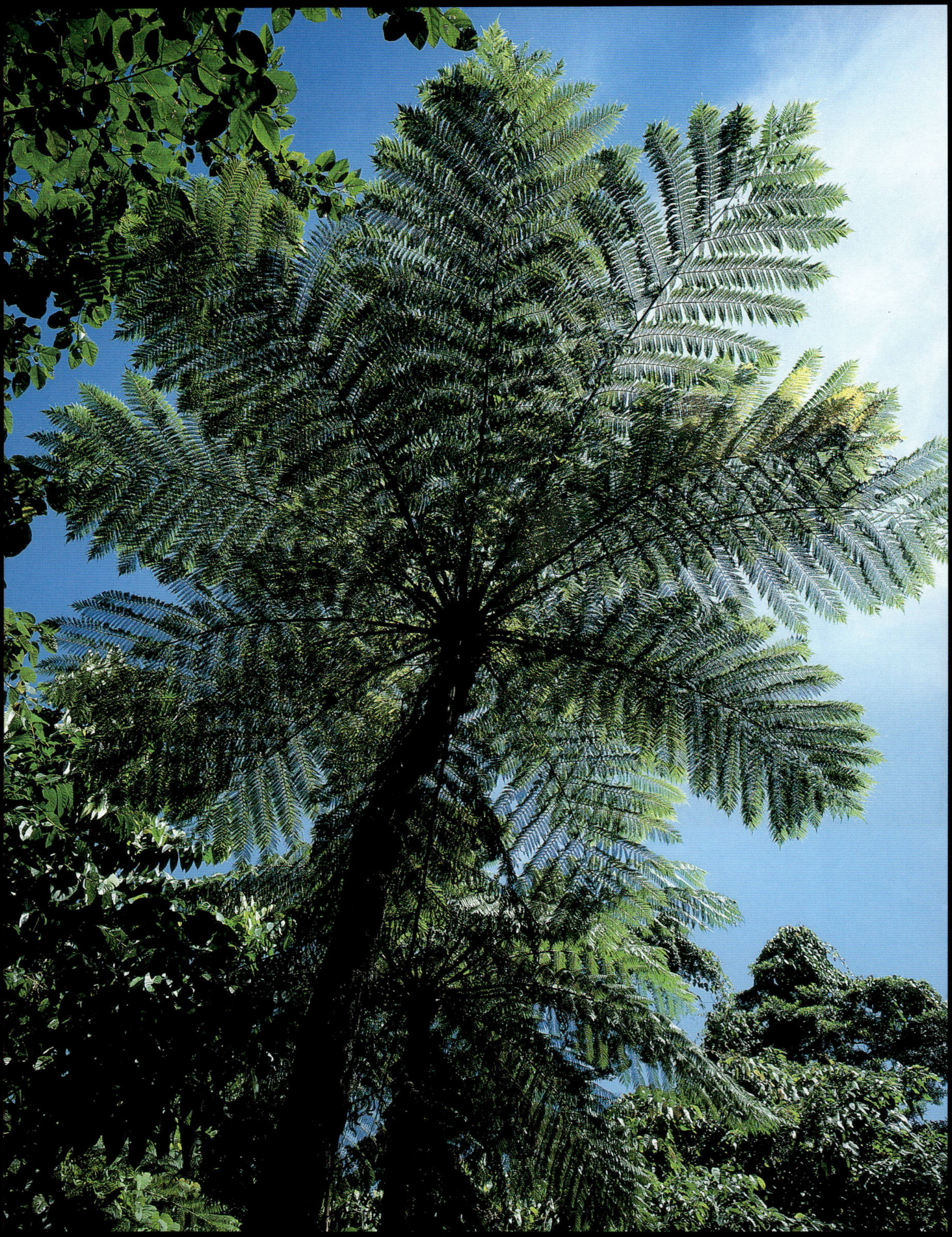

Tree fern, Daintree National Park, Queensland, Australia. This view was taken just off the main road. Unfortunately the first place I could park was about a kilometre further on and, as a result, I had a bit of a walk. It was also on a blind corner, which was something of a hazard, considering that my tripod was set up on the road edge. This image was spot-metered for the green fronds.
Mamiya 7II + 43mm lens, Velvia.

I have seen some absolutely outstanding images taken on this format, although some subjects lend themselves better than others. It is easy to see how subjects on a grand scale such as the Grand Canyon fit the format well, but a creek in my local wood is less likely to be amenable to the panoramic treatment – or so I thought, until I saw the brilliant work of Peter Lik on a recent visit to Australia. Some of his finest 6 x 17cm panoramic studies depict woodland scenes – often with a creek – and they are truly amazing. So amazing in fact, that I bought a Fuji GX617 with a 90mm lens. With this format you need to have foreground interest that leads into the subject from the edge of the frame, creating a 3-D effect as the eye moves across the frame to more distant landscape elements. This is something that is not always easy to achieve.

Some photographers feel that this format stretches things a little too far. While a well-executed 6 x 17cm image looks great blown up as a large fine art print, it looks rather less impressive in a magazine or as a diminutive postcard. The dimensions of the average magazine restrict the reproduction size of a 617 panoramic so much that little detail is visible. If the full horizontal edge is printed across the page, only a shallow vertical edge is available. Most books that use this format are produced in a short but wide format to realise the full potential of the format. Given this restriction, I wonder whether, for editorial use at least, the smaller Hasselblad Xpan wouldn't be a more cost-effective way of producing pans. This camera takes the same aspect ratio as a 6 x 17cm, but on 35mm film. The camera is once again a rangefinder design that employs 30, 45 and 90mm lenses. The Mamiya 7II can also use 35mm film to expose this 3:1 aspect ratio via a special insert (Bronica also offer a similar option). Much cheaper, although more basic than the bespoke pan cameras, are two models made by Tomiyama which are available in 6 x 17cm and 6 x 24cm formats.

There are also a number of cameras available that use a rotating drum to move the lens, which exposes the film through a slit on a curved film plane. These exist as 5 x 12cm and 5 x 17cm cameras, and are manufactured by Noblex. These are very interesting cameras, and are generally cheaper than the non-rotating versions discussed above.

Every photographer has his or her own preference. Many opt for a 6 x 12cm panoramic format over the 6 x 17cm one. While 6 x 17cm seems more *de rigeur* these days, 6 x 12cm gives a very pleasing 2:1 ratio that is generally easier to compose and allows greater magnification for editorial use. It is also cheaper. Bespoke 6 x 12cm cameras with interchangeable lenses are made by Horseman (the SW612 is now available with movements) and Linhof's Technorama 612 PC II. However, a cheaper way into panoramic photography is via 6 x 12 roll film backs that attach to 5 x 4in view cameras. These allow roll film economy and pan format on a camera type that permits a wide range of movements giving extreme depth of field, and which use some of the highest-quality optics available today. This is how I take many of my pan formats, using a 6 x 12cm Horseman roll film back on my Ebony SV45 TE 5 x 4in field camera.

Considerably cheaper than the above pan options is the masked 35mm format that many SLRs offer, whereby the blades shutter off the upper and lower sections of a 35mm frame. The cheapest option of all is available on APS cameras. A full-frame negative has data imprinted at the point of exposure that instructs the printing machine to produce a panoramic print.

Large-format photography

For many years this category of photography (typically 5 x 4in, 5 x 7in and 8 x 10in) has been considered the province of the true professional. For many jobbing photographers who previously used large format and film for high throughput product shots, etc., the reality is that digital photography has taken over from sheet film. It has become far easier and cheaper for professionals to swap to digital capture on medium- or even 35mm format. This switch to digital means that rather than professionals, it is keen amateurs and fine art photographers (many fashion photographers continue to use this format) who, by demanding the absolute highest photographic quality available, are keeping alive this, the ultimate film format. There is simply nothing to compare with a huge, vibrant 5 x 4in Velvia transparency taken with one of the latest generation of large-format lenses like the Schneider Super-Symmar aspherical 110mm XL (equivalent to around 32mm in 35mm format). While many large-format landscape photographers are extreme enthusiasts, a select few have become world-famous professionals. These experts extract visions of the natural world onto celluloid and successfully market their work as fine art of the highest imaginable standard. There is one book that I always bring to the attention of people who are not sure what I mean by professional fine art landscapes. This is *Stone Canyons of the Colorado Plateau* by Jack Dykinga (published by Harry N. Abrams). Dykinga's large-format images are simply superb, and most people would be happy to have any one of them grace their wall as a fine art poster or print.

So, what is large format all about? Simply, you take pictures using a slow, bulky system with umpteen knobs and levers, view the world upside down and hide (some might say draw attention to yourself) by cloaking your head under a black cloth. Well, the first large-format Velvia transparency that you take on your view camera will justify all the complexity involved. Because the huge view you

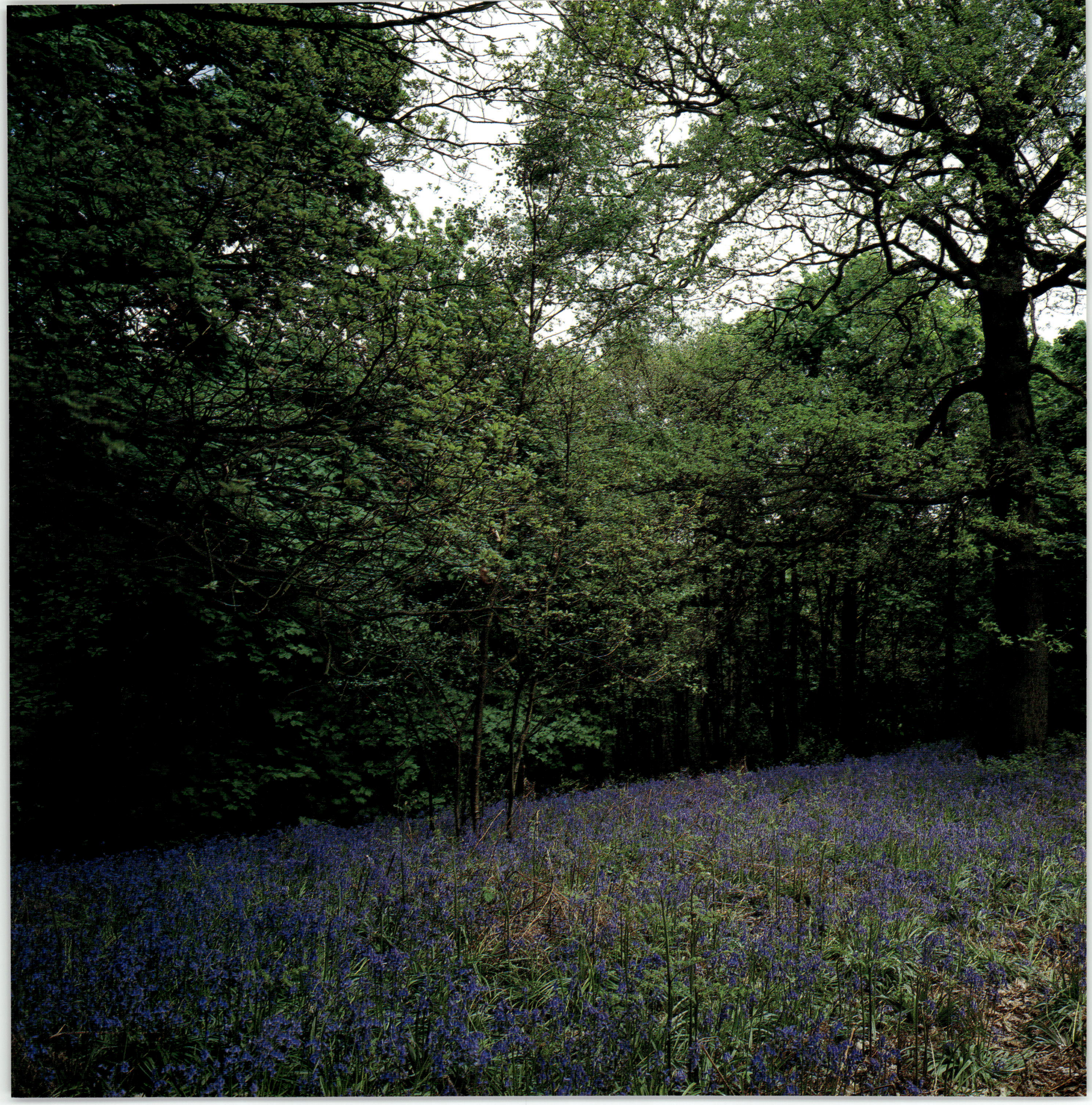

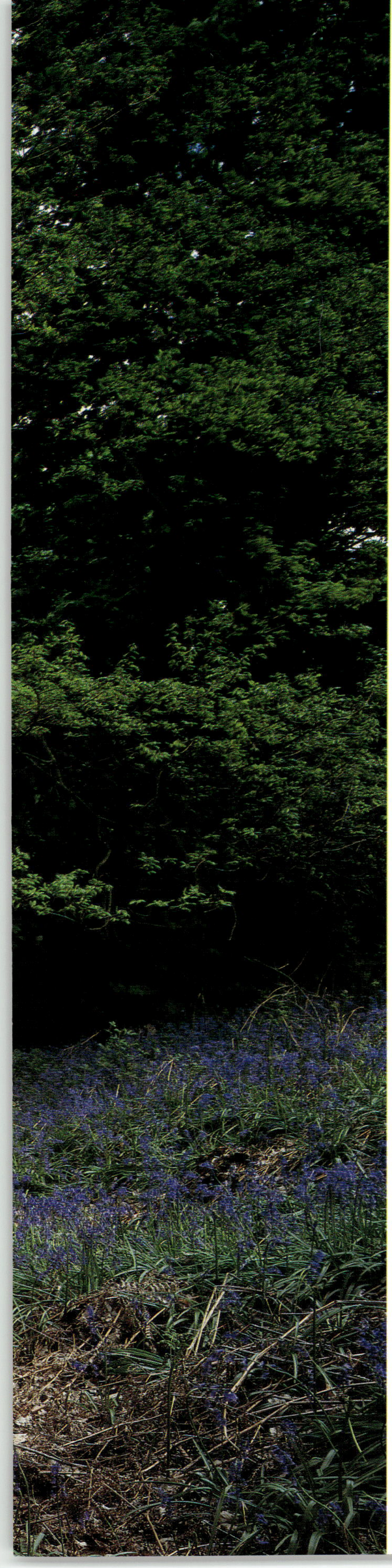

This shot was taken in my local woods. Given a choice between 5 x 4in or 35mm formats, a picture editor will select the larger format, which offers the ultimate in image quality and tonal range (if we conveniently forget 5 x 7in and 8 x 10in formats). This is particularly true for images taken on Velvia. ***Ebony SV45TE + 80mm Schneider Super-Symmar XL lens, 8 seconds at f/32, Velvia.***

see through the ground glass back of a view camera is reversed and inverted, it actually helps you to compose the shot. The view appears as a series of lines, shapes and tones which produces a graphic abstraction of reality that aids the compositional process. The logical part of your brain is supervened by the artistic part and, as a consequence, the final picture is inevitably better.

The choice of view camera for landscapes comes down to two main types: either a metal technical field camera such as Linhof's Master Technica Classic and 2000, Horseman's FA and HD, or the 45AII and 45AX by Toyo. Alternatively, a number of manufacturers – Ebony, Wista and Gandolfi, for example – make wooden field cameras. How do you choose the right type for you? Well, it took me six months to decide on the right large-format outfit. Initially I was going to go for a Toyo 45AII because I had seen the incredible pictures taken by Graham Osborne of the Pacific Northwest. This camera seemed to have it all. Its bellows permit extreme wide-angle lenses down to 47mm, while longer lenses can be used for telephoto and macro imaging. It folds up neatly and has a good range of movements. I had pegged this camera as the best metal field camera for my needs. However, as the various options vied for my attention, along came the Ebony SV45TE. This is a legendary folding view camera made for landscape photography. It is superbly crafted from super-strong, non-warping, straight-grained ebony wood and solid titanium (TE). It is a camera without compromise or, according to Ebony, 'a classic imitated but never equalled'. It certainly offers a lot: 35mm (very extreme wide-angle) to 800mm telephoto lenses via interchangeable bellows and film backs (6 x 12cm, 6 x 9cm and 6 x 7cm), oodles of movement, and a rear-viewing bellows which avoids the dreaded black cloth. I was sold on this camera after talking to the supplier, who offered me an excellent deal once I bought a few Schneider lenses to go with the camera. I believe I made the right decision; Ebony is widely regarded as being the manufacturer of the world's best wooden field cameras.

There are around 30 manufacturers of large-fomat cameras worldwide, and it is up to you to make your own mind about which is the one for you. There is no shortage of advice, particularly on the web. Remember, go for a portable camera that offers the best movements and accepts the largest range of lenses. Some cameras are not particularly compatible with wider-angled lenses, so do look into this. Don't take the salesperson's word on anything; find out for yourself from independent sources. I won't tell you what I read about termites and wooden cameras after purchasing my choice, but I will think twice about taking my Ebony to the tropics. In India, during a two-week stay, our wooden bedroom cupboard was 50% recycled by these insidious beasties. So, as a precaution, I

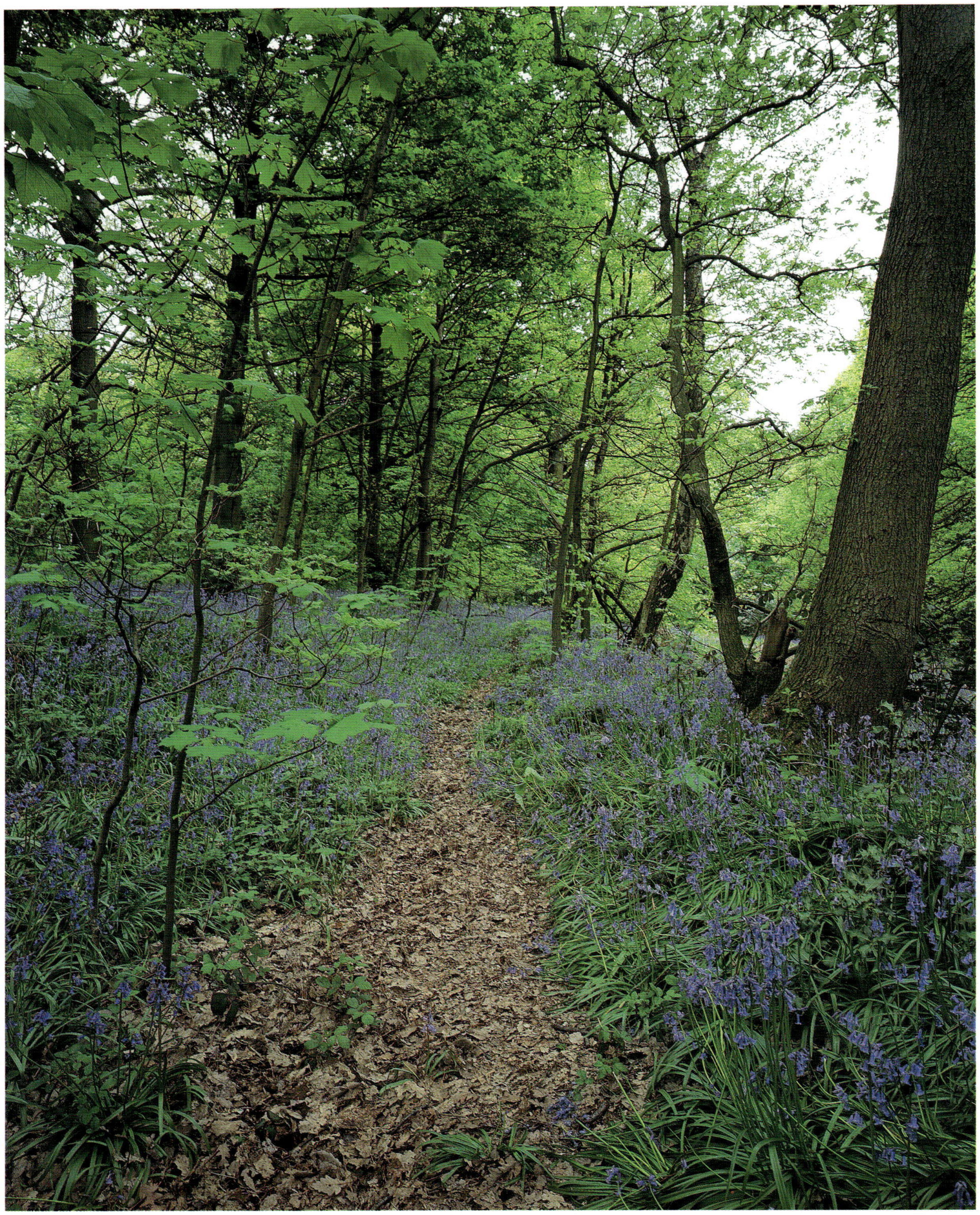

A further spring woodland scene taken with my 80mm lens and Ebony view camera. The strong 3-D structure of the trees prevents much camera movement. See page 15 for the 5 x 4in view of a rape field which used front tilt to enhance depth in the field.
Ebony SV45TE + 80mm Schneider Super-Symmar XL lens.

wrapped my Fuji G645Wi in about three bin-liners – not that termites like plastic and glass, but I slept easier anyway.

What does a field view camera look like? It is essentially unchanged from plate cameras of the nineteenth century. It is basically a lens-bellows-box with a glass back. It has various hinges, knobs and racks that permit movements to control perspective and parallel lines; that is, they alter the plane of focus and do other clever things.

Front rise and fall

If you want to shoot a stand of trees yet keep all the trunks parallel, this would be difficult on an ordinary camera where you would tend to angle the camera upwards to include the whole scene. By placing the view camera back parallel to the trees, and employing front rise, you avoid the problem of converging verticals (most people have experienced this when shooting tall buildings). Along with rise (and incline bed), fall (and drop bed) and shift are other parallel movements that move the lens up, down or sideways relative to the centre of the ground glass.

Front/rear tilt and swing

I think front tilt is the most important movement available to the landscape photographer. It allows you to shoot a landscape, such as a hay meadow, and have objects near to, and far from, the camera in focus simultaneously. Setting an aperture of f/22 or smaller and tilting the lens forward creates the much-extended depth of field necessary. This phenomenon is based on the Scheimpflug rule which states that three planes – the subject, lens board and film planes – must either be parallel to one another, or meet at a common intersection along their planar axes, in order to enhance apparent depth-of-field. (Theodor Scheimpflug was awarded a patent for his work on this phenomenon.)

A similar enhancement of depth of field can be obtained if the back is tilted (front and rear tilt can also be combined for even greater effect). By using rear tilt you also exaggerate the size and shape of foreground objects. The same extension of depth of field is given by front and/or rear swing (or shift bed). Like rear tilt, rear swing also alters the shape of objects. In this case it would extend depth for a parallel subject such as a picket fence or dry-stone wall. With my Mamiya 7II, the best I can do to obtain good depth of field with a similar subject is choose a point of focus, select a small aperture, and hope for the best. Any camera without movements will never match the capabilities of a view camera.

From a purely artistic viewpoint, all this messing around with complex image-control and camera movement actually assists in obtaining a better picture. The reason for this is that even before setting up your camera on its tripod, the effort involved in exposing a sheet of film means you have spent time thinking about your picture. This considered approach seldom enters your mind when shooting off 35mm film, machine-gun fashion. Quite apart from composing the shot and setting movements in place (all done under the dreaded dark cloth with a magnifying loupe), you must load your film back and film, take a hand-held meter reading, set shutter speed and aperture and, finally, cock your shutter and fire. It is certainly hard work, but it is worth it. Fortunately, some of the effort can be removed by replacing the traditional double-dark slide with the Fuji Quick Load System. This allows you to easily and conveniently load sheets of Velvia in daylight, without the need to load and unload dark slides in a light-tight changing bag, which brings with it the attendant hassle and risk of dust contamination. Alternatively, Kodak produces an equivalent system. It also becomes easier and cheaper if, as previously mentioned, you use a roll film back. I use the Horseman 6 x 12cm back, but other, smaller formats are also available.

Large-format lenses are among the best optics available. What allows them to be used for perspective changes via camera movements is their large image circle (the diameter of the total area focused at the film plane). The larger this diameter, the more rise and fall available to you.

When selecting my lenses, I went for one of the largest image circles available in a wide-angle lens. The Schneider 90mm Super-Angulon XL has a huge image circle at f/22 of 259mm. This is even large enough for a 5 x 7in format. However, as I do a lot of international travelling and cabin baggage is limited, weight is a big issue. This wide-angle lens weighs in at a massive 665g (1.47lb), and also requires a large, expensive 95mm wide filter.

So, there is more to selecting a lens than specs on paper. In the field you are better off with light, high-performance optics. This fact only dawned on me after I had spent ages making my initial lens selection. This selection came down to a 47mm XL, 72mm XL, 90mm XL and 150mm lens. The 72mm has many of the same size and weight issues as the 90mm. The 47mm was a bit too extreme. So, with quality and portability an issue, I finally opted for a selection that bucked the trend of 75, 90 and 150mm, which is what many landscape photographers start off with. I went for the latest generation of aspherical Schneider lenses – Super-Angulon 58mm XL, Super-Symmar 80mm XL, Super-Symmar 110mm XL and Apo-Symmar 150mm – supposedly among the best you can buy. The two Super-Symmar lenses are part of a line-up that represent the world's first aspherical large-format lenses. The 110XL is widely considered the best that there is. The following table gives the specs on my particular lenses.

Model of Schneider lens	Focal length	Max f-no	Min f-no	Image circle at (f/22)	Total rise in landscape format (mm)	Total rise in portrait format (mm)	35mm equivalent*	Weight (g)	Filter (mm)
Super-Angulon XL	58mm	5.6	32	166	9	8	15–18mm	320	67
Super-Symmar XL	80mm	4.5	64	212	39	34	21–25mm	271	67
Super-Symmar XL	110mm	5.6	45	288	83	76	28–32mm	425	67
Apo-Symmar	150mm	5.6	64	220	44	39	38–45mm	250	58

*Note: *35mm focal length value depends on which source you take. A typical range of values quoted in the literature is given.*

Clearly, the table shows how aspherical lenses reduce weight and produce optics with wider maximum apertures. This increases light transmission when focusing on a ground glass screen and permits much easier focusing in dark environments such as at dusk or with woodland scenes. Compare the f/4.5 80mm Super-Symmar with the f/5.6 Super-Angulon 90mm XL mentioned above, or with its cheaper non-XL f/8 cousin. Compare, too, the weight differences and filter sizes. Also of paramount importance are image circles, all of which are excellent, particularly the amazing 110mm lens. This lens produces image resolution in terms of lpm up in the mid-70s – that is really good, believe me.

It is probably worth reiterating that depth of field is the same for a 110mm lens be it on a 35mm or a 5 x 4in camera. Obviously, on the larger format you have the option of camera movements such as front tilt to enhance the field of focus. The table below gives the depth of field for a series of focal lengths on large-format Schneider lenses at f/32.

With the technical considerations out of the way, you are probably wondering whether you can afford a large-format outfit and, if so, whether or not you have the stamina to carry it around with you. In reality you will find that the camera and back with two lenses weighs about as much as a typical 35mm kit. The cameras generally weigh no more than their medium-format counterparts, and in many cases are lighter. So, weight isn't much of an issue. Price is always an issue with expensive hobbies but, again, the best lenses compare in price to Mamiya 7II lenses, perhaps even being slightly cheaper. Because so few exposures are made with large-format lenses, second-hand optics are a real bargain. These lenses are made to last a lifetime, and should be fine when bought second-hand from a reputable dealer.

It is often said that 150mm and 90mm lenses are the ones to start off with. As I've said, I bucked the trend. I was so pleased with the perspective offered by my Mamiya 65mm, that I wanted something equivalent in large format, for example the aspherical 110mm XL. I heard that 90mm is not always quite wide enough, which is why some photographers also carry a 75mm lens. I thought I could save money by replacing both these focal lengths with a single lens: the aspherical 80mm XL. This meant I had some cash left over for an extreme wide-angle lens, a 58 XL, that I use for capturing a very broad landscape perspective. For a more standard view, I have a 150mm lens.

Point of focus	47mm	58mm	72mm	90mm	110mm
5ft	1.56ft ➔ ∞	2.04ft ➔ ∞	2.58ft ➔ 84.38ft	3.12ft ➔ 12.57ft	3.19ft ➔ 11.54ft
20ft	2.03ft ➔ ∞	2.94ft ➔ ∞	4.20ft ➔ ∞	5.35ft ➔ ∞	6.12ft ➔ ∞
200ft	2.24ft ➔ ∞	3.39ft ➔ ∞	5.18ft ➔ ∞	7.97ft ➔ ∞	8.45ft ➔ ∞

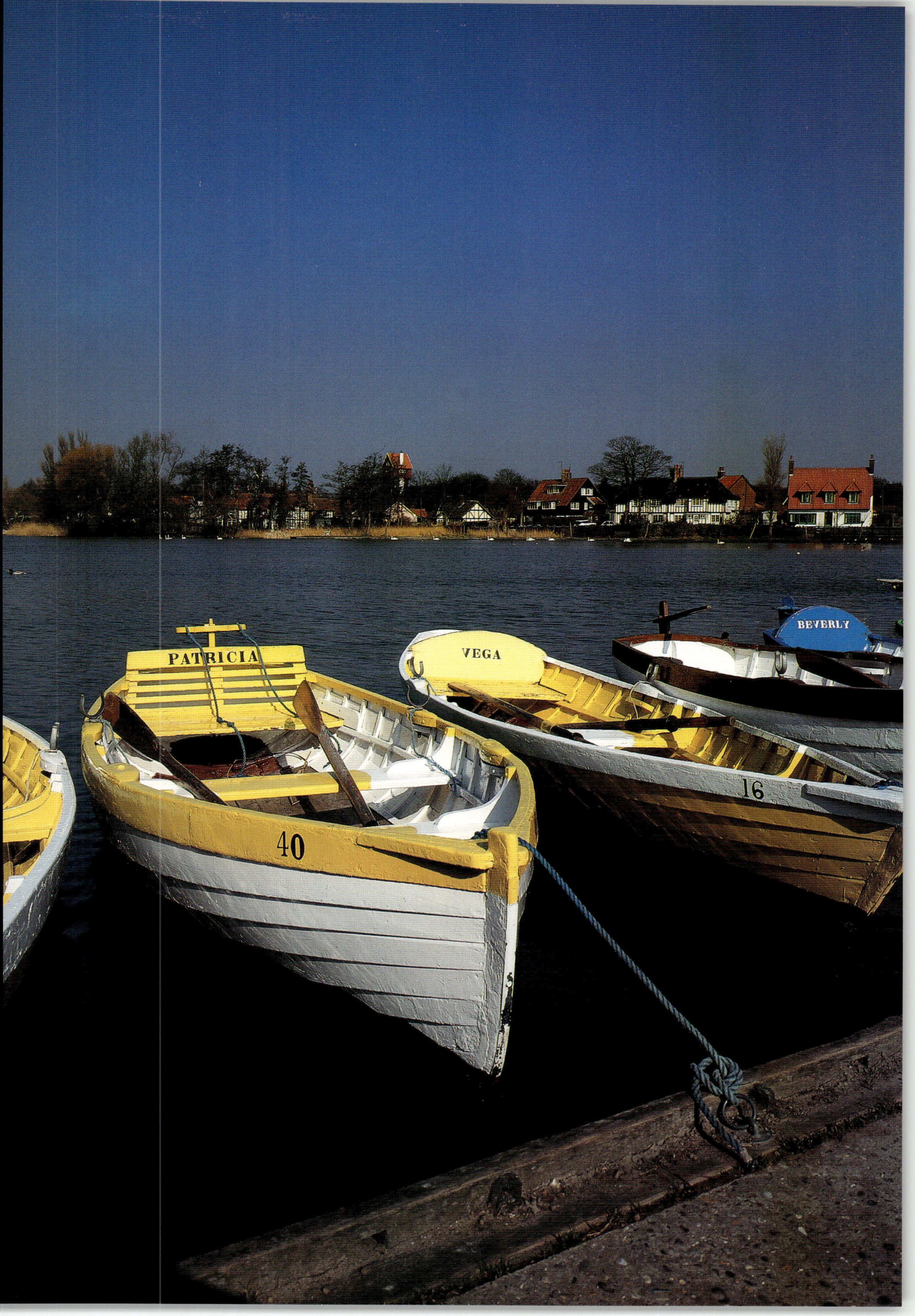

This shot of moored boats was taken with my Fuji GSW69III, and metering was with an incident meter held immediately in front of the boat. Taken at Thorpeness Meare, Suffolk, England.
Fuji GSW69III, 1/60sec at f/11–16, Velvia, tripod.

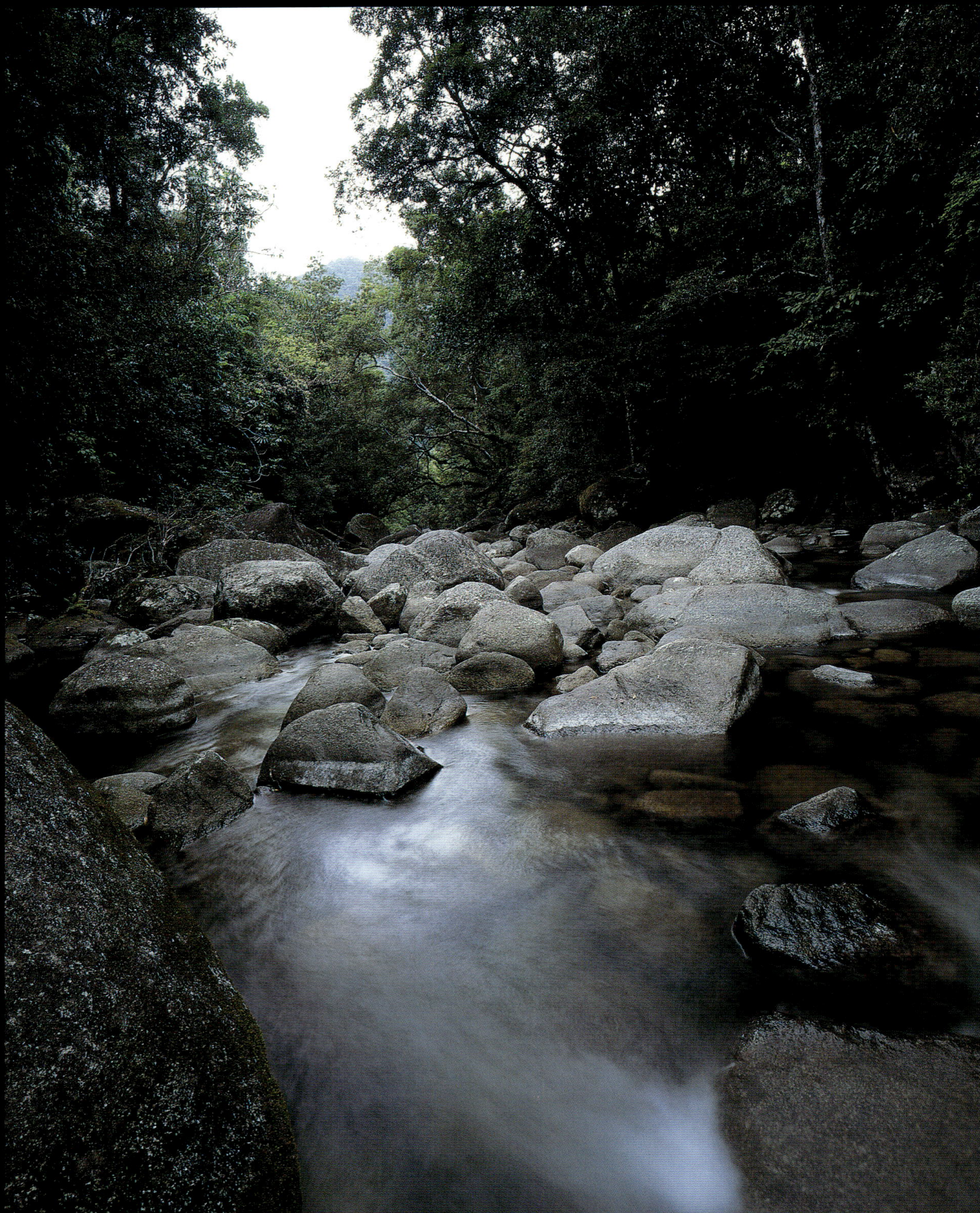

This image of a cascading Australian river offered me a metering problem because of the level of contrast in the scene. I opted to use a reflected spot reading off a large, neutral grey rock in the river. This was roughly equivalent to using an 18% grey card.
Mamiya 7II+ 43mm lens, Velvia.

Exposure meters

I have given this subject a separate heading of its own simply because it is so important, particularly in the context of large-format photography where the cost of a wrong exposure is so high relative to the other formats. However, it is not necessary to review all meters, past and present. Suffice to say that most modern meters by manufacturers such as Minolta, Gossen, Sekonic and Pentax are accurate and reliable, given some familiarity. Beware old meters – they may no longer be accurate enough for exposing transparency film.

My own meter is the Sekonic L-508 zoom master, which offers incident and spot (1°–4°) reflected ambient metering. I bought this to replace my old Sekonic Flashmate L308B which, while brilliant, did not offer spot metering. With the advent of my interest in large-format photography, I felt that spot metering was an essential metering option to facilitate correct exposure on the expensive sheet film.

Incident light measurements record the light falling on the subject via a Lumisphere dome. Therefore, the subject's colour or reflectivity does not unduly influence the exposure value. This is generally considered to be the most accurate way of exposing for the majority of subjects and scenes.

Reflected metering reads the intensity of light reflected from the subject, and will bias the meter according to variability in tone colour and contrast because all meters see their subject as an 18% neutral grey. Thus subjects lighter than 18% grey reflect more light and result in exposures that render them darker, and vice versa. Therefore, in landscape photography where you are often metering distant objects over a wide area of view, highly reflective surfaces and extreme contrast including back-lit situations, a reflected spot reading can be very useful. In fact, my zoom spot meter can average two or three exposure readings from critical areas of highlight and shadow, providing suggested optima for the overall scene. With reflected measurements in general, using an 18% neutral grey card placed in front of the subject avoids aberrant readings due to reflections and colours that bias the meter reading.

A further reason why I like my particular meter is that it will meter down to 30 minutes for really long exposures. Also, while less relevant to landscape photography, the Lumisphere retracts for flat copy work, and the meter will measure both flash and flash plus ambient.

While large-format cameras have an obligate need for the judicious use of an exposure meter, many medium-format cameras have accurate in-built metering these days. However, many of them – such as my Fuji GSW690III and Hasselblad 500CM – do not. Some people still prefer to use a hand-held incident meter reading than rely on their medium-format camera's reflected meter reading. Personally, down to four seconds I am happy to rely on my Mamiya 7II's automatic exposure system. 35mm SLR cameras are now so good at assessing exposure with their various matrix, multisegment and/or spot metering options that it would be a complete waste of money to buy a separate hand-held meter to use with them.

Travelling with camera gear

This is a very sore topic with many photographers. How do you get all the gear and film you need past the airport check-in desk? With a paltry 5kg cabin baggage allowance you can take film plus either a large-format camera and a couple of lenses or a medium format with one or two lenses, a 35mm plus two or three light lenses. There is no allowance for mix-and-match unless you are happy to consign fragile and expensive camera gear to the hold, which is not something I would recommend. The only item of kit that I place in the hold is my tripod, which I wrap in beach towels and store in my suitcase. Also, many airports have introduced a whole new generation of super X-ray machines capable of scanning hold luggage for suspect electronic devices. Reports show that they can damage film, particularly APS film. The bottom line is that if you want to keep your film safe in your hand luggage, you need to cut down on your camera equipment. The only way I can get around this thorny problem is to spread my equipment out as part of my family's hand luggage allowance. It is interesting that I invariably have my hand luggage checked and weighed in the UK, but have never had it weighed in any other country. Things seem far more relaxed and photographer friendly elsewhere, in the United States in particular (or at least until recently). Before the terrorist outrage at the World Trade Centre in New York, I thought the authorities in the UK were overly obsessed with bureaucracy, particularly with issues of safety, but all photographers have to rethink this in light of this tragic event.

I have a fantastic Billingham bag for my camera gear, but it weighs a lot and will therefore accrue fewer air miles in the future than lighter bags by Tamrac and Lowepro, which are fine for most of my travel needs. I always carry some bin liners with me in case it pours with rain. They also help if I want to lay my kit out on a wet forest floor. Whether a bag is waterproof or not is of little consequence to me, because I always coddle it in a refuse bag should the need arise. I protect my electronic cameras from water, but a little splash or two on a view camera isn't cause for concern.

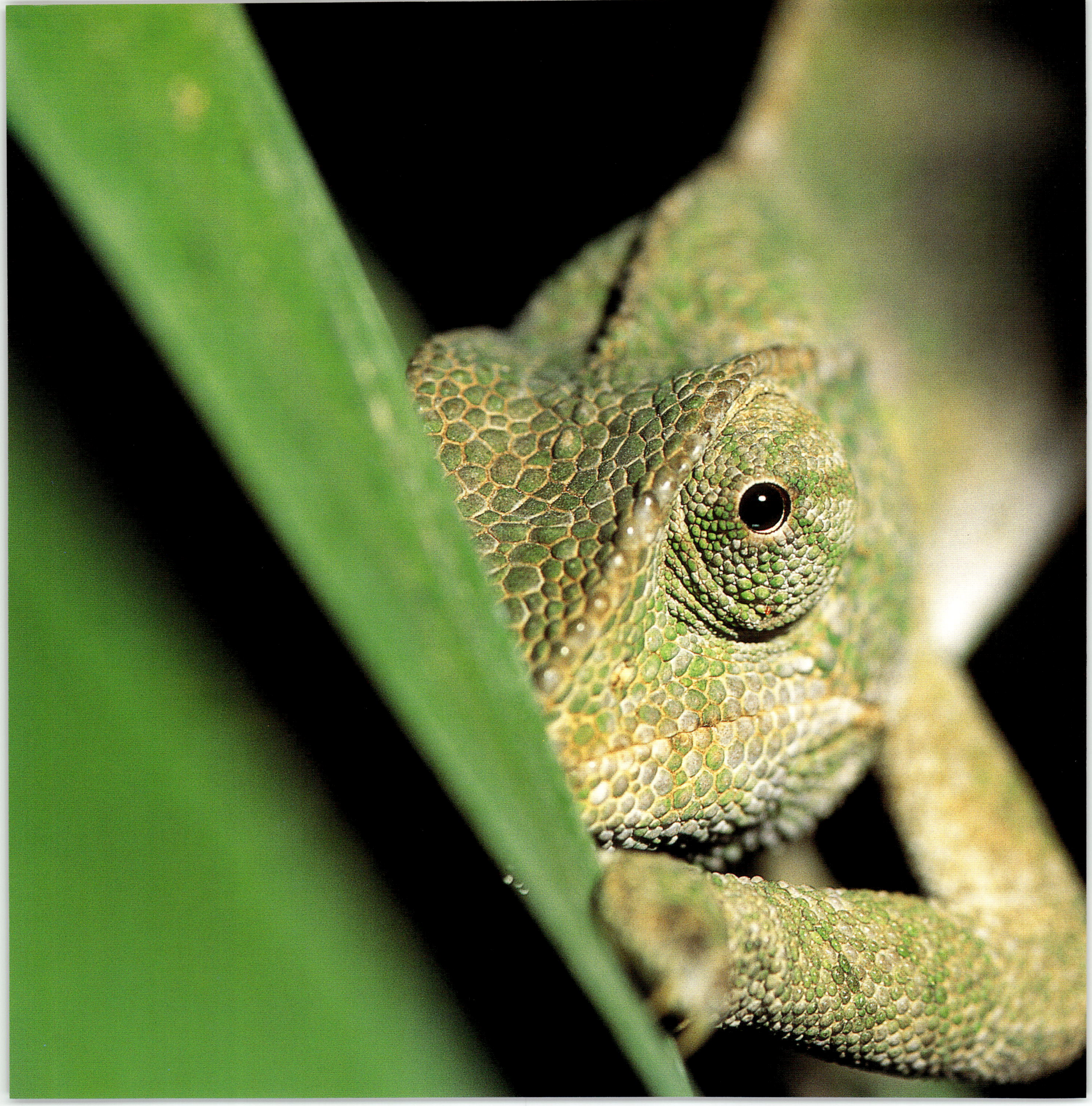

Many photographers pigeonhole themselves as landscape photographers. Such exclusivity is a mistake. It is always best to diversify as much as possible on a shoot. For instance, while photographing Cypriot landscapes, I took the time to shoot a mini project on chameleons. To do this I needed to take a greater range of gear than would be required for landscapes alone. I shared out my kit with travelling companions to comply with airline weight restrictions for cabin baggage. This, and the two images which follow, show differing aspects of these most beguiling creatures.
All three images: Pentax MZ5n + 100mm macro lens, off-camera TTL flash. Apertures were f/11–16.5.

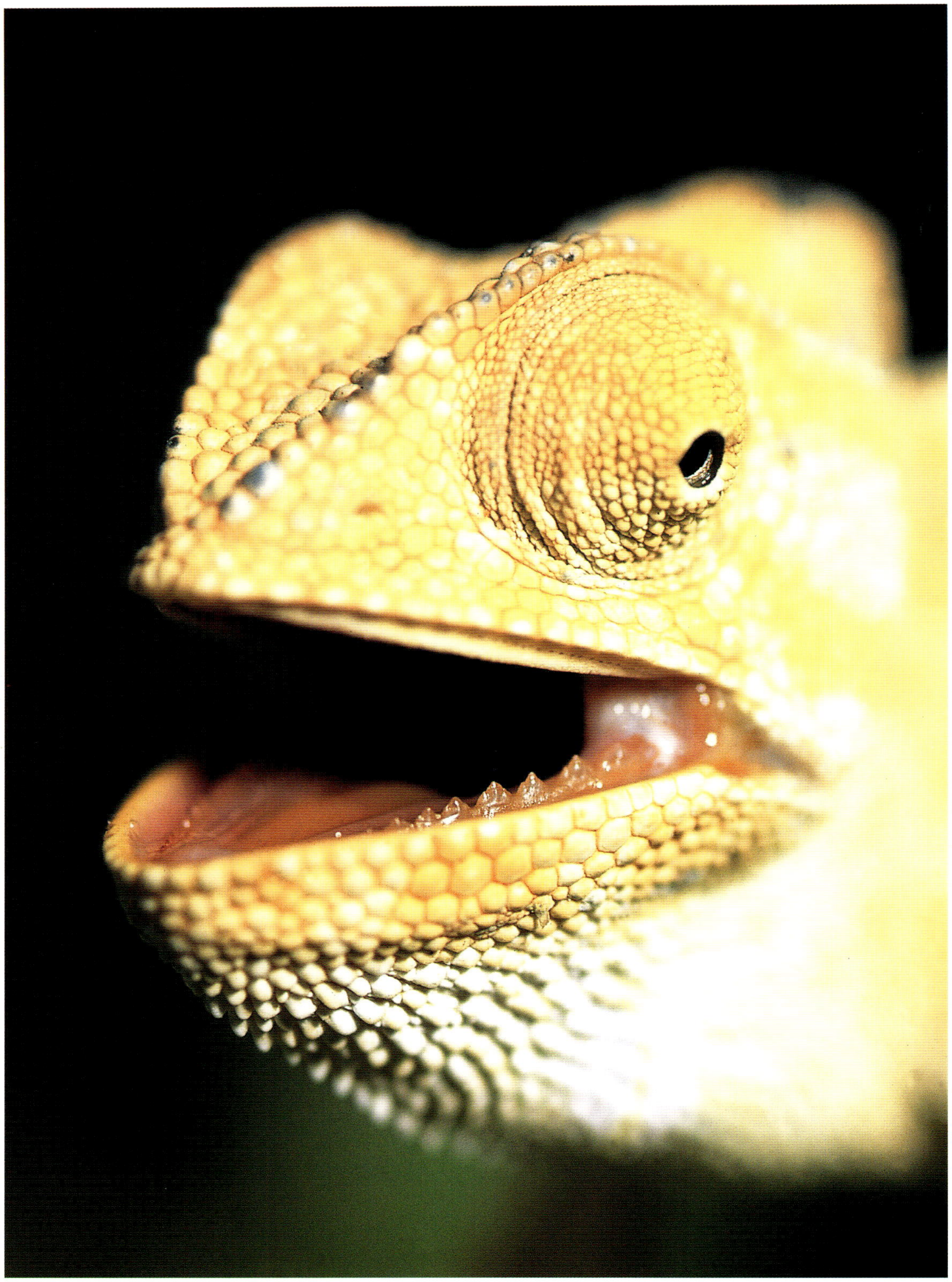

It should be patently obvious that in many poorer countries you are inviting trouble if you openly advertize your expensive camera equipment. Chances are you will be mugged or worse. Photographing landscapes means that you tend to be in wilderness areas, away from the urban centres where most crime occurs, but it pays to be discreet anyway. Even away from the hustle and bustle of towns, don't leave your camera in your hire car on full view. If you do, you are inviting theft – and remember, insurance policies tend to exclude theft from cars. In any event, unattended cars can get hot very quickly, and your camera and lenses will rapidly deteriorate. Adhesives that bond lens elements in place may melt. I remember once leaving a bottle of water in my car for 30 minutes in Key Largo. When I came back for a drink it was almost hot enough to scald me. Think what that could do to a lens or camera.

I have already mentioned the problem of termites eating view cameras in the tropics. Actually, there are real problems in the tropics during the wet season. You should store film in hermetically sealed containers, preferably with activated (blue) silica gel. This is more important for exposed and fast films than slow and unexposed films. Cameras and, importantly,

This portrait of a chameleon has real impact.

lenses, should also be protected from humidity. Lenses can soon sprout a fungal culture between the elements. And again, when you arrive home, process your films immediately. In very cold climates you should avoid autowinding and rewinding; stick to manual operation if possible. This is because at low temperatures, film becomes brittle and sprocket holes tear very easily. Even at home you need to be careful.

At your departure airport on your return home, you always have to send your exposed film through a security X-ray machine. This is unavoidable, so there is little merit in worrying about it. I must admit, I often wonder how film-safe some third world X-ray machines are. Despite this, the value of lead bags is equally unclear and may simply lead to the X-ray machine operator turning up the power to investigate the shielded bag further. Elsewhere, I have no problem with putting my new unexposed film through the hand luggage X-ray machine, since I have never noticed any detrimental effect. If in doubt, my advice is to ask for a hand search. This is a particularly good idea where extensive use of domestic flights within a country means your film would otherwise incur a substantial cumulative dose of radiation. In the United States, the Federal Aviation Authority have a ruling which entitles anybody to a hand search upon request.

This image was taken specifically to show how seamlessly the chameleon blends into its environment.

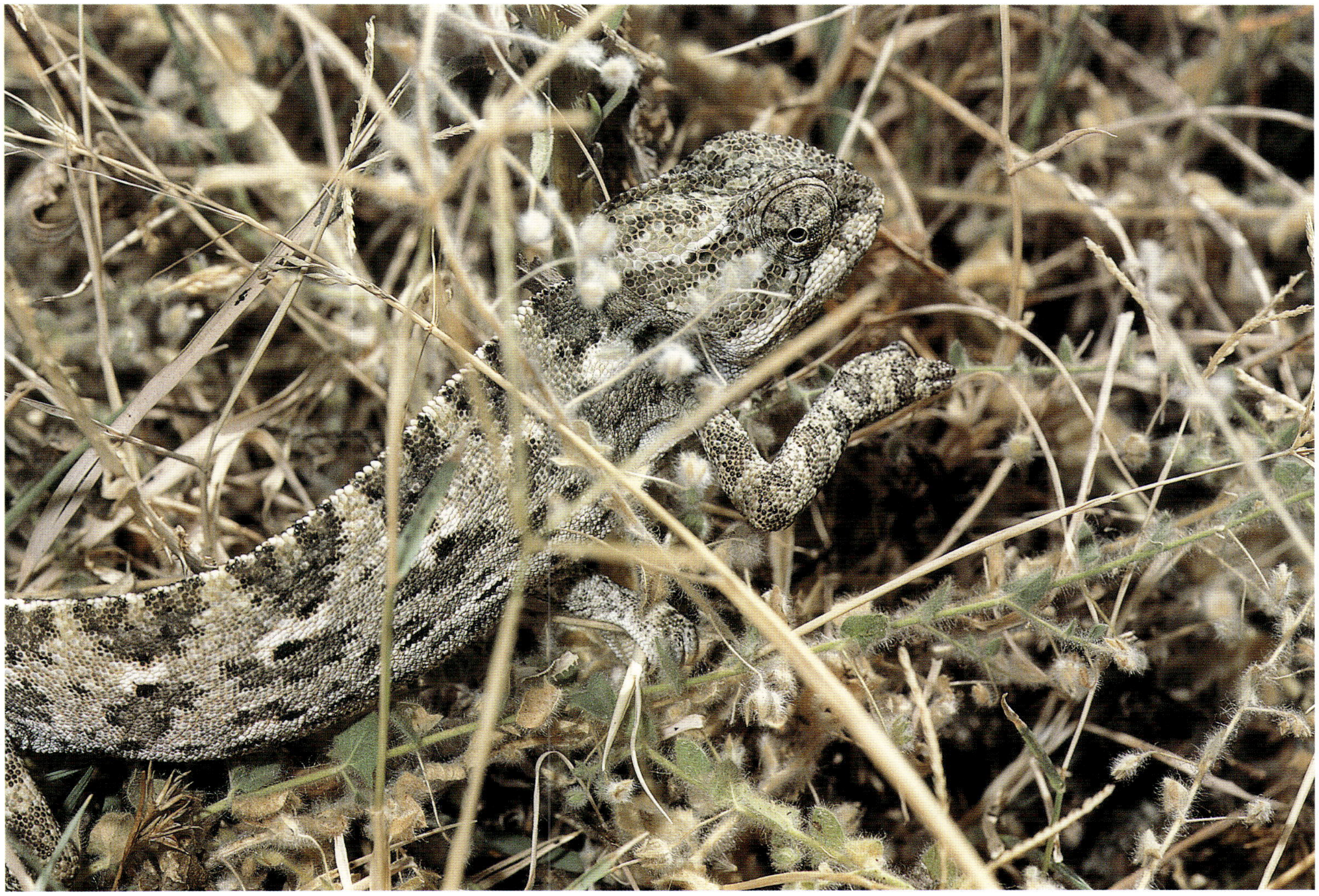

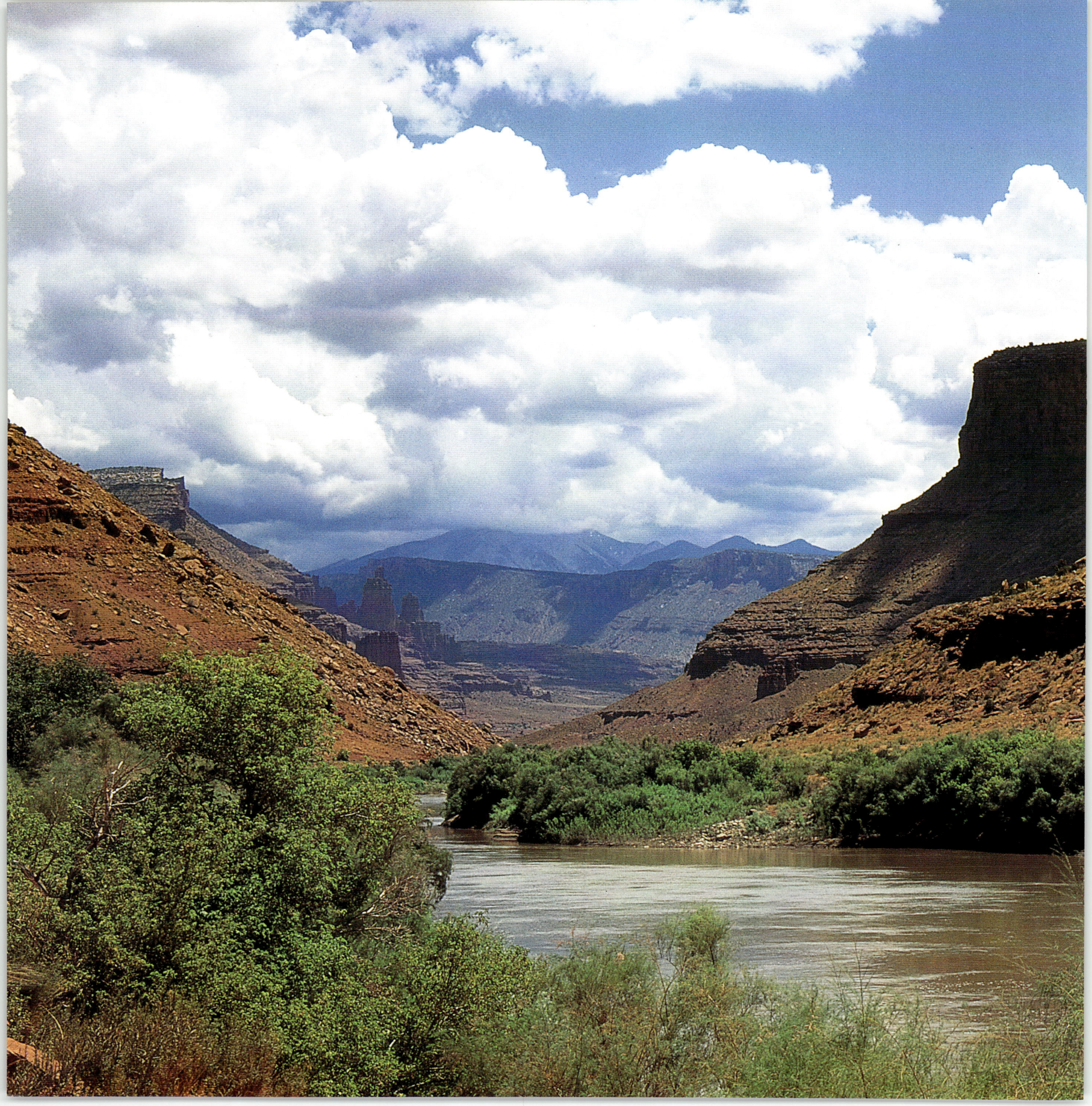

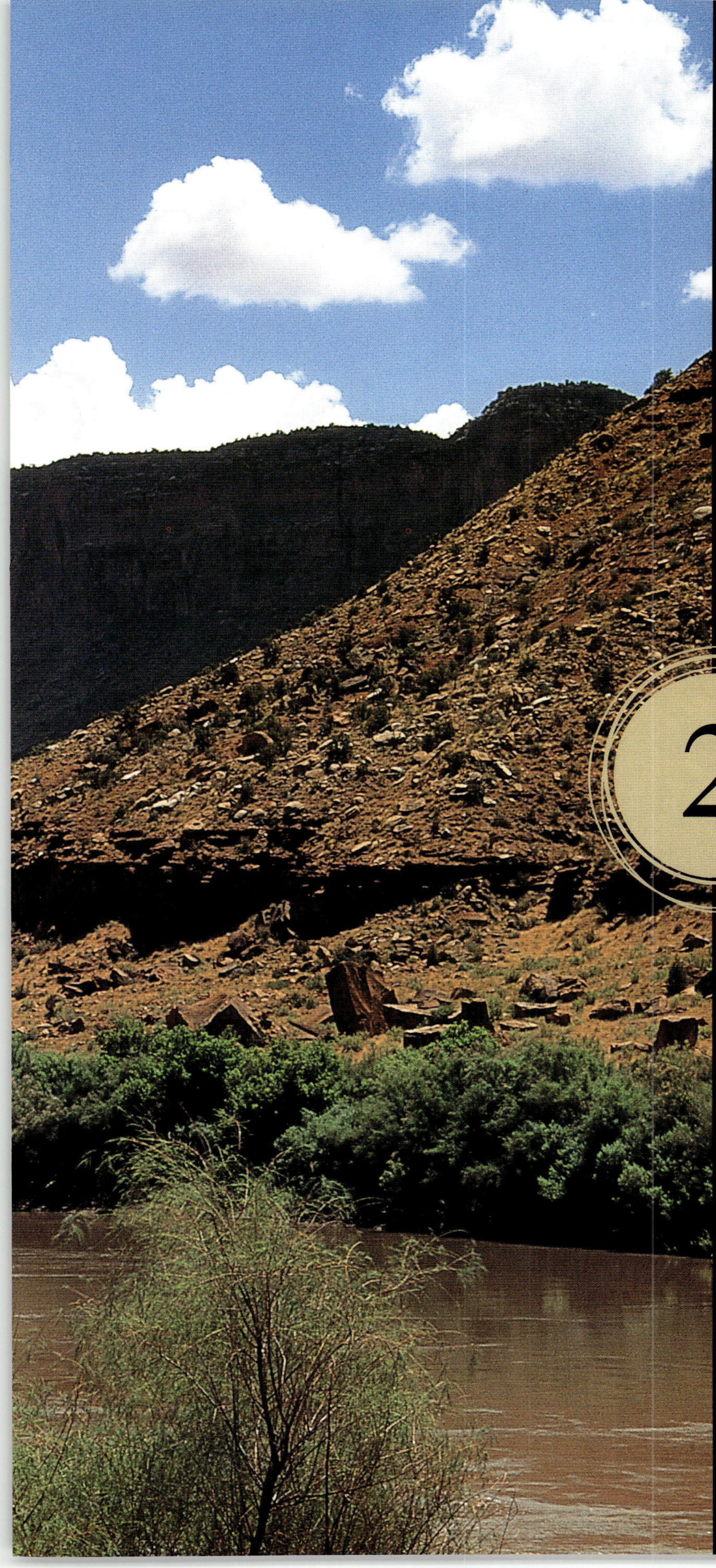

2 In the Field

Every environment offers the landscape photographer a different set of challenges. This chapter describes those habitats which, for me, are very special; places where you can make superb landscape photographs. It is the spirit of nature that draws me to these very different landscapes to practise my craft, and each section covers both the pleasures and pitfalls of photographing them. Although a major component of this section, I have not limited my discussion to the natural world. Included is a section on cityscapes which offer some fantastic photo opportunities for producing arresting landscape images.

Temperate woodland

In Britain, where I live, temperate woodlands arguably form the island's most precious natural asset and need considered protection. Embodied in even the smallest fragment of these ancient woods is both the history and the future of a nation. If this, the most beautiful of natural environments disappears, how can we ensure our own survival into the not-too-distant future? My local wood is special to me. I walk in it for solace, study it for interest and photograph it for pleasure. Saturday is the best day, because everyone goes to the new local shopping mall. This leaves the whole wood to me, and virtually no-one else – a landscape and environmental photographer's dream.

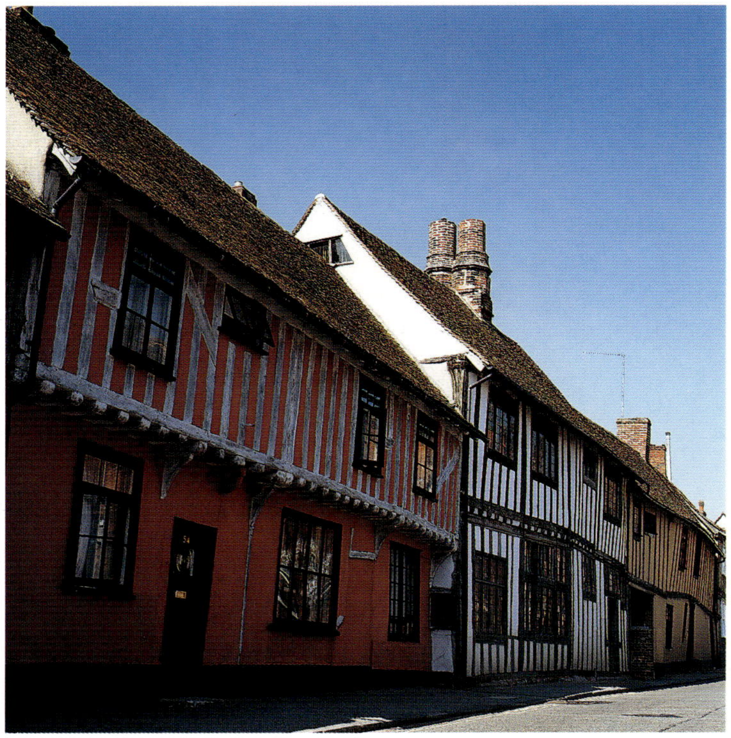

The larger the wood, the greater the diversity of habitats that exist, and the more niches there are for plants to occupy. This leads to more interest for the photographer. For example, in a single large area you can come across soil that is well-drained and soil that is damp, so the chemistry and hence acidity may also vary. Some areas, too, may be regularly bathed in sunlight while others are almost permanently shaded. Additionally, the more established a wood is, the greater the variety of life contained within.

Thus, precise characterization of any given woodland is difficult. In fact, although today's mixed woodland is often derived from ancient wild wood, many are dominated by a single species of tree. Stands of either ash, beech or oak are common. To understand the origins of a wood, however, one needs to understand the region's agricultural history, too. Although the dominance of a species of tree may change as a result of alterations in land usage over the years, its carpet of spring flowers can remain in perpetuity and reflect the true ancient character of the woodland site. Some plant species, however, are clear indicators of human activities in woodland areas. Stinging nettles grow on enriched soils and indicate cattle may have been stalled there at one time. Now they provide a feast for vanessid butterfly caterpillars. Foxglove seeds persist in the soil's seed bank for half a century, only germinating when freshly opened woodland lets light permeate to the floor. Similarly, rosebay willowherb invades newly bared and disturbed land, especially after a fire when there is a rapid release of nutrients, hence the plant's alternative name – fireweed. Large stands of foxglove or fireweed can be extremely photogenic, particularly if shot in the muted light of a cloudy sky. Perhaps one of the most incongruous woodland plants is the

These half-timbered buildings were built with oaks that grew 1000 years ago. Pictures like this might be used as an effective complement to a portfolio on woodland. Submitted to a magazine it illustrates an interesting facet of woodland history. Taken at Lavenham in Suffolk, England.
Hasselblad 500CM + 80mm Carl Zeiss Planar lens.

rhododendron, which was not native to woodland but widely planted by the Victorians as pheasant cover.

Woodland wildlife has a different face for each season. I favour spring when anticipation of the dawning summer reaches its zenith with a pageant of colour provided by carpets of bluebell, wild daffodil and aromatic garlic. Along with the warm spring sunshine dancing through the canopy of immature leaves, the glory of woodland flowers provide me with the most potent antidote to the damp chill of winter.

In Britain, coppiced woodland provides perfect open conditions for the spring flowers which are the envy of nature photographers from Continental Europe. In fact, bluebells are virtually unique to Britain, forged by ancient management but tempered by a distinctly dank temperate maritime climate.

Woodland is a stratified mosiac of verdant life, from the crisp mat of patterned leaf litter, rich in fungi and creepy crawly decomposers, to the impenetrable canopy of ancient, broad-leaved trees. So dense is it that even in the height of summer only flecks of light can penetrate to illuminate the shady interior. This dappled light contrasts so strongly with the shade that it is an exposure meter's worst nightmare (even an all-singing, all-dancing SLR TTL meter with the latest multisegment technology). It is not a problem if you get in close for macro portraits of wild flowers, since these are generally bathed in a uniform light. Yellow archangel, lesser celandine, bluebells, campions, wood avens and other spring and early summer plants are easy to shoot close-up for intricately detailed photographs. A 100mm macro lens and tripod can be used for close-ups, or you could go for a

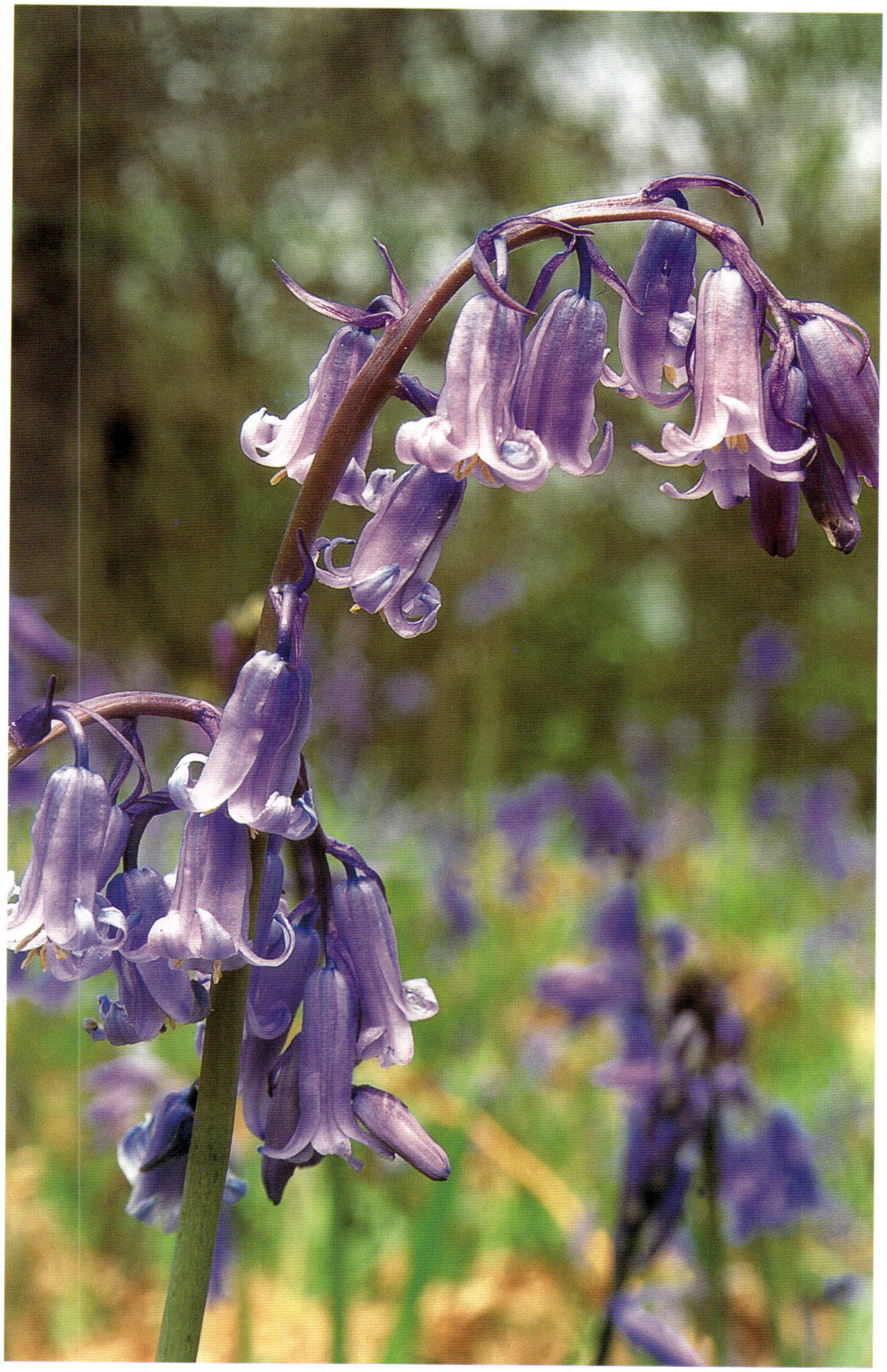

To get this close-up of a bluebell I added a Nikon 3T dioptre and used the built-in RTF for fill-in flash.
Pentax MZ5n + 28–70mm zoom lens, Nikon 3T dioptre, tripod.

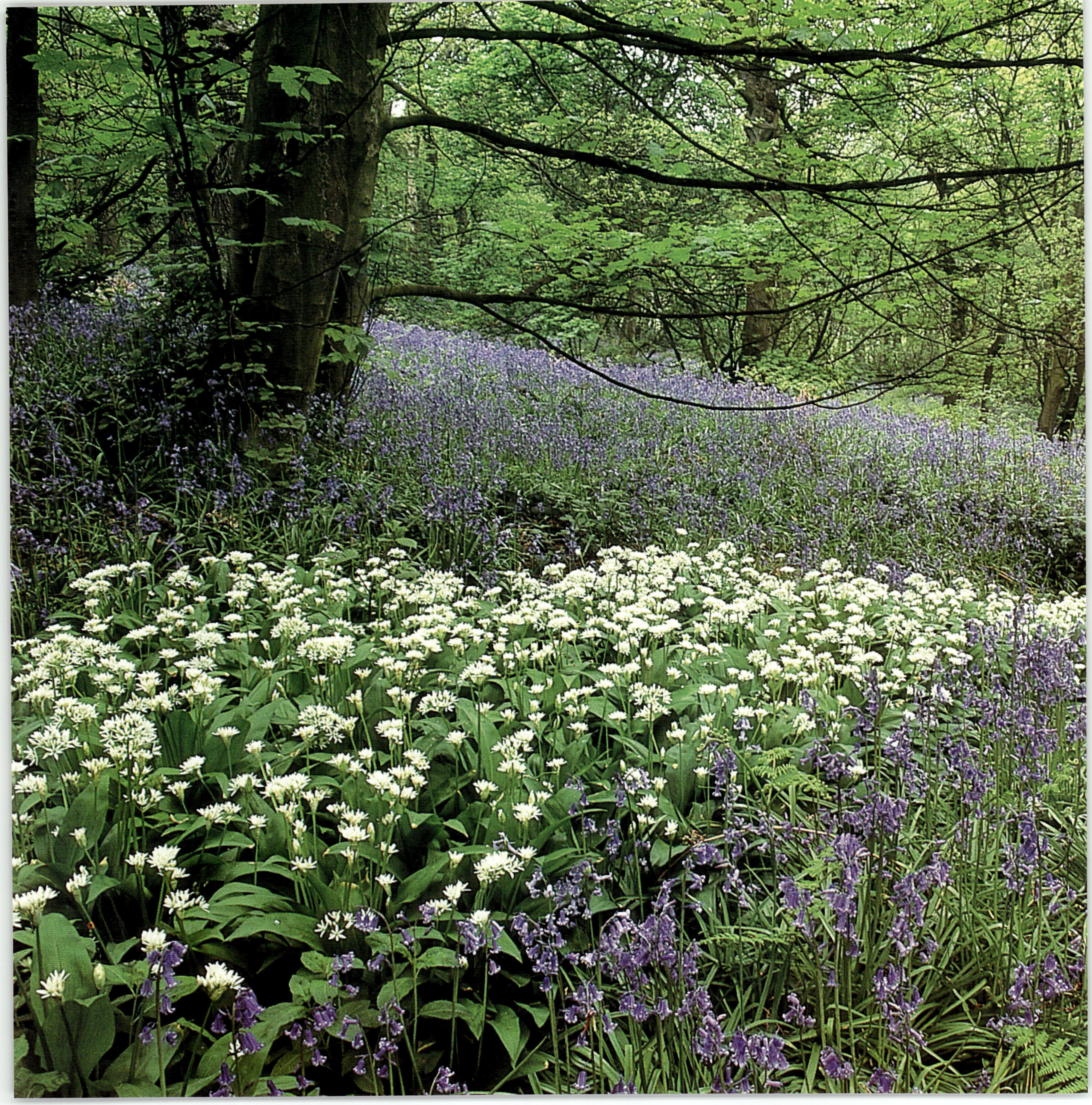

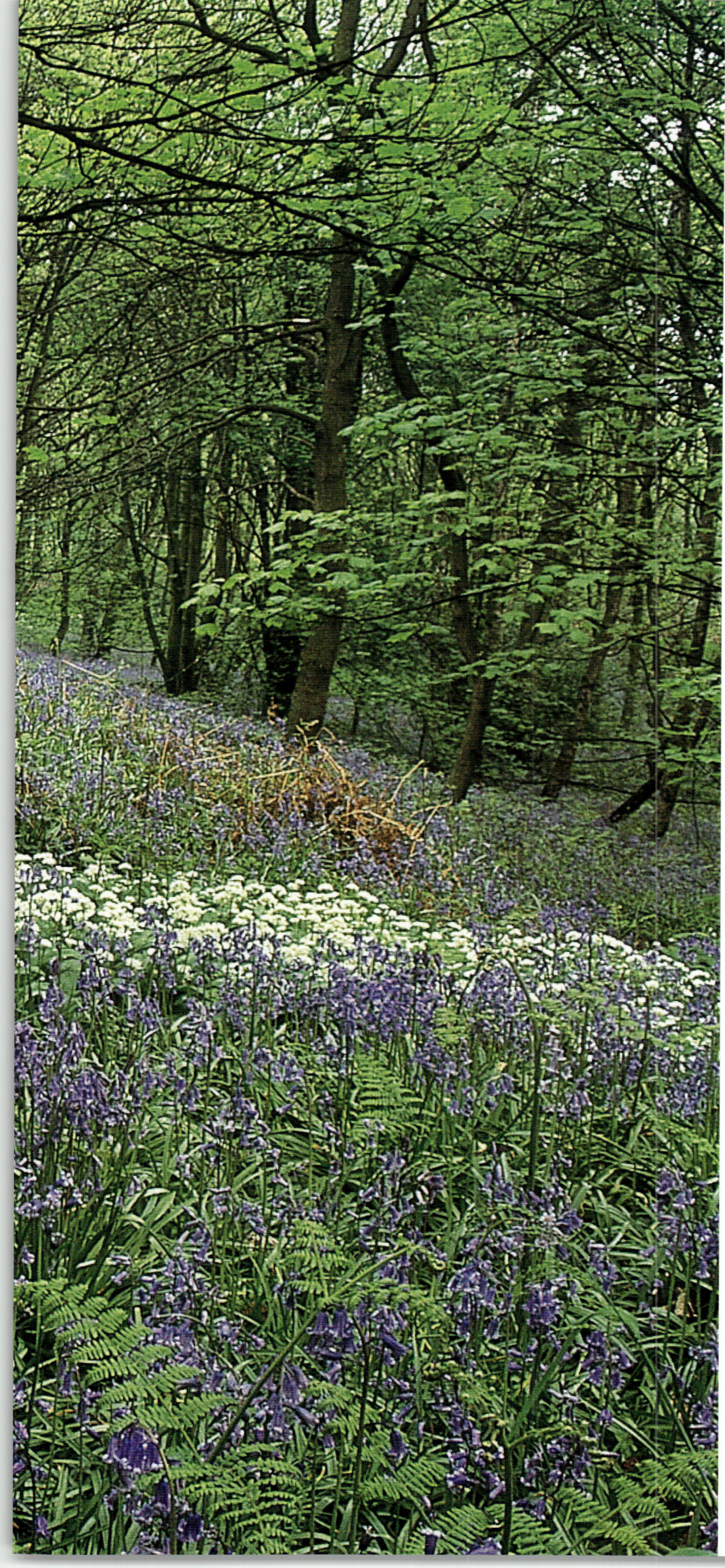

different type of close-up using a wide-angle, large-format lens like the Super-Angulon or Symmar XL series. These enable you to capture detail, yet with a bit of lens or rear tilt, add infinite depth and render the whole macrocosm in focus. With a lens that has a narrower angle of view you can employ TTL flash for fill-in lighting, or bounce light back into the shadows with a white reflector to compensate for any contrast that might be present. Given a choice, I personally prefer spring flowers en masse to isolated blooms; few would argue that a broader vista offers the landscape photographer the greatest impact and sales potential.

To photograph an entire carpet of bluebells, lesser celandine or wild daffodils with sharpness from close-up to the distant horizon you need to use a wide-angle lens (typically 24–28mm in 35mm format). 28mm is probably my favourite (it is also the cheapest lens in this class), since anything with a wider perspective can cause distortion. Having said that, this can also add interest to a scene. To maximize the depth of field you need to use the principle of hyperfocal distance. The hyperfocal distance is the precise point of focus where everything from half that distance up to infinity is within the depth of field. In order that sharpness extends from the nearest bluebell in the foreground to the most distant oak tree, pre-focus the lens by placing the infinity mark over the f-stop index corresponding to the aperture you have selected. The working aperture should be f/22 or f/32 if possible. The closest point of focus will be directly opposite the f-stop on the other end of the lens barrel scale. This sort of shot requires a sturdy tripod since exposure times are invariably long under the dense canopy. I usually select the manual focus 28mm lens on my Pentax LX. I would have to guess this critical focus setting on the autofocus Pentax 28–70mm f4 lens that I use with my Pentax MZ series cameras. Fortunately, the autofocus algorithms are spot-on when it comes to creating acceptable depth of field. All I do is set aperture priority, f/16.5 or f/22 and use multi-point autofocus. This superb aspheric lens has razor-edged sharpness and delivers the goods. It goes without saying that you should pick a day with good visibility (low water vapour), preferably with cloud cover to provide soft, diffuse lighting and avoid excessive contrast discussed above, and without wind.

In the past I have always gone for a camera-free walk in my local woods, seen a photogenic vista of bluebells and been forced to return with my gear. However, last year I made more effort to study

I used Velvia for these bluebells and ransoms. This incredibly fine-grained emulsion augments sharpness and vibrancy. Taken in Yorkshire, England.
Pentax MZ5n + 28–70mm zoom, Velvia, tripod.

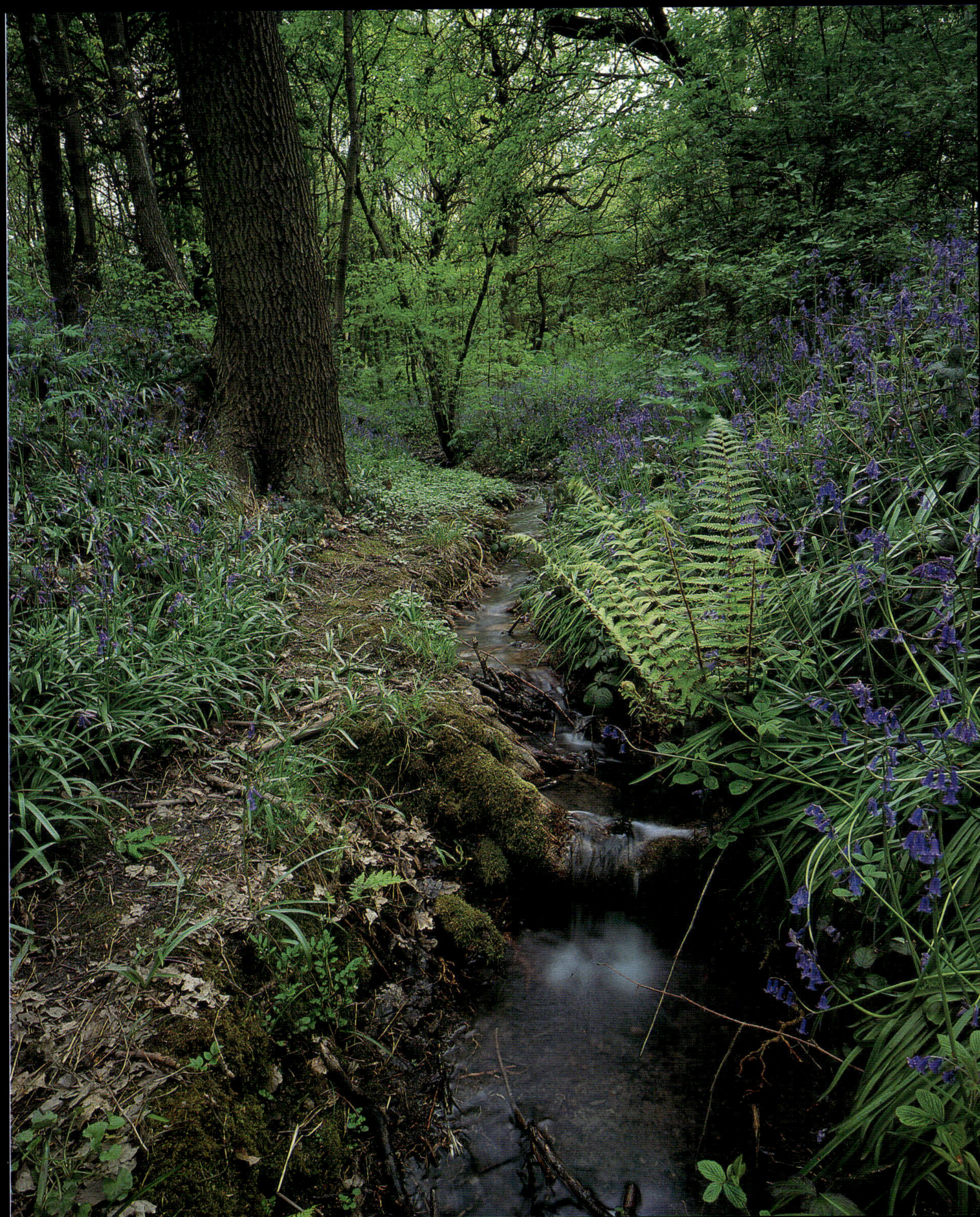

Detailed studies in woodland are best achieved with a wide-angle lens and medium- or large-format equipment. This shot of a small cascade surrounded by bluebells was taken on my Mamiya 7II and 43mm lens. I was forced to straddle this rivulet to take the picture. Sadly, 24 hours later, kids had uprooted the fern and a flagpole from the neighbouring golf course had been thrown into the stream. Taken in Yorkshire, England. *Mamiya 7II + 43mm lens, Velvia, tripod.*

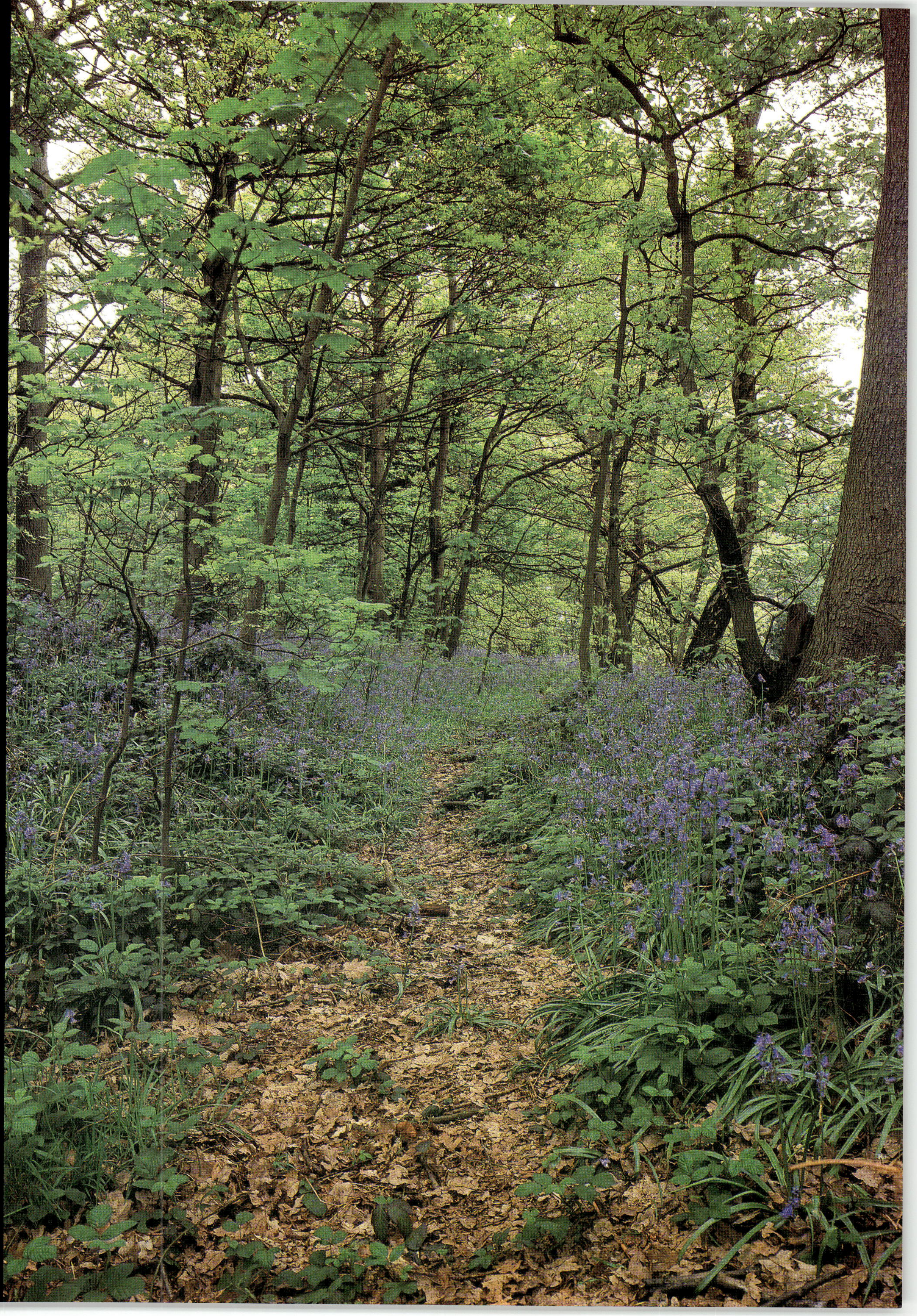

This 6 x 9cm portrait of a path lined by bluebells is one of my favourite shots. *Fuji GSW69III, 1 second at f/22, Velvia.*

the events surrounding our spring bluebells. The following diary shows that only one week out of four was really suitable for shooting bluebells at their best, and this had less to do with film, filters or lenses and more to do with the relative bracken growth and light. In fact, there is an interesting relationship between bluebells and bracken that the photographer cannot afford to ignore. They coexist in nature because bluebells flower early in the spring, catching the light before bracken forms an umbrella of fronds overhead. Underground they coexist because bracken rhizomes occupy deeper ground than the shallow bluebell bulbs. Photographers have to time their visit before bracken dominates the scene.

Diary

26th April
Bluebells still not at their peak in shaded areas of woodland. In sunny glades, however, they have reached their best. Photographed them en masse and close-up in glades. Ransoms not out, young bracken only 4in (10cm) high and dwarfed by the bluebells.

3rd May
Bluebells growing in shady woodland are at their peak. Ransoms growing in shade are also flowering, providing diazo contrast with bluebells. Bracken 6in (15cm) high but not yet overly intrusive. Shot best spring flower images of the year in soft, overcast light. Yellow archangel also starting to flower.

10th May
Bluebells are now past their best – getting leggy with bracken now at least 12in (30cm) in height and disrupting bluebell carpet. Ransoms and yellow archangel are still flowering.

17th May
Bluebells very leggy and completely overshadowed by bracken. Ransoms and yellow archangel – which appears to be at its best – still flowering.

As I write this, it is once again spring in my local wood. I have not kept a diary this year, but this spring follows a very cold and wet winter. The consequence of this is that flowering has been held back and all the various species of flowering plant have synchronized somewhat. This year, in early May, the unexpectedly cool weather

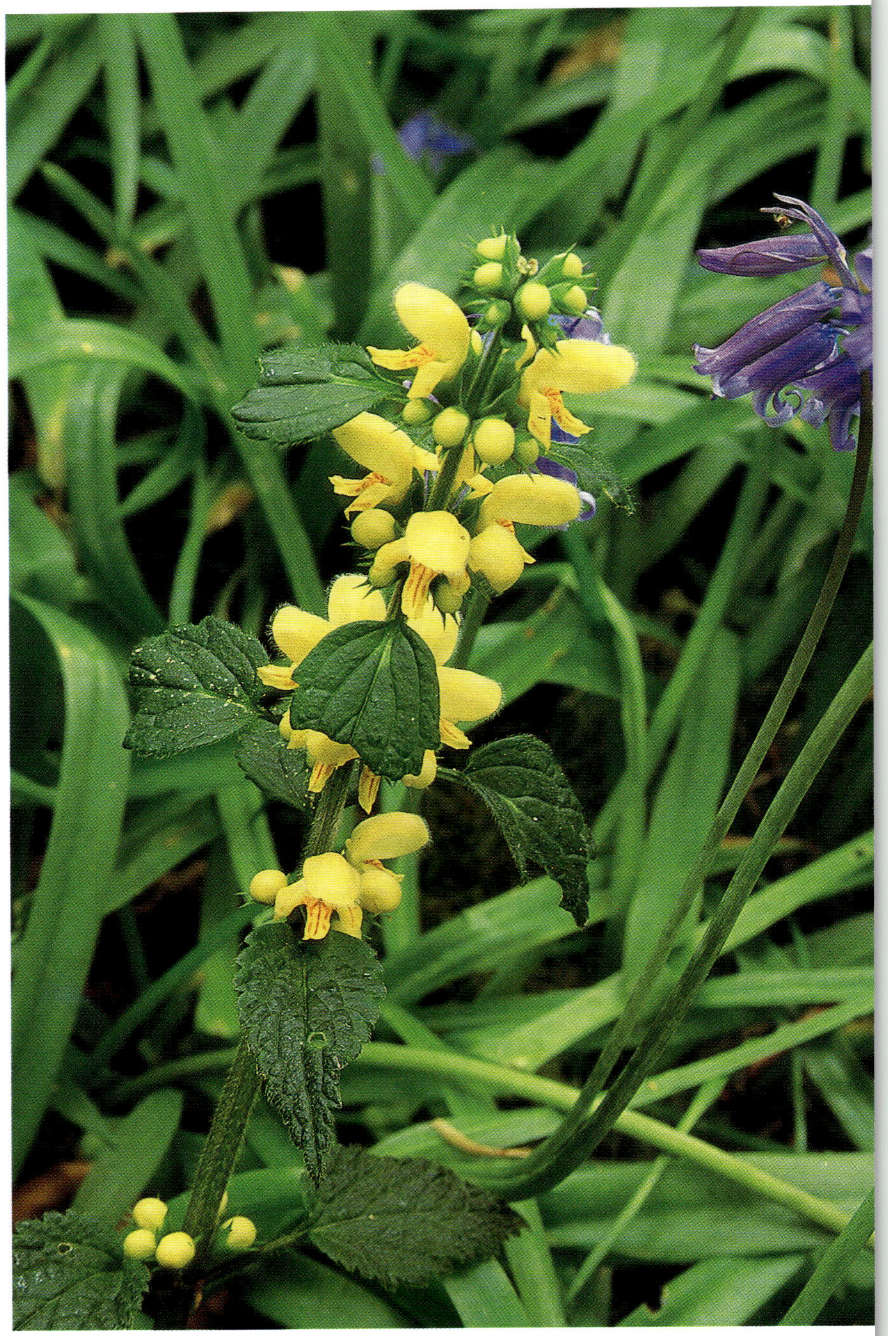

Yellow archangel is an indicator of ancient woodland and generally appears just after the bluebells reach their zenith. *Pentax 28–70mm zoom lens, Nikon 3T dioptre, tripod.*

Foxglove in close-up.
Pentax LX + 100mm macro lens, off-camera TTL flash.

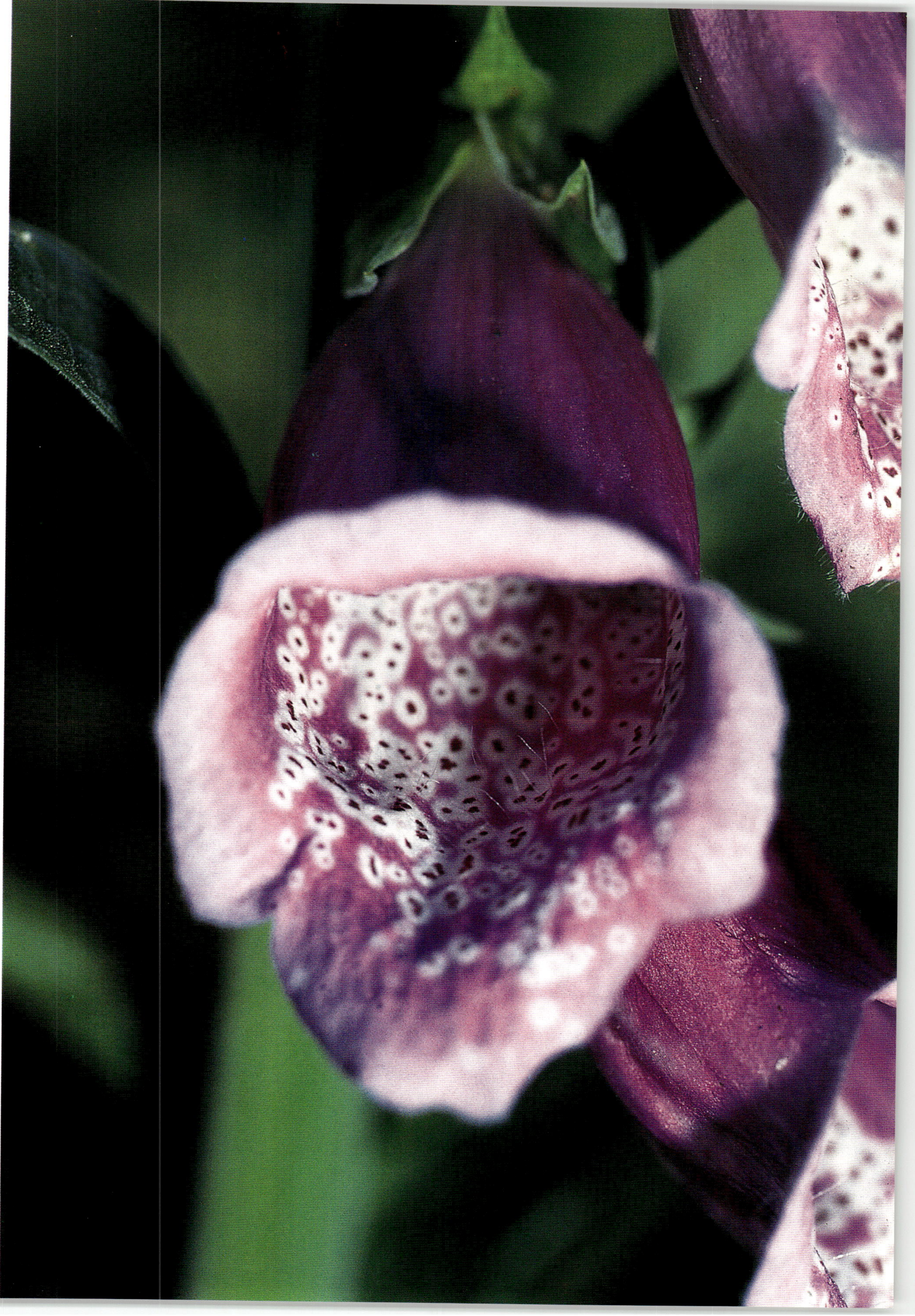

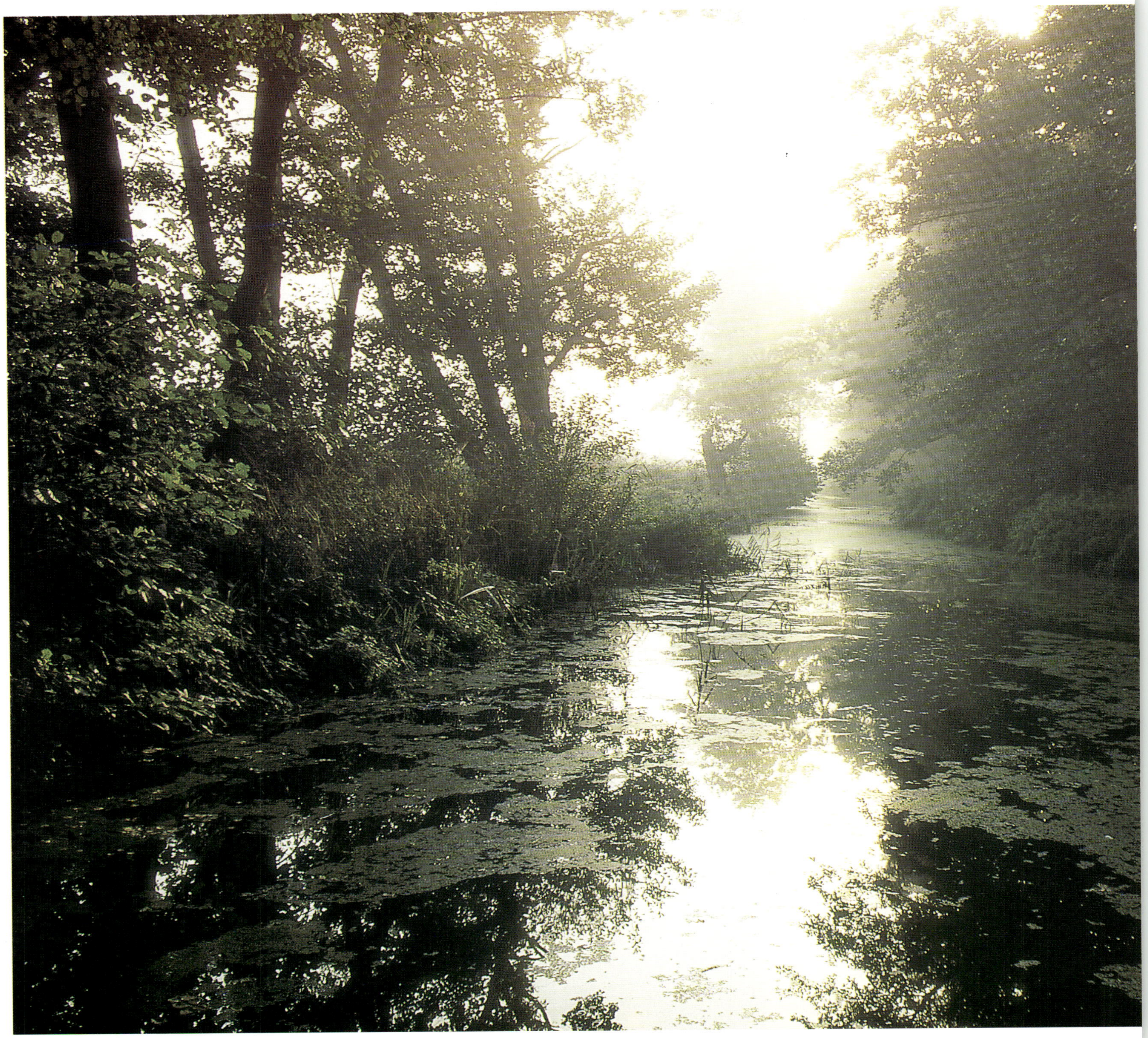

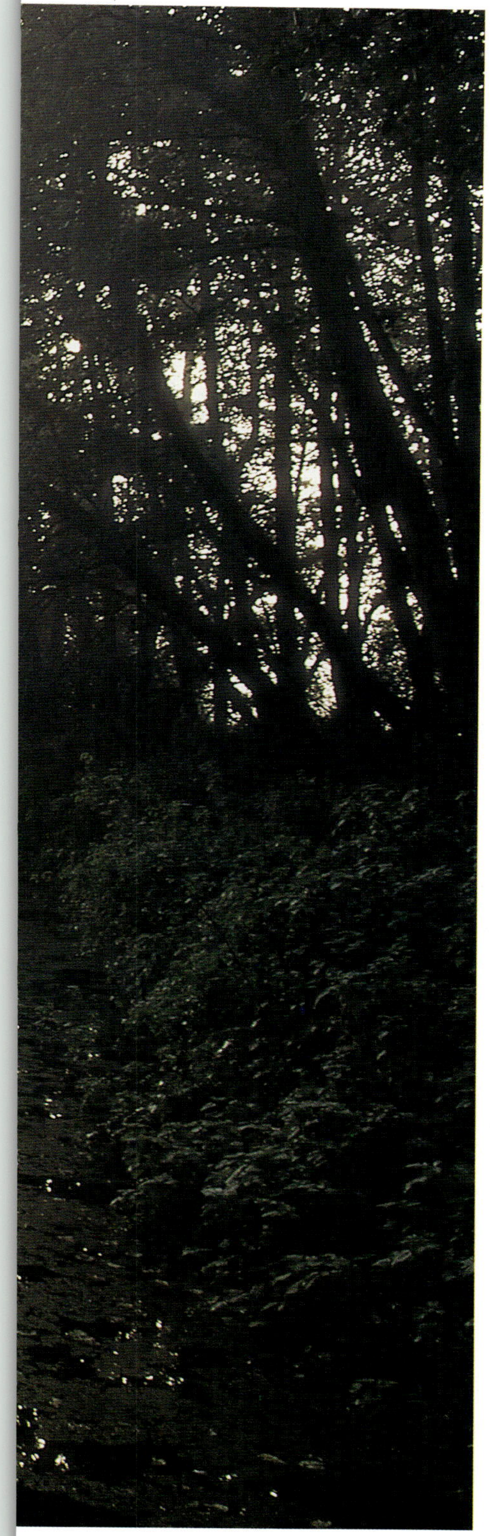

Contre-jour photography using a reflected centre-weighted TTL meter. This photograph was shot against the light in an autumnal woodland. ***Pentax SLR + 28mm prime lens, 1/125sec at f/16.***

means early flowering plants such as celandine are still in bloom, while later flowering plants in sunnier glades such as bluebells are also out. However, the stage of growth is more akin to mid-April last year. I have to confess, I am dying to get out with my Ebony camera and shoot a couple of new vantage points I discovered over the winter, but the flowers are still simply not right. What do you bet that the floral display will just achieve its optimum and it will begin to rain and not stop until the flowering peak has passed? I would definitely recommend keeping a diary of your environment in line with the changing seasons; the more familiar you become with the nuances, the better informed your plans for photography during the year and the more interest you are likely to capture in your images.

As spring moves into summer, the floral character changes. In June, flowers like bugle and creeping jenny carpet damp woodland floors, while tall and erect foxgloves look like sentinels standing guard over a woodland whose biomass is swollen to its maximum potential. These species form attractive subjects for the photographer (and nectar-seeking insects, particularly bees). Other summer woodland flowers to look out for are wood avens, betony and hedge woundwort: a plant whose smell lives up to its name.

At the end of the season, russet autumn colours often last for only a brief week or two. As a photographer you must achieve a compromise between waiting for the leaves to turn gold and beating the winds which liberate them from their fragile grip. At this time of year the sun remains very low in the sky which necessitates the use of a lens hood to prevent flare, although good-quality optics like the 80 and 110mm Schneider aspherics should help to avoid this problem. Given good-quality glass, it is always worth having a go at contre-jour photography (shooting directly into the light) for spectacular images of the sun's globe through golden leaves, or even bare branches. Compare the 35mm contre-jour image (opposite) taken with TTL centre-weighted metering (reflected) that was overexposed by two stops, with the image on page 76, which was taken with a 6 x 6cm Hasselblad. The 6 x 6cm image is also contre-jour but an incident meter was used in the dominant lighting zone. In this latter image, only half a stop extra exposure was given to that indicated. As discussed in the previous chapter, the TTL reflected light meter is calibrated to mid-grey (see page 19). In order to turn the bright sun to a mid-tone, the TTL meter stops the lens down dramatically. I would be surprised if any TTL meter could cope with this lighting situation. Even with 35mm SLR photography, it is sometimes best to use a hand-held meter to take incident readings in the dominant zone of lighting. Despite this I still bracket by up to one-and-a-half stops if I have a potentially good image in my viewfinder. My own feeling is that a little overexposure suits a woodland scene best. This means you can retain all of nature's perfect detail on the final transparency.

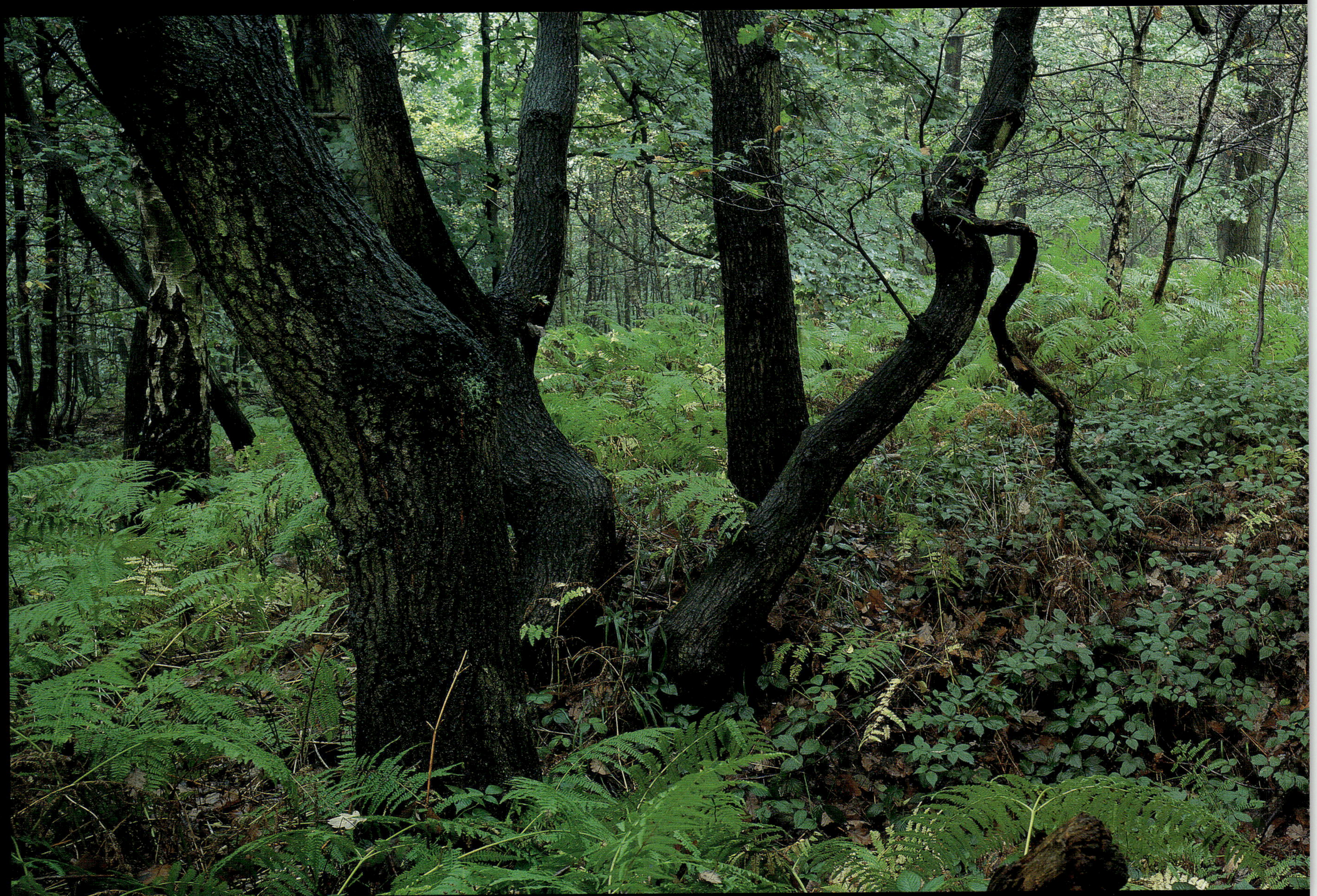

6 x 17cm panoramic slide of an early autumn woodland. To be sure of the right exposure, my daughter held up a grey card which I spot-metered from with a hand-held Sekonic exposure meter. I then allowed one extra stop to compensate for light lost due to the neutral density graduated centre spot filter that is required with this ultra-wide lens. There is much to be said for having an assistant with you when using big cameras; it began to pour with rain just as I took this frame and my daughter held an umbrella over the camera. Taken in Yorkshire, England.
Fuji GX617 + 90mm lens, 6 seconds at f/32, Velvia.

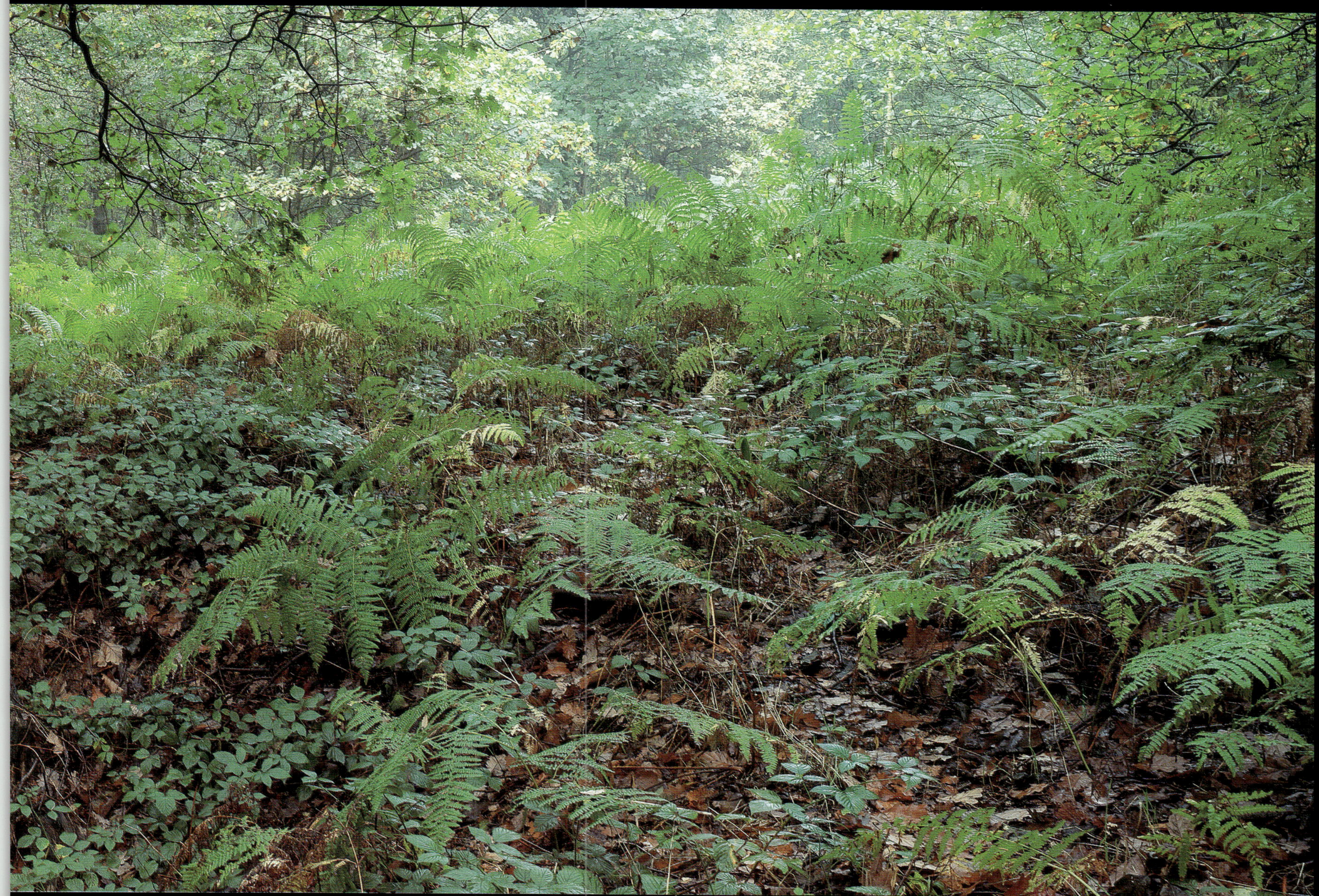

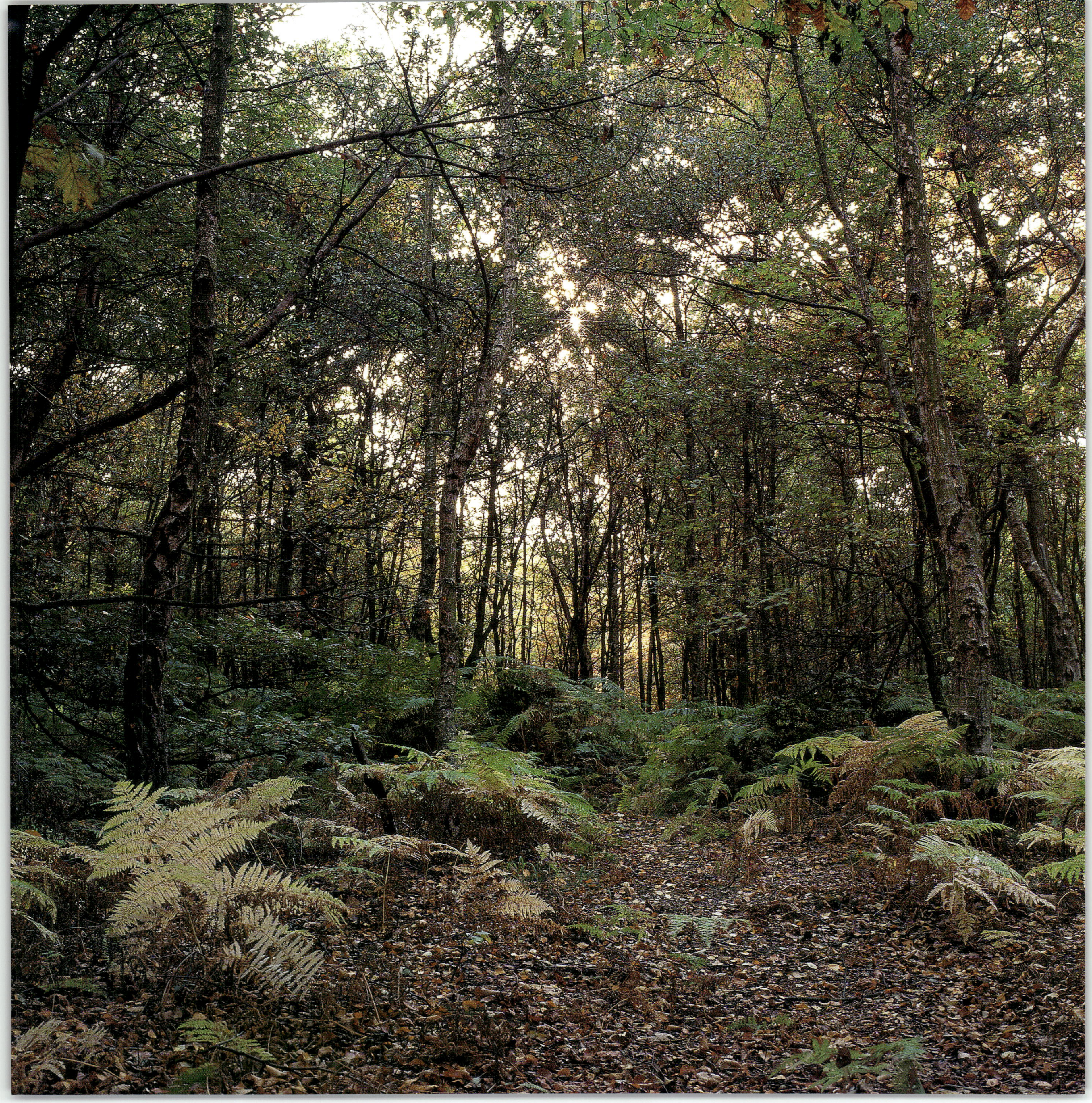

The complexity of an oak woodland ecosystem is such that the photo opportunities are only limited by your imagination. Supplement your landscape shots by photographing buds, flowers, fruits, leaf and bark patterns; the list is almost endless. Learn to read the signs. A patch of nettles is home to many butterfly caterpillars, which make elaborate communal tents out of the leaves. Bring home some caterpillars, pot up some nettles and photograph the process of metamorphosis. Watch out though – as some species emerge from their pupal stage, blood-coloured haemolymph goes everywhere. You have to see it to believe it. Images like these that get in close add to your woodland portfolio, and can only help sell your work. In winter, when the only plants are leafless trees, introduce other elements to your pictures such as flowing streams or, better still, waterfalls (see pages 114–139).

Tropical rainforest

Like Conan Doyle's mythical lost world, the misty rainforest that cloaks the Great Dividing Range in tropical northern Queensland is home to strange and sometimes dangerous creatures. For Europeans, this is the most distant tropical rainforest on our planet. Although safe by South American and African standards, it has its hazards: death adder, taipan, paralyzing ticks, aggressive cassowaries and Daintree ulcer. The latter is a disease of unknown aetiology that causes the unlucky victim to simply rot to death. While uncommon, it is well described and has parallel conditions in South America and Africa. If you survive all these pleasures, you are sure to get caught by the stinger tree, whose heart-shaped leaves have silica-like hairs that break off in your flesh and inject venom akin to snake poison; a treat that creates localized pain for months on end (I'm told waxing the affected area helps). I won't even mention the enormous estuarine crocodiles and box jellyfish. Actually, like most visitors, I survived these dangers. The biggest problems for me on a recent trip to the Daintree National Park in Queensland were, a) rain, b) sun and c) finding the animals to photograph in the first place.

Before arriving, I was particularly keen to take 6 x 7cm rainforest landscapes on my ultra-wide 43mm lens (21mm on 35mm format). As this lens cost a lot of money, you can imagine that I wasn't too keen to use it in the incessant drizzle that I encountered. However, having travelled 12,000 miles to capture this remarkable environment and since I was unlikely to return for some time, I did just this. Imagine the scene: a Briton abroad in baggy shorts, tee shirt, erect umbrella and Mamiya 7II on a tripod, standing ankle deep in a muddy rainforest creek timing three-minute exposures on Velvia because of the gloom of the rainforest interior. After a set of well-bracketed exposures, I place a dustbin liner over the camera and move on. Before doing so, I remove the dozen or so leeches that are fully or partially engorged with my blood. Well, this is how it went for the first four days as I shot the extensive tracts of pristine upland rainforest, the remarkable rivers and beautiful waterfalls. Fortunately, by the time I hit the lowland rainforest, the rain had gone, but the sunshine which replaced it provided the heaviest contrast I have ever come across. I made the most of it by shooting back-lit foliage such as palm fronds and wild ginger leaves. In the two weeks I spent in the rainforest, I only had a couple of perfect dry, but overcast days for photography. Diffuse light from a cloudy sky provides even illumination that is free of shadows and highlights, and this yields the best images of woodland wherever it is.

Using my 43mm Mamiya lens I managed to get a wide perspective on the forest and achieve an excellent depth of field, something I could not easily have achieved with my usual 65mm Mamiya lens. I also made good use of my Sekonic L-508 in its spot-meter mode. In certain locations it was indicating an average of one minute at f/22. At the end of the day up to three minutes was sometimes required to compensate for reciprocity failure (see the table on page 22). All this effort was certainly worth it as these are among the oldest rainforests on earth and, biologically, some of the most interesting. The Daintree rainforest, divided into Mossman Gorge and Cape Tribulation sections, is a remnant of the vegetation that once covered primeval Gondwana Land, the great southern landmass that existed before continental drift created Antarctica, Australia, Africa and South America. It is a true privilege to shoot landscapes in such a beautiful, ancient and pristine wilderness – even with leeches between your toes.

Far more frustrating than the leeches was attempting to photograph the secretive animals that inhabit the forest. Most only come out at night and those that do come out during the day are perfectly camouflaged. My major targets for this project were the unusual Boyd's rainforest dragon and various tree frogs that inhabit the forest. If you look at any literature for the forest, its facilities and local businesses, they seem invariably to have a tree frog or dragon as their emblem or motif. To be honest, this was one of those rare occasions where I definitely needed some help. The owner of a small B&B where I was staying took me out spot-lighting for tree frogs, and a local Kuku Yalanji Aborigine helped me to find a forest

Contre-jour photography using a hand-held incident meter. This shot was taken during autumn.
Hasselblad 500CM + 80mm lens, 1/125sec at f/16, Velvia, tripod.

dragon, which was perfectly camouflaged despite its large size. Just how many had I walked past without knowing, I wonder?

Often, the best landscape compositions are not always the most famous. The better-known ones, such as Mossman Gorge, tend to have more people and consequently more litter to contend with. From a photographer's perspective, it was preferrable shooting the small tributary creeks rather than the Mossman River itself, since these were generally prettier babbling brooks overhung by vines, palms and other rainforest vegetation.

Although the Daintree National Park at both Mossman and across the Daintree River in the Cape Tribulation section are the most famous rainforests, I preferred the Wooroonooran National Park, particularly its Bellenden Ker sector. It was here that I found excellent photographic sites for my rainforest project.

Photography can be very frustrating. When I arrived in Queensland, I studied the local postcards to see if I could find some worthy locations. One stood out above all the others. It was a panoramic card of the rainforest at Mount Lewis National Park. I set a day aside to find this location and the remarkable view in the postcard. I spoke to local people who might have known where the scene in question was located but, unfortunately, no-one could help. I drove up to the end of the bitumen on the Mount Lewis Road and then hiked for five miles – all uphill – with my tripod and Mamiya before giving up the quest, and returning to my car. Ten miles in humidity and heat for nothing. Well, I did shoot one scenic view, but it wasn't a patch on the one I was after.

To sell a complete story about a landscape you need to photograph its diverse component parts, not simply the most scenic aspects. So in Queensland I shot cassowaries: icons of the Australian rainforest.
Pentax MZ5n + 100mm macro lens.

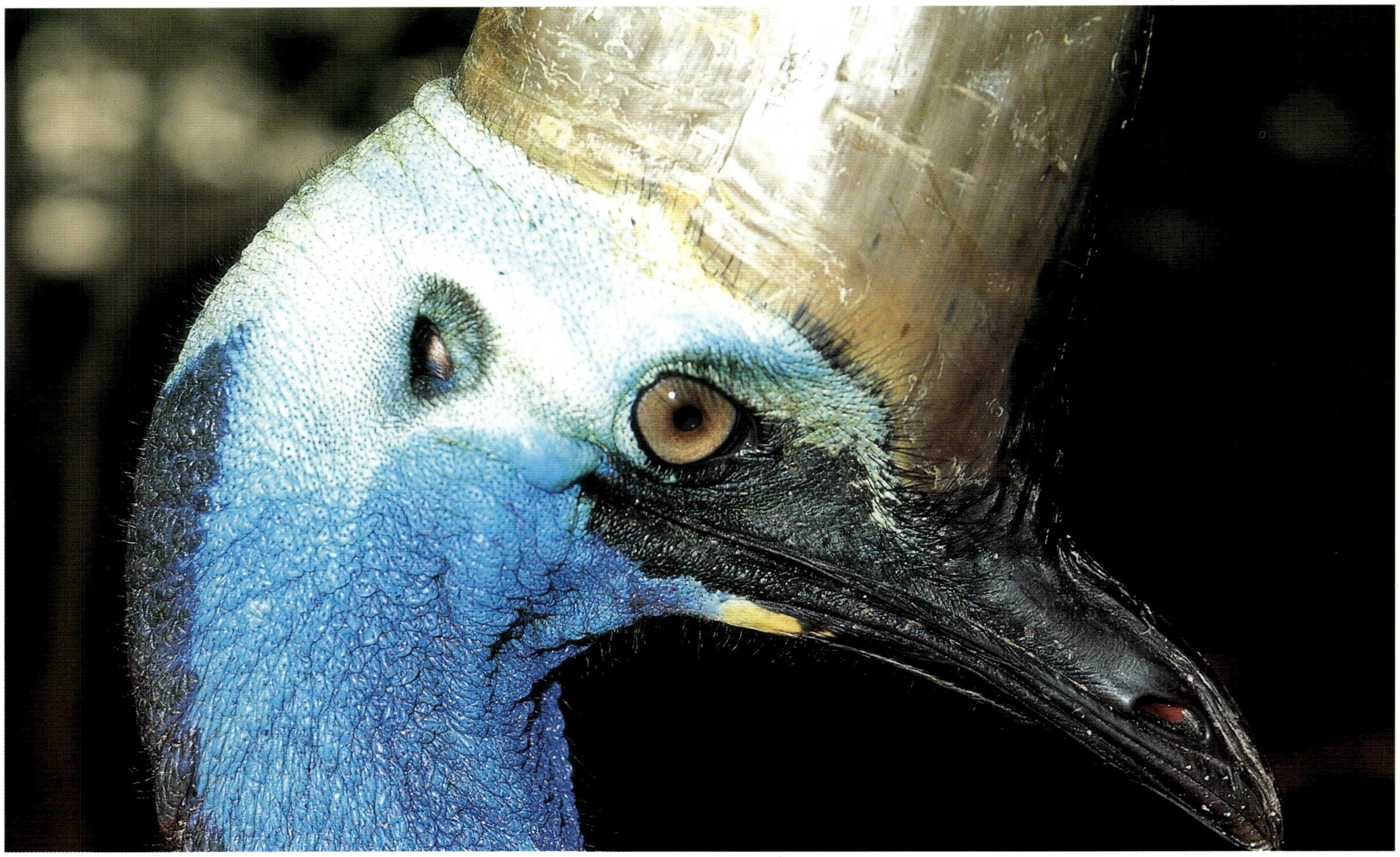

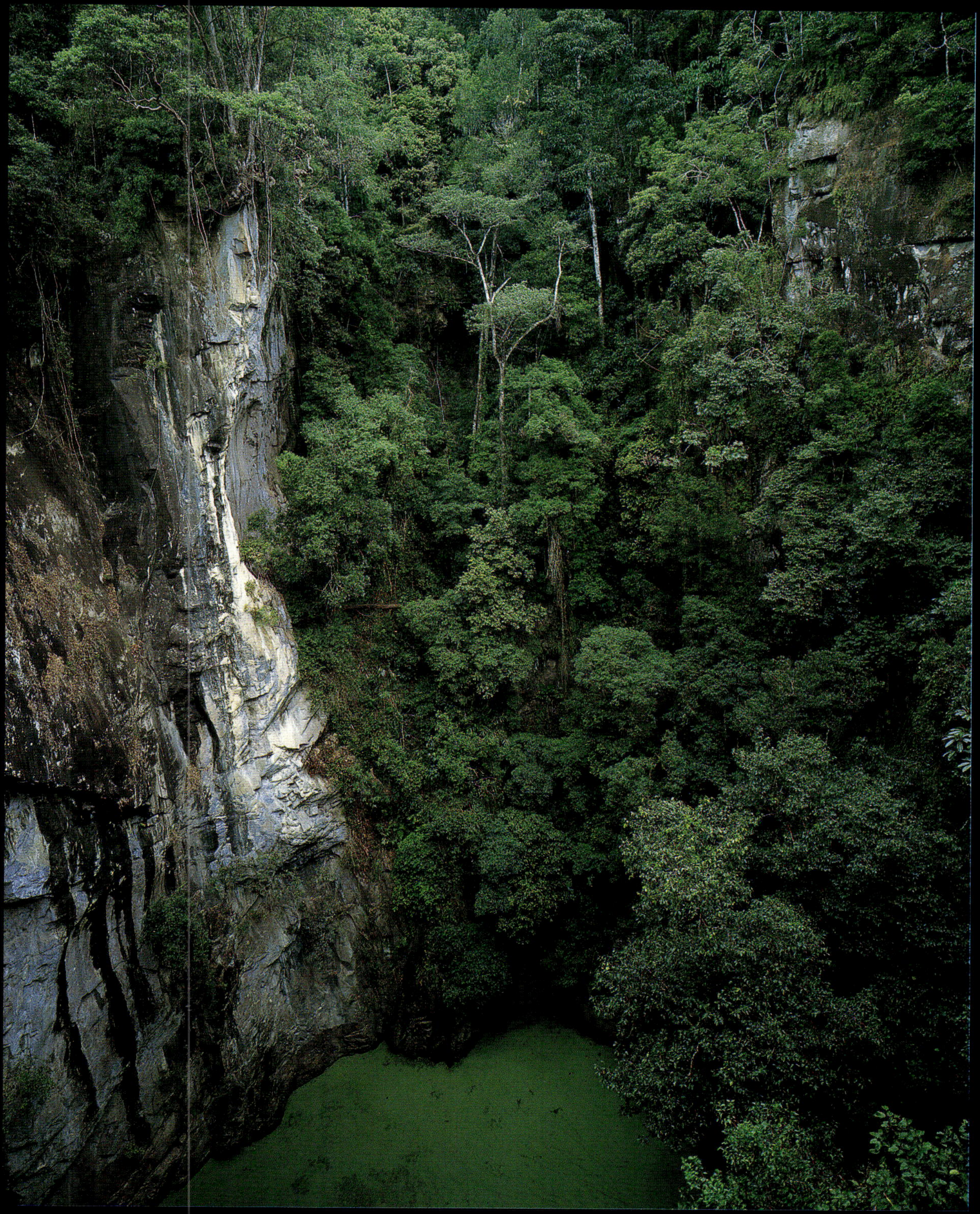

Mount Hypipamee National Park, Queensland. This diatreme was created by volcanic activity. Today it is a deep, eerie crater with a green lake at its base. The edge of the diatreme is broken up with evocative rainforest vegetation. The wooden platform on which I set my tripod was very bouncy, and I needed to take real care to avoid any movement when taking this shot.
Mamiya 7II + 43mm lens, Velvia.

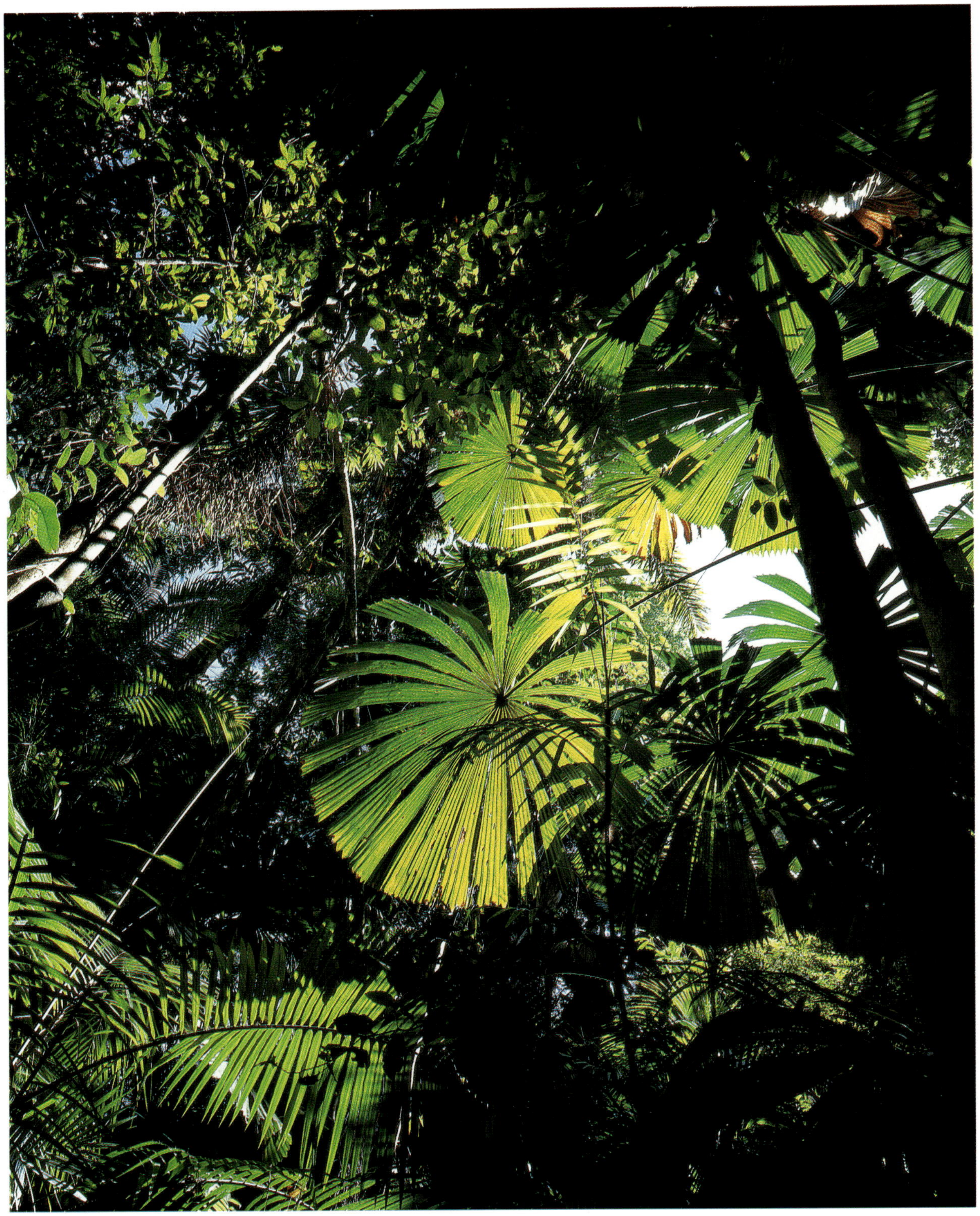

Licuala palms back-lit against an unrelenting tropical sun. This shot was taken in the Daintree rainforest and was bracketed extensively. Only the most extreme exposure compensations were successful. *Mamiya 7II + 43mm lens, Velvia, tripod.*

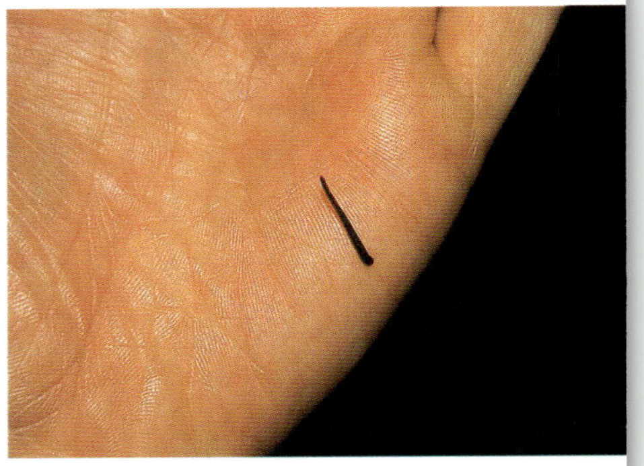

Portrait of a leech attempting to feast on my blood. This little fellow had found his way a bit too far up my leg for comfort. Taken in upland rainforest, Atherton Tablelands, Australia. *Pentax MZ5n + 100mm macro lens, TTL flash.*

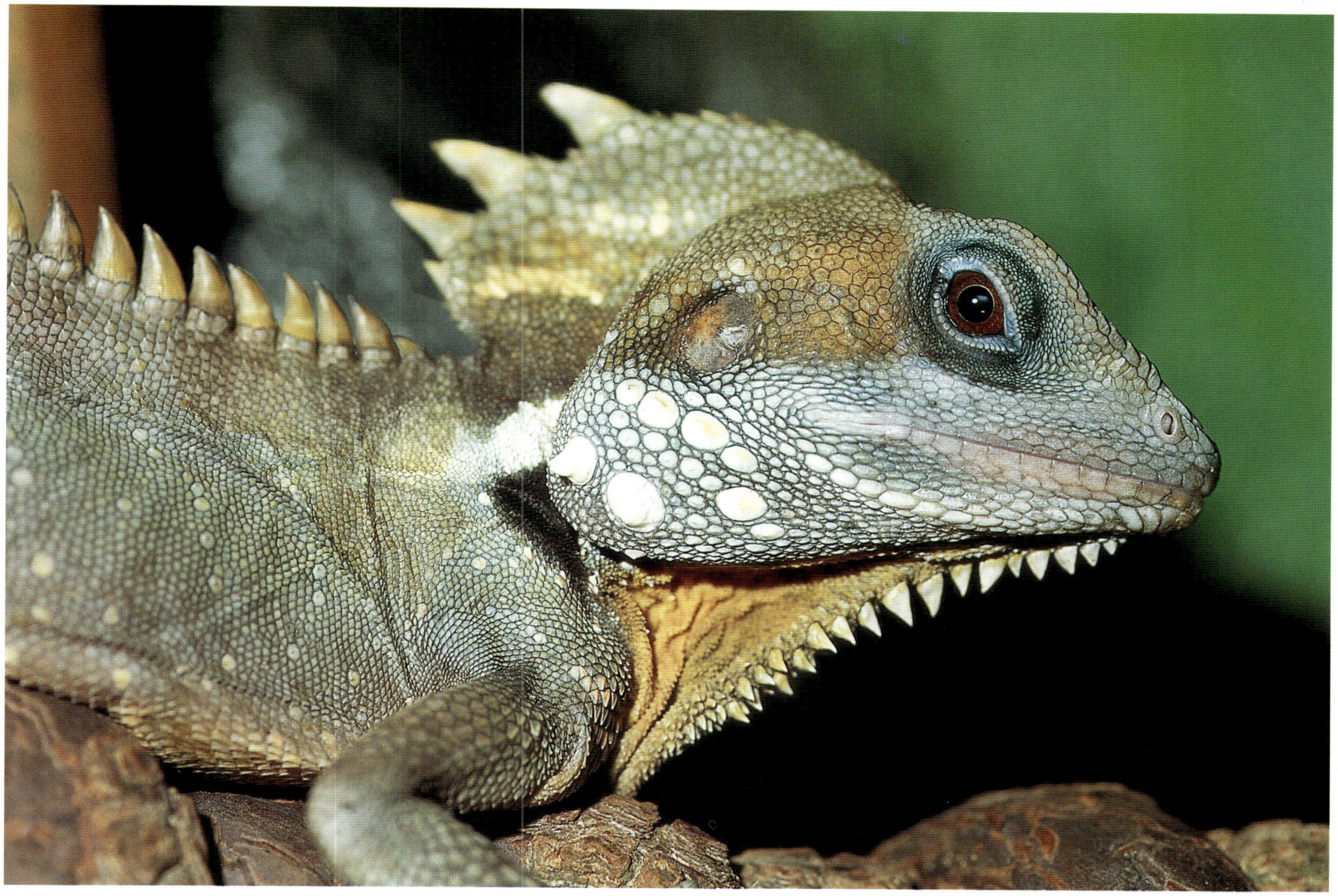

Boyd's rainforest dragon, tropical rainforest, Queensland, Australia. *Pentax MZ5n + 100mm macro lens, f/11.5, TTL flash.*

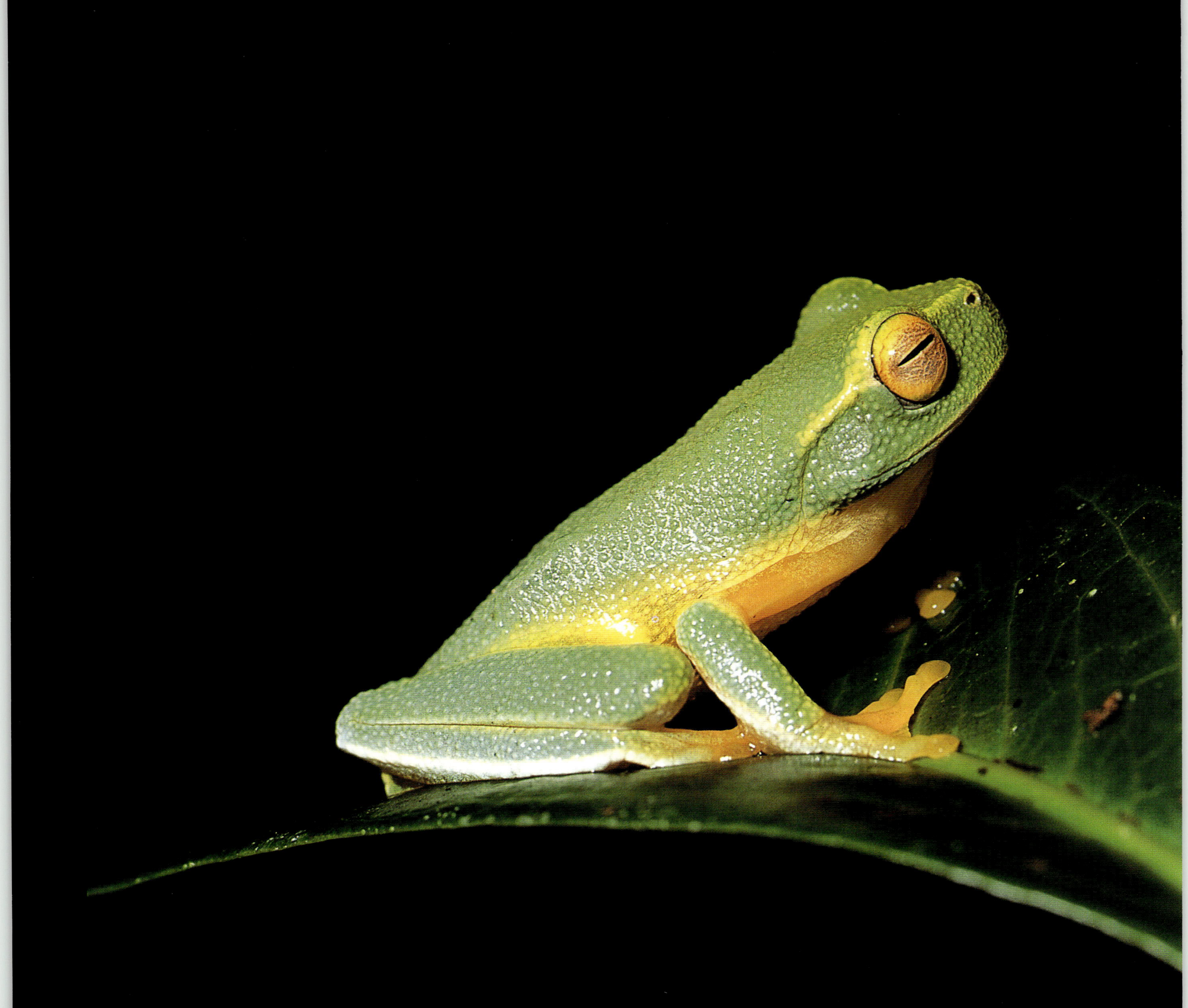

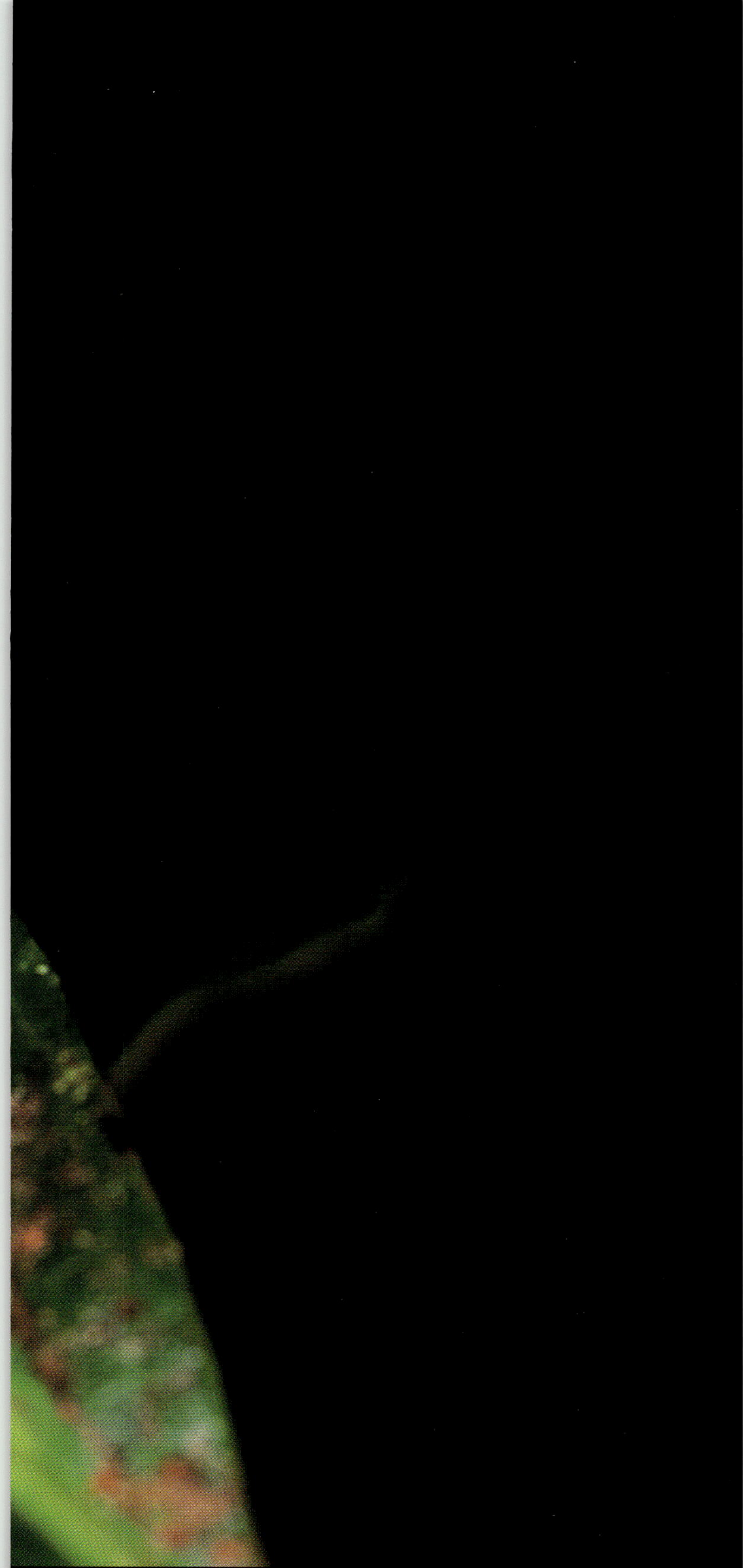

Dainty green tree frog, taken in Daintree National Park, Queensland, Australia. To help me focus and ensure a sharp picture, my daughter shone a torch on this diminutive creature which I photographed at about 10pm one evening. *Pentax MZ5n + 100mm macro lens, TTL flash.*

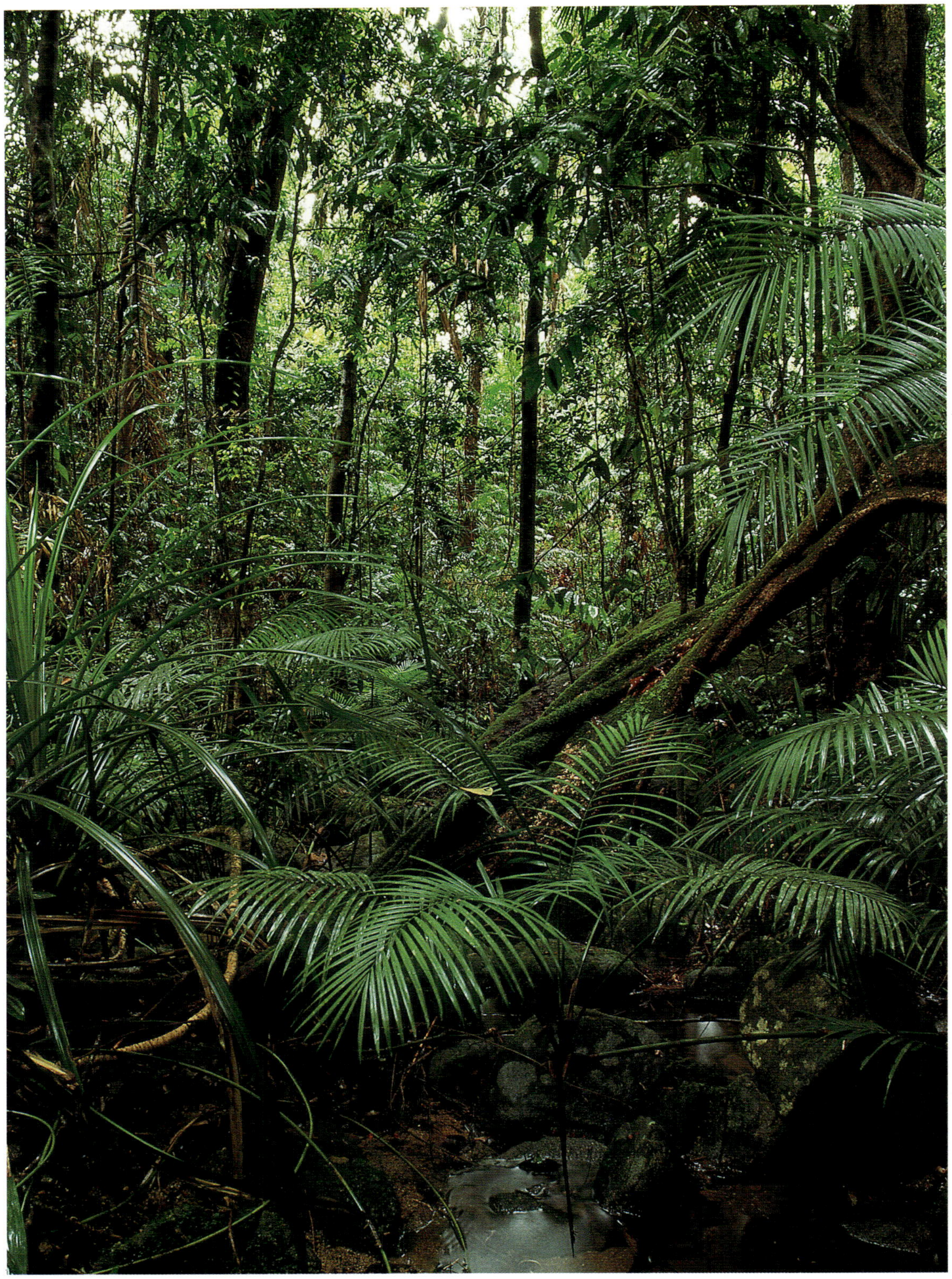

Rainforest stream, Bellenden Ker section of Wooroonooran National Park. A sturdy tripod was precariously set up between and on slippery moss-laden stones. *Pentax MZ5n + 28–70mm zoom lens, 30 seconds at f/16, tripod.*

This recently fallen tree was a difficult shot in the dappled light of the rainforest. I used a hand-held spot meter reading to judge the exposure.
Mamiya 7II + 43mm lens, Velvia, tripod.

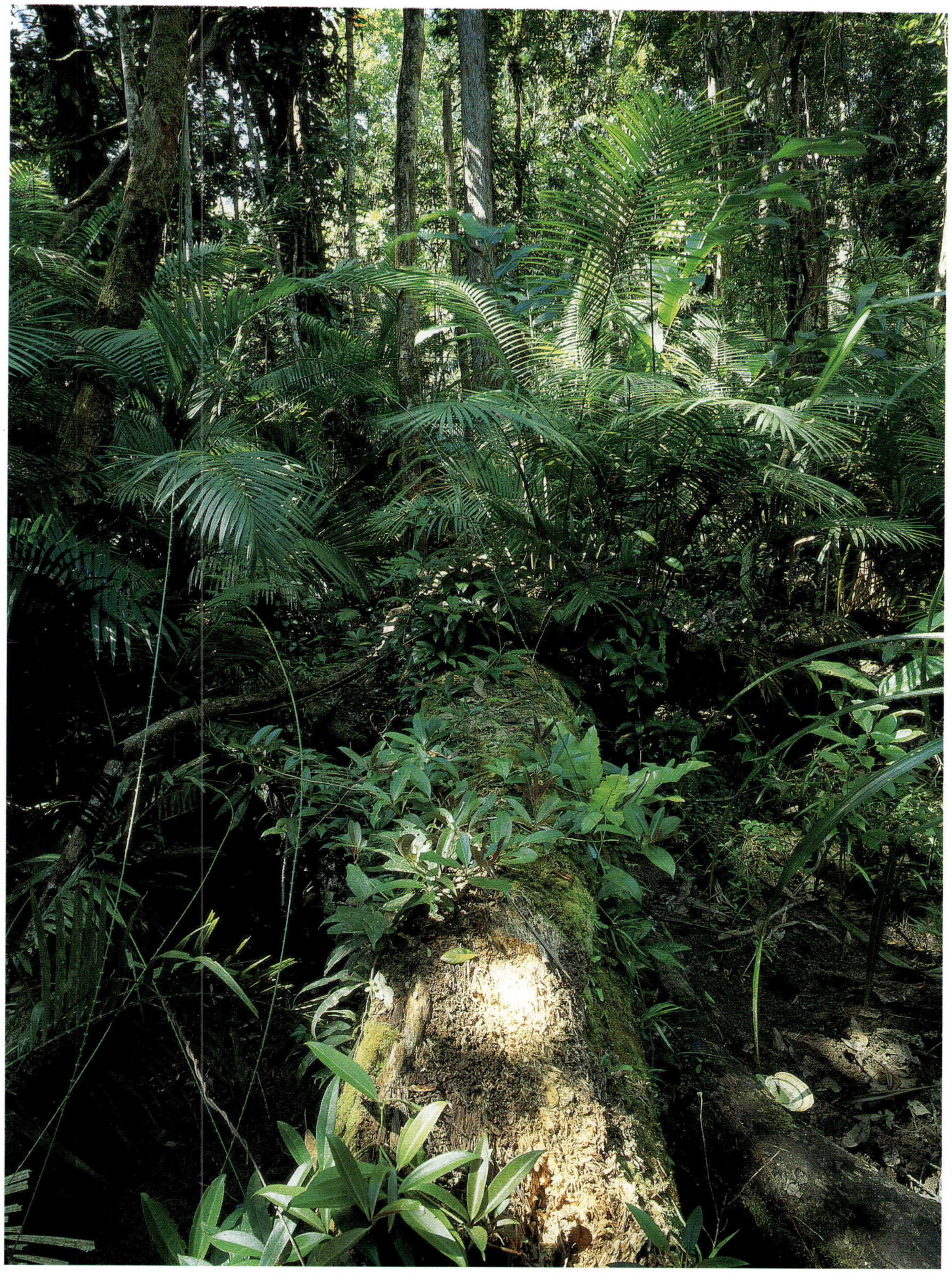

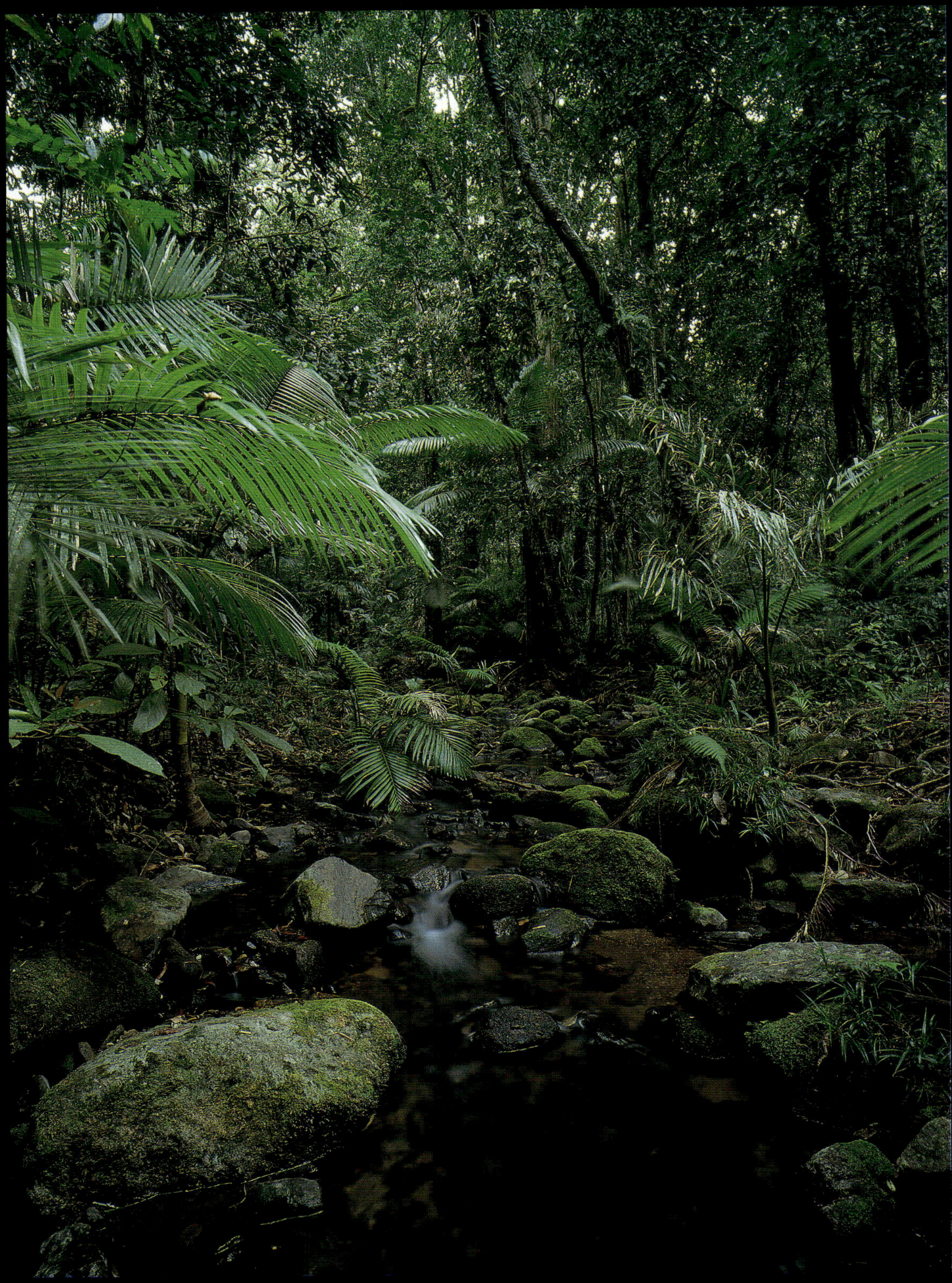

This is one of my all-time favourite shots. It was taken from the middle of a small creek in Mossman Gorge. Conditions were perfect: overcast and wind-free. I used Velvia for its beautiful rendering of punchy greens even in low light conditions. Taken in Daintree National Park, Queensland, Australia. *Mamiya 7II + 43mm lens, 8 seconds at f/16, Velvia, tripod.*

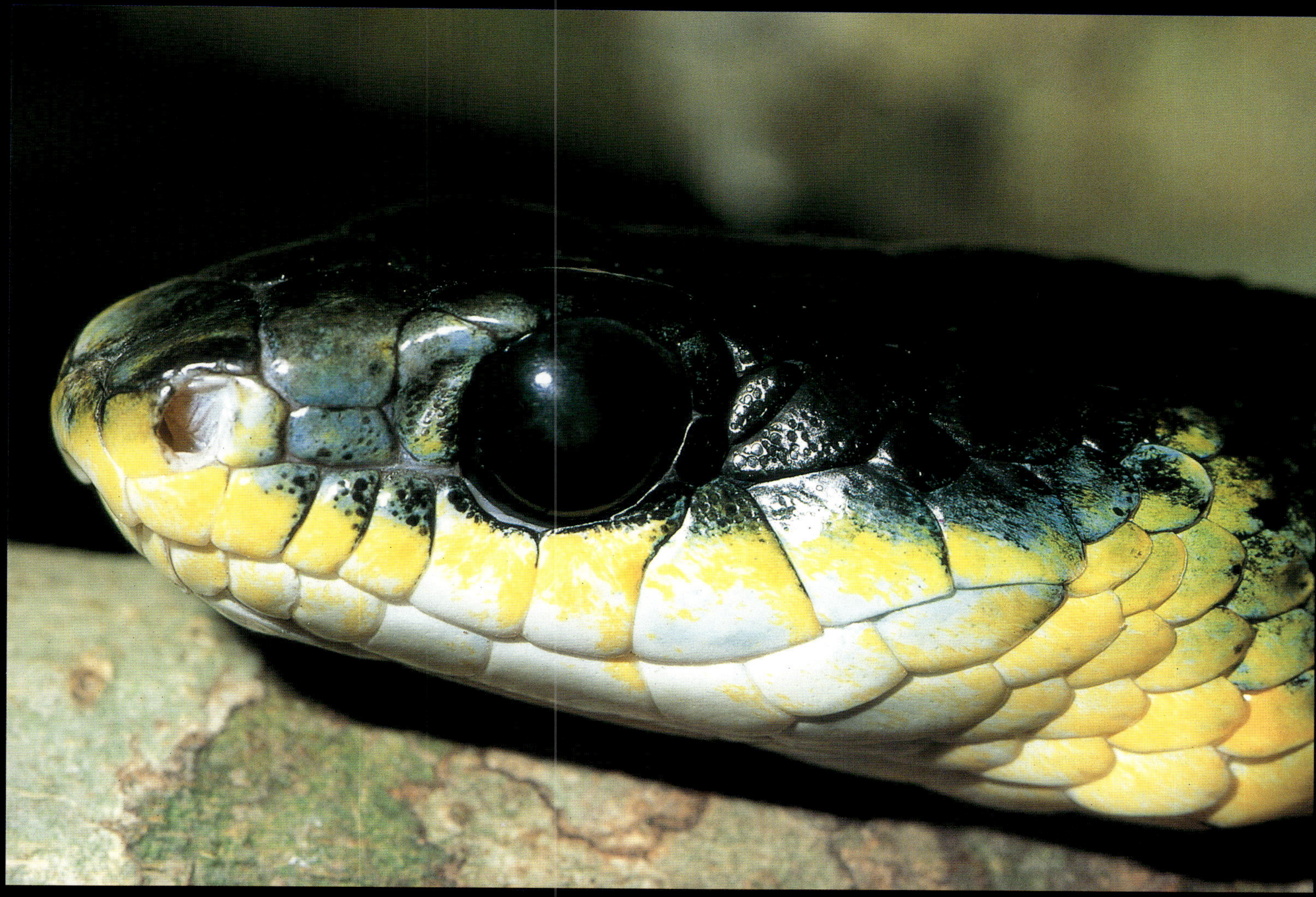

The green tree snake can often be seen at the open edges of rainforest environments. Taken in Queensland, Australia. *Pentax MZ5n + 100mm macro lens, off-camera TTL flash.*

Hot, dry environments

Typically, one would probably define an arid landscape according to annual rainfall or some other geophysical or meteorological factor but, for the purposes of this section, I use the term to broadly describe any hot, dry environment. I have travelled extensively in the southwest United States, arid areas of Australia, North Africa and the Mediterranean. All these places loosely fulfill my criteria of an arid landscape for a substantial part of their year. Summer in the southwest United States is prone to bursts of monsoon rain, while the top end of Australia bakes in the southern winter, but floods with water in the wet summer months. In fact, the Aborgines actually recognize six separate seasons in Australia's top end: Yegge, Wurrgeng and Gurrung (during the winter months); and Gunumeleng, Gudjewg and Banggerreng (during the summer months). The Mediterranean, of course, has a cool, damp winter.

Despite seasonal and geographic variations, there are several photography-related characteristics that arid landscapes seem to share, apart from the obvious hazards of heat and dust. The light – especially at the start and end of each day – is truly phenomenal in its clarity and warm, vermilion hues. Also, plants and animals can be quite unusual-looking so as to survive what are generally hostile environmental conditions. For instance, in the States columnar and barrel cacti provide interesting, photogenic forms, while pandanus, ancient cycads and Darwin woolybutts characterize the arid top end of Australia and are equally photogenic. Madagascar's baobab tree and Mexico's boojum are also intriguing subjects.

These environments can sometimes offer a unique photographic perspective on the cycles of nature. During August, Litchfield National Park in Australia's Northern Territory is tinder-dry. While driving in the Tolmer Gorge region of the park we were suddenly engulfed by flames lapping at us from the open forest. Visibility dropped to zero in the smoke, sending the occupants of the car into a momentary panic, until we drove out of the flames into a world of charcoal-encrusted trees. I immediately got out my camera and started shooting this soot-laden, surreal world. I was aware of the routine burning of the undergrowth to maintain the diversity and vigour of life in this mostly arid environment, but hadn't expected to see it first hand. Every now and then, a party of wedge-tailed eagles mopped up the reptiles and insects being flushed out by the tide of flames. It was a fascinating spectacle to behold.

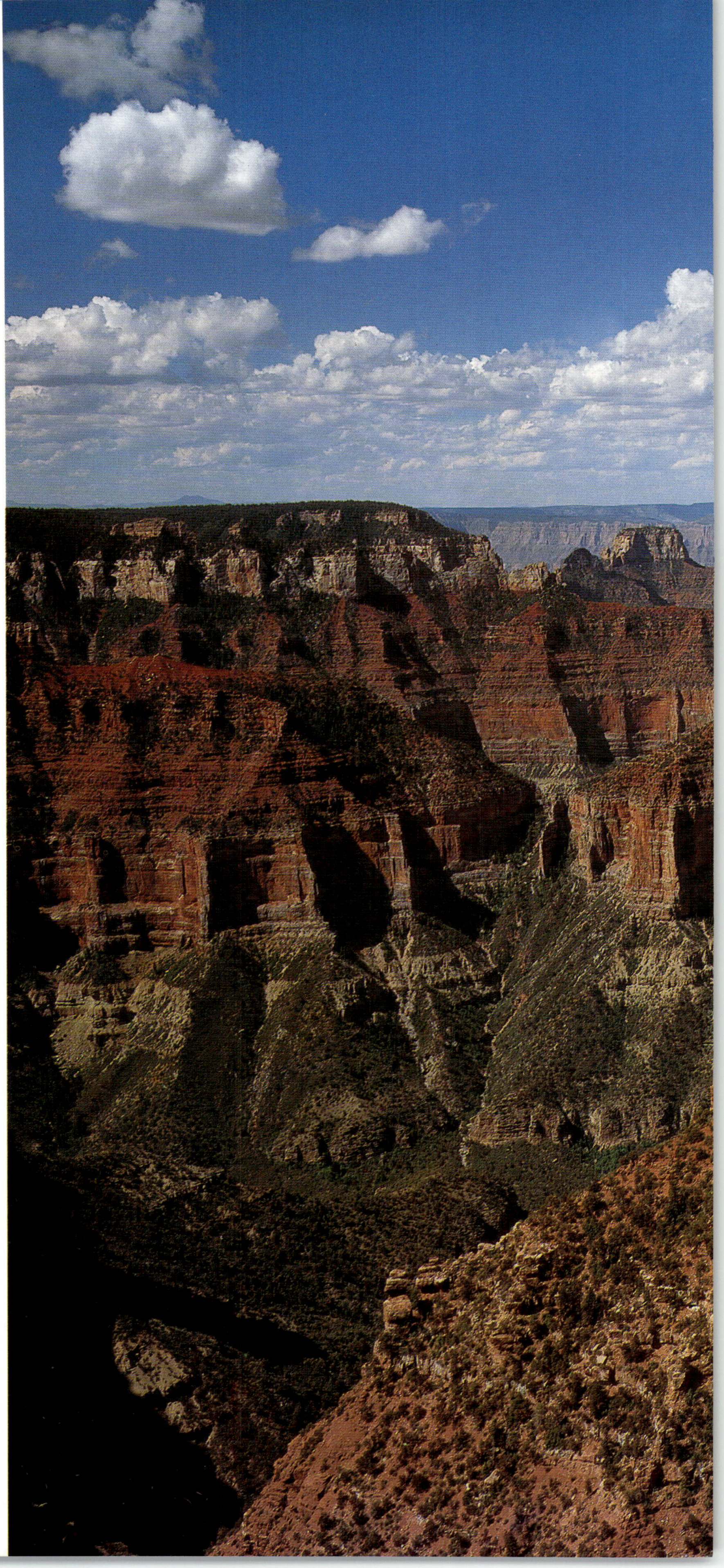

View from Point Imperial, the highest point overlooking the Grand Canyon from the North Rim.
Fuji GSW69III, Velvia, tripod.

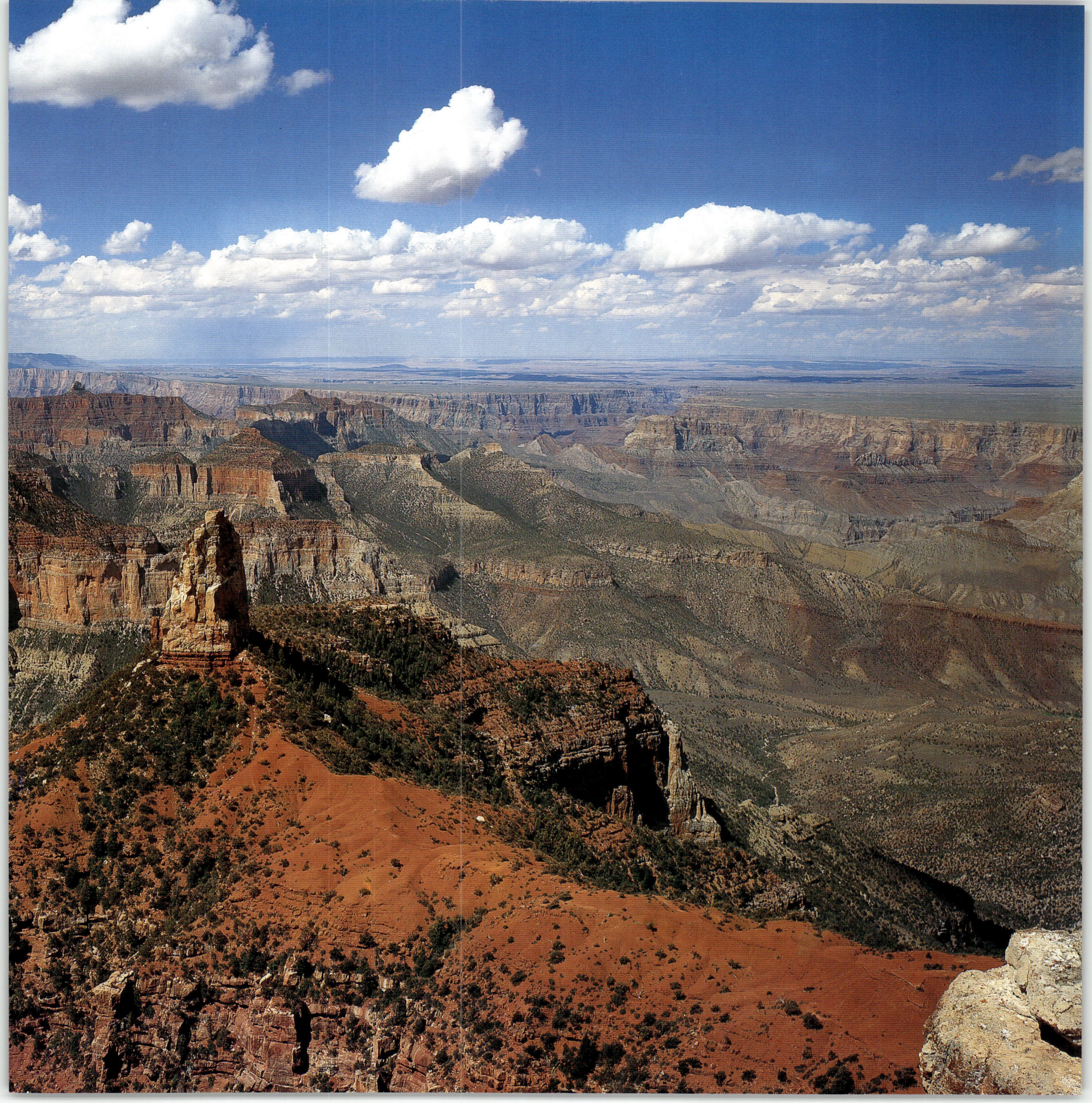

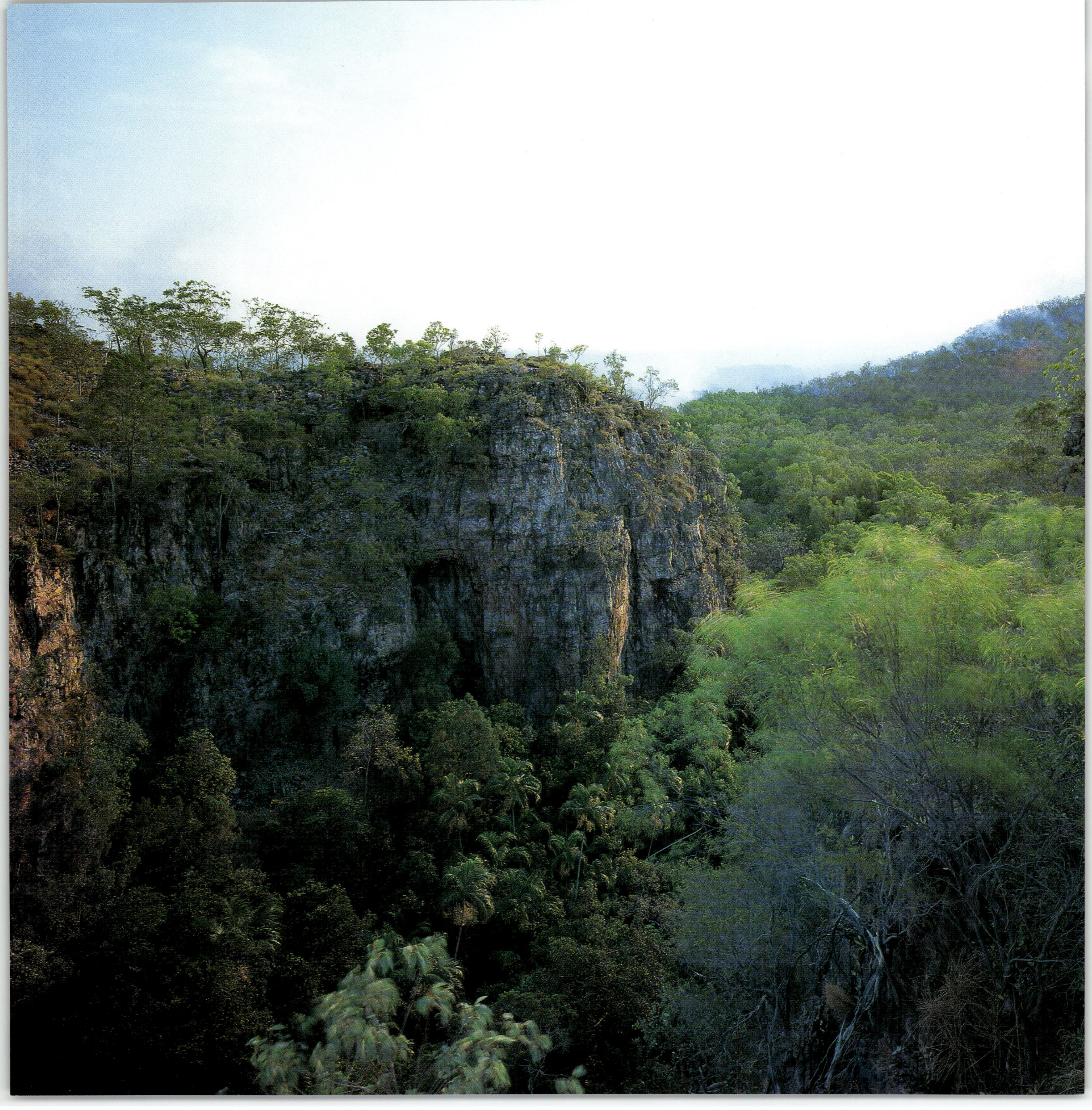

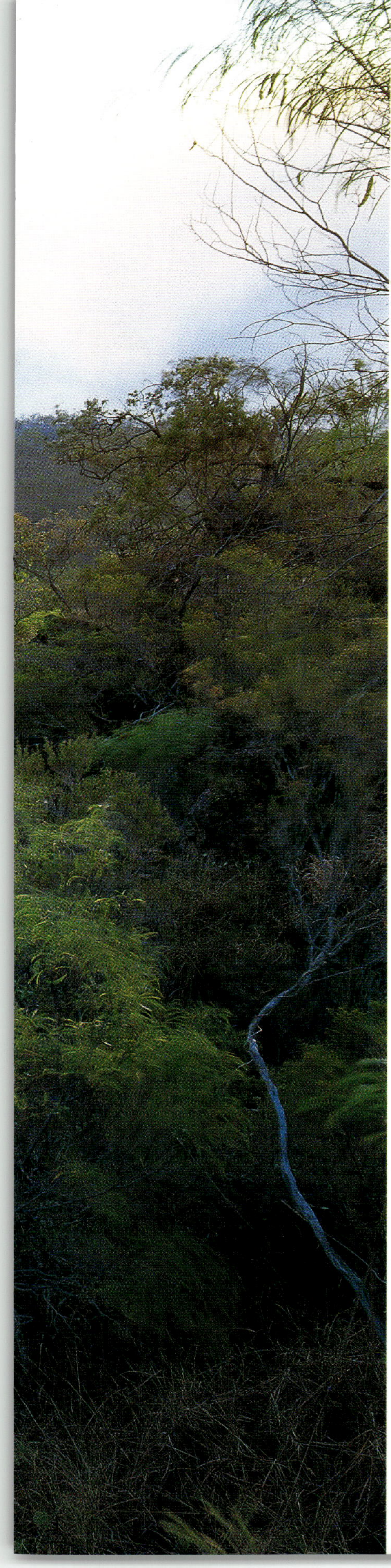

This 6 x 7cm shot of the Tolmer Gorge in Litchfield National Park was a revelation when I got it back from the lab. I knew they were carrying out controlled burns while we visited the gorge, what I didn't know was that I had caught a tracery of the flames on a distant hillside. I hadn't realized that I had captured it because I was using an ultra-wide 43mm lens, which shrinks detail. Additionally, I was delicately poised on a rather unstable wooden platform, and so could only shoot when other people stopped moving about – an approach that was very distracting. Taken in the Northern Territory, Australia. *Mamiya 7II + 43mm lens, Velvia.*

While at the time I was pleased to capture this large-scale housekeeping operation on film, it wasn't until later, having spoken to local residents that I realized the burning was, for some, a contentious issue. Aborigines and local farmers burn every three to five years, while the areas I saw burn were set alight every year. Some felt this was too often and was having an adverse effect on the fauna, particularly emus and frilled lizards. Other locals I spoke to felt it was appropriate to burn in the adopted manner. The burning, I was told, is done in a methodical way using a grid system. Helicopters lay incendiary devices to burn in strips leaving unburned areas as a wildlife refuge in between (these being burned in subsequent years). The grass only burns during the day, with evening moisture extinguishing the fires. If burning were less frequent, the grass layer would build up and burn with a heat and ferocity that would kill even the trees. As it is, flora such as gum-like Darwin woolybutts have a layer of insulating bark extending halfway up their trunks which protects them from the fires that, for aeons, have been ignited naturally by the frequent lightning strikes; a perfect example of how evolution has tuned a species into its environment. Animals should not be adversely affected by the burning as they can escape to unburned grids or go underground.

It will be interesting to see how this issue develops. I certainly noticed how, even in the height of the dry season, the burned charcoal ground was beginning to turn green with new, sweet shoots of grass fed by latent moisture in the soil, attracting the agile wallaby community to gather at these spots. It occurred to me that ancient Aborigines may have used this as a mechanism to guide the whereabouts of their animal food sources, for these were certainly the only places we saw marsupials in any numbers in this arid region. There is huge potential for an environmentally led photo essay on this subject. Recognizing such opportunities and acting upon them is what gives you an edge on the competition and can make you a successful landscape and environmental photographer.

Paradoxically, photography in this hot, bright, arid environment requires a similar approach to that in cool, dark, wet rainforest environments. That is, while rainforests require additional exposure to compensate for the film's reciprocity failure (a fairly inexact science in my hands), arid regions often need additional exposure to compensate for the bright light that fools the meter to underexpose.

In terms of potentially life-threatening situations, if rainforest photography has its obstacles, it is preferrable to shooting the open savannah forests of the Northern Territory. Photographers have to contend with being encrusted by flies as if you were a corpse, and a few bite with extreme ferocity. Just walking up the wrong creek can be dangerous; if a crocodile misses you, scrub typhus, Ross River fever or Bahmar Forest virus might get you instead. When I visited,

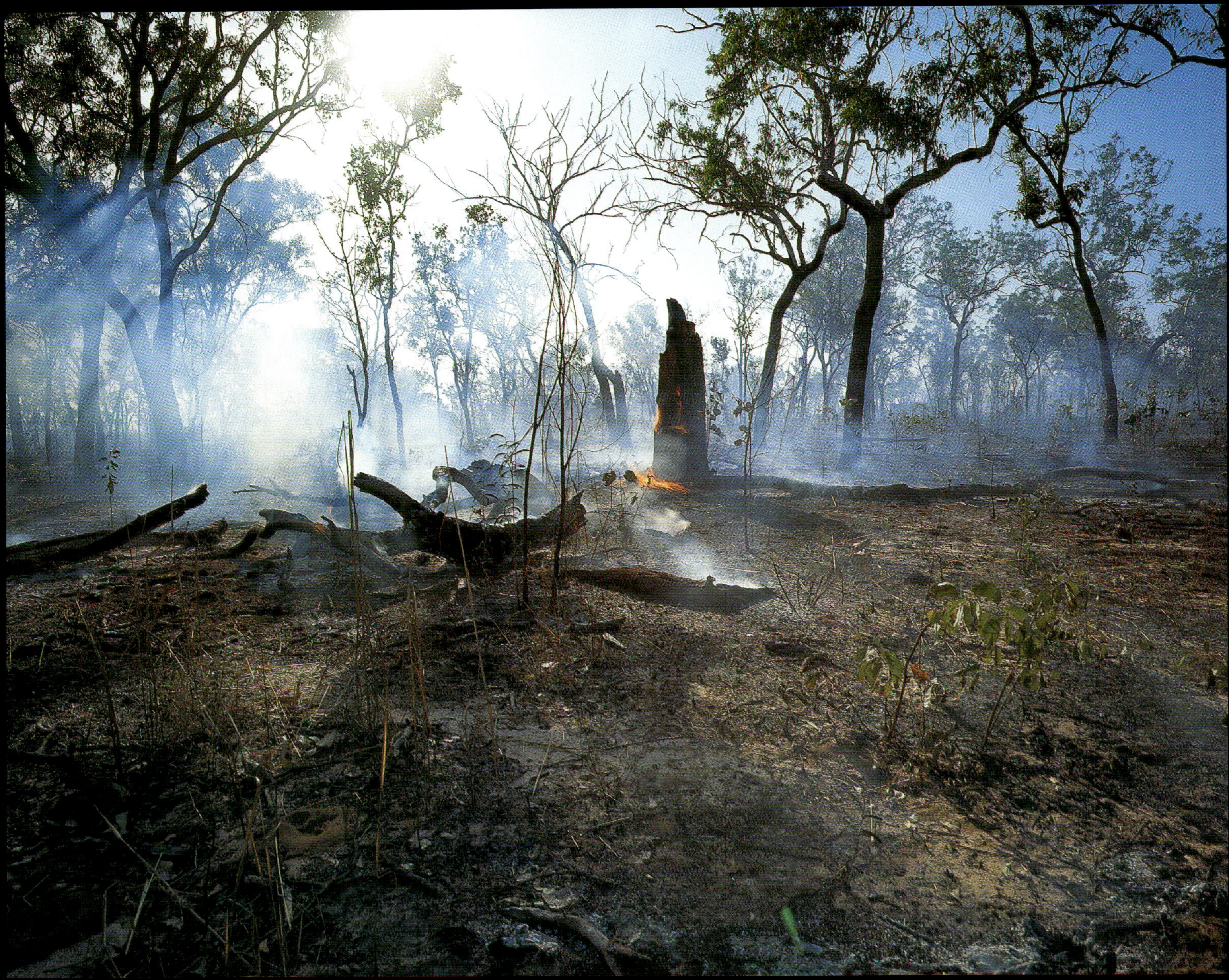

The aftermath of a controlled burn in Litchfield National Park. To maintain the ecological vigour of the landscape, rangers periodically burn sections of the endless sea of arid savannah woodland. My tripod survived the experience intact, despite being set up in hot ash. Taken in the Northern Territory, Australia.
Mamiya 7II + 43mm lens, Velvia.

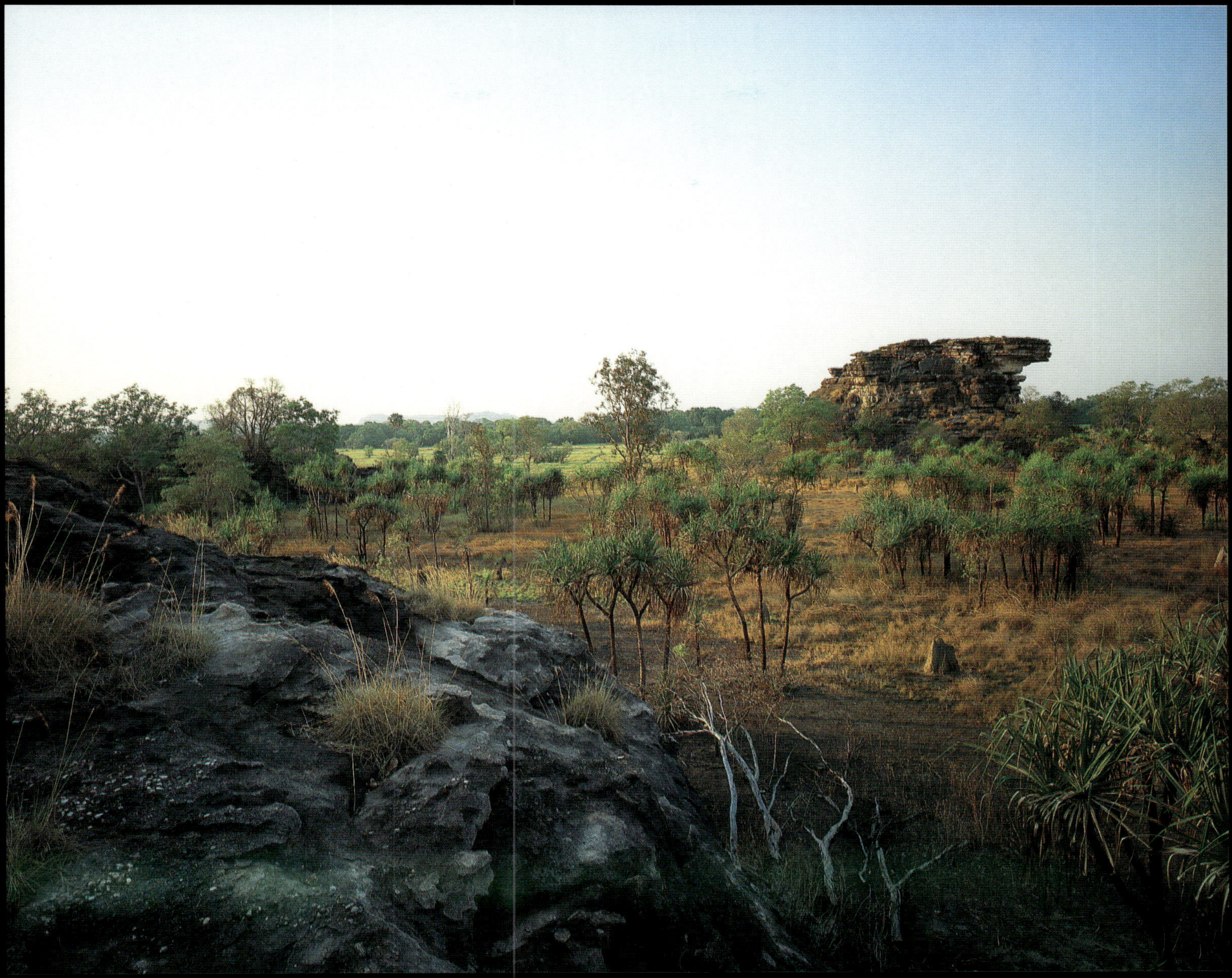

Small sandstone outlier of Arnhem Plateau with pandanus palms in Kakadu, Northern Territory. This was taken at an important Aboriginal art site; ideal for taking pictures of rock art for a photo essay.
Mamiya 7II + 43mm lens, Velvia.

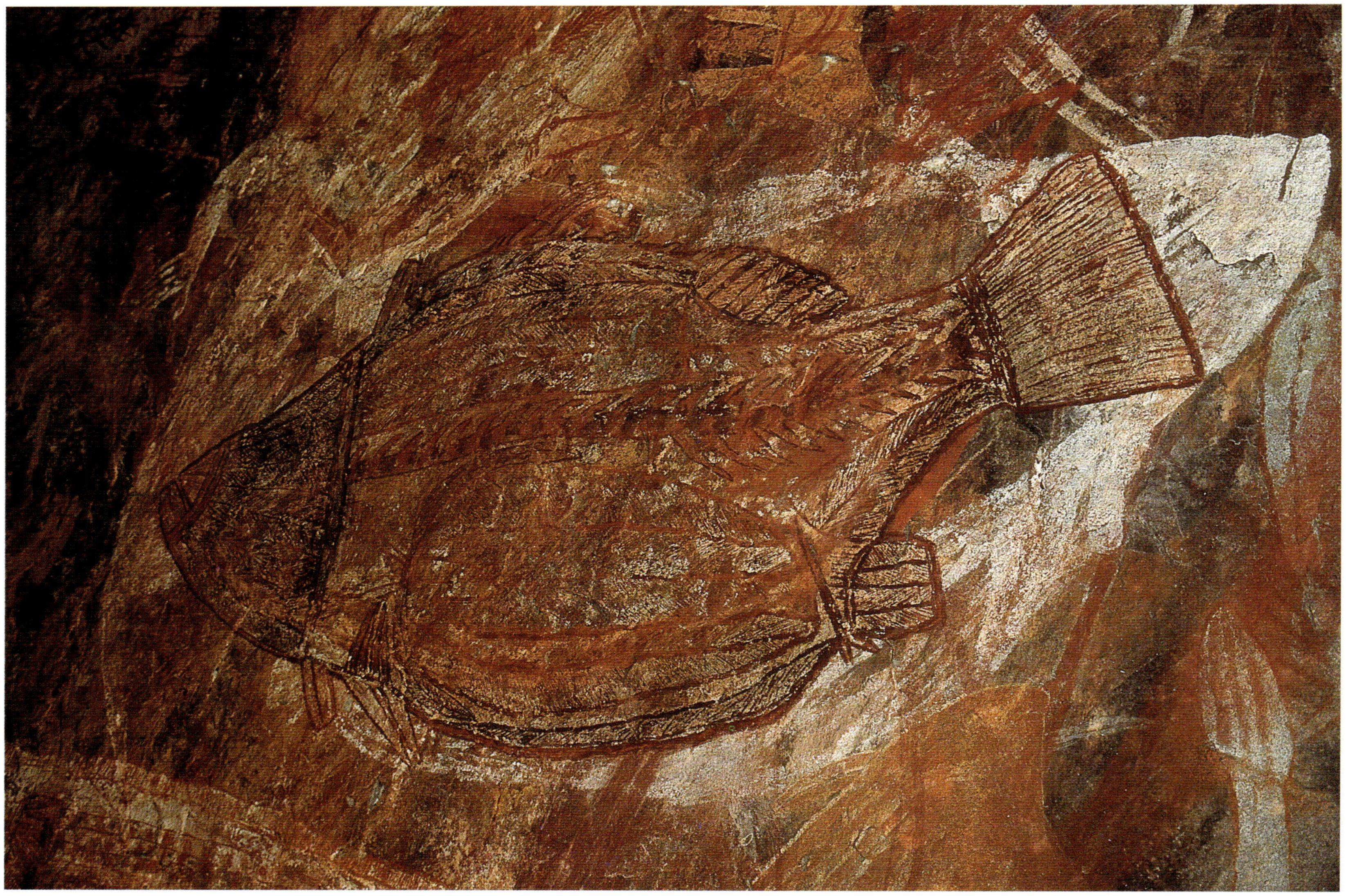

warning signs about some of the tropical diseases you can pick up in the top end of Australia were not wasted on me. One local explained how she had picked up scrub typhus from mites in the soil at Litchfield's Wangi Falls: very nasty indeed. She also once had Bahmar Forest virus, while her son and husband had contracted Ross River fever, which meant enduring six months of arthritic, chronic fatigue. These diseases are therefore very real and must be considered serious threats on your travels.

For 20 years I have enjoyed insect photography, but a few days in the Northern Territory is enough to cure anybody of this passion. Flies are constantly after the salts in your sweat, while some are after your blood. Sometimes it is impossible to swap a 120 roll film

Aboriginal rock art depicting a barramundi. Taken in Kakadu National Park, Australia.
Pentax MZ5n + 28–70mm zoom lens.

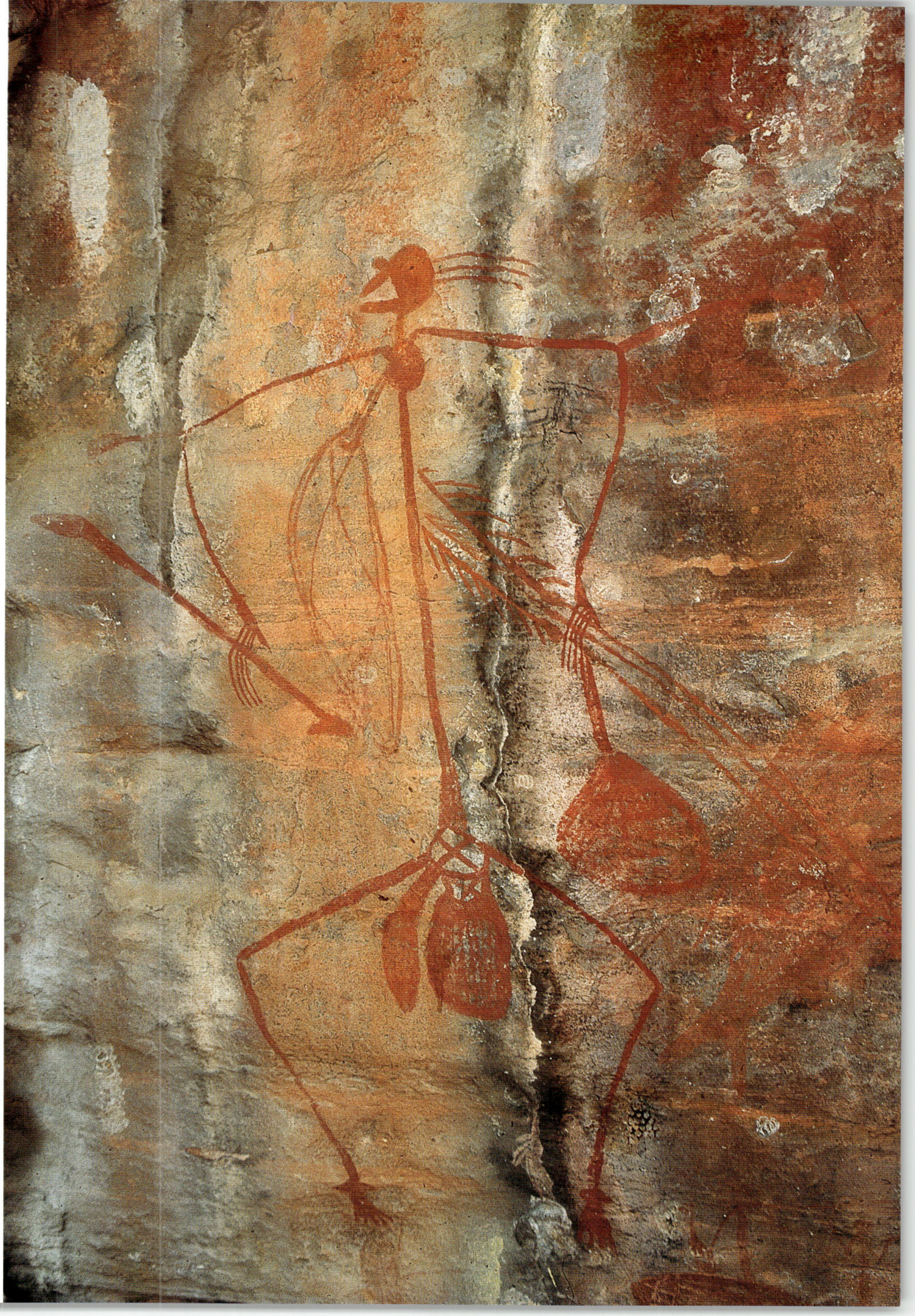

Aboriginal rock art depicting the story of Mabuyu, Kakadu National Park, Australia.
Pentax MZ5n + 28–70mm zoom lens.

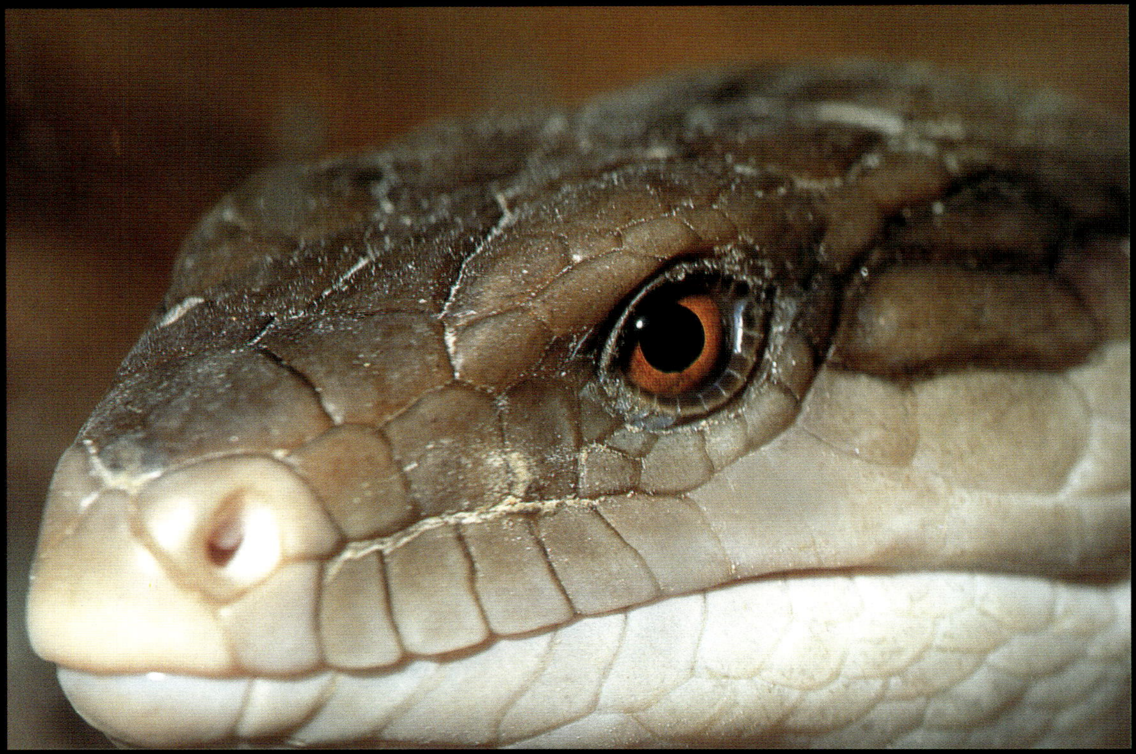

Blue-tongue lizard, Australia.
Pentax MZ5n + 100mm macro lens, off-camera TTL flash.

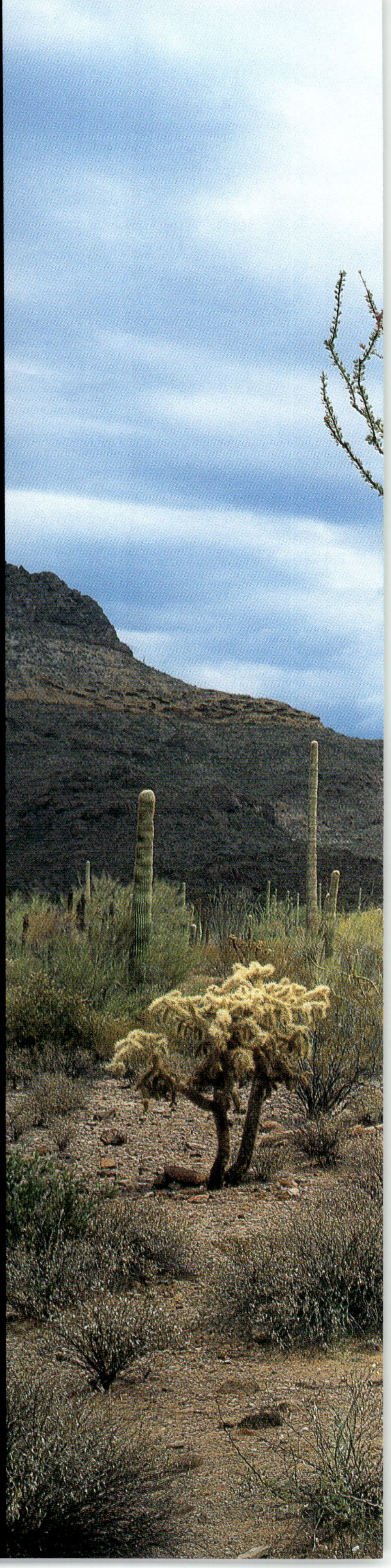

Organ Pipe Cactus National Monument in Arizona was at its best with a brooding summer monsoon sky that hung menacingly behind my composition of saguaro cacti and bizarre ocotillo.
Mamiya 7II + 65mm lens, Velvia, tripod.

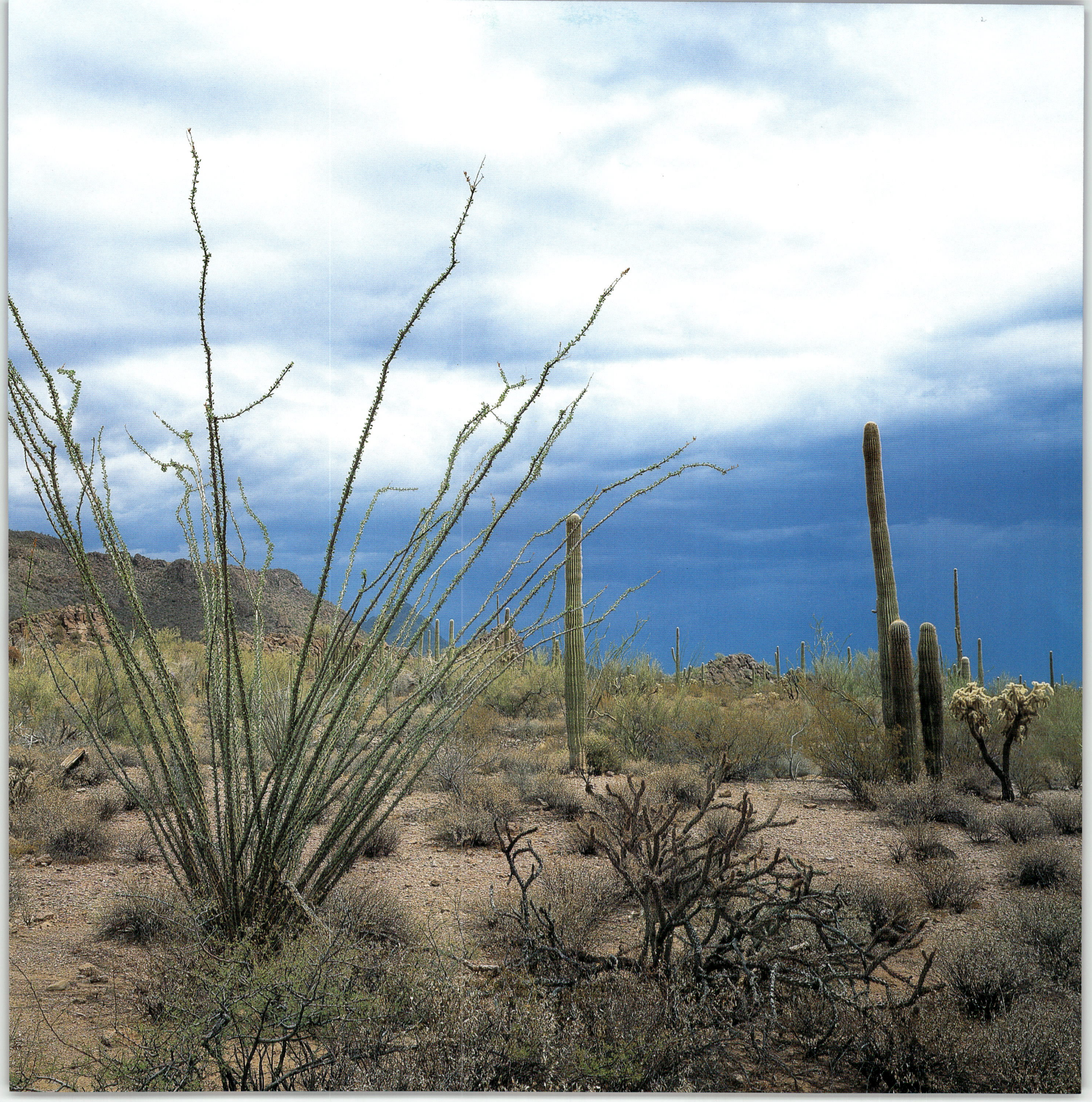

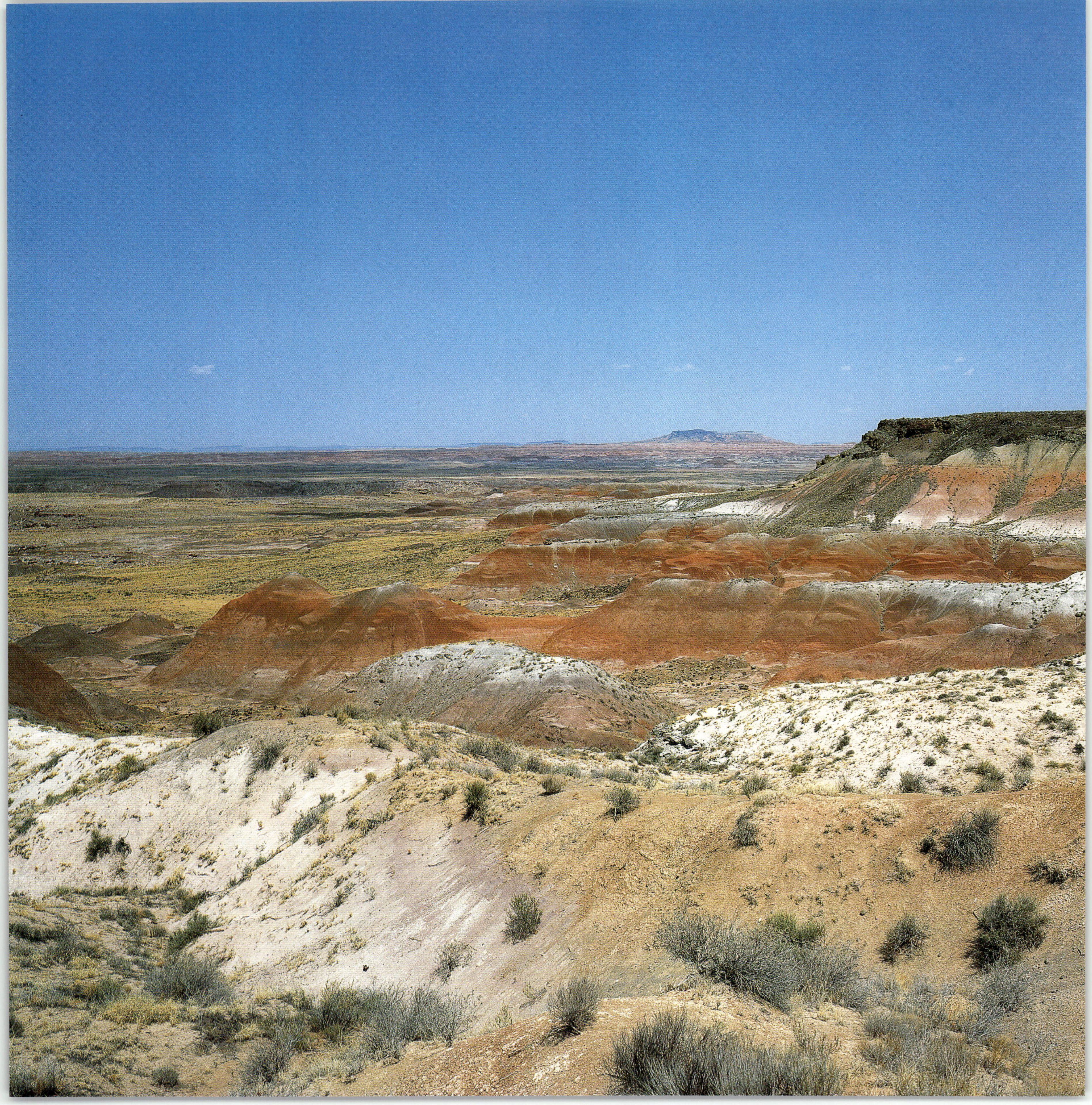

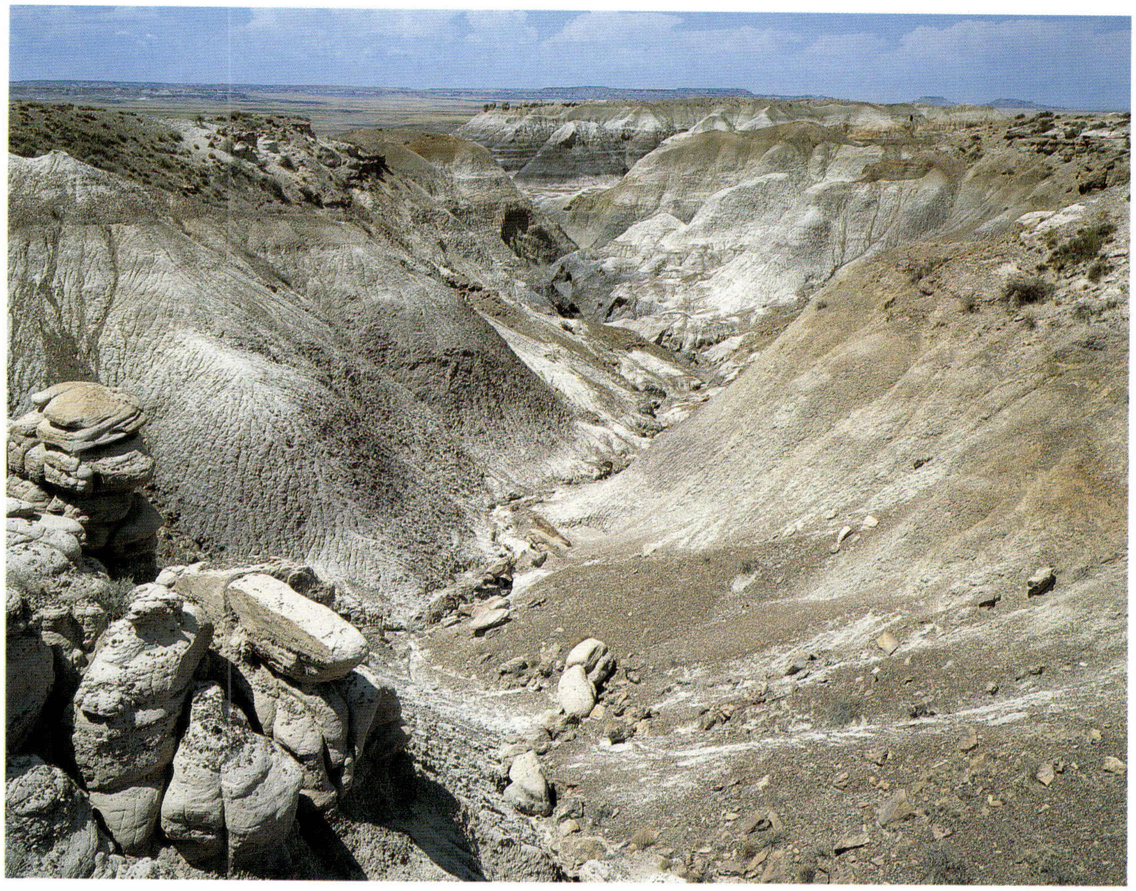

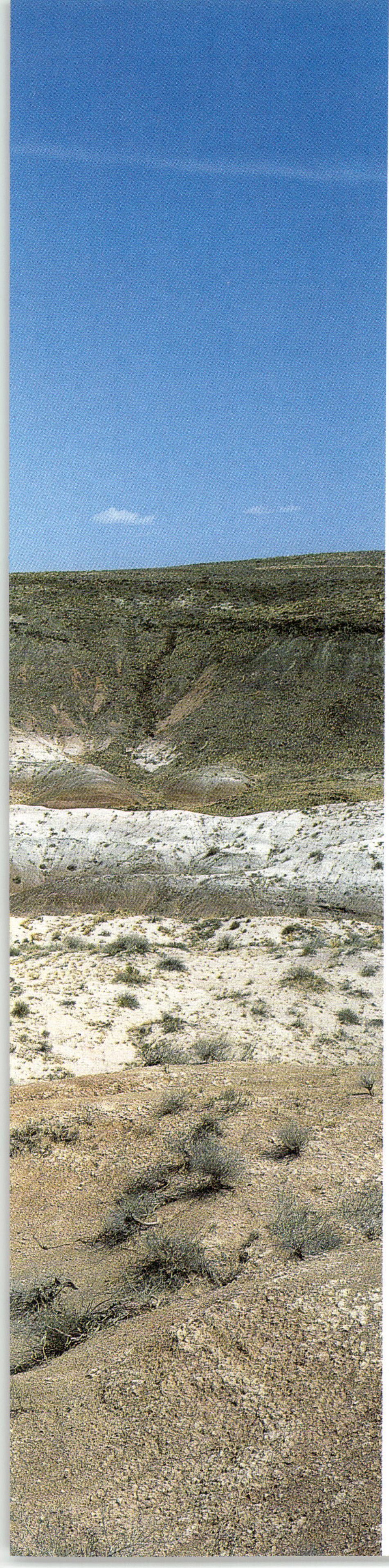

Blue Mesa, Painted Desert National Park, Arizona. They don't call these areas 'badlands' for nothing. I bracketed over the recommended exposure. *Mamiya 7II + 65mm lens, Velvia, tripod.*

Painted Desert, near Holbrook, Arizona. Again, I bracketed this shot. *Mamiya 7II + 65mm lens, Velvia, tripod.*

without incarcerating a fly or two in the camera back. In fact when I was jotting the notes for this chapter, I had to take refuge from an army of green ants.

While the closed world of rainforest begs for an ultra-wide lens such as 43mm on 6 x 7cm (21mm on the 35mm format), open savannah woodlands and wide deserts don't require such extreme measures. I would go for 65mm on my Mamiya 7II (32mm in 35mm format) or a 28mm lens on my 35mm kit. For instance, in Organ Pipe Cactus National Monument in Arizona, I used my Mamiya 65mm lens almost exclusively as it has the perfect perspective for desert environments. This environment is true desert with familiar trees being replaced by unusual floral life forms such as organ pipe and saguaro cacti, and ocotillo: a strange plant that looks like an old-fashioned TV aerial.

Although both Australia's top end and Arizona's Organ Pipe Cactus National Monument are extraordinarily dry and hot for much of the year, I found the best photographs were obtained in those places where water intruded into the landscape. In the Arizona

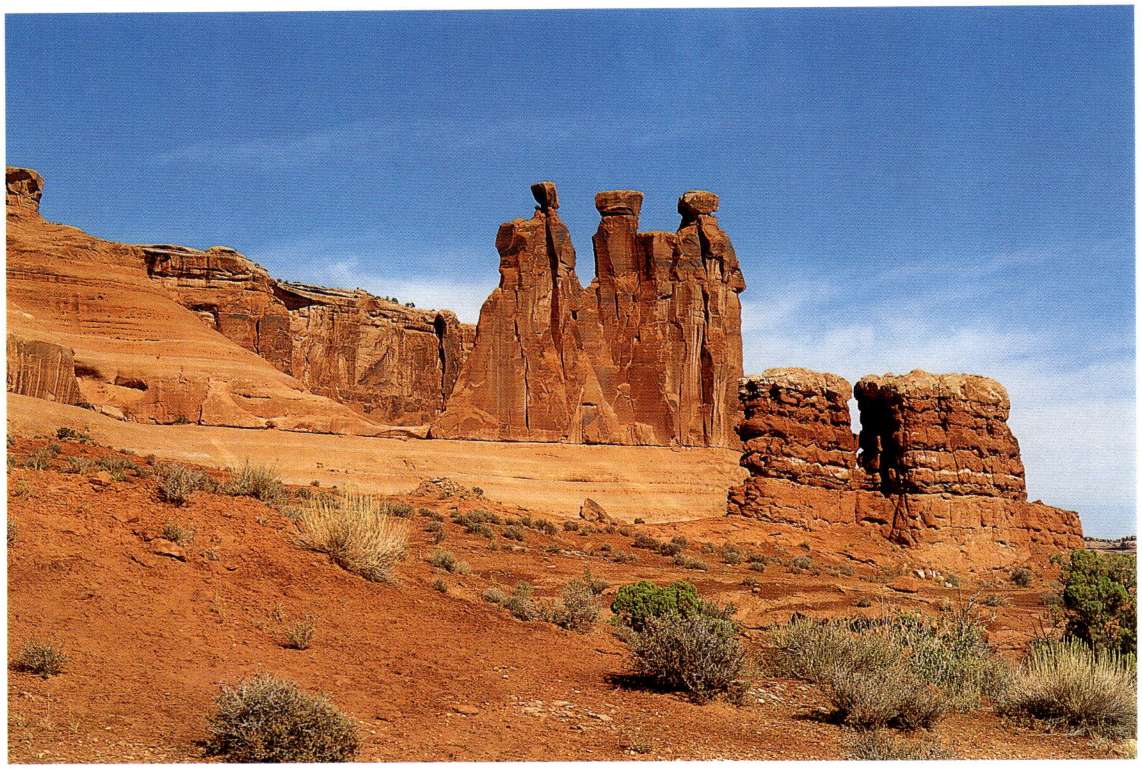

Three Gossips, Arches National Park, Utah. *Pentax MZ5n + 28–70mm zoom lens.*

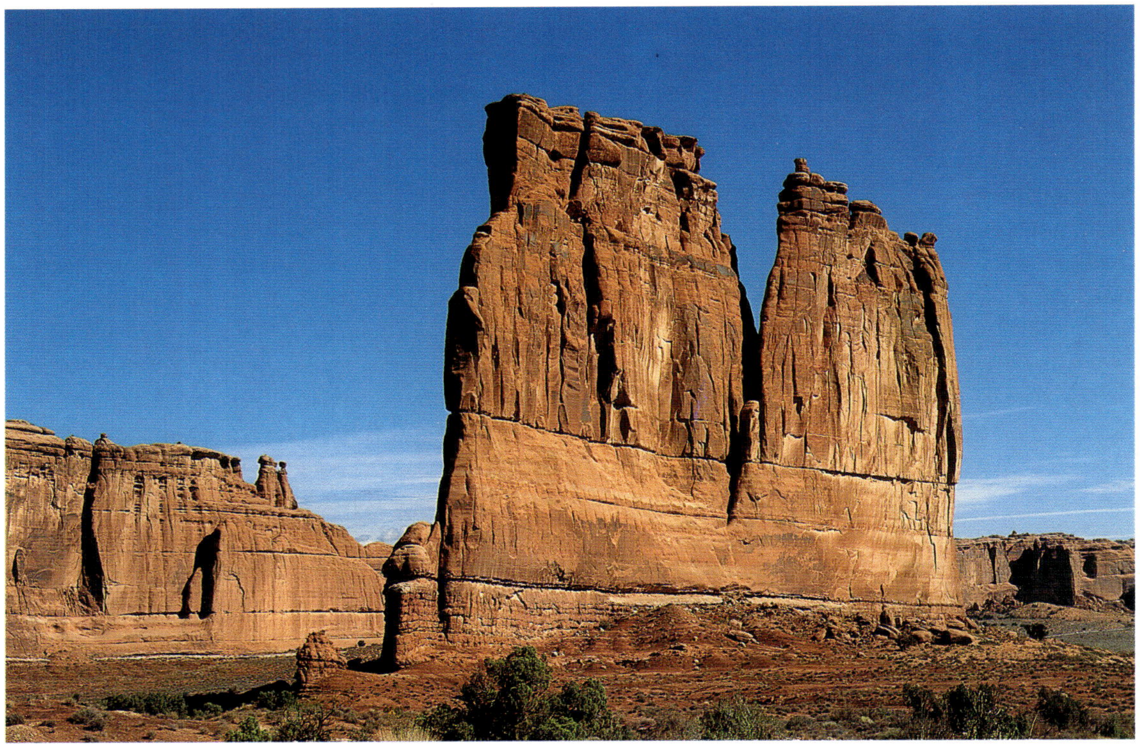

Tower of Babel, Arches National Park, Utah. *Pentax MZ5n + 28–70mm zoom lens.*

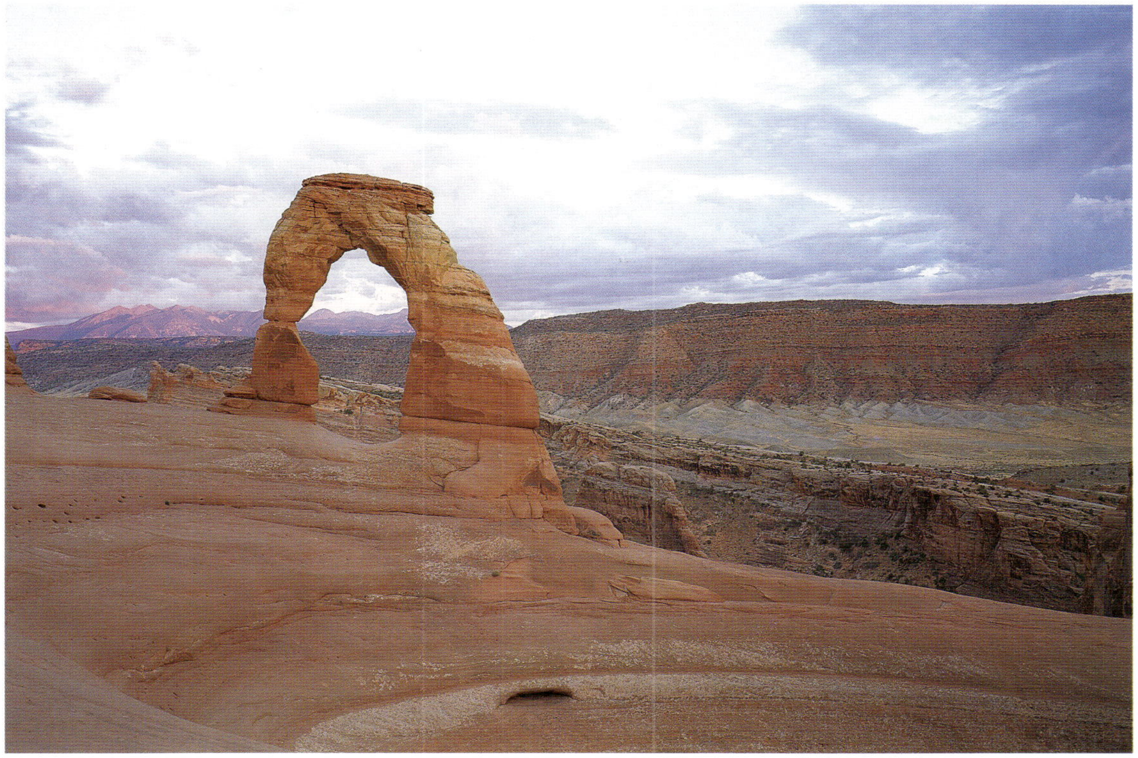

Delicate Arch and La Sal Mountains at sunset. taken at the Arches National Park, Utah. ***Fuji GSW69III, 2 seconds at f/5.6–8, Velvia.***

desert, the cacti looked at their best against a blue-grey, moisture-laden monsoon sky. In Australia, the best images I obtained in the arid winter were those where sinuous creeks and delicate waterfalls bisected the parched land. Consider, too, how much better a Mediterranean scene looks with an azure sea included in the frame.

Water is not always necessary to spice up a landscape photograph in arid climes, where other elements can be equally effective: consider the archetypal acacia tree against a fiery East African sunset or sculptured giant sand dunes in Namibia. Indeed, where natural geological features have been carved out of the land, nature often provides photographers with the best opportunities. Nowhere on earth is this truer than southern Utah where the arid Colorado Plateau has been metamorphosed into a wonderland of natural sculptures.

In fact, just as with Gondwana's ancient rainforests in tropical northern Queensland, many arid lands, particularly those of the Colorado Plateau (Great Basin Desert), have a special character that draws me in and stimulates a basic need in me to photograph these magical places. Increasingly these days, I try to catch the essence of nature in a way that reflects her primal forces. In so doing, I like as far as possible to remove evidence of human influence and concentrate on a view of the world that appears to have been unaltered from a time long since passed. In Britain, there are few opportunities to do this, although some master photographers such as Joe Cornish manage to do it with great skill.

The russet-coloured rock formations in Utah provide beautiful photographic compositions at any time of day – forget the old chestnut about not shooting at midday. Formations like the Three Gossips, Tower of Babel, The Organ and Delicate Arch are almost as good at midday as they are at sunset. A bright blue polarized backdrop against the orange rocks is very striking on Velvia; just remember to shoot as indicated and bracket upwards with your exposures. These latter formations are found at Arches National Park, the setting for sequences in Ridley Scott's film *Thelma and Louise*. Southern Utah is just full of such marvels: Capitol Reef, Zion and my favorite – Bryce Canyon – to mention just a few.

Of all the places I have photographed, nowhere can compare to Bryce Canyon for its beauty and splendour. The view from Sunset Point is one of the most photographed spots on our planet, for good reason. Every evening a plethora of visitors line their cameras up on the palisade of hoodoos and distant Powell Point to catch the various shades of colour from orange to pink to purple which are reflected from the rocks as the sun sets. I was no exception, despite plagiarizing a million photographers before me. My slides were very

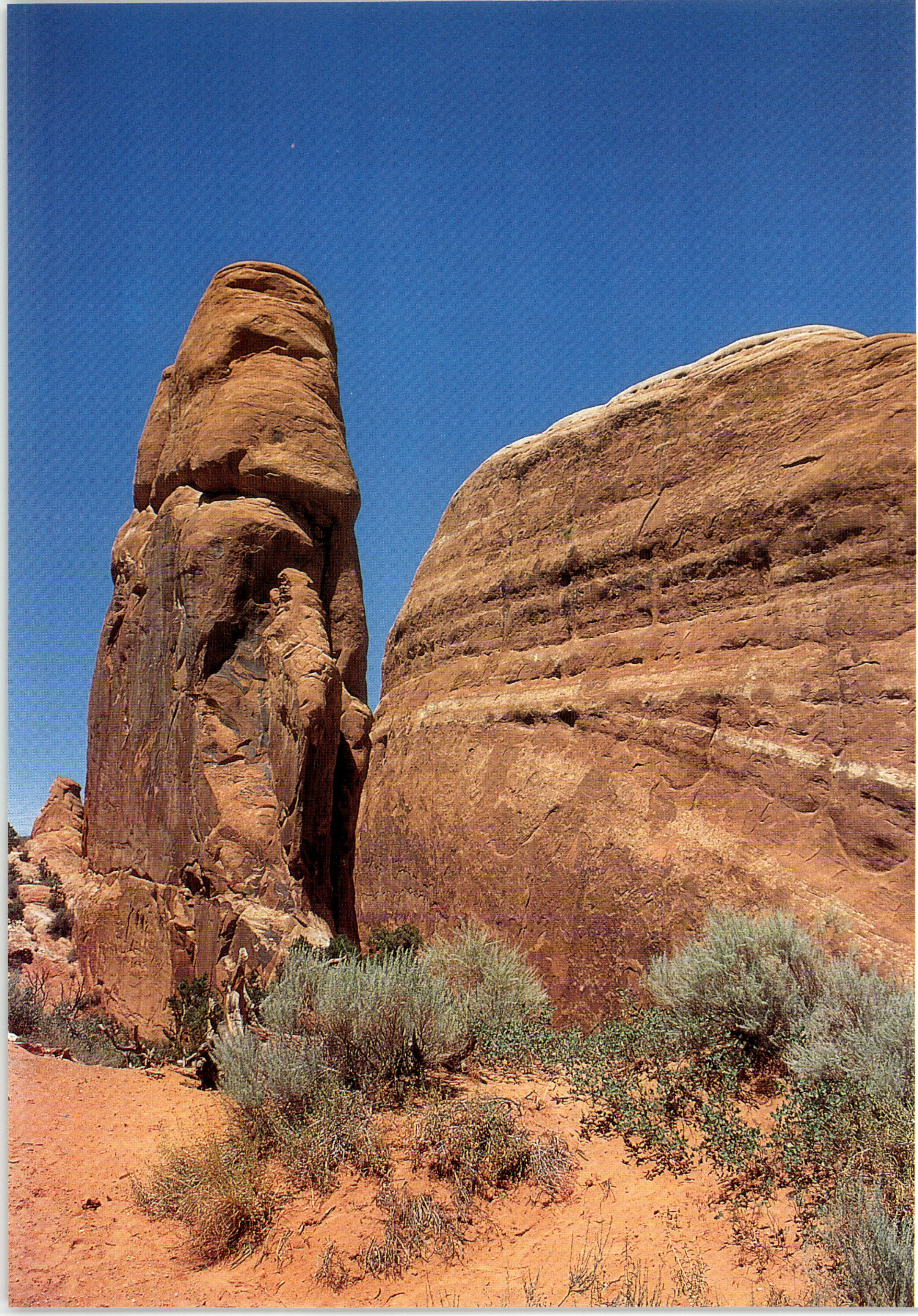

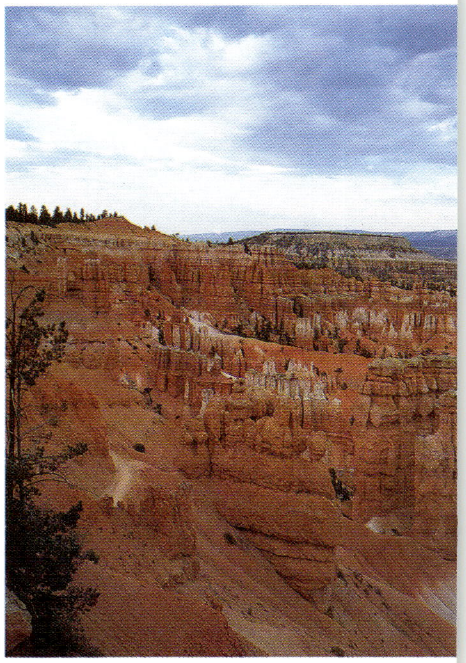

Sunset Point, Bryce Canyon. This shot was taken just below the rim where the slide opposite was exposed. I really like this shot for its own picturesque qualities, although the site afforded the opportunity to take other kinds of images. *Mamiya 7II + 65mm lens, Velvia, tripod.*

Sandstone fins, Devils Garden, Arches National Park, Utah. *Pentax MZ5n + 28–70mm zoom lens.*

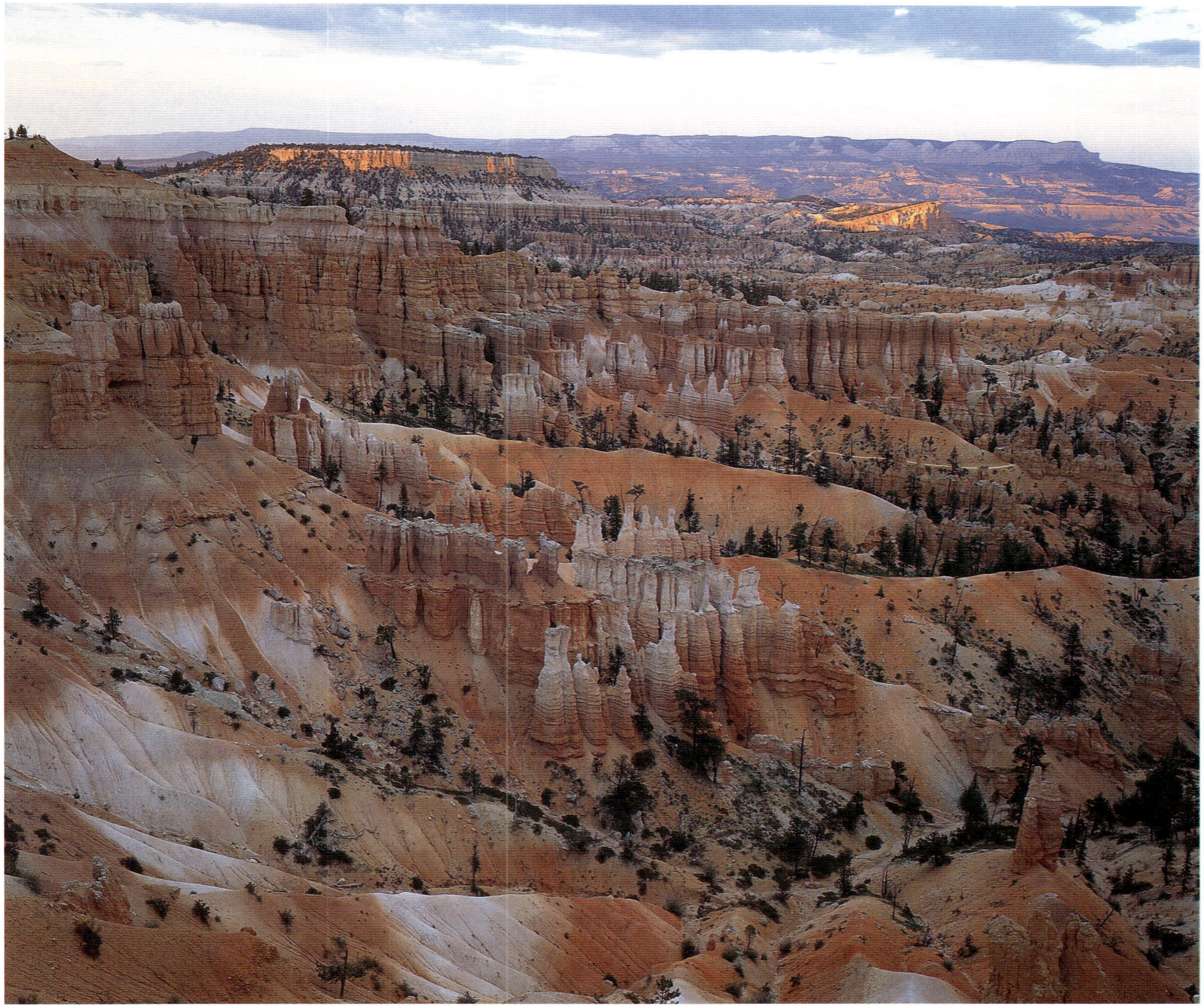

Sunset Point, Bryce Canyon, shortly before sunset. This is a popular view, for good reason. It is definitely worth scouting around for less familiar vantage points. This shot and the previous image illustrate the endless potential for unexpected views around every corner.
Mamiya 7II + 65mm lens, Velvia, tripod.

pleasing and portrayed a timeless and ancient landscape just as I had intended – so what if I follow in the footsteps of others? Of course such places also offer possibilities for original perspectives: for example, from below the canyon rim or from other less popular locations in the park. All you have to do is engage your imagination. Using a good map and carrying out local research can prove very

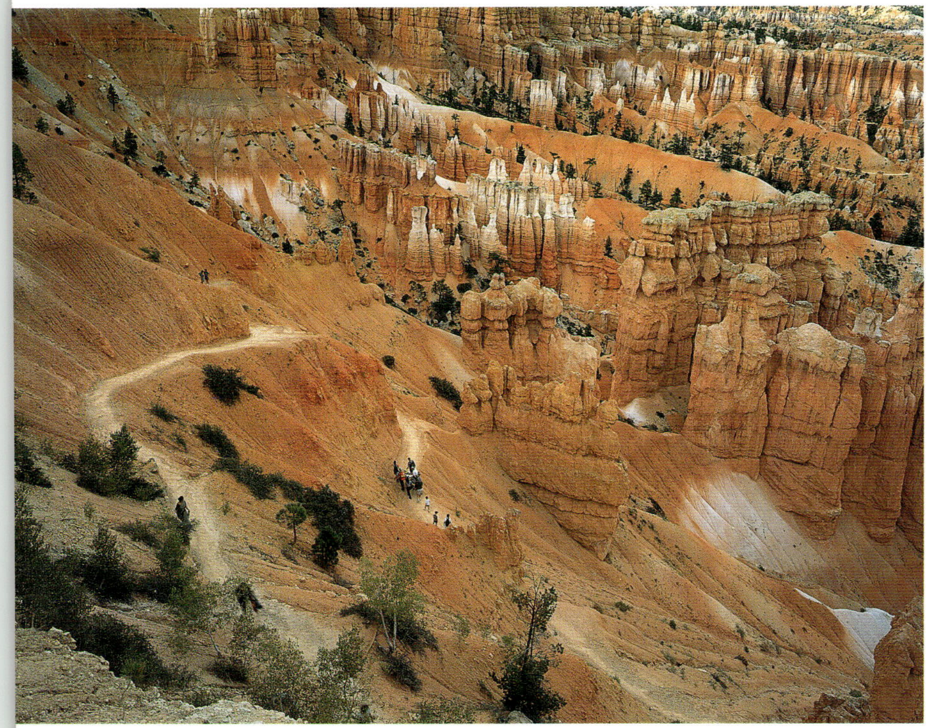

Sunset Point, Bryce Canyon. My visit to the site alerted me to the news that a walker was being carried out of the canyon by stretcher. Timely pictures like this are newsworthy, and show a side to the environment that most people don't get to see.
Mamiya 7II + 65mm lens, Velvia, tripod.

useful in seeking out worthy natural environments for photography. Over the years I must have amassed one of the best local map collections for photogenic locations of anyone in the world (I love maps). Very few of Bryce's visitors, for instance, will visit the nearby Grand Staircase Escalante National Monument – which was only relatively recently afforded the protection it justly deserves, by former President Bill Clinton. Areas of the park are accessible only by helicopter, but otherwise you are in 4WD terrain, although some of it is better explored on horseback. In this vast wilderness you can really do some original photography. I shot Grosvenor Arch, but wasn't able to penetrate deep into the landscape – nothing for it but to go back another day. If you want to see the photo opportunities that I missed, take a look at Jack Dykinga's *Stone Canyons of the Colorado Plateau*.

Still, the relatively lesser-known formations and arid regions of Australia's top end created an opportunity to shoot more original material. Here, I tried to shoot subjects that were off the beaten track

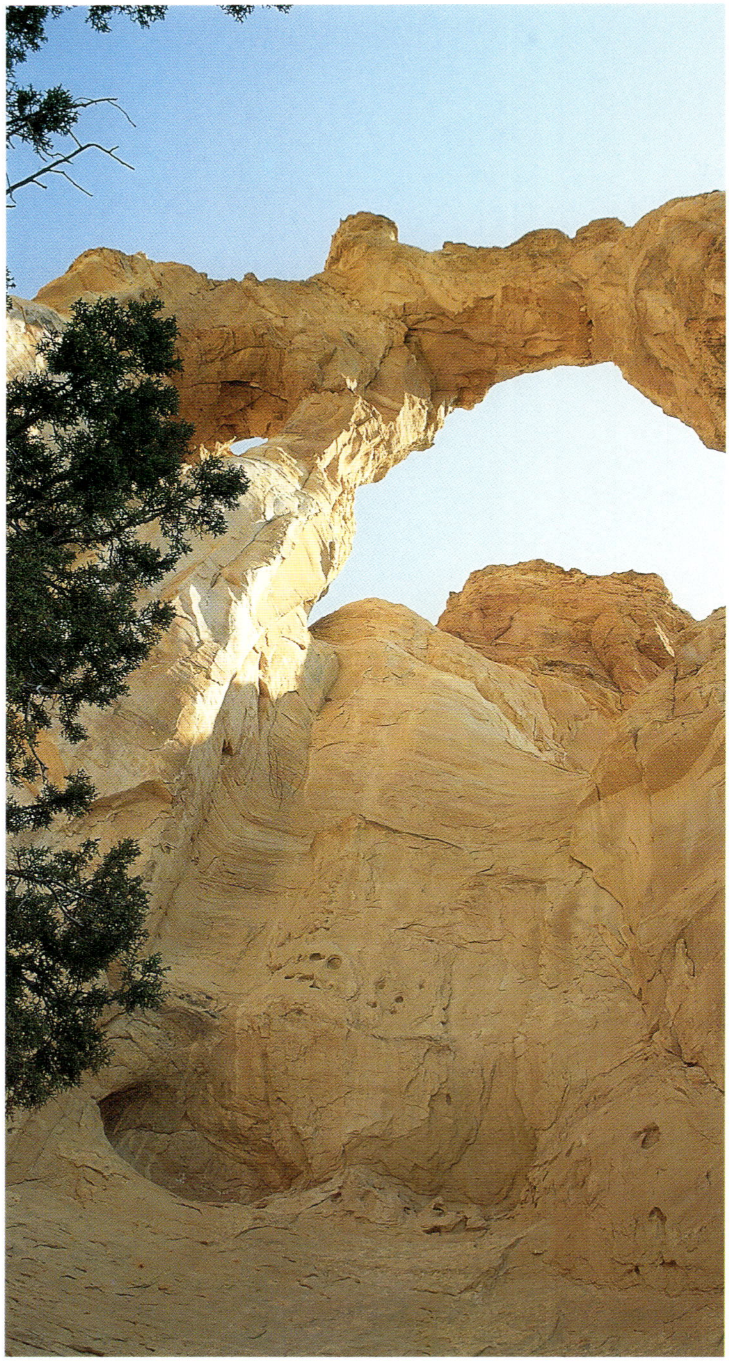

Grosvenor Arch, Grand Staircase Escalante National Monument, Utah. One of the most arid environments I have ever visited; the sun was hot beyond belief on this particular day.
Pentax MZ5n + 28–70mm zoom lens, tripod.

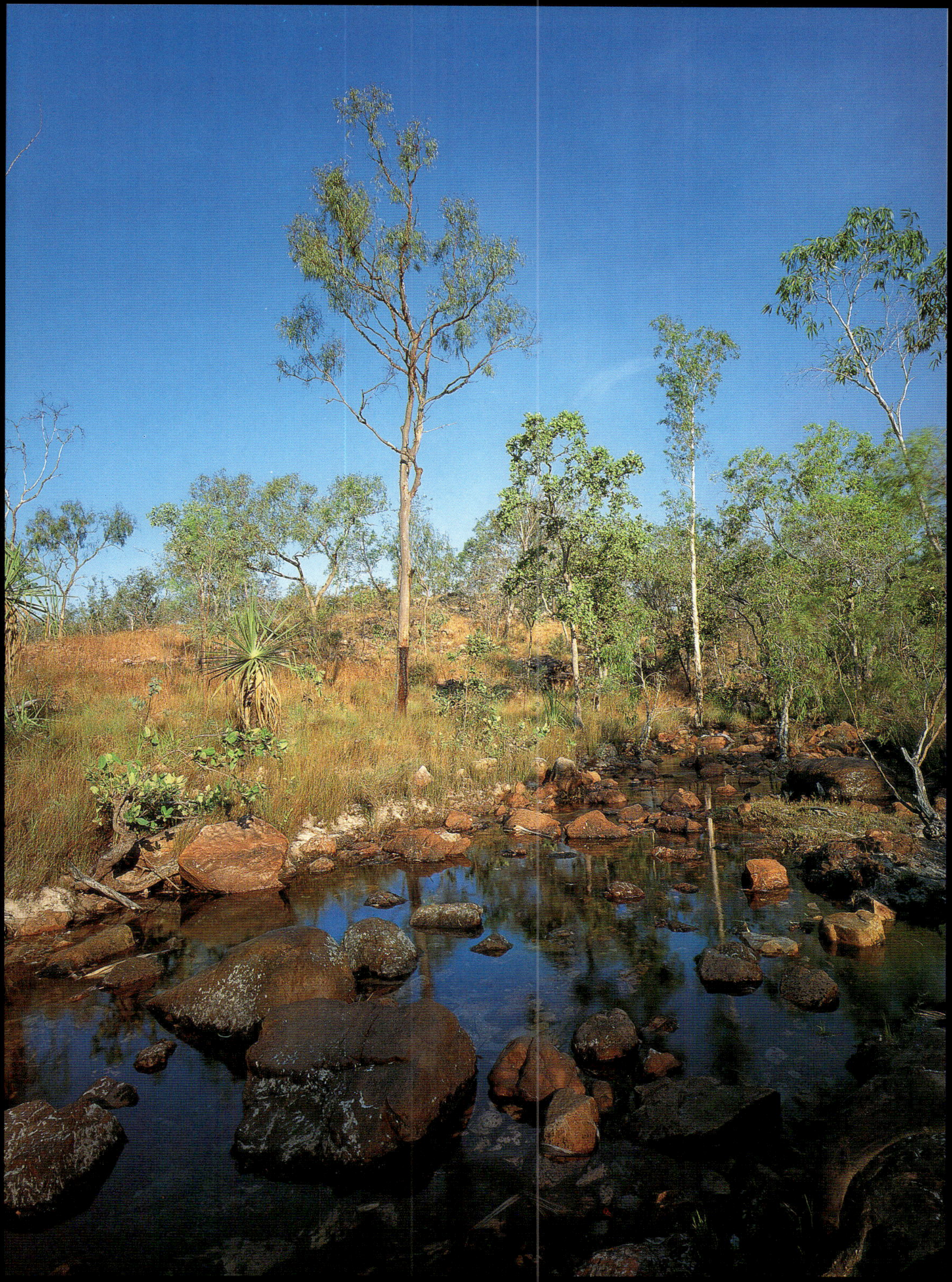

Tolmer Creek is a watery ribbon through an arid land in Australia's Litchfield National Park. By shooting late in the day, the harsh blue cast of midday is replaced by the warmer light at the red and orange end of the colour spectrum. *Mamiya 7II + 65mm lens, Velvia, tripod.*

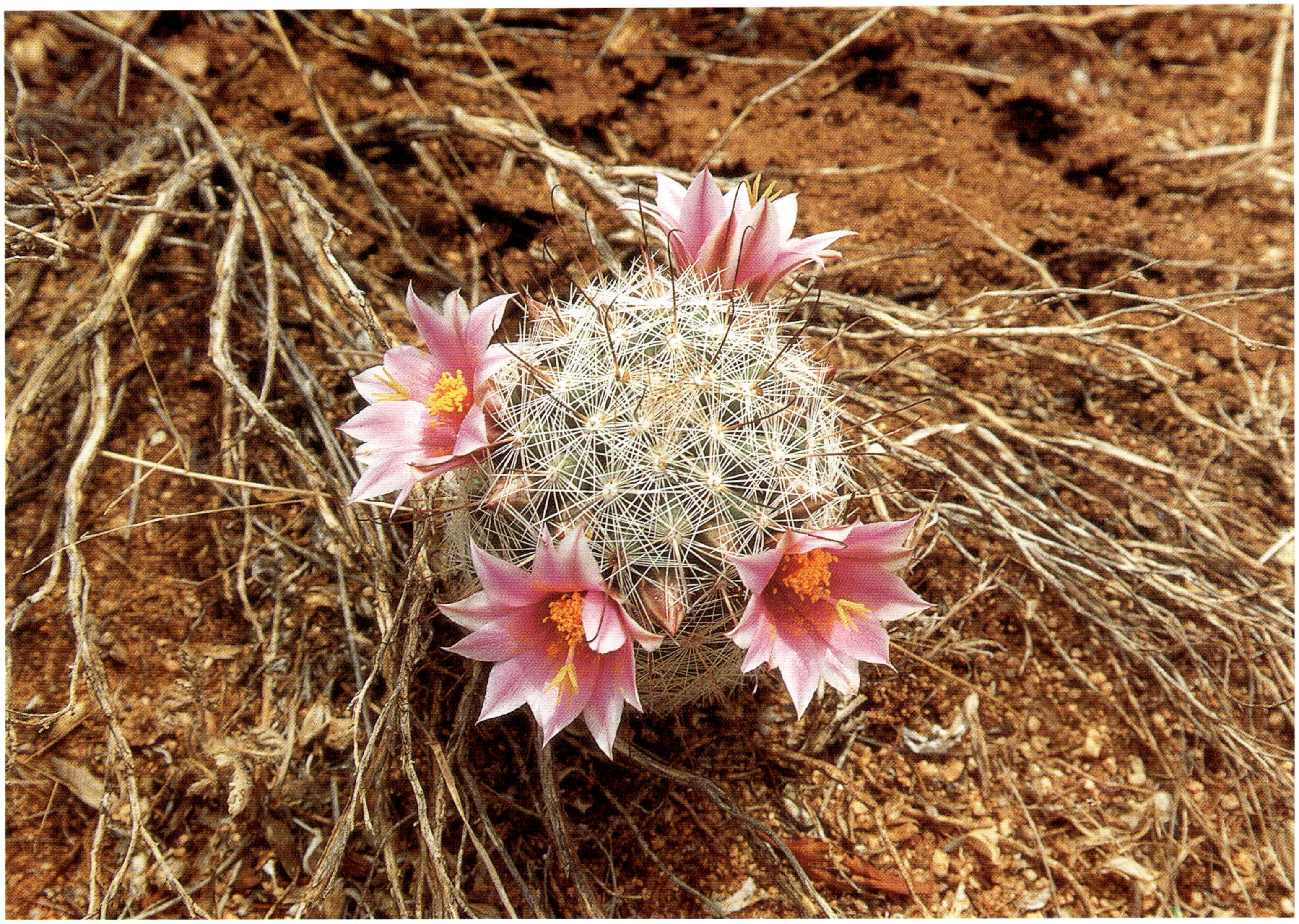

Tangled fishhook cactus in bloom, Sonoran Desert just outside Tucson, Arizona.
Pentax SLR + short zoom lens, Nikon 3T dioptre, 1/8sec, Velvia.

such as the enchanting Tolmer Creek on the sandstone plateau of Litchfield National Park. By shooting around 40 minutes before sunset, the harsh aridness of the day changes into a seemingly verdant landscape. My efforts at Tolmer Creek were treated with some suspicion by a yellow-throated monitor lizard 1.5m (4 1⁄2ft) long, who didn't seem too happy with my presence.

Remember, there is always something unique or photogenic in a hot, dry region. While slick rock is *de rigeur* in the southwestern United States, in the top end of Australia, rare magnetic termite mounds are a photographic must.

Even though the sun shines a lot in arid environments, I still resort to a tripod for all my landscape shots. Shooting at f/16 on Velvia can still yield slowish shutter speeds in the sun. As in all environmental photography, the landscape is but one facet of the whole. Within the landscape, one should capture the animals and plants that are component parts of this world. In the deserts of the United States, I have shot cactus flowers, lizards and rattlesnakes which characterize and symbolize this ecosystem. In Australia's top

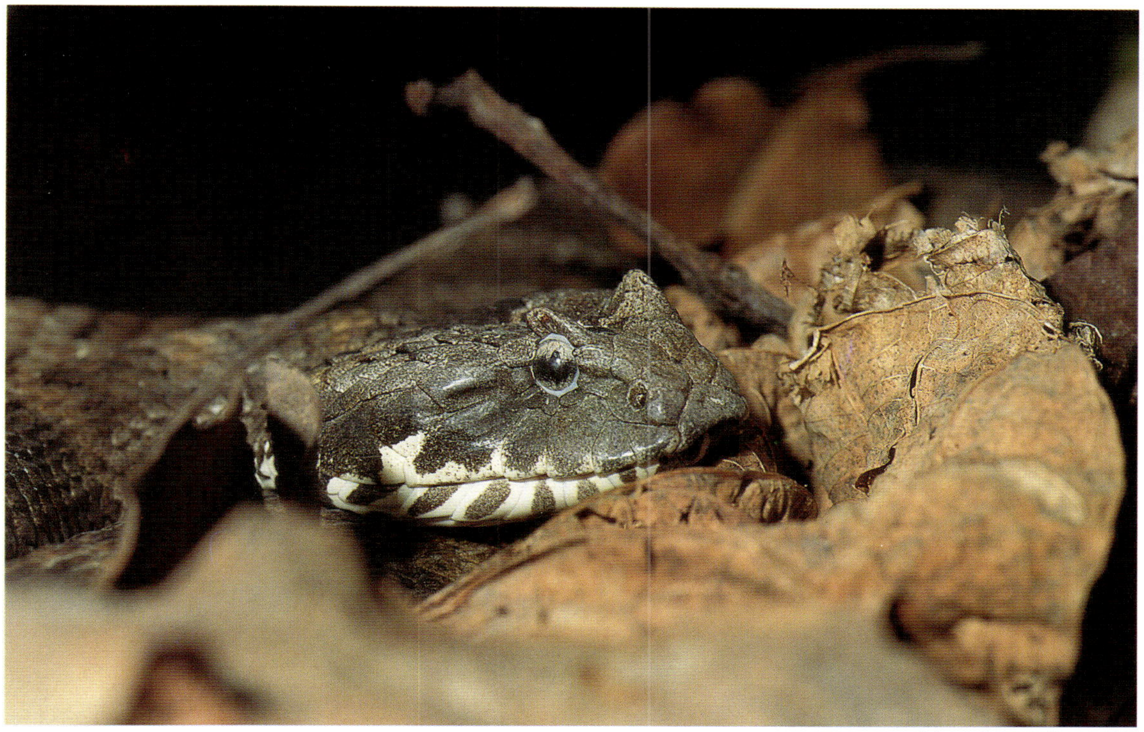

Death adder. This lethal species is found at the top end of Australia.
Pentax MZ5n + 100mm lens.

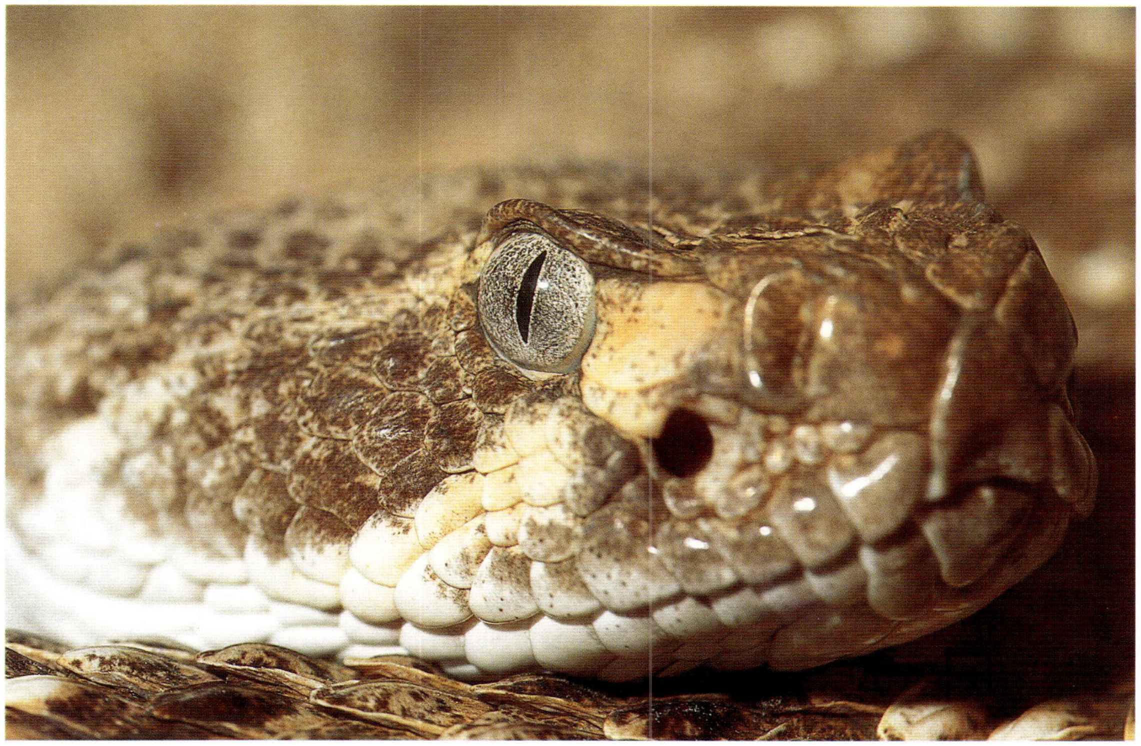

Western diamondback rattlesnake. Shots like this symbolize an image of America and complement desert landscape photographs in a way that will augment the potential for picture sales.
Pentax MZ5n + 100mm macro lens.

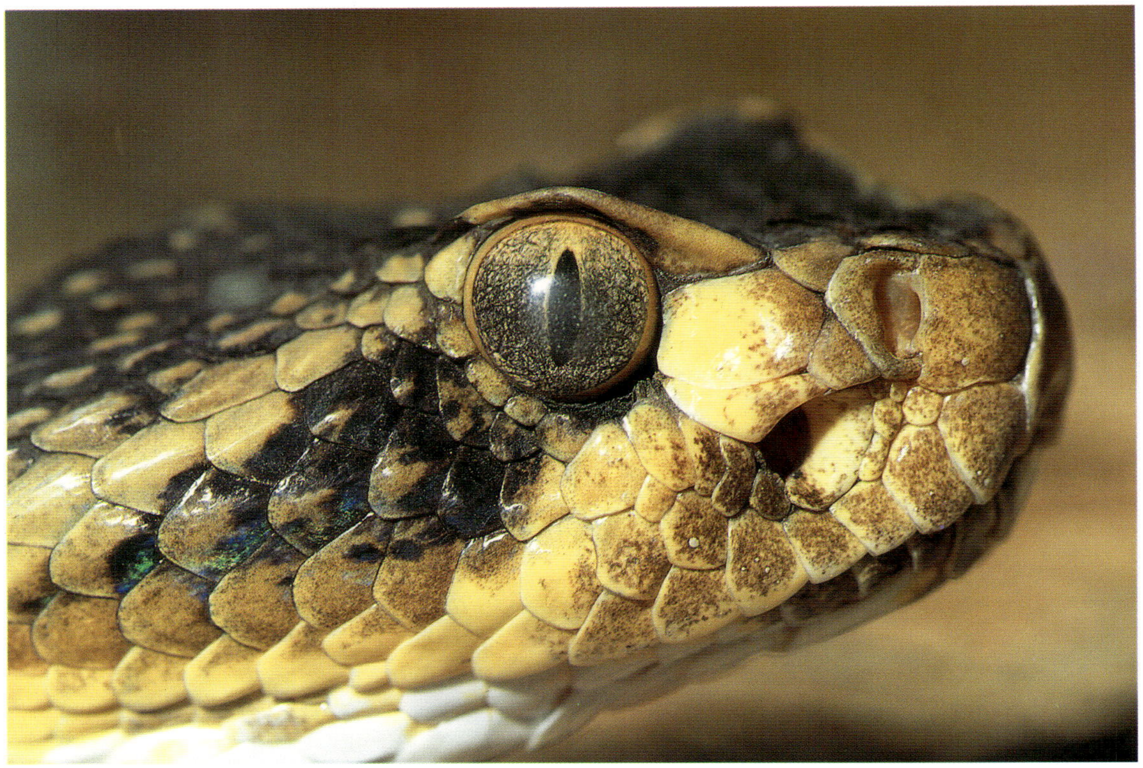

Mojave rattlesnake: the most feared of all American rattlers. When in verdant livery, it is also one of the continent's most elegant snakes. I came across a particularly vivid green specimen high in the Chiricahua National Monument near the American/Mexican border. *Pentax MZ5n + 100mm lens.*

end, I have shot emus, frilled lizards and death adders to supplement my landscapes. By doing this you come away with a complete photographic record of the environment. You can then, for example, submit a comprehensive photo essay to travel and nature magazines or, in my case, prepare a chapter for a book.

If there is one photo theme that defines hot arid landscapes in my mind it is their remarkably intense sunsets. Of all the sunsets I have witnessed with and without a camera, whether in the

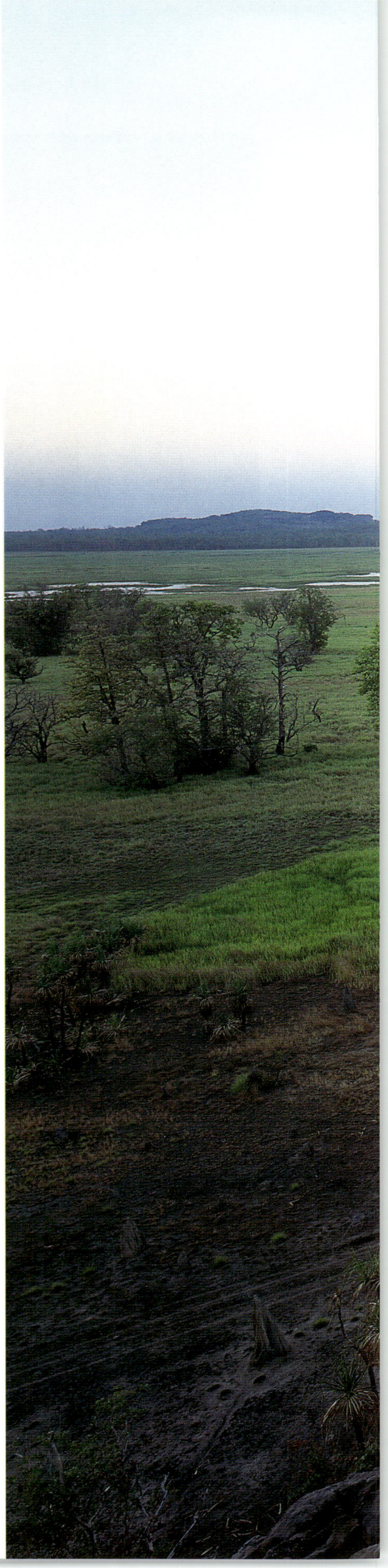

This is the best image of the impending Kakadu sunset I managed to achieve from the classic lookout over the Nardab flood plain. Not bad, but I prefer the one I took of silhouetted pandanus trees from a far more prosaic setting (overleaf). The sun's orb is just out of frame to the left. Shots which included the sun were highly underexposed, losing nearly all of their vital detail. I chose this particular view because of the waving grasses, which created essential foreground interest. You may think this is a green and verdant land but, for most of the year, away from the flood plains, this is an arid and extremely hot environment.
Mamiya 7II + 43mm lens, Velvia, tripod.

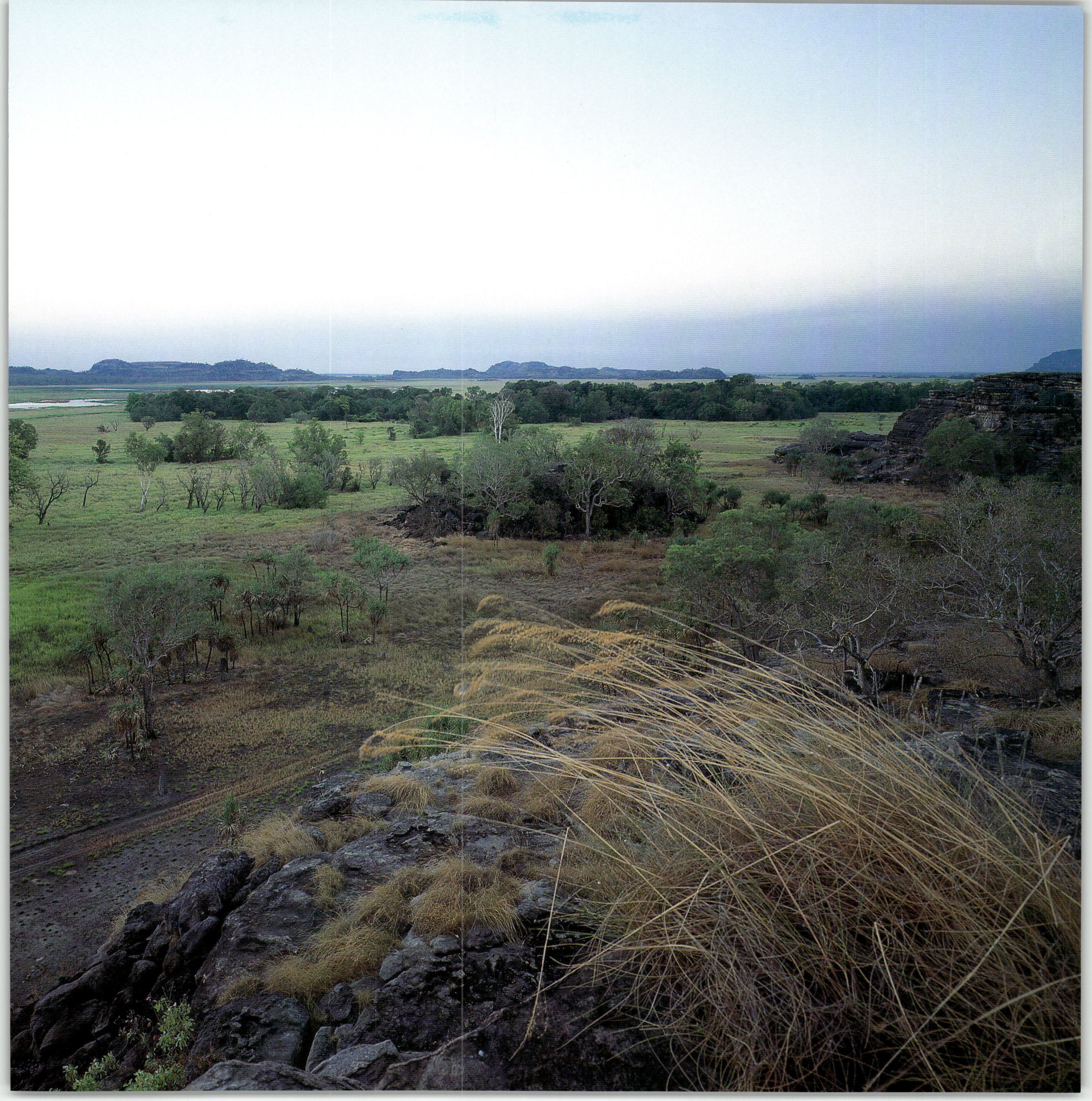

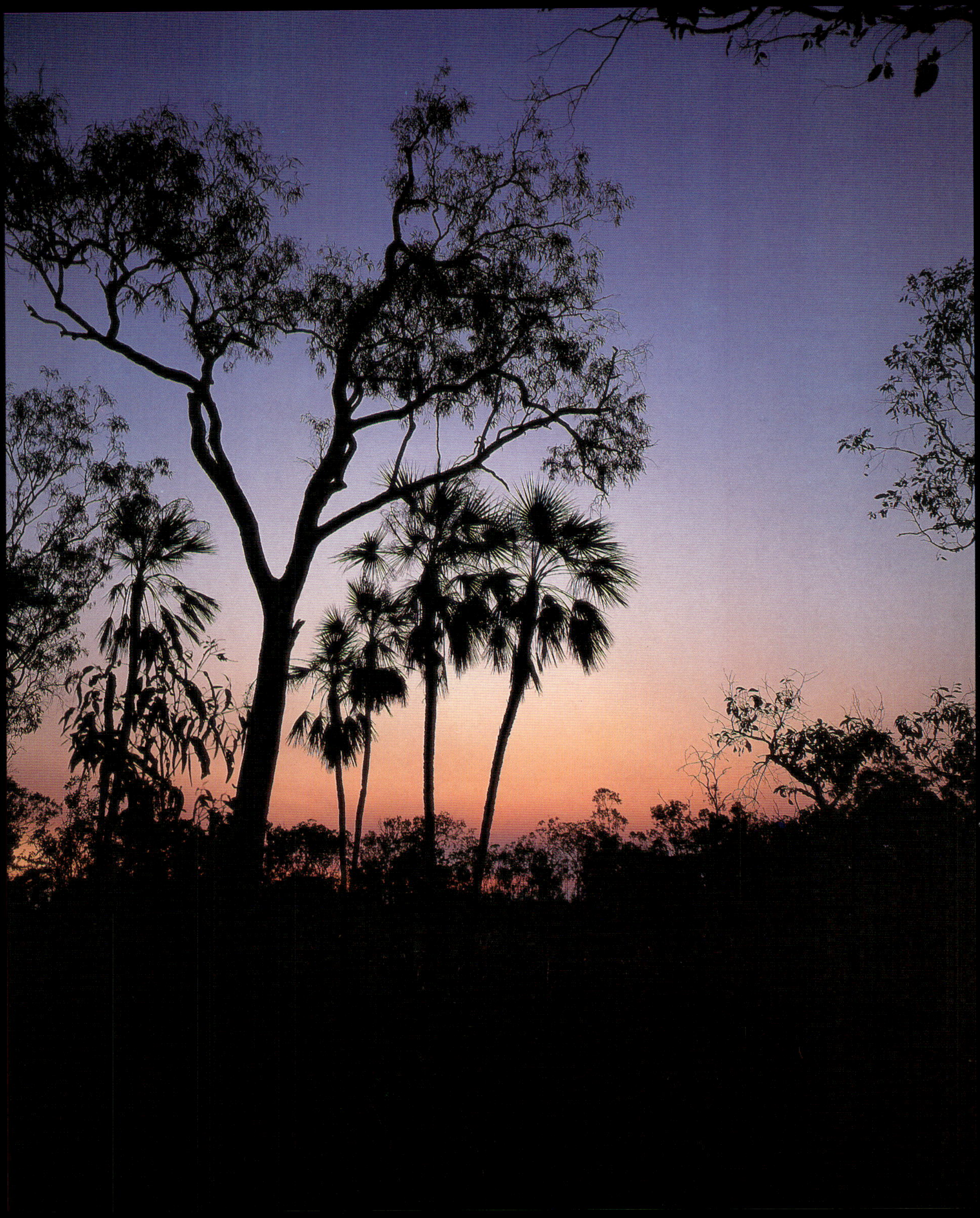

Silhouetted pandanus palms at sunset. Although a far more mundane setting than the Nardab flood plain, this is a strong composition. Unfortunately no focusing or exposure forethought was possible due to a dense plague of mosquitoes that were quite unbelievable in their thirst for blood. .
Mamiya 7II + 43mm lens, tripod and torch.

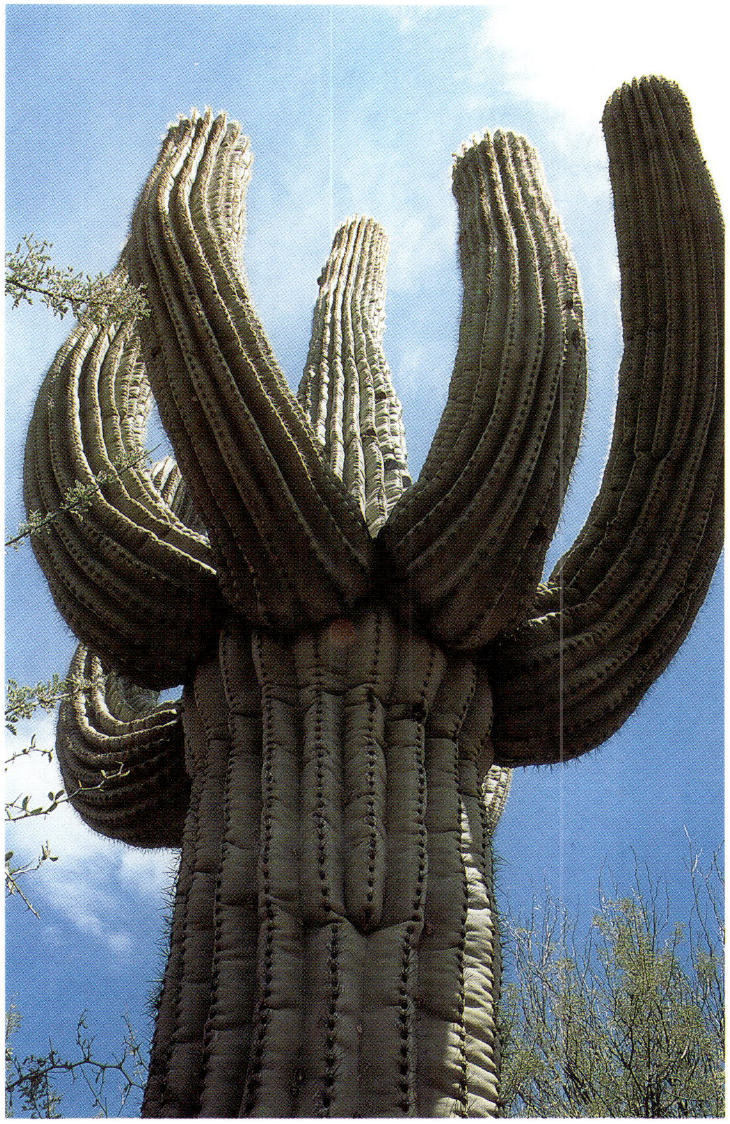

Saguaro cactus near Payson, Arizona.
Pentax MZ5 + 28mm lens.

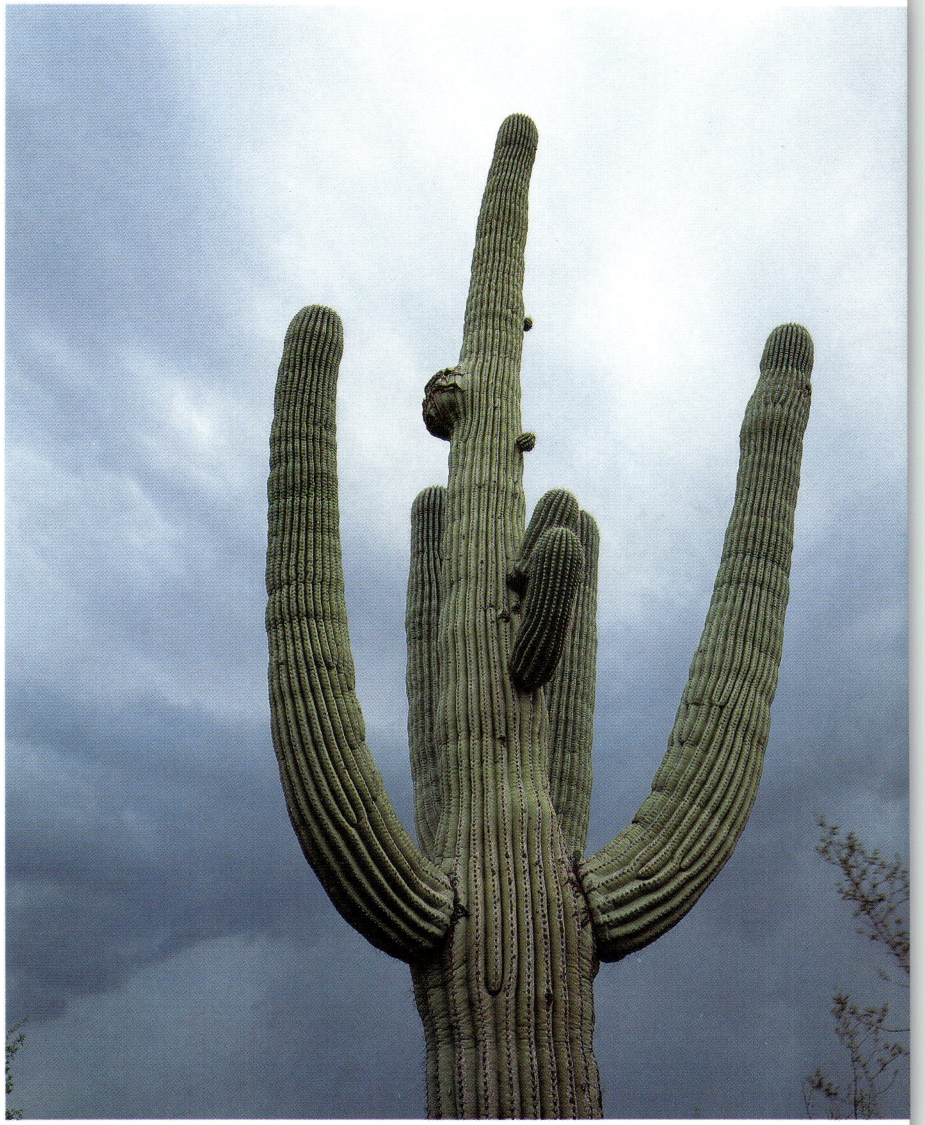

Saguaro cactus and brooding monsoon sky, Saguaro National Monument-East, Arizona.
Mamiya 7II + 65mm lens, Velvia, tripod.

Californian deserts, high Utah deserts or deserts of the Middle East, none can compare to those I was privileged to view in Australia's top end. Be warned though, a remarkable transition can occur as the sunset reaches its climax: Kakadu is a complex mosaic of wetlands with, in winter, extensive and extremely arid open savannah woodland. (Savannah woodland represents 80% of Kakadu, a national park roughly the size of Wales.) I had been told that the best place to witness sunset here was the Aboriginal art site at Ubirr (of 'Crocodile Dundee' fame). Well, I drew the short straw when I turned up here to shoot the setting sun over the Nardab flood plain, it was one of the poorer sunsets I had seen in the top end and, to be honest, not really the best vantage point for serious photographers. The next day I drove around frantically as the sun began to set looking for a pandanus (screw palm) to silhouette against the fiery

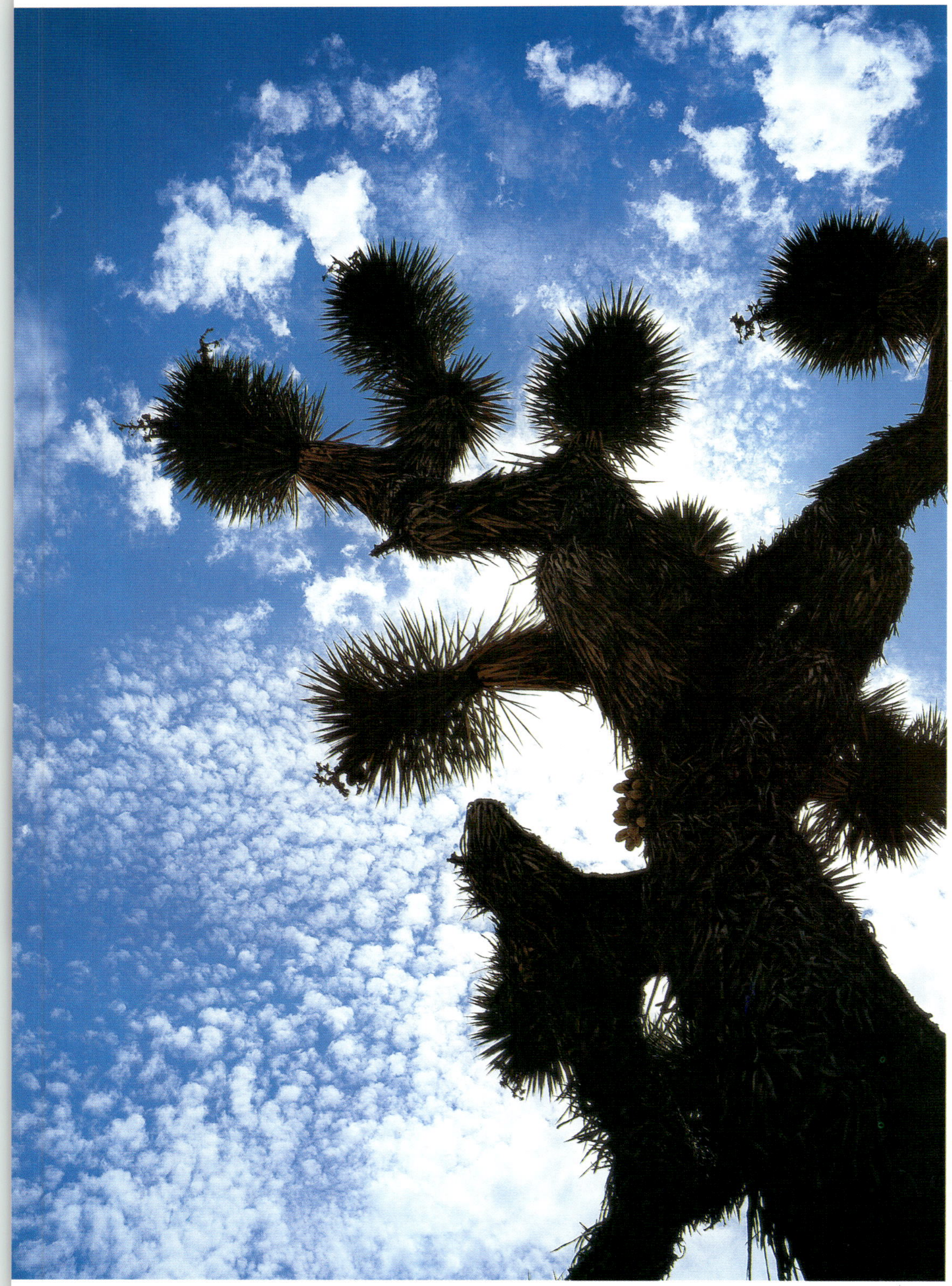

Joshua tree, Joshua Tree National Park, California.
Mamiya 7II + 65mm lens, Velvia, tripod.

Pandanus screw palm, Kakadu National Park, Northern Territory, Australia.
Mamiya 7II + 43mm lens, Velvia, tripod.

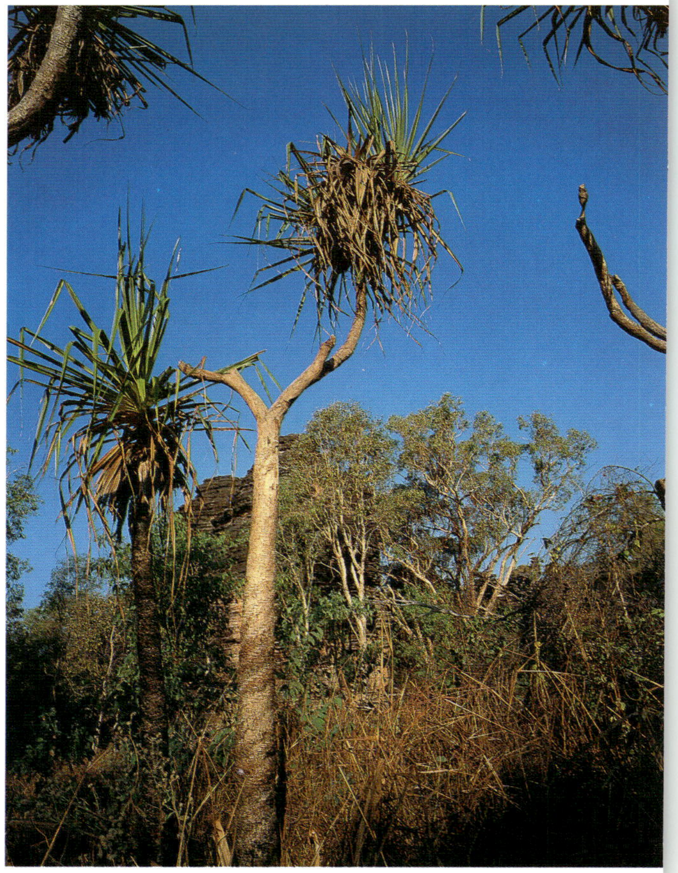

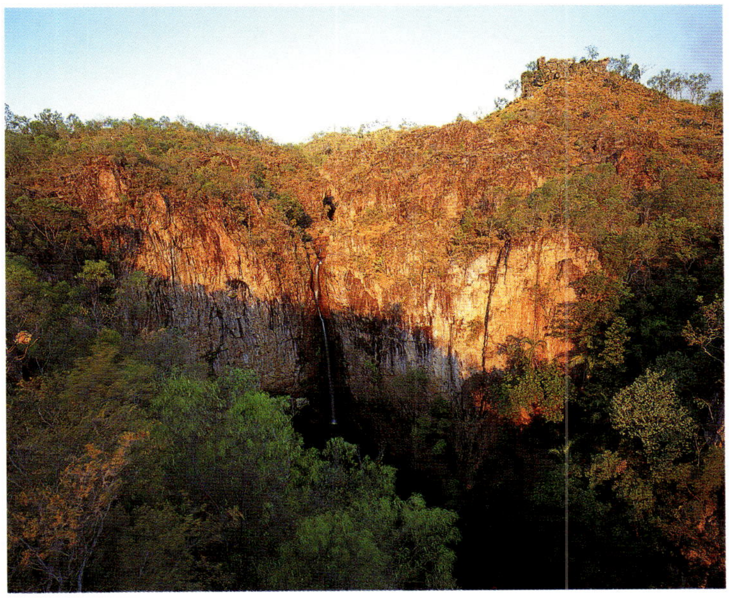

globe; not an easy task since, while this is an extensive parched landscape with open woodland, there is seldom a horizon open enough for sunset photography. Fortunately, I found some cleared land and two isolated pandanus just as the sun was disappearing below the horizon. I shot one roll of Velvia with my Mamiya 7II and 43mm lens. Then, in the space of 30 seconds, just as the colours were deepening into a good sunset, the air came alive with billions of mosquitoes. Somehow, despite being bitten to hell, I loaded the next roll of film and shot ten images without any attention to f-number, focus or shutter speed. What a sight my wife and I must have been, dancing around and slapping ourselves, my wife with a torch in her hand, me with a cable release in mine. With mosquitoes at night and biting flies during the day, Scottish midges are nothing by comparison. The price we photographers and our families pay for a good picture. Fortunately, not all arid environments have such annoying insects.

A tall, thin, cascading waterfall in Tolmer Gorge, Litchfield National Park, Northern territory, Australia. Water sculpted this landscape, but it seems insignificant and lost in what is otherwise a large, parched, hot land. *Mamiya 7II + 43mm lens.*

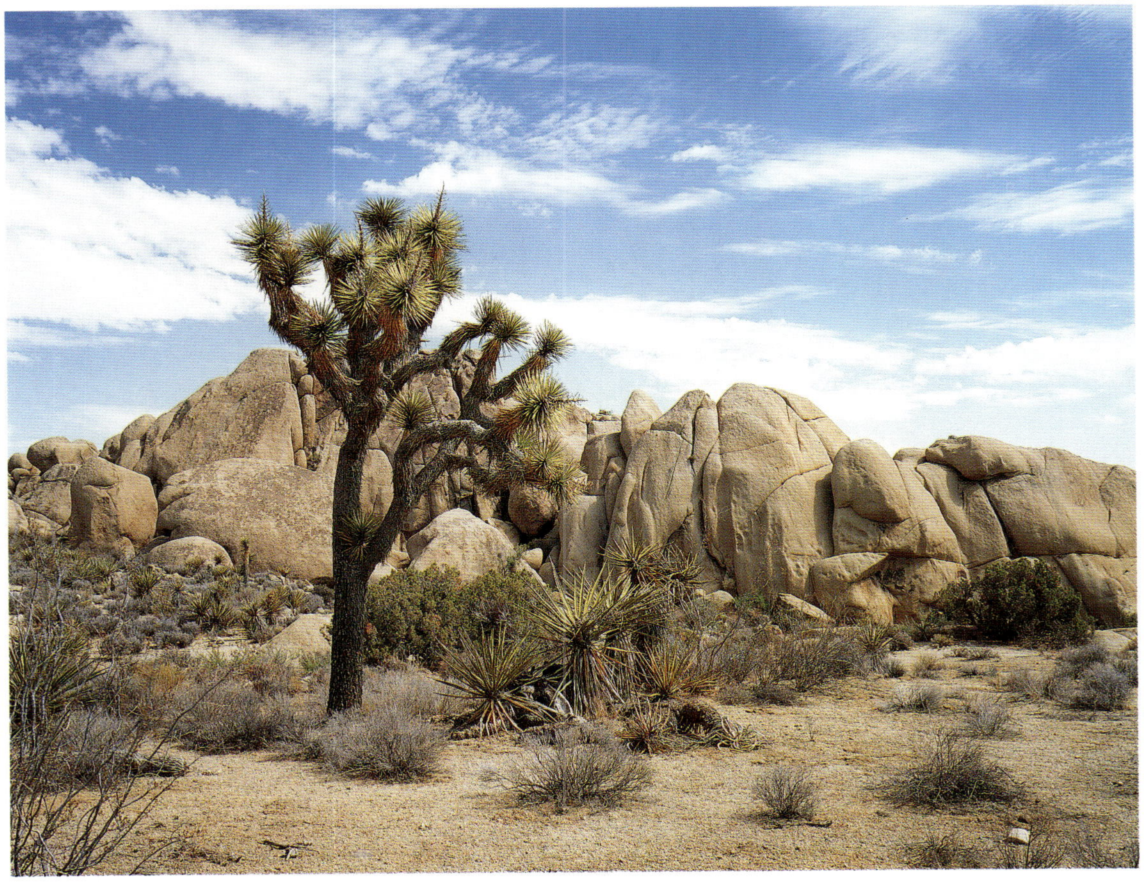

Joshua tree and rocky outcrop, California. I like this photograph because its surreal quality reminds me of a prehistoric world in which the Flintstones might have lived. *Mamiya 7II + 65mm lens, Velvia, tripod.*

Remember that arid environments come in many forms and each differs quite significantly in its character: stereotypical deserts like South America's high Atacama and California's low, parched Death Valley; colourful deserts like Arizona's Painted Desert (a paleontologist's dream); sculpted deserts like the Great Basin and the savannah woodlands of Kakadu and Litchfield in the Northern Territory. Whichever arid environment you find yourself in, search out the photo opportunities: sunsets, ecologically significant features, classic views and the animals and plants that form part of these dry worlds.The best shots I have seen of the American West and other arid regions around the world have, for the most part, been taken in the warm, low-angled light that only really exists early and late in the day. If you cannot shoot at this time of day, perhaps because you are passing through a scenic region and unable to break your trip, you should think about employing 81 series warm-up filters to counteract the strong blue element of the midday light in the world's hot, sunny, arid regions. While I am no great fan of filters – I don't even use polarizers these days – the 81 series warm-up filters are absolutely essential in my opinion. They allow midday photography in sunny climates, and work really well with Velvia, a film that always makes blue skies really blue (see page 34 for more information on using filters).

Water

Coastlines

Every country with a seaboard has its own seaside stereotype. Knotted hankies, lobster-red complexions, bingo and noisy arcades represent familiar facets of the archetypal British seaside. However, away from the piers and rollercoasters is a more sedate world where lobster pots, weathered fishing boats and pink-washed cottages engender a very different, but no less photogenic seaside spirit. Here architect-designed follies replace helterskelters, fishing boats replace boats for day-trippers. Further afield, idyllic, palm-fringed, tropical beaches provide the opportunity for taking images which are imbued with a feel-good factor that is hard to match with any other subject.

The sea and the seaside

By itself, the sea can produce rather flat, featureless images. It often needs a second element to enliven the scene and create a sense of depth. This could be the sun rising or setting with its alluring watery reflections. For those of us who photograph at a more humane time of day, try to include foreground interest. A breakwater is ideal and allows you to introduce a sense of movement with ripples or crashing waves.

Sunset over the Timor Sea. I took this dramatic Darwin sunset with a relatively cheap compact Pentax 738s. I loaded Velvia and braced myself as best I could.

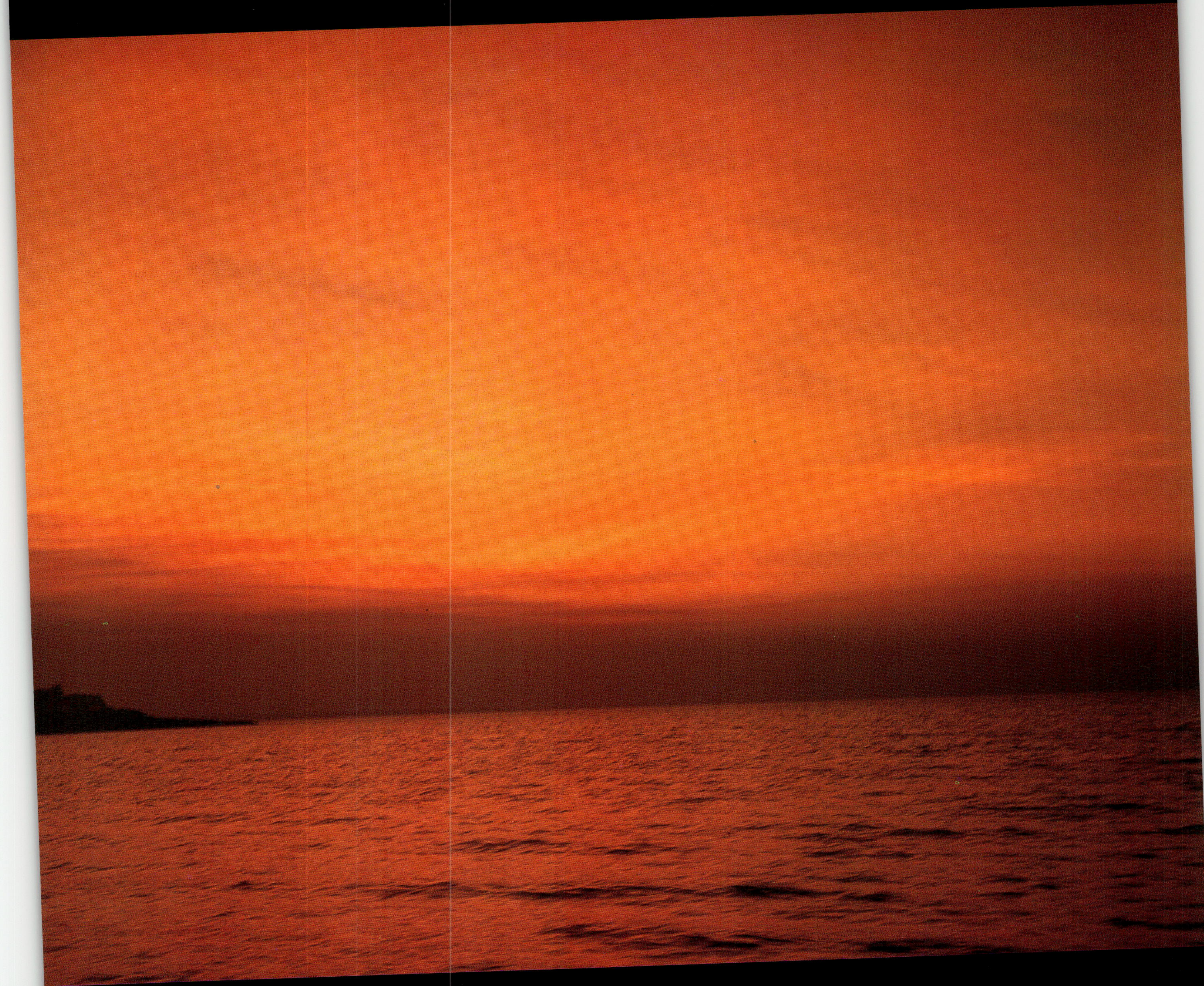

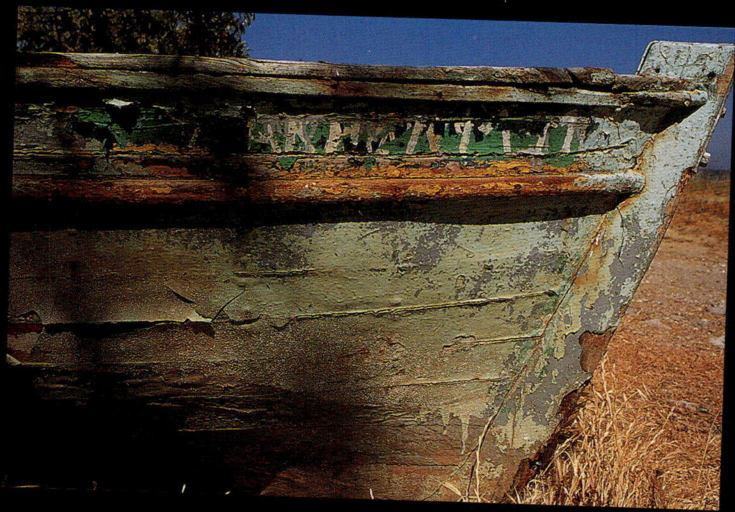

Weathered fishing boat with peeling paint, Lesbos.
Pentax LX + 28mm Tamron lens, hand-held.

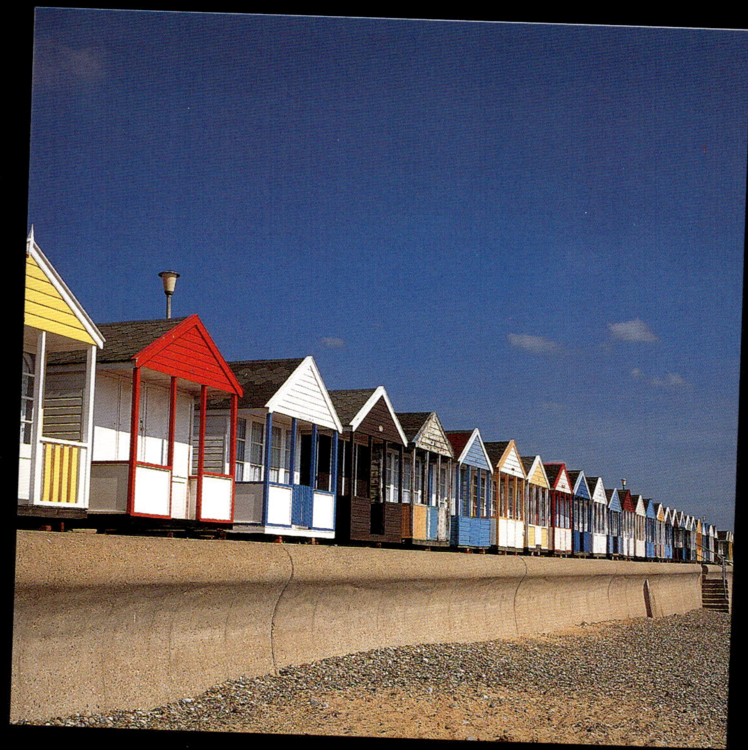

The emphasis of this 6 x 6cm image is colour, which is why it has sold many times. The square format is less of an issue. Taken at Southwold in Suffolk, England.
Hasselblad 500CM + 80mm lens, 1/60sec at f16, Velvia, tripod.

This 6 x 6cm image, taken at Dunwich beach, Suffolk, England, has isolated this inshore fishing boat from the rest of its environment.
Hasselblad 500CM + 80mm lens, 1/60sec at f/11.5, Velvia, tripod.

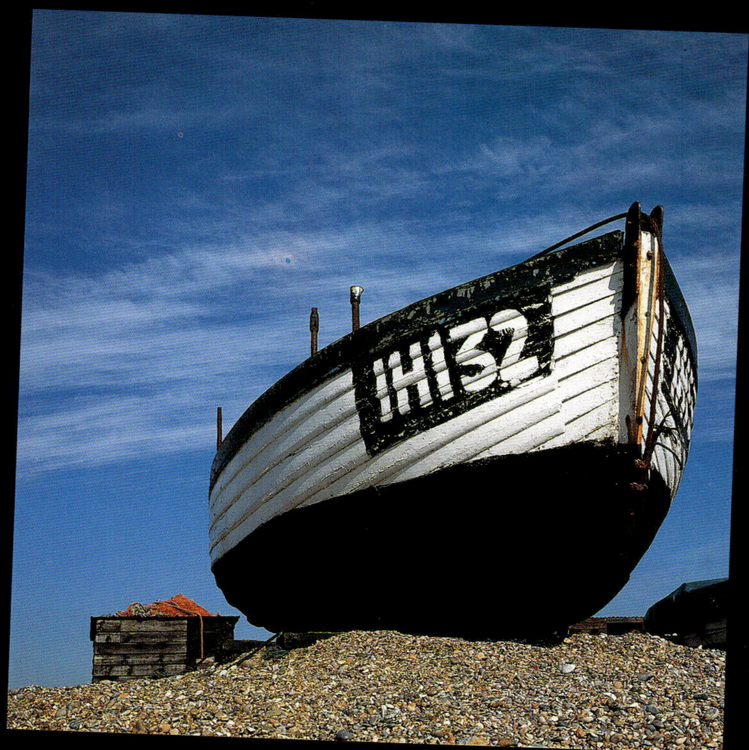

This 6 x 9cm image has placed this decaying boat beside the River Alde into a broader natural landscape.
Fuji GSW69III, 1/30sec at f/11, Velvia, tripod.

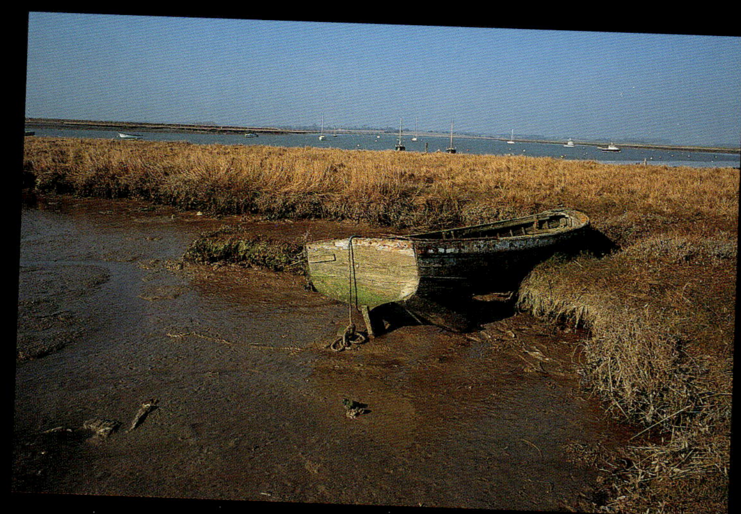

The seaside is an ideal place to learn about contre-jour photography. Shoot into the sun or towards a highly reflective sea and your meter will be fooled into underexposing the scene. The resultant silhouettes may be what you desire. Alternatively, bracket at half stops up to +2 stops to compensate for this huge quanta of light. If you can't stretch to medium or large format, a 28–80mm lens on 35mm is ideal for shooting the sea, although a longer telephoto suits sunrise or sunset photography. I have even used a simple compact to shoot the tropical setting sun in Darwin, Australia. I loaded Velvia, took aim, braced myself and pressed the button. The result was some excellent sharp, vivid and interesting images.

There is something about old, wooden, inshore fishing boats which transcends the modern world and makes them particularly photogenic, especially when a beached hulk has bright, weathered paint. Depending on its location, go for either a standard lens and a tight crop to isolate the boat or a wide-angle to include it in its environment. You should use a tripod to ensure the weathered detail on the hull is rendered sharp, and try to avoid a cluttered and distracting background as it is best to keep the picture simple for maximum impact. The previous slides show how a 6 x 6cm and 6 x 9cm camera can both make the most of boat shots. The 6 x 6cm shot isolates the fishing boat from its environment, while the 6 x 9cm image places the decaying boat within a broader, natural landscape.

Seaside buildings are always photogenic, too. Look for a palisade of wooden bathing huts with a colourful and varied livery. Shoot with Velvia, on a bright sunny day for results with impact (for more impact, you could also add a polarizer). A 28mm (or medium-format

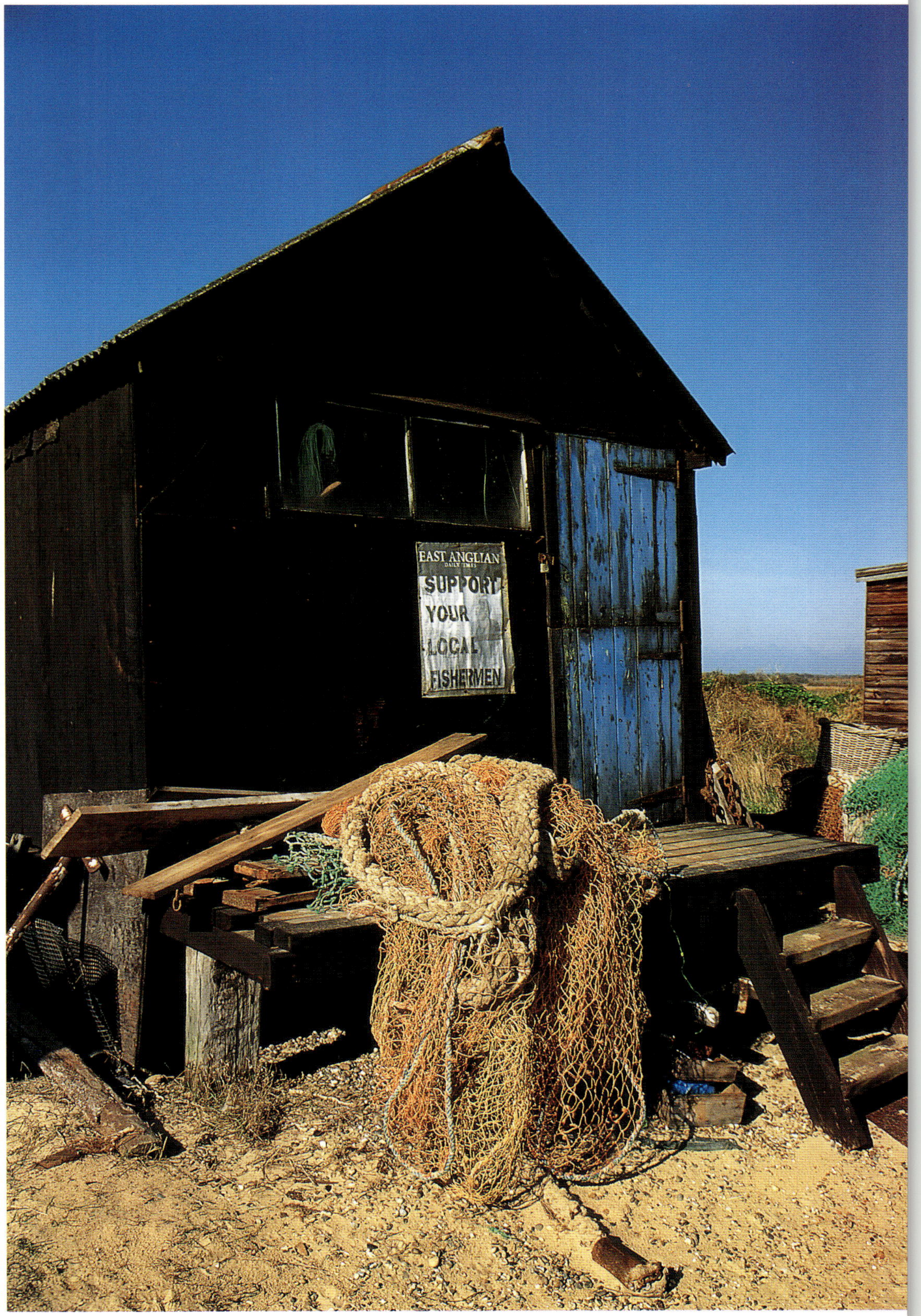

I love rustic fishing huts of this type. A good place to photograph them is Walberswick in Suffolk, England.
Pentax + 28mm lens, tripod.

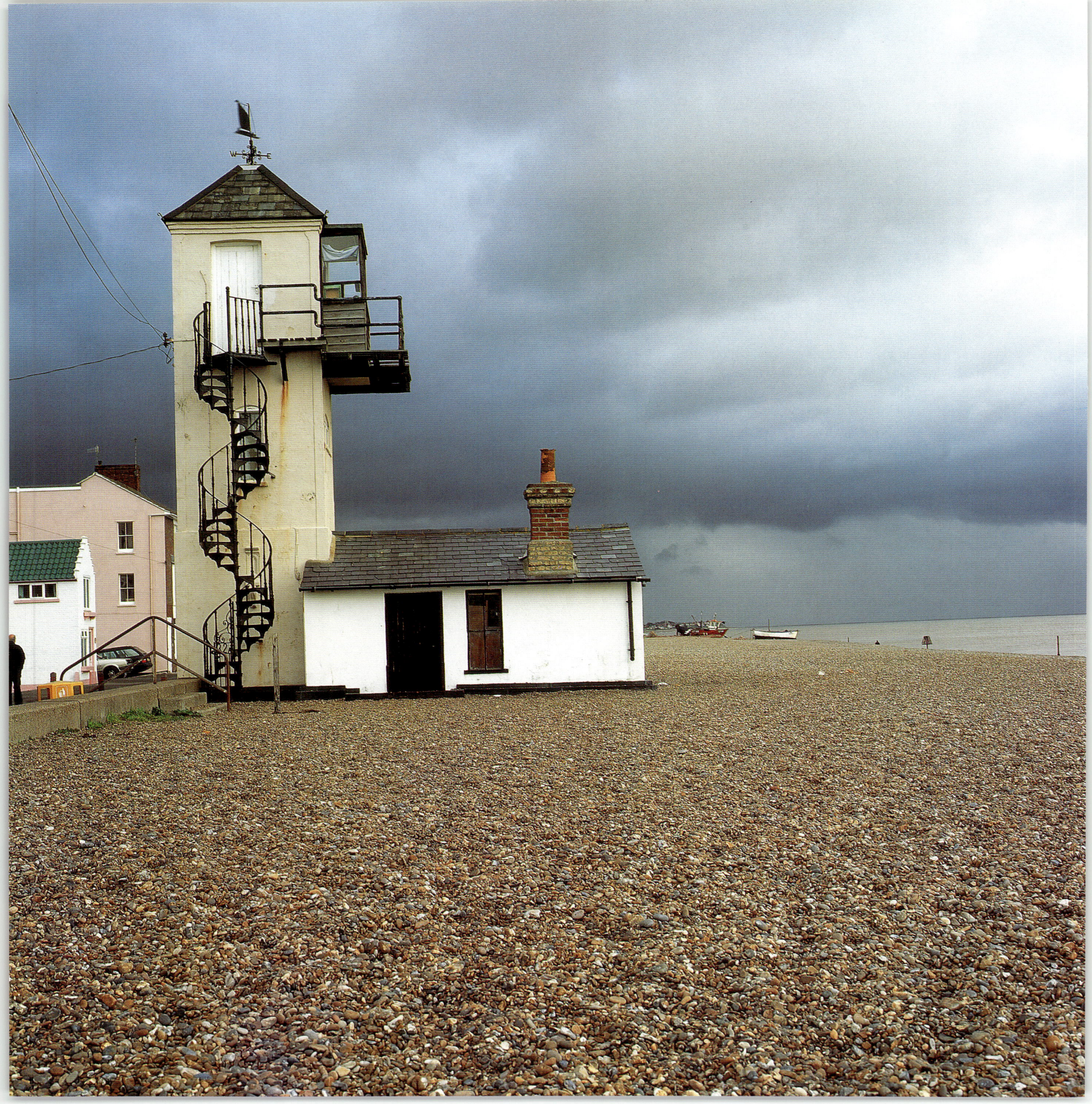

South Lookout, Aldeburgh, Suffolk, England. The 6 x 6cm format makes the most of the shape of the building in a positive way. *Hasselblad 500CM + 80mm lens, 1/15sec at f/11.5, Velvia, tripod.*

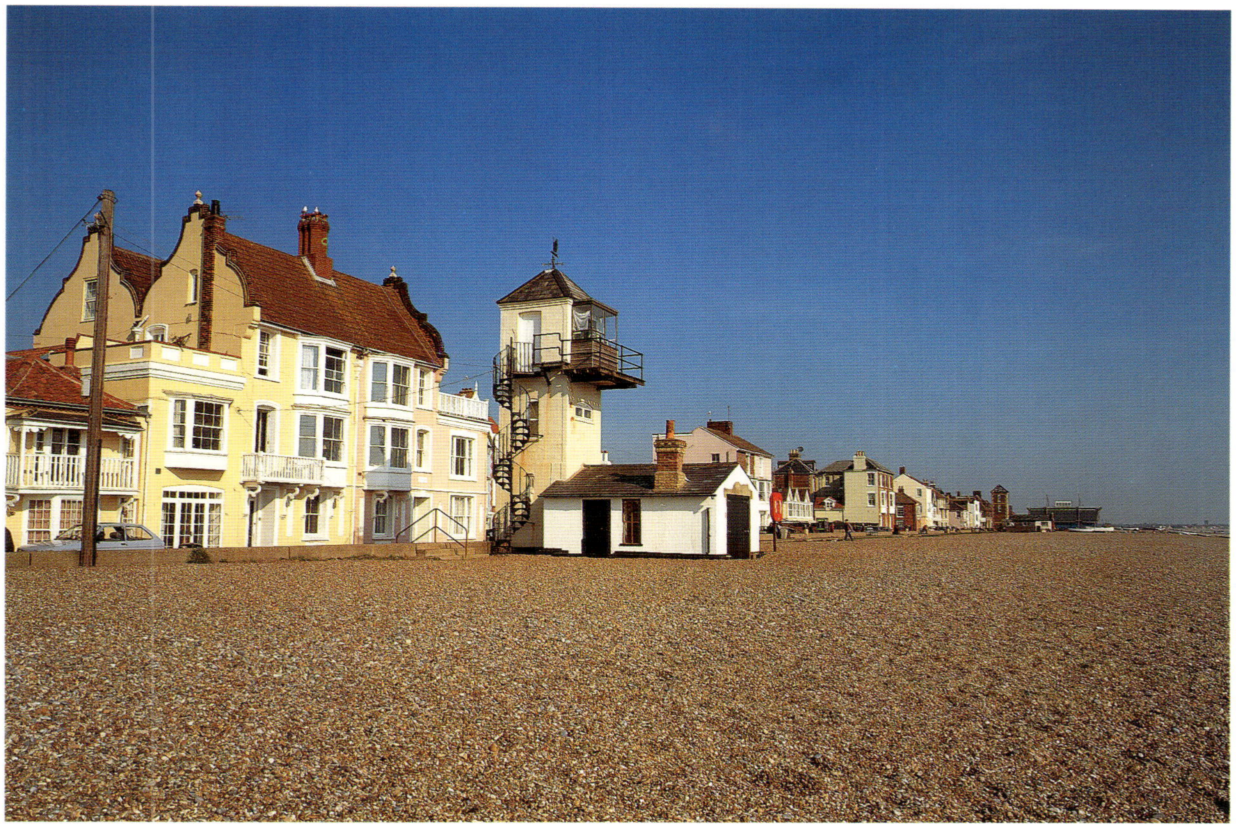

South Lookout, Aldeburgh Suffolk. The 6 x 9cm format also emphasizes the shape of the building. You just need to have the patience to play around with the viewfinder until the composition works. *Fuji GSW69III, 1/60sec at f/16, Velvia, tripod.*

equivalent) up to a standard lens will give a good perspective. Again, the 6 x 6cm camera can be used to good effect in landscape work as the Southwold image shows. Interestingly, the 6 x 6cm Dunwich beach shot and this one are both bestsellers and have been used editorially at least four times. Small rustic fishing huts are my favourite subject. They are always in a permanent state of dilapidation and evoke a true sense of the seaside. Since they are usually shades of black with occasional highlights of orange fishing net, you should bracket up to –1 EV.

Coastal towns often contain follies or unusual buildings that characterize the local landscape. Check out local postcards to identify some and try to shoot them from the same angle as on the postcard, but then look for a more unique perspective. Coastlines also have many castles and forts. For example, there are a plethora of Martello towers on the east coast of Britain. Look also for lighthouses, windmills and windpumps. I have shot one such folly (South Lookout) on both square and rectangular formats. The results indicate that it is how you set up the perspective of your subject in the viewfinder which counts for more than the appropriateness of either format for a given subject. Ultimately, I think that both formats work if you take your time composing the subject.

Estuaries and marshes

This is one of my favourite environments in which to shoot: dense reed marsh on the coastal fringe. Look for patterns in the reeds where they have been cut for thatch. You should try to find a focal point in the dense reedy sward such as an old building or windpump, or a pattern of open water. The following image of a disused, dilapidated windpump was bathed in constantly changing light, which is the most frustrating of problems when using a hand-held meter.

Mudflats contain all manner of subjects: the rotting, skeletal hulks of old vessels, seaweed-draped quays, gulls on knarled posts driven deep into the mud. If you have the time and patience, you can collect shots of redshank, dunlin, oystercatcher and other common waders.

Living in Yorkshire, in the north of England, I am fortunate to have access to some marvellous varied seascapes. Classic limestone

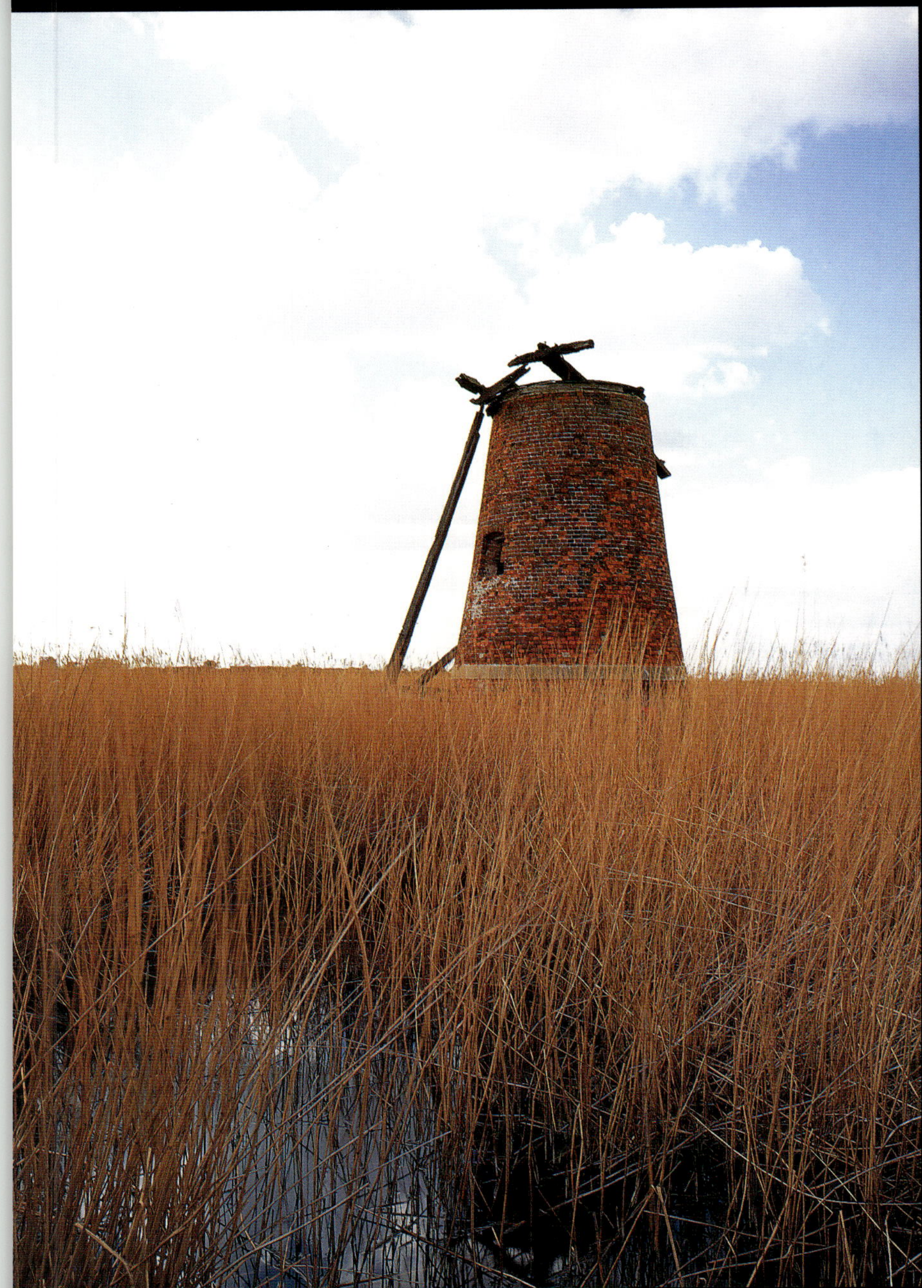

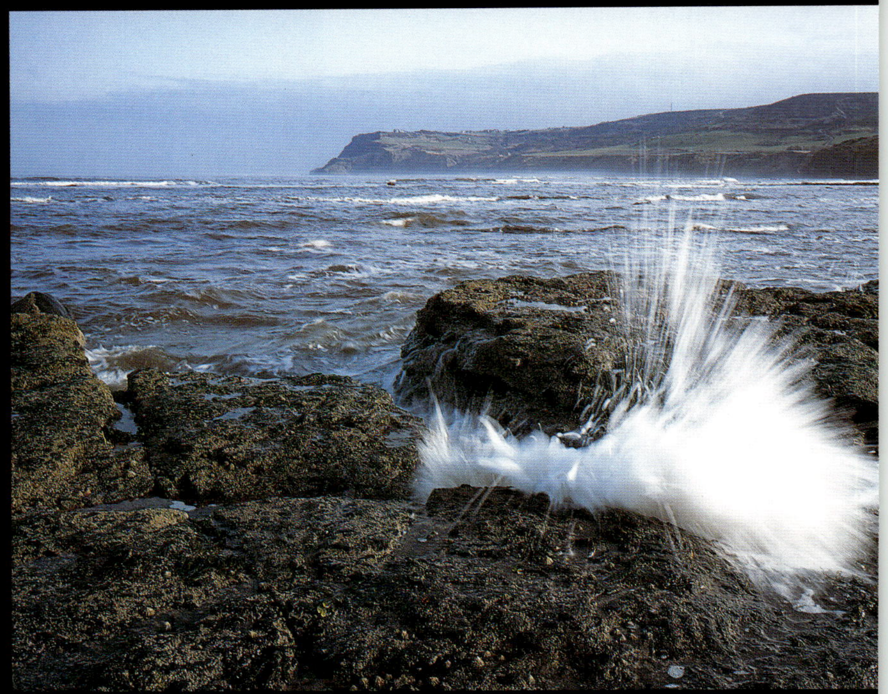

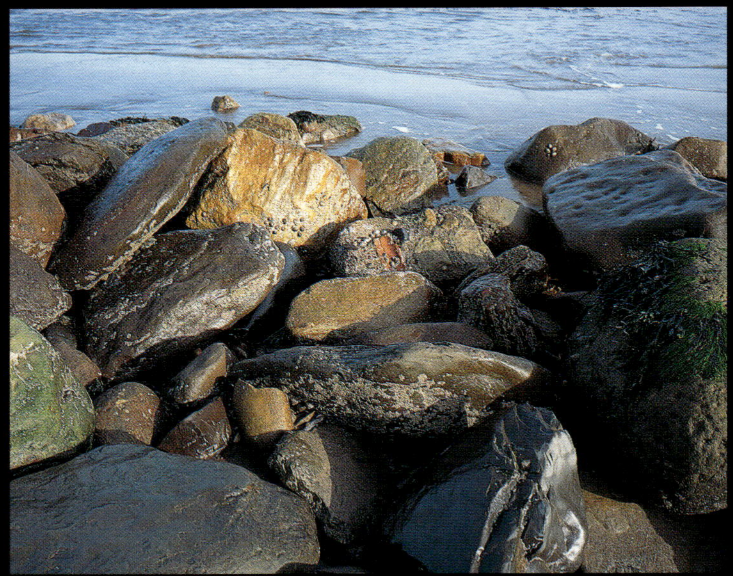

Landscapes such as this reed marsh can be improved by adding rustic human elements. The disused windpump is on Dingle Marshes in Suffolk, England. The light metering was difficult due to rapidly changing conditions and extreme cold, which made a hand-held meter difficult to use.
Fuji GSW69III, 1/30sec at f/11, Velvia, tripod.

I shot this image of spray jetting up from the waves and breaking over a rocky brig at Robin Hood's Bay, North Yorkshire, England.
Mamiya 7II + 65mm lens, Velvia, tripod.

Wet stones always make an attractive subject for coastal photography.
Mamiya 7II + 65mm lens, Velvia, tripod.

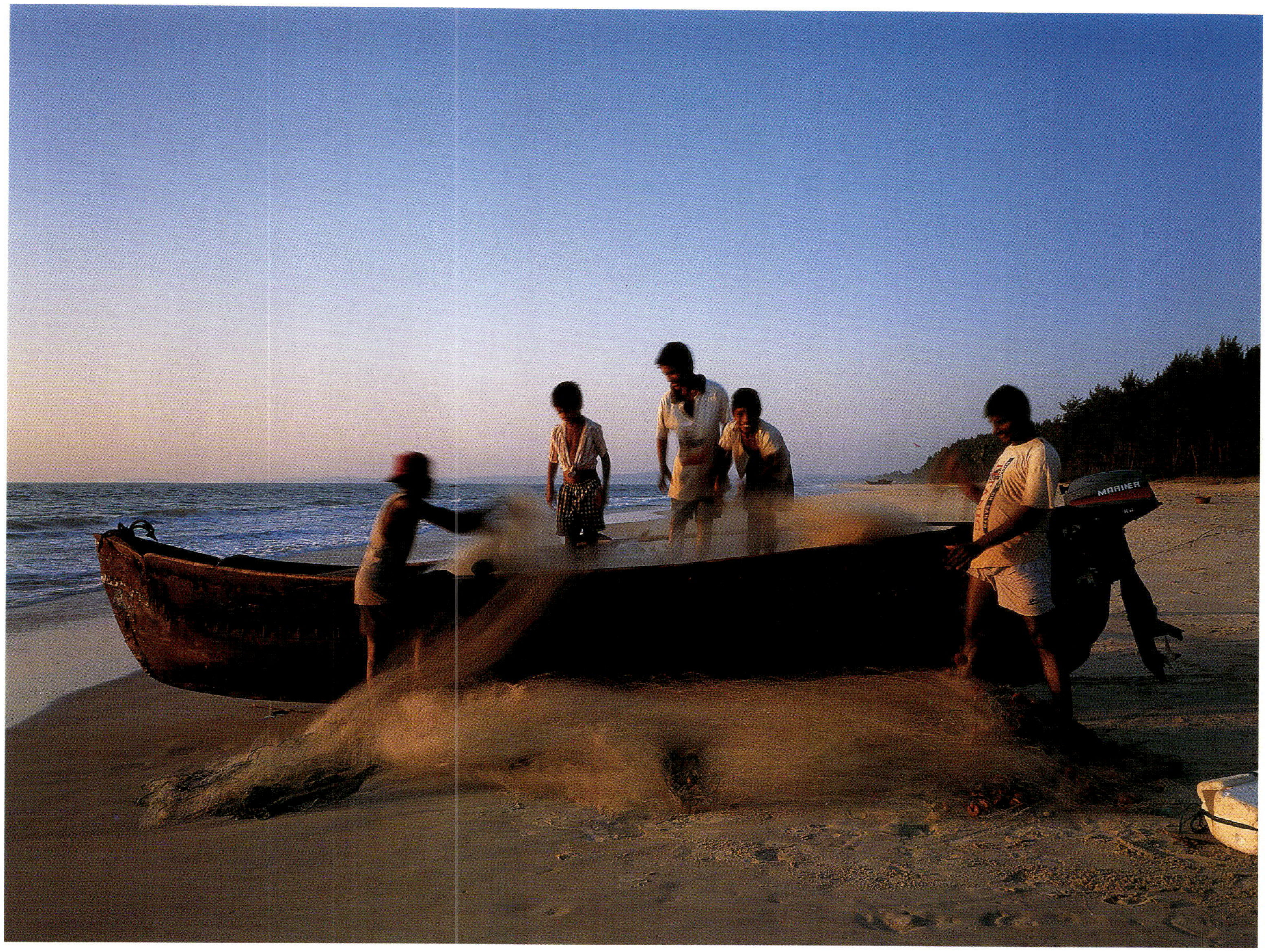

cliffs can be found at Bempton where, in early summer, gannets, puffins, cormorants, kittiwakes and razorbills amass to raise their offspring. Rocky brigs project their sinuous arms out to sea at Robin Hood's Bay, while sandy coves hug the land at Runswick Bay and Sandsend. I love trying to catch sea spray on film, particularly as the waves impact on a rocky brig, which renders water as a photogenic frothy, white curtain (providing action in an otherwise passive landscape). I have spent many an hour trying to catch the pinnacle of this display on my Mamiya, usually with a wide-angle lens. Saltwater and sand are anathema to both modern electronic and

These fishermen let me photograph them for a few rupees. They had just returned from sea and were sorting their catch. The beaches of Goa in India where this picture was taken are extremely photogenic.
Fuji GA645Wi, Velvia, tripod.

older mechanical cameras, so take precautions to protect your gear. Several times I have yanked my tripod-borne camera out of harm's way just in the nick of time. I generally use Velvia, pre-focus where I

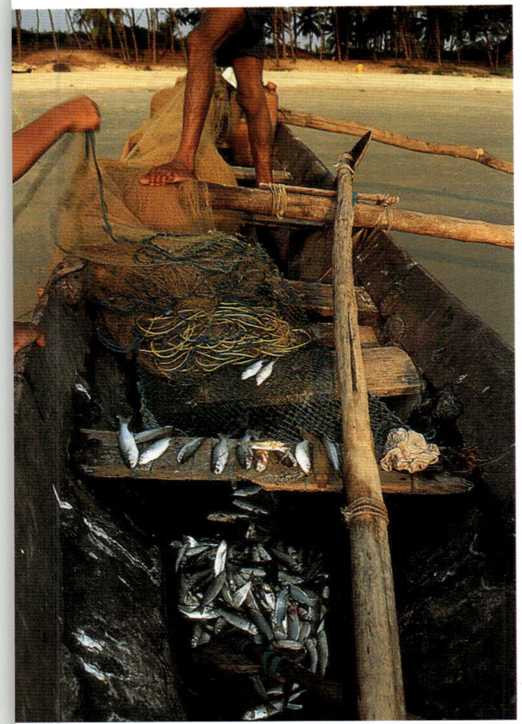

I used 35mm equipment for this picture, shooting hand-held to provide increased flexibility to capture the essence of the Goan fishermen's enduring ritual.
Pentax MZ5n + 28–70mm zoom lens.

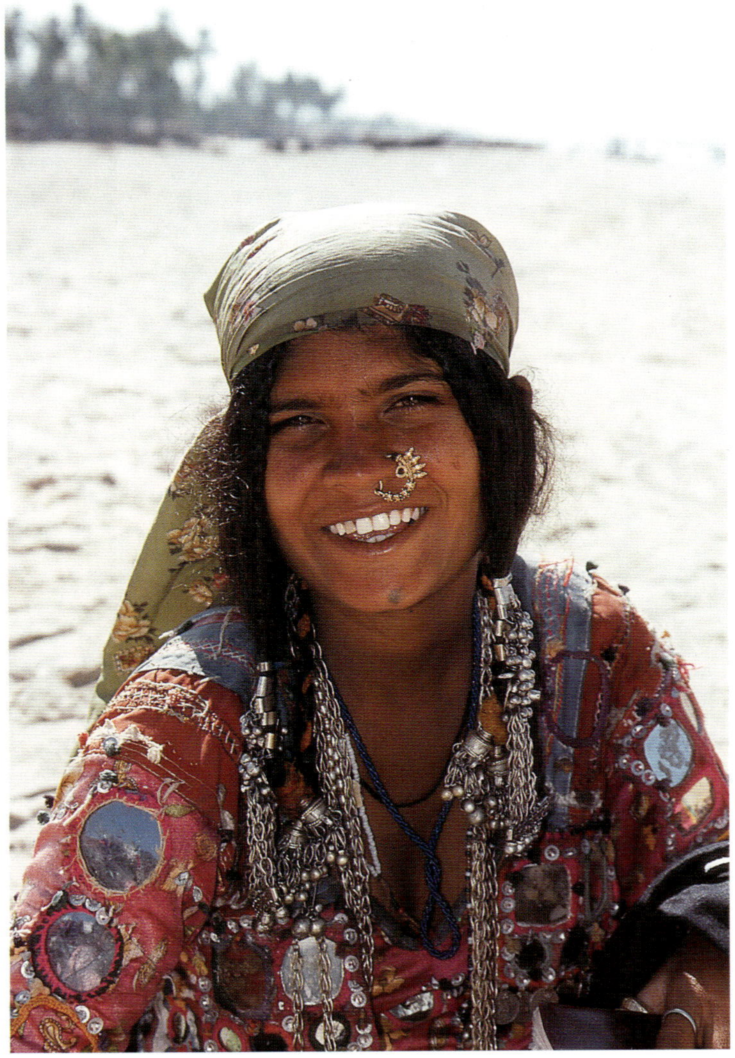

Even in the height of the tropical day, beaches provide a panoply of interesting material to photograph. Beach traders in India are always colourful and photogenic.
Pentax MZ5n + 28–70mm zoom lens.

expect the wave to break on the rocks, and set at around f/16–22. A telephoto lens would keep the camera out of harm's way, but reduce the depth of field, which I like to maintain wherever possible.

For many keen amateur and professional photographers, the object of seascape photography is to conjure up a conceptual image, for example palm trees on golden sands lapped by a calm, turquoise sea. These clichéd shots are generally taken at places like La Digue in the Seychelles, and help sell a dream through an idealized image. Concept images of this nature are great for selling pictures through libraries, but I prefer to add interest such as fishing boats with nets being repaired or reeled in. Goa in India is an excellent place to catch local fishermen at work on beautiful, tropical beaches. I have caught this on my Fuji GA645Wi at sunset and in the height of the day on my 35mm kit. I paid a few rupees for the privilege, and was allowed to set my 645 rangefinder up on its tripod and shoot away as they sorted out their catch. I tried to record everything: nets being folded, fish piled up in the boat, etc. I returned the following evening and repeated the procedure with my Pentax 35mm kit. A 28–70mm zoom was quite adequate, using the built in RTF flash of my MZ5n to provide a little fill-in lighting.

Quite often it is impossible to catch a beach empty enough to produce a classic library shot of palms, sand and turquoise sea. You need to get up early to avoid the crowds. There are, however, other ways to tackle the problem. In Queensland I was frustrated not to be able to find a classic view, devoid of people and churned-up sand. What I ended up doing was finding a lone rock to act as a focal point in the foreground in a sea of sand. I shot directly out to sea and incorporated a small, offshore tropical island in the frame. For me the scene conjured up a remote and beautiful tropical beach free from human intervention – that is, apart from the lady who did a pirhouette for me in front of my 43mm wide-angle lens momentarily before I exposed the frame. It seems she thought the picture needed something to liven it up.

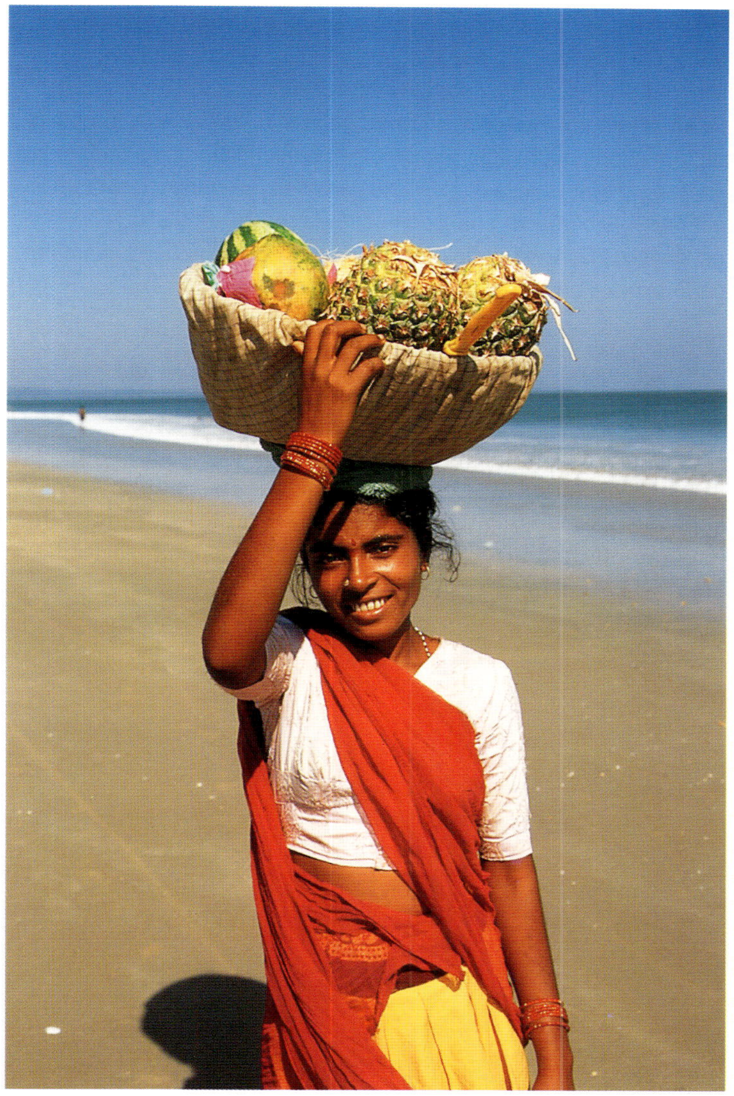

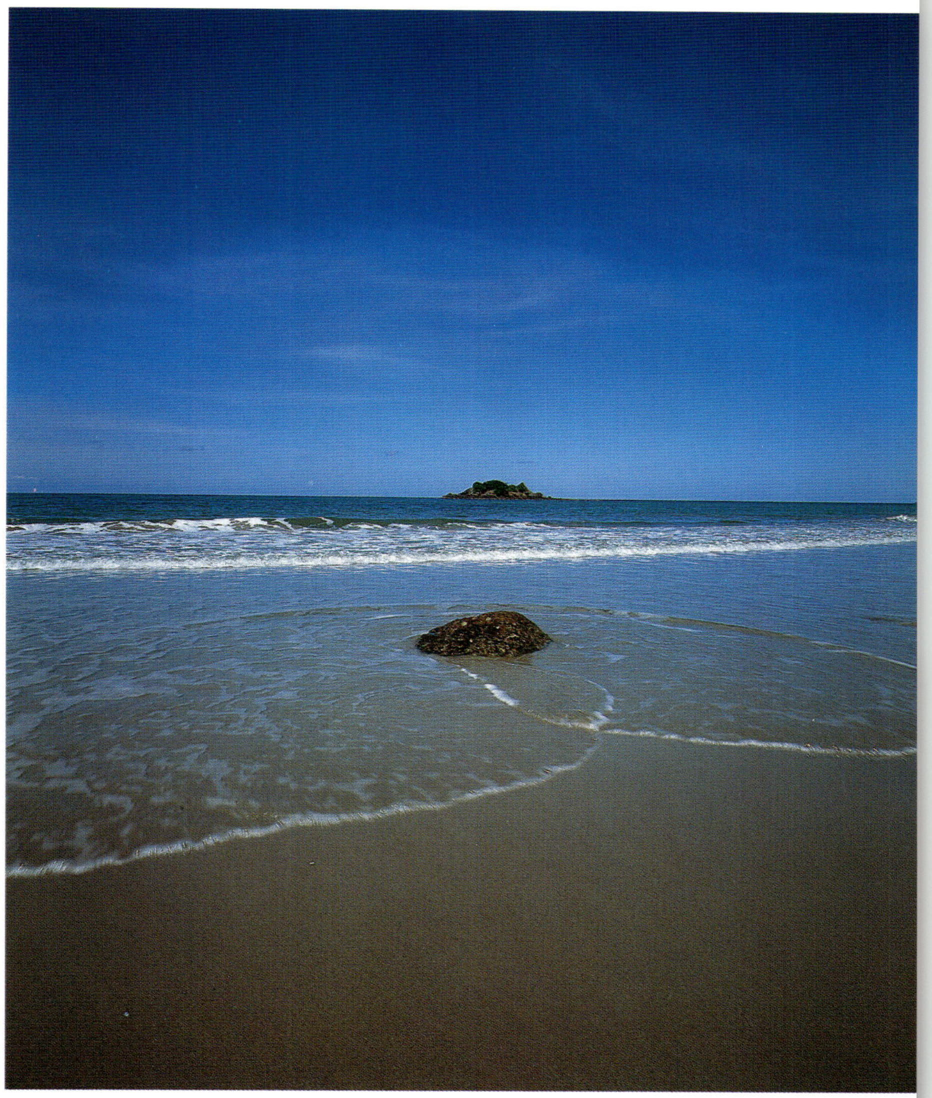

Beaches, particularly hot, sandy ones can be cruel places for cameras (for humans, too). Grains of sand will ruin even the best camera, while heat can damage film, delicate mechanisms and bondings. I never hang around on sandy beaches in hot climates with my camera unless I'm waiting for a sunset. Sunsets can often be quite incredible with a glassy sea reflecting vermilion hues from the dropping sun. Fortuitously, the automatic exposure control of a camera will read to underexpose sunsets, enhancing all colours.

If, like many photographers, you have difficulty finding a people-free, palm-fringed beach, do as I did in India: shoot a coconut palm silhouetted against a fiery setting sun. It doesn't matter much about

Looking out towards the Great Barrier Reef, I saw this lone island with a rock in the immediate foreground. As the beach was littered with walkers, I aimed out to sea to try and catch the essence of a tropical seaside location without the crowds. ***Mamiya 7II + 43mm lens, Velvia, tripod.***

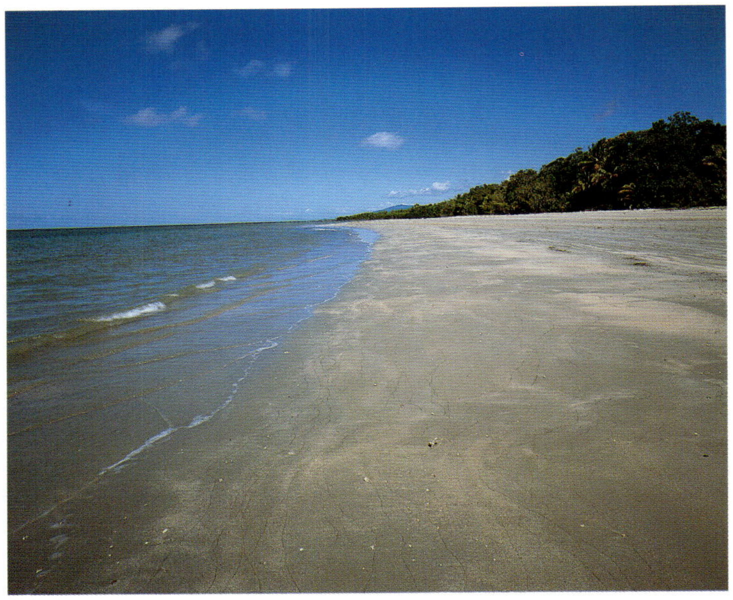

the rest of the landscape. I found an isolated, straggly palm next to the sea which, by day, was quite ugly, but made an excellent silhouette to act as a foil for the tropical sunset.

Just remember one basic photographic rule whenever shooting on a beach in bright light: bracket by overexposing up to two stops (in half-stop increments). This is just in case the metering system is not capable of reading the scene accurately. As discussed previously, they tend to be calibrated to 18% grey and will, therefore, underexpose brighter than average scenes like tropical beaches.

This is perhaps more akin to the classic view of an idyllic beach. This series of shots should include two similar scenes showing overhanging palms, but guess who forgot to take the lens cap off his rangefinder? Taken in Queensland, Australia. *Mamiya 7II + 43mm lens, Velvia, tripod.*

I was really fortunate to have this boat with a paraglider attached appearing in view just as I was framing the sunset. It adds further interest to an already engaging view. *Pentax 738S, Velvia.*

This gorgeous sunset was taken in Goa, India. The palm actually looked rather scruffy in daylight, but it was perfect as a silhouette to complement the sinking sun.
Fuji GA645Wi, 1 second at f/22, Velvia, tripod.

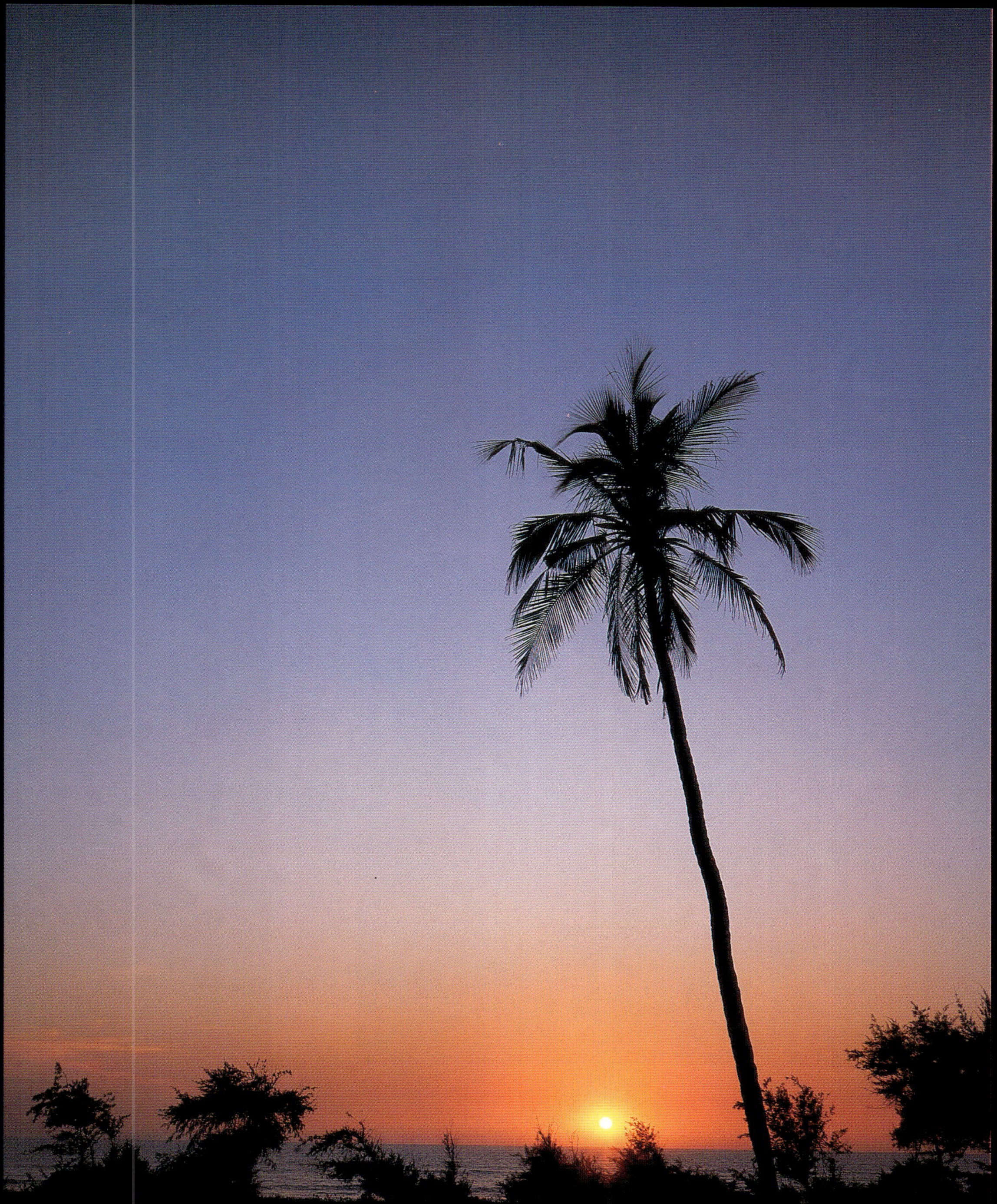

Still water

By still water I mean lakes, reservoirs, ponds and all variations on that theme, from puddles to billabongs. Just as well-executed imagery of tropical beaches conjures up an idyll that makes us wish we were there, so still water engenders a sense of calm and tranquillity. Reflections and gentle ripples in water contribute to this feeling of serenity. Again, although one should perhaps be thinking along concept lines when supplying libraries with shots of still water, I still prefer to look for some detail and story in an image. For example, what could be more different from the 6 x 6cm Hasselblad shot of Rydal Water taken in the height of winter in the English Lake District, and the 35mm images I took in the height of the Australian winter at Yellow Waters Billabong, an isolated backwater spilling over from the South Alligator River. One was –2°C the other +35°C. The Rydal Water shot would not look out of place on a calendar, postcard or box of chocolates. In other words, it sells a concept more than a story. The reflections of weeping paperbarks in the receeding waters of the South Alligator River billabong not only

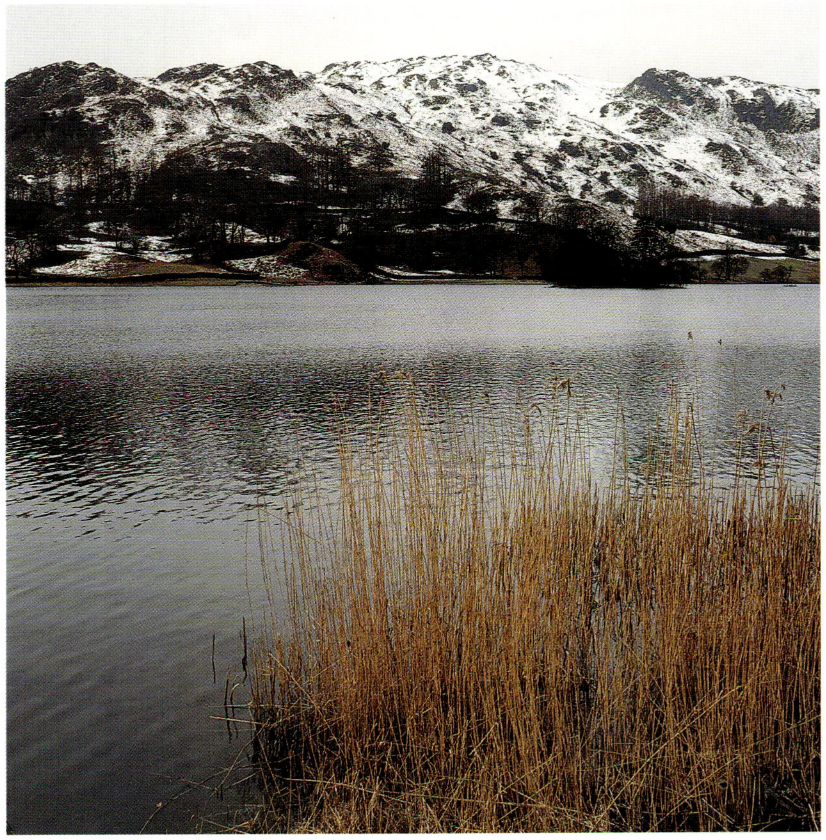

Rydal Water, Lake District. Pictures like this are staples for chocolate box manufacturers. *Hasselblad 500CM + 80mm lens.*

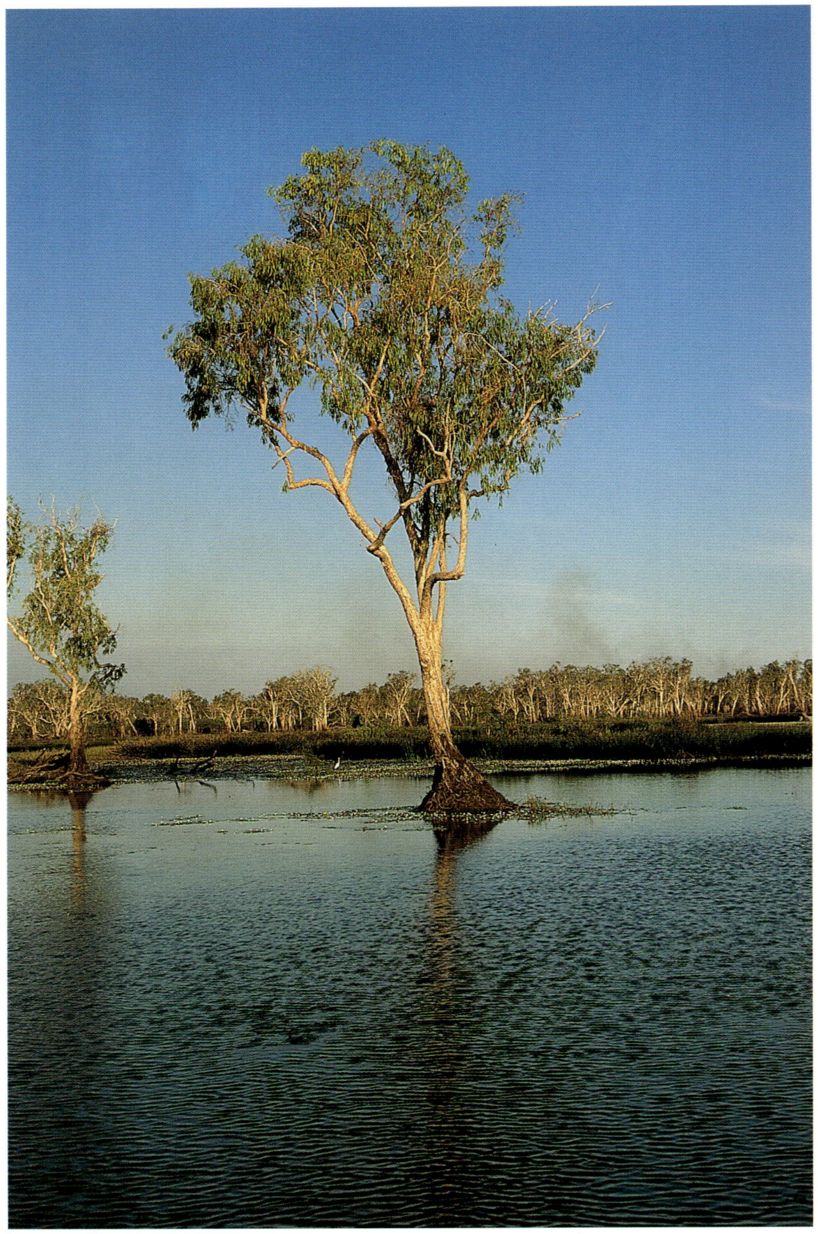

I shot this paper bark at dusk in Yellow Waters Billabong, Kakadu Australia. The tree and its reflection were taken, hand-held, from a boat. *Pentax MZ5n + 28–70mm zoom lens, Velvia.*

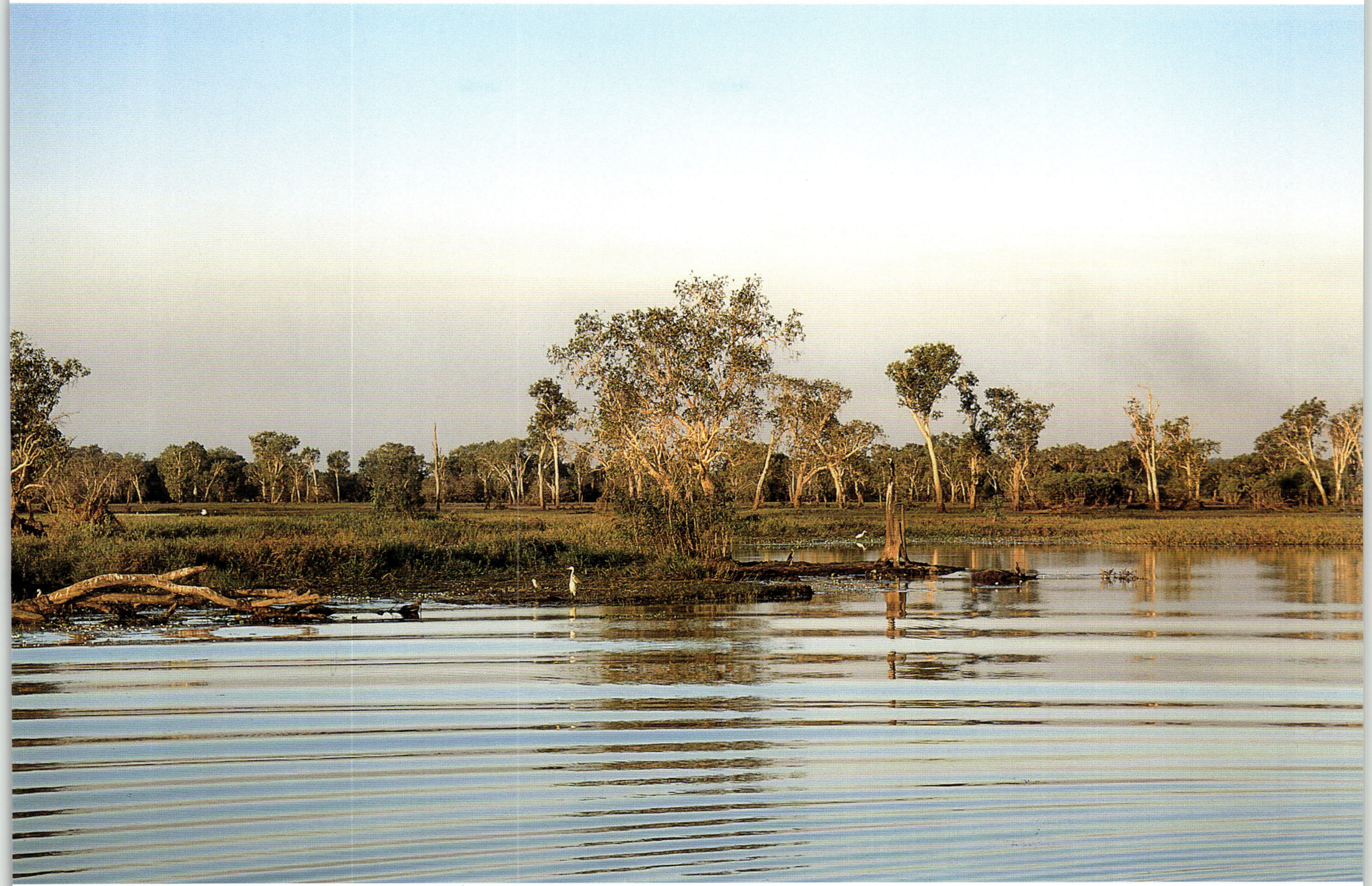

reveal an infinitely more complex ecosystem than Rydal Water, they go further in satisfying many of the criteria that qualify an image as fine art. The same is true of the Menara Pavilion in Marrakesh and its watery reflection (overleaf). Both the billabong and pavilion images are unusual and, while as images they are complete, they also have a certain mystique. The same cannot be said of the Rydal image. This is just one of the qualities which, while difficult to articulate, separates a fine art image from a pretty record shot.

I took this view of the water's edge at a billabong just before dusk. It was taken, hand-held, from a boat. I love the way the light, birds and the texture of the water conspire to engender a real 'wish I was there' feeling.
Pentax MZ5n + 28–70mm zoom, Velvia.

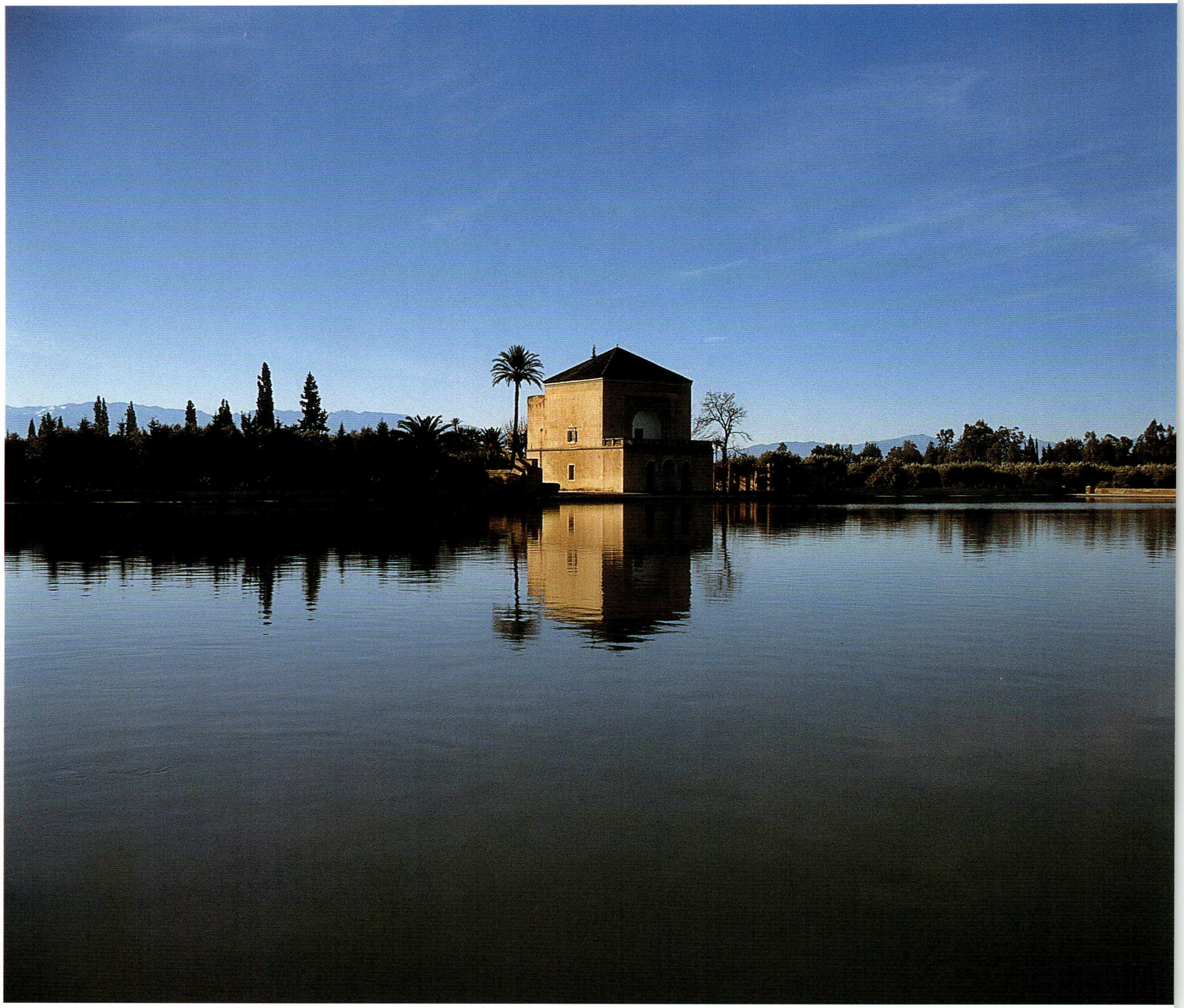

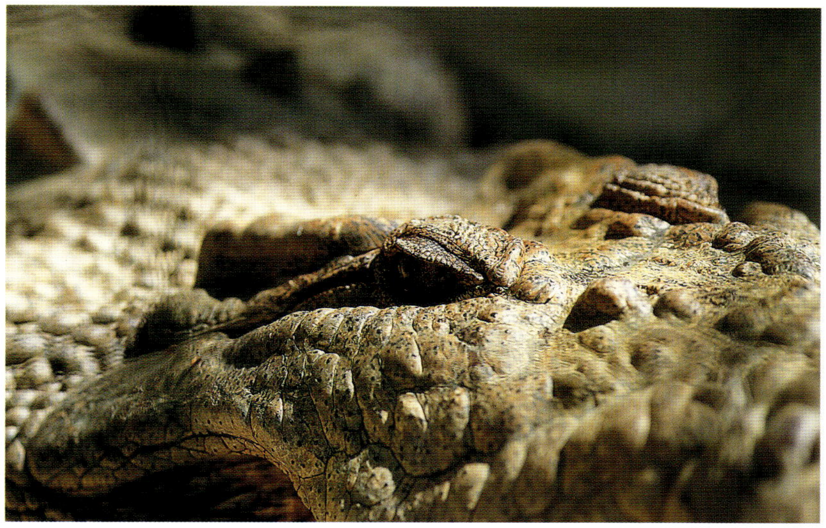

If you photograph an environmental scene – an Australian billabong, for example – you have to shoot some of the creatures which inhabit it, especially when they are as interesting as saltwater crocodiles. Unsurprisingly, I didn't take too much notice of the setting for this close-up 'Saltie' shot. *Pentax MZ5n + 100mm macro lens.*

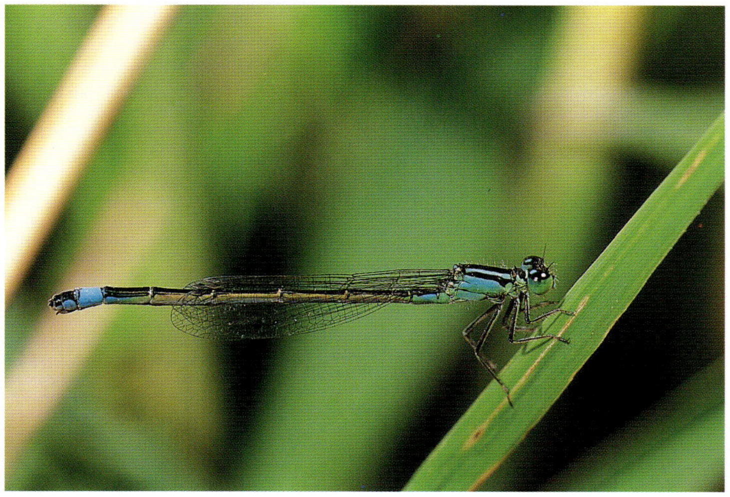

One of the reasons why I like the environment around still water is the profusion of interesting creatures that can be found in its proximity. This image of a blue-tailed damselfly was shot on waterside vegetation using a macro lens and TTL flash balanced with the ambient exposure. *Pentax LX + 100mm macro lens, Velvia.*

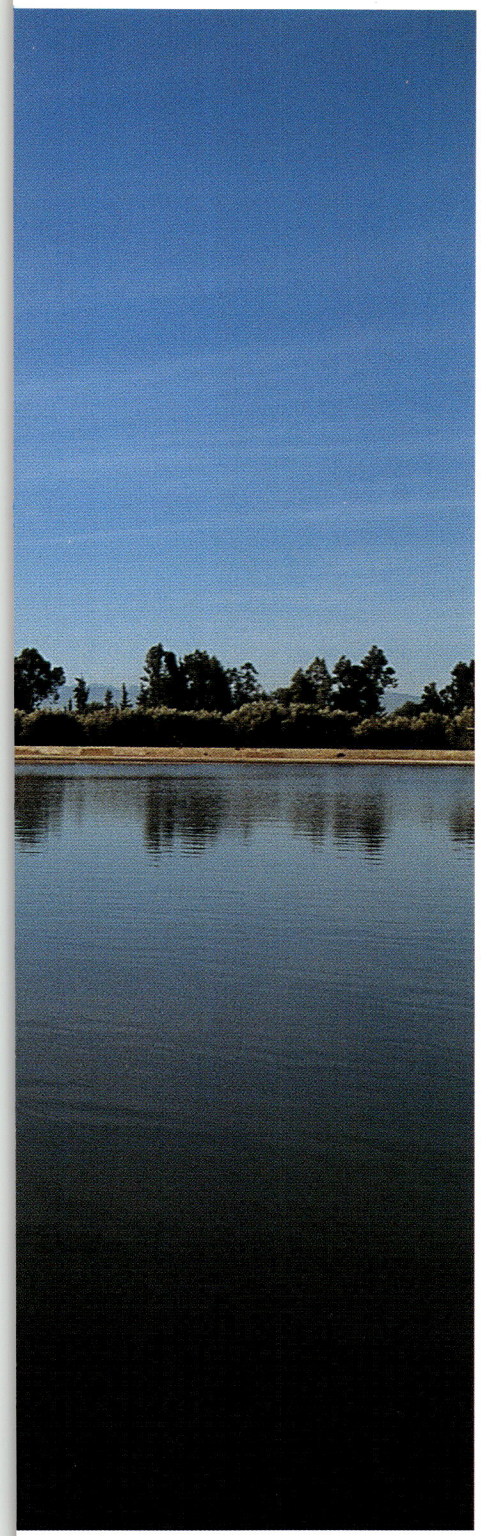

Menara Pavilion, Marrakesh, Morocco. *Pentax MZ5 + 28–70mm zoom lens, Velvia.*

In terms of environmental photography, it is not hard to accumulate several diverse images, all held together via their intricate association with a billabong. For example, billabong trees at sunset, gum trees reflecting in the still water, estuarine and freshwater crocodiles, Australian pelicans, darters, jacanas, monitor lizards, lilies, flood plains, etc. In one afternoon you can easily have a complete set of images to reflect the whole landscape and its component parts. The same cannot be said for all environments. Rydal Water may have many moods to shoot according to time of day and season, but it would not be so easy to photograph the lake's component parts in a way that offers the diverse interest and shows the vibrancy of a Northern Territory billabong.

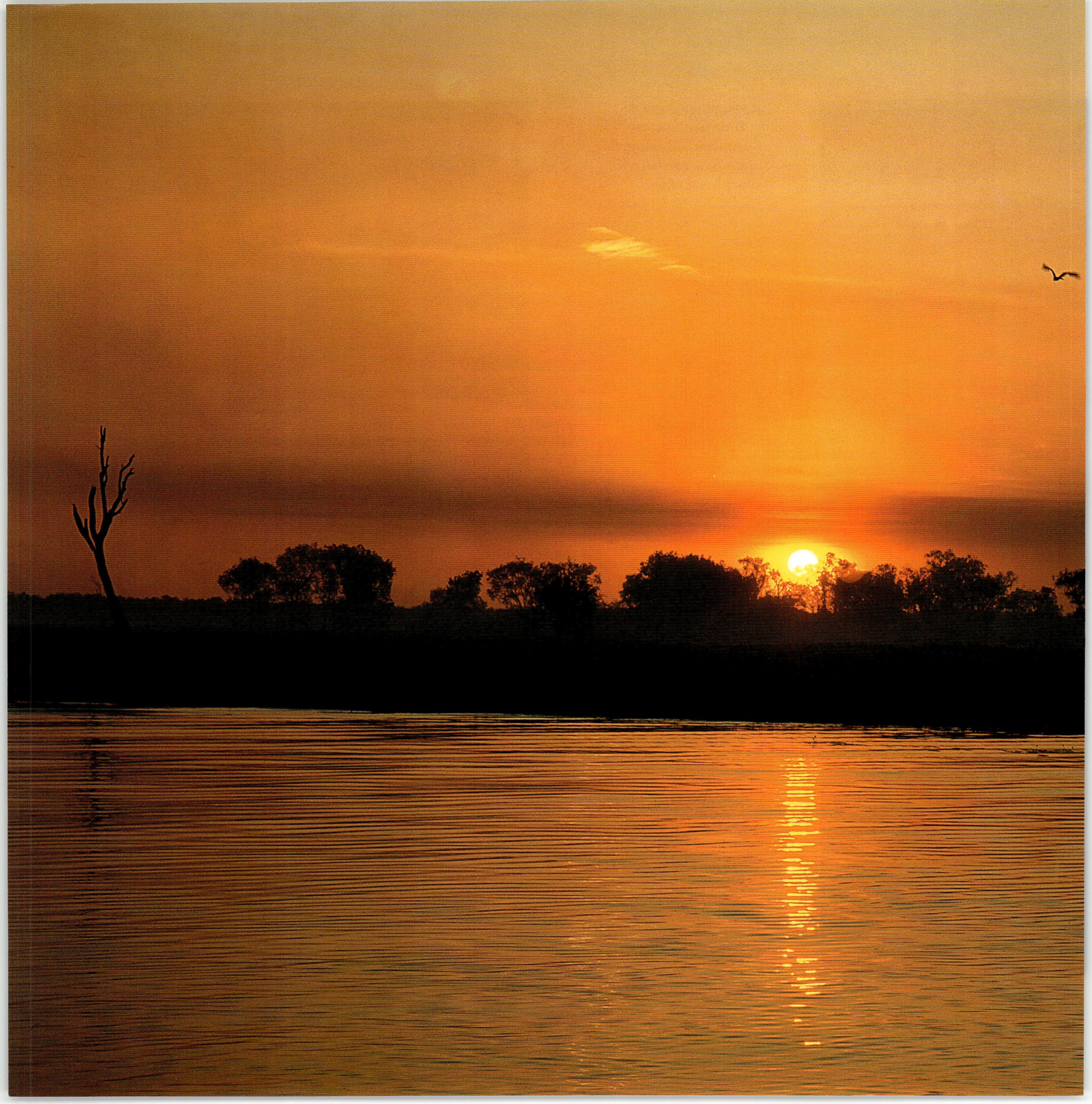

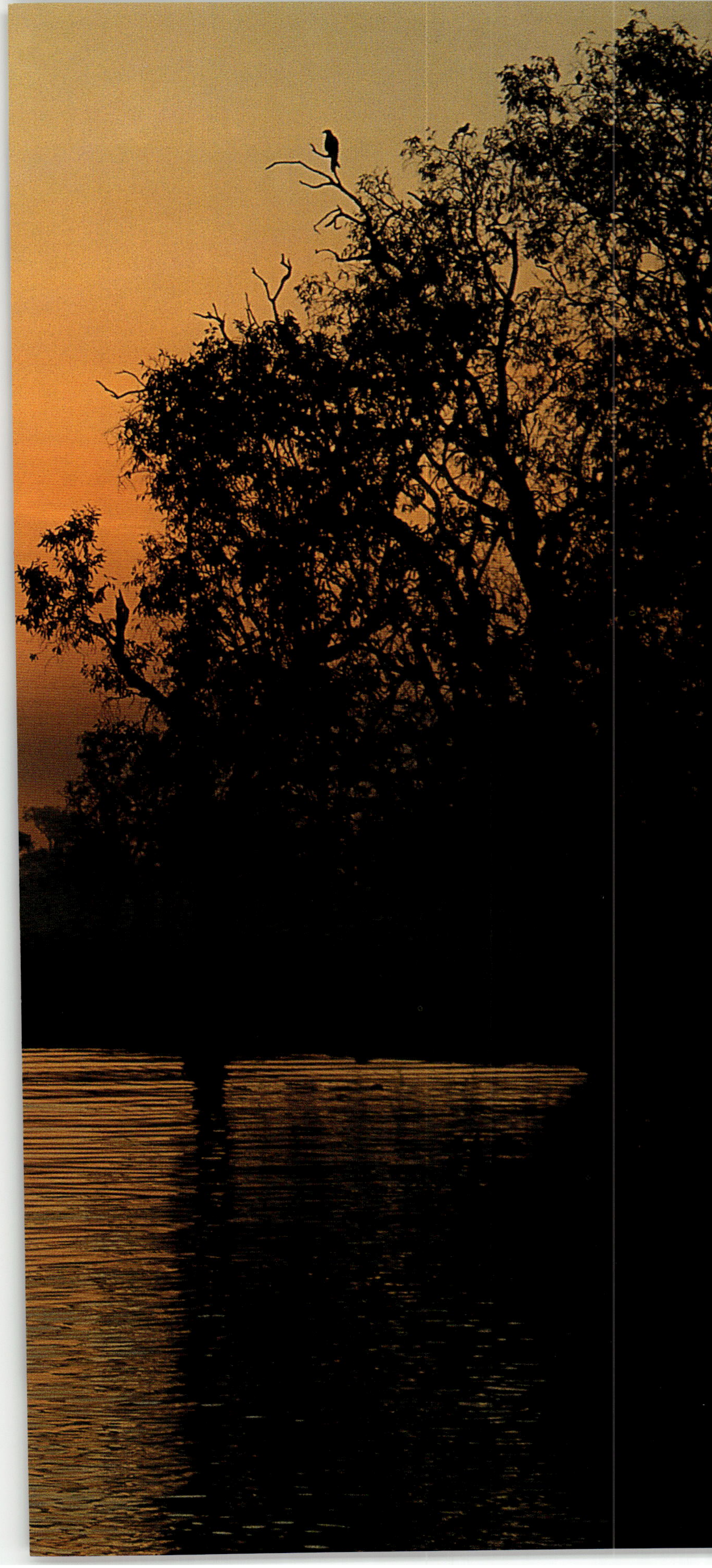

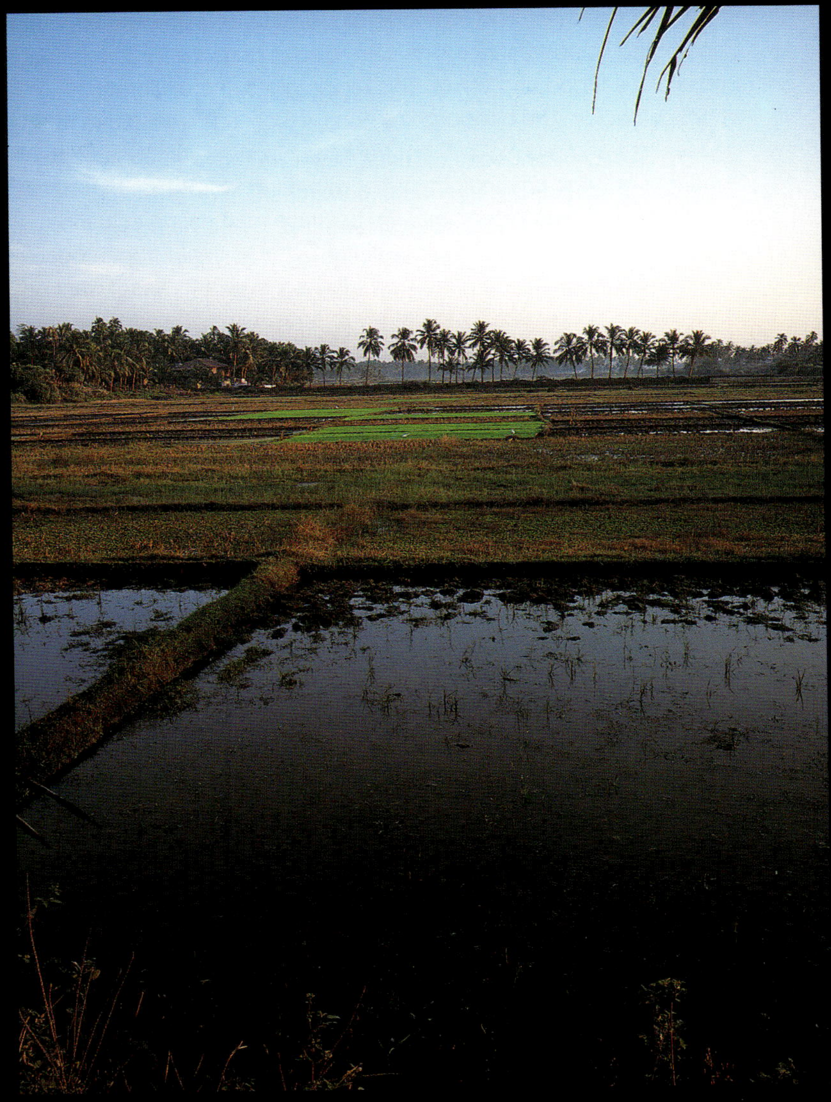

Silhouette of a raptor at sunset. Taken at Yellow Waters Billabong, Kakadu National Park, Australia. *Pentax MZ5n + 28–70mm zoom lens, Velvia (and mosquito repellant).*

Here is an interesting example of still water, just before dusk. I stayed in a small guesthouse next to this flooded paddy field in India. It was brilliant to sit and watch all of the herons, kingfishers and raptors feeding. *Fuji GA645Wi, Velvia, tripod.*

Of course these two examples of still water require very different photographic approaches. The Lake District begs the largest format possible, a tripod and Velvia. This recipe gives sharp, vibrant transparencies. The billabong, by comparison, requires 35mm equipment and more of a shoot-from-the-hip style. Although I did shoot billabongs on medium format with a tripod from their shoreline, I wouldn't recommend it because man-eating estuarine crocodiles are thick on the ground. Far better to shoot from a boat using 35mm equipment hand-held, and a range of lenses. I went on two billabong boat safaris to get my images. I imagine everybody thought I was a bit odd. On the second trip, every time wildlife was spotted, the pilot drew the boat to a halt. I would then move to the opposite side of the boat to everyone else and shoot the landscape. Free from competition, I could use the boat railings to stabilize the camera and even manage to shoot an amazing landscape at f/16 on Velvia in the failing light of dusk.

Despite the obvious opportunities for a range of photography in the given examples, whenever travelling abroad, I probably make more of the total environment than I do at home. This is because it is often a one-off opportunity for me, and I do not want to waste the possibility of capturing every facet on film. In my own country I like to make more use of medium- and large-formats for lakes and reservoirs. This allows me to spend more time and make as much of a single scene as possible from an artistic viewpoint, which is not so easy to achieve in the limited time frame of a journey abroad.

Flowing water

If still water elicits a feeling of serenity and calm, flowing water has connotations of cleansing freshness and purity which, photographically, provides an excellent means for selling concepts, from toothpaste to lemonade.

My favourite flowing water scenes almost invariably contain a waterfall or cascade of rushing water. Waterfall images are actually quite hard to mess up. However, to get the very best from a waterfall image there are certain rules to follow. First and foremost is safety; wet rocks are almost always slippery and plunge pools can be deep and treacherous. From a photographic viewpoint, if foaming white water dominates a scene it will often require extra exposure to compensate for its unnatural brightness. I have given up to +1.5 EV stops in the past to get this right. I feel that the best waterfall shots contain plenty of foreground interest, for example water swirling around emergent rocks or a frame of luxuriant foliage.

Many countries have areas rich in waterfalls. I am fortunate to live near one such area in the Yorkshire Dales, and to have travelled to another, quite remarkable area where delicate, moderate and cataclysmic waterfalls abound. This area, on the Atherton Tablelands

The Colorado River is at its best as it flows through Professor Valley, USA.
Pentax MZ5 + 28–70mm zoom lens.

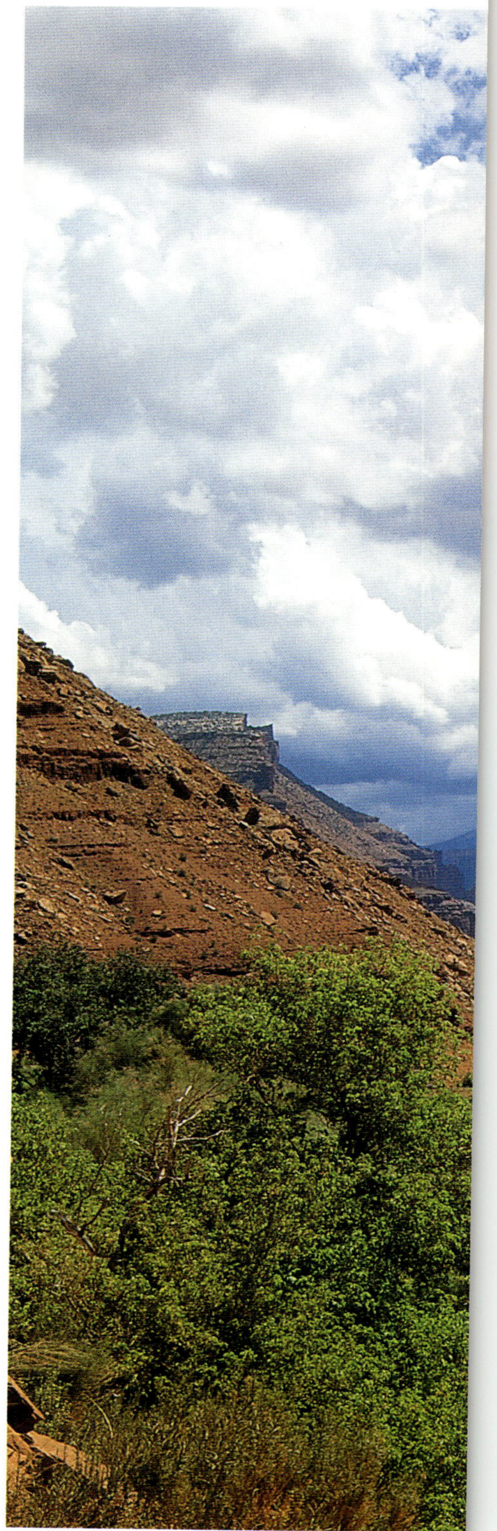

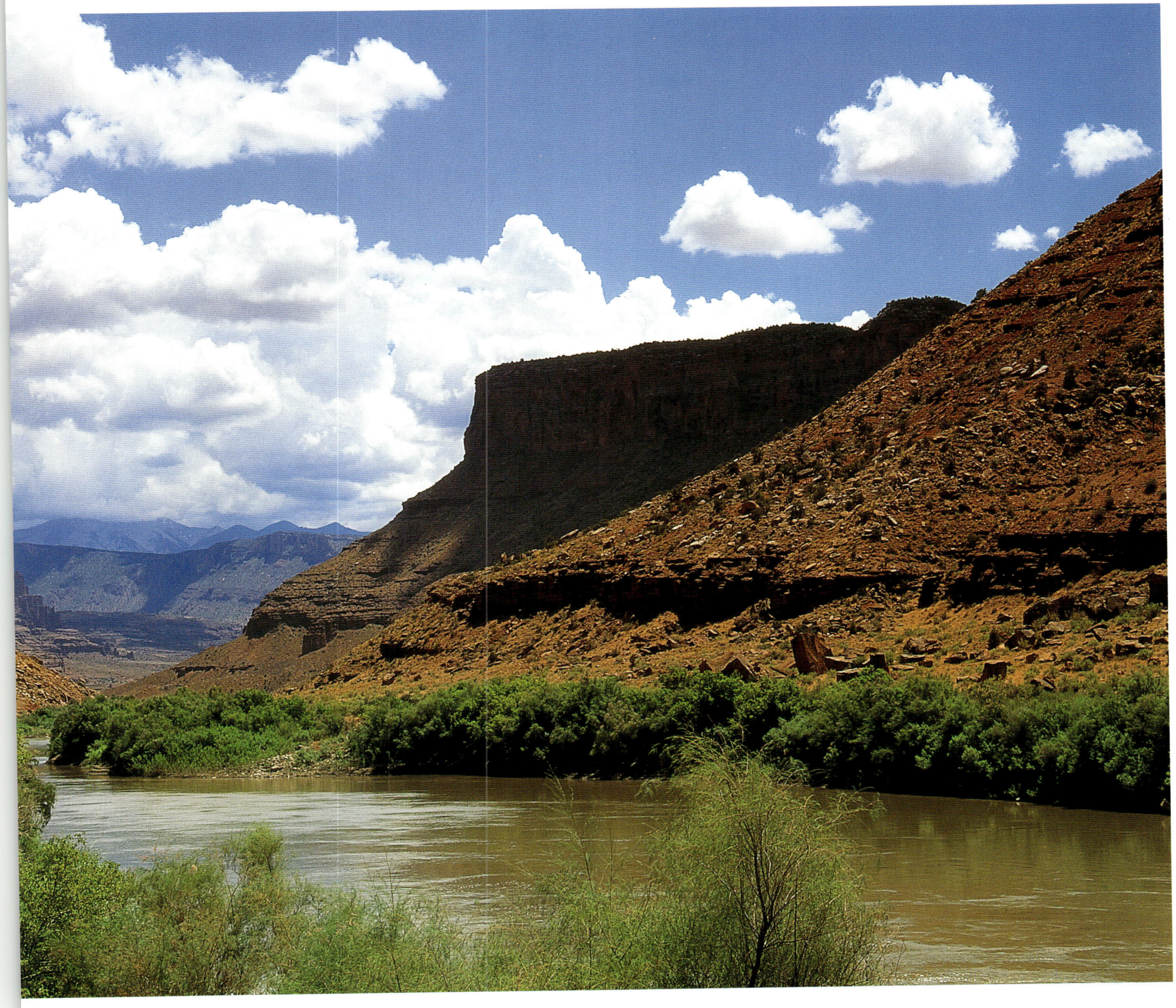

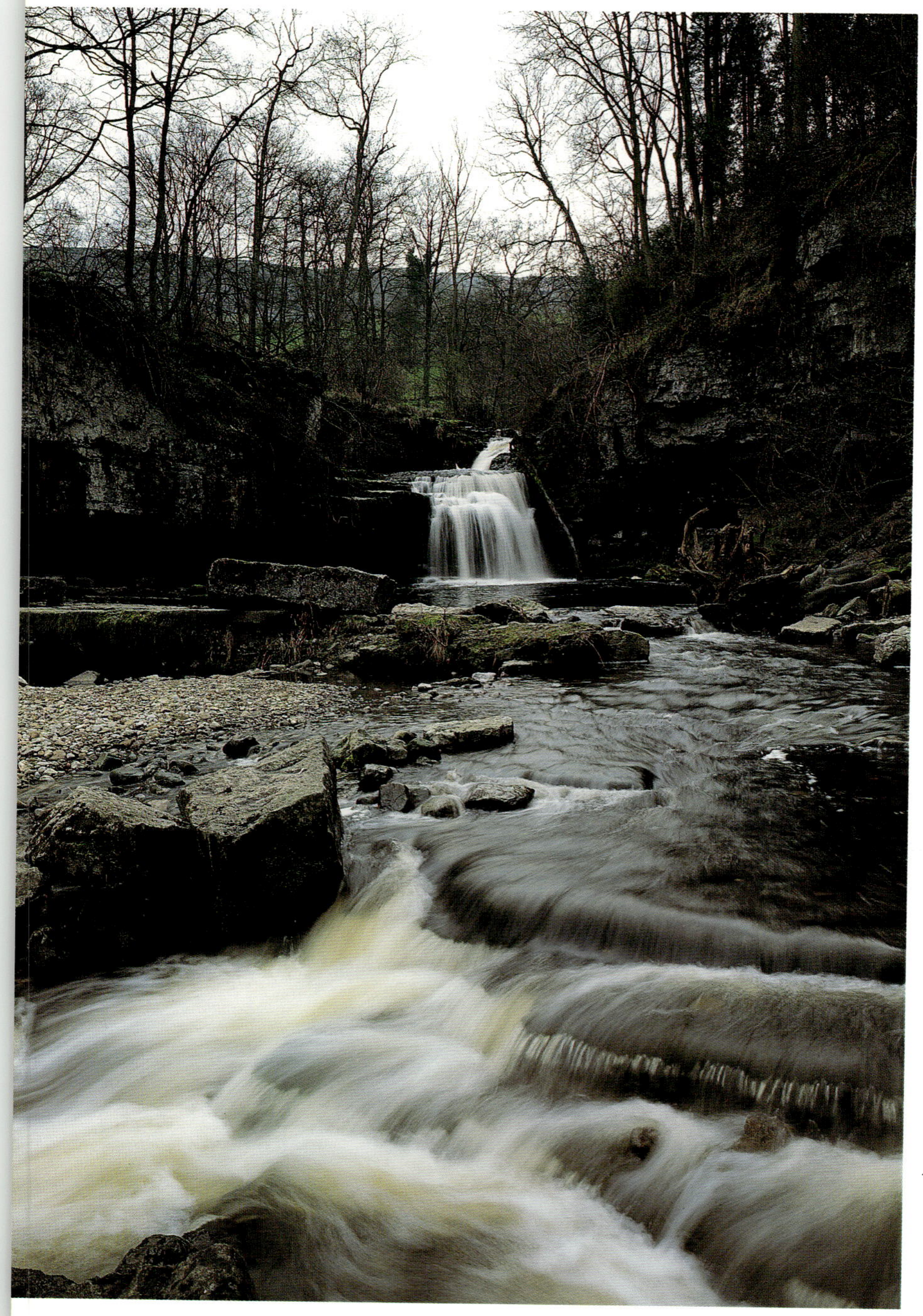

West Burton Waterfall, Yorkshire Dales, England. In this image, the waterfall plays second fiddle to the swirling foreground water.
Fuji GSW69III, Velvia, tripod.

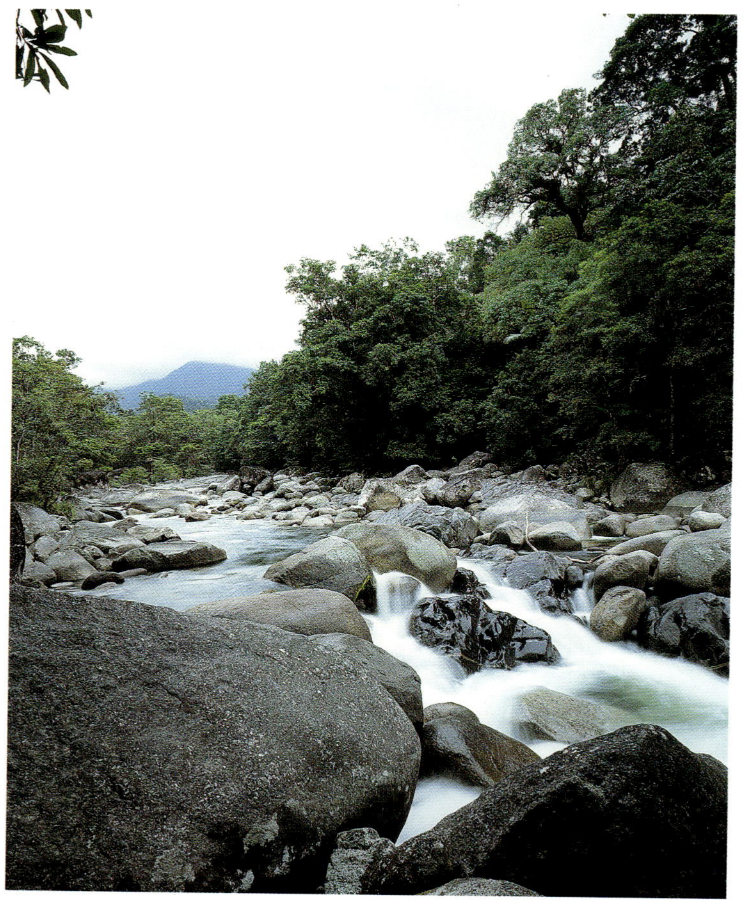

This shot evokes all those connotations – cool, fresh, zingy – often associated with fast-flowing mountain streams. I was delicately balanced amidst the white water to take it. Queensland, Australia.
Mamiya 7II + 43mm lens, tripod.

in Queensland contains, without question, some of the world's most photogenic cascades. Even the names are exotic: Millaa Millaa Falls, Zillie Falls, Ellinjaa Falls. If, by comparison, the Yorkshire Dales contain relatively humble waterfalls, they do let you get really close so you can integrate turbulence around rocks at the base of the falls. My two favourite Dales waterfalls are West Burton Falls and East Gill Force, but don't overlook Hardraw Force either. This is the tallest waterfall in England and can only be accessed through the Green Dragon pub near Hawes; a particularly attractive feature of these falls (see page 30). Unfortunately, many of the Atherton Tablelands falls are not as easy to get close to; even in the dry

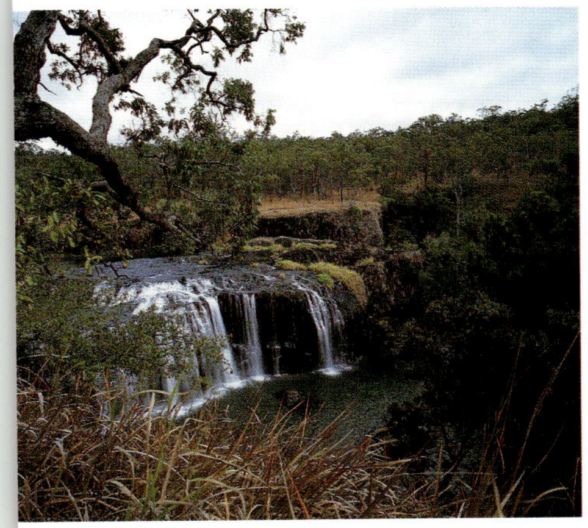

This picture shows Millstream Falls, the widest cascade in Australia. I purposely placed the tree branch to lead into the scene, and the grass to give foreground interest. I used f/22 to maximize the depth of field.
Mamiya 7II + 43mm lens, f/22, Velvia, tripod.

I took several views of Millaa Millaa Falls on the Atherton Tablelands, Queensland, Australia. This one was a straight 35mm shot.
Pentax MZ5n + 28–70mm zoom lens, Velvia.

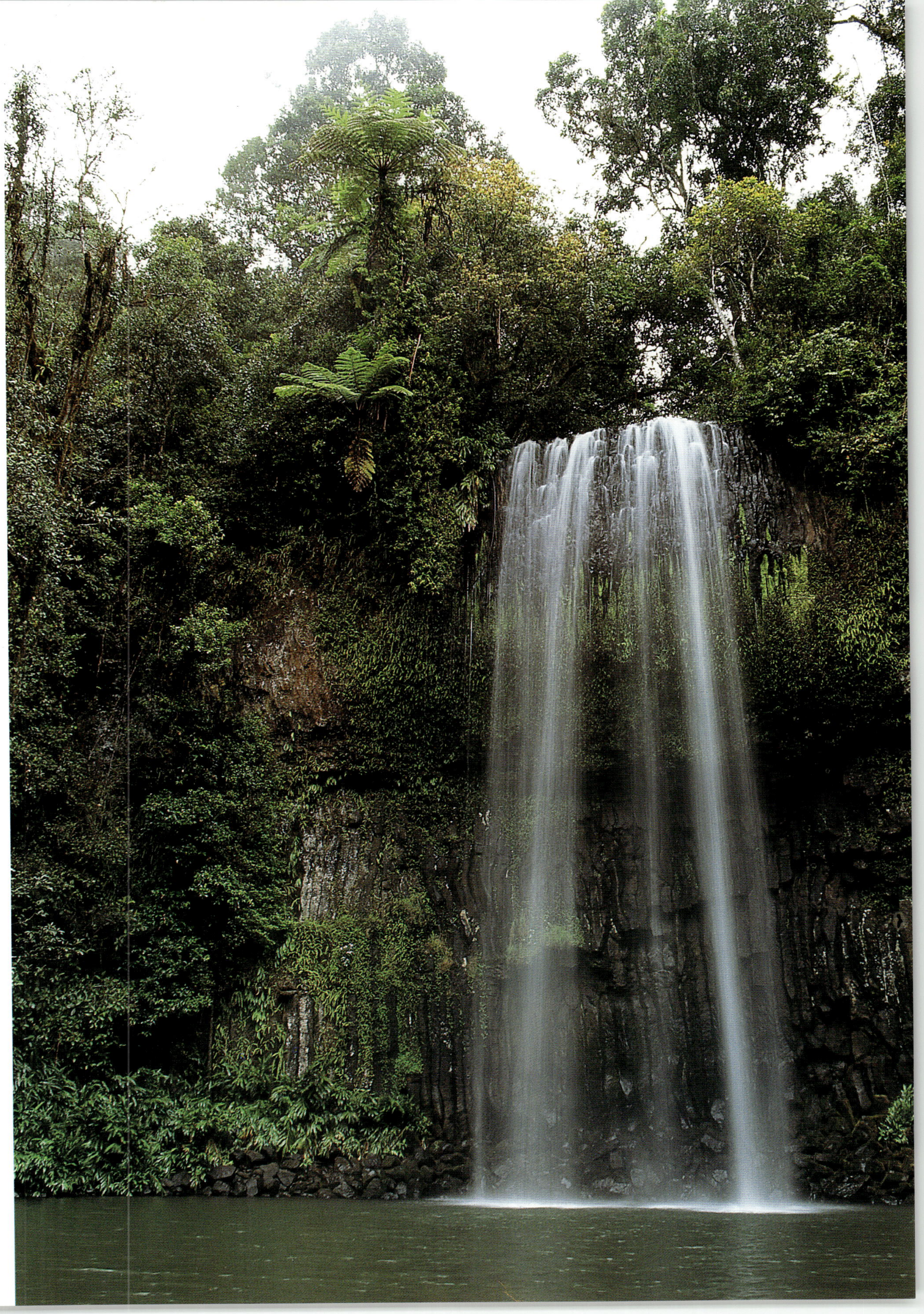

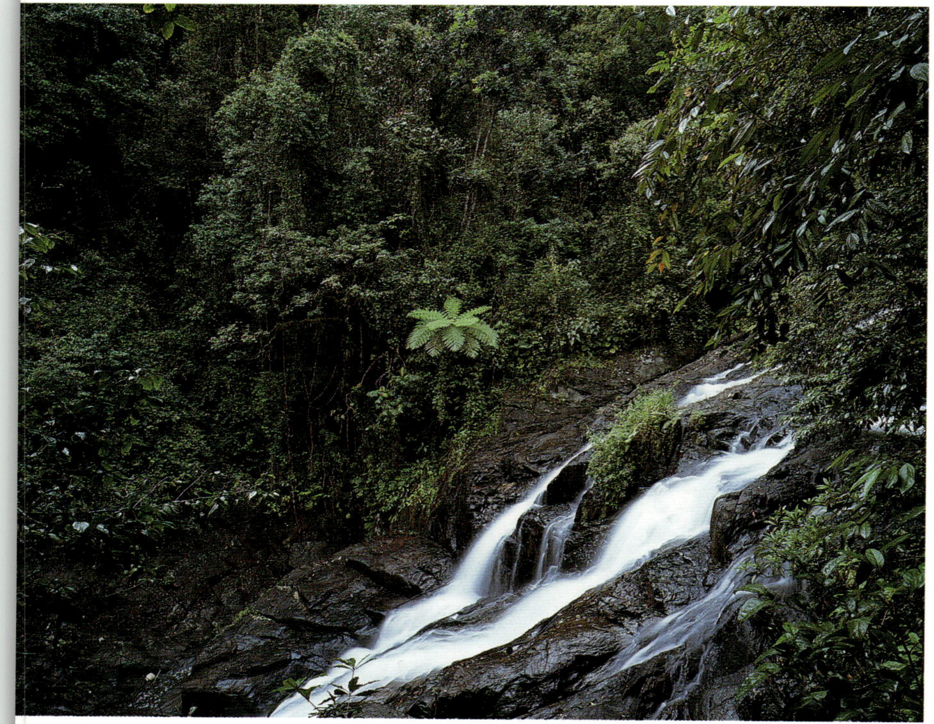

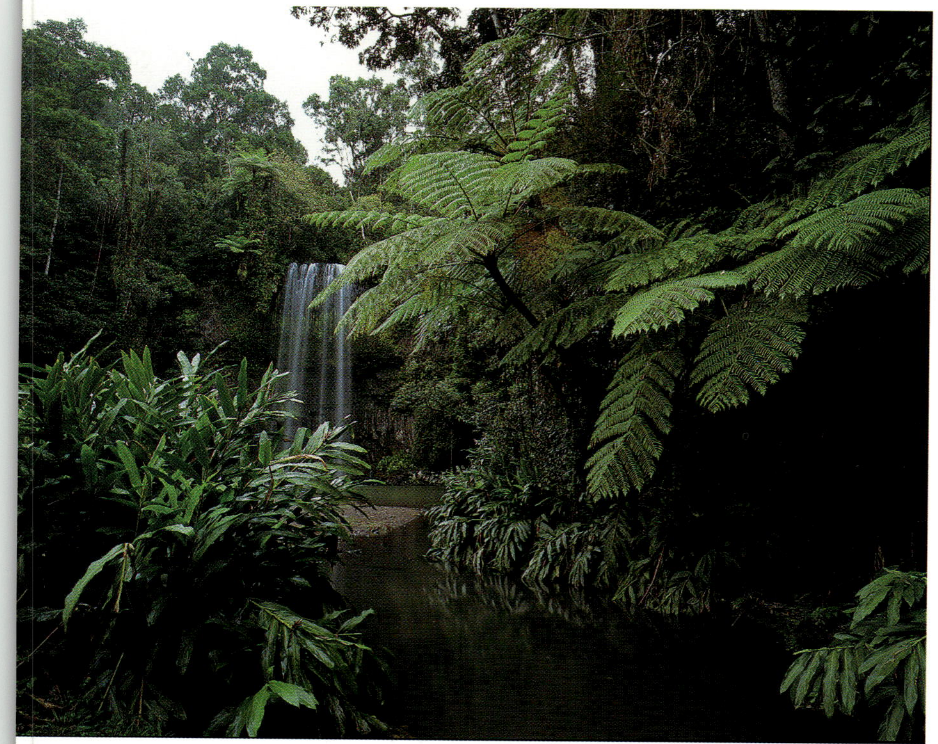

These shots of Lower Dinner Falls (top) and Millaa Millaa Falls (bottom) place the cascade as a secondary feature to the surrounding tropical vegetation. The latter required considerable patience while waiting for a people-free view.
Both images: Mamiya 7II + 43mm lens, Velvia.

Taken at Watendlath, Lake District, England, this view of a winter stream in full spate has the perfect foil of a snowy mountain backdrop.
Hasselblad 500CM + 80mm lens, Velvia, tripod.

season they can remain a raging torrent of steep, powerful white water. I shot the iconic Millaa Millaa Falls with both 35mm and 6 x 7cm formats using 28mm and 43mm lenses respectively. This tall fall is quite gentle, but has a large plunge pool, making it relatively inaccessible for close-up shots. My favourite falls on the Atherton Tablelands is Lower Dinner Falls. These are found in Mount Hypipamee National Park and are truly spectacular, as much for the magnitude of the cascading water as for the surrounding tropical vegetation. Mists here provide the icing on the cake, creating typical evocative rainforest vistas.

Big falls require either extreme wide-angle lenses to encompass the entire scene, or telephoto lenses to concentrate on the impact on the plunge pool area. I always use Velvia which, being a slow film, allows long exposures that blur water movement. The same effect can be arrived at by using neutral density filters.

In order to achieve some of my images, I have been forced to go rock-hopping across some really fast white water. As careful as I try to be, on more than one occasion I have nearly fallen in; indeed, my tripod once went swimming away down the Barron River. So, do be very careful in fast-flowing waters.

One of the biggest problems of photographing the very best waterfalls is that everyone wants to do the same, and you can end up vying for elbow room with other photographers. Worst of all, you can end up waiting forever for a photographer-free view which is very frustrating (please excuse the hypocrisy). This was particularly true at Millaa Millaa where a brief break in the incessant rain meant I had a two-minute window to shoot the falls, as did half a dozen other photographers. I carried on shooting until my Mamiya was well-soaked. It didn't seem to do it any harm, thank goodness. And I got some excellent uninterrupted views.

Although I have discussed exotic and spectacular falls, don't overlook three or four-inch cascades in small rivulets and becks. Some of my favourite flowing water shots are of delicate ribbons of

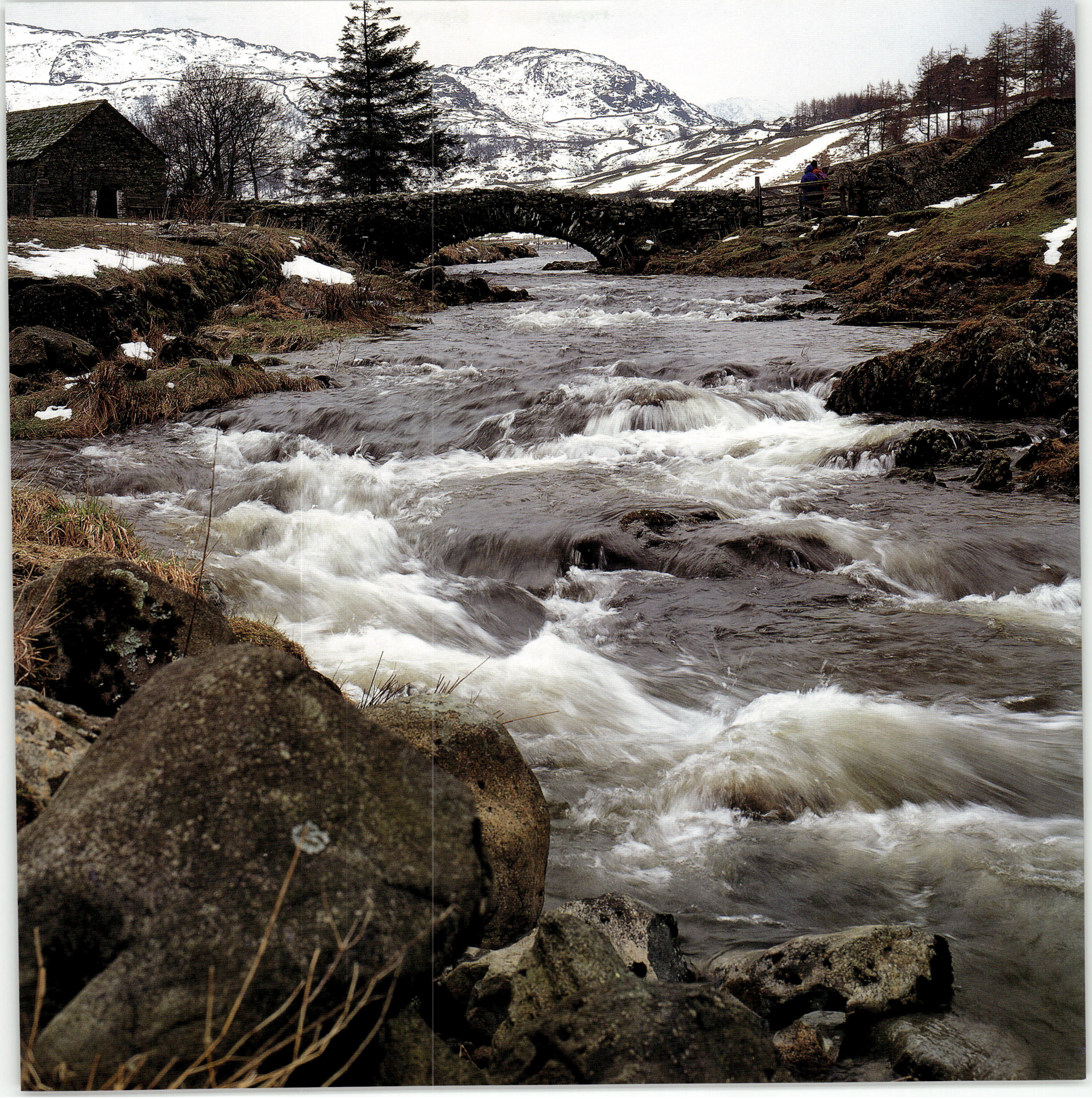

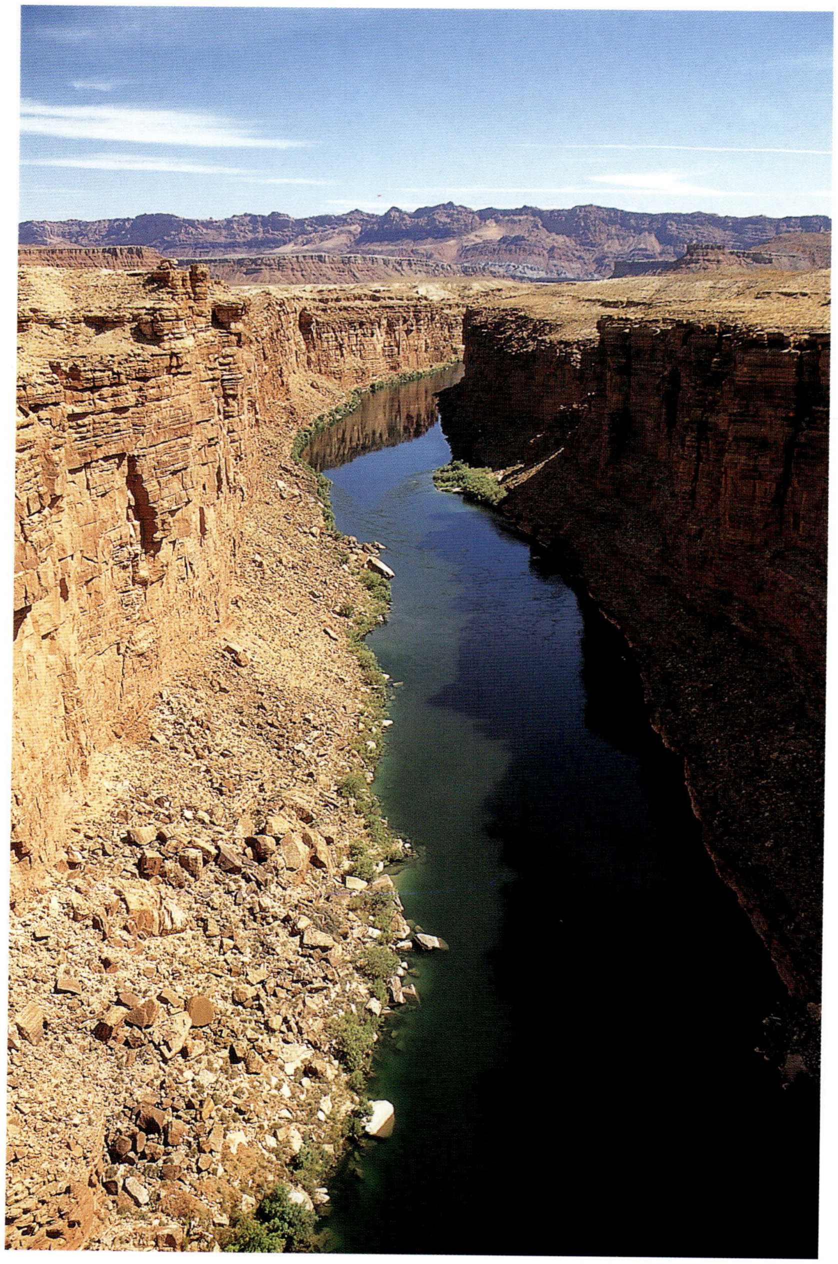

In strong sunlight, contrast becomes a real issue. This picture of the Colorado River has a large EV range (between left- and right-hand sides of the image), and might well have been improved with a neutral density graduate filter. However, it still works quite well, and portrays this mighty river and its surroundings in a powerful and evocative manner.
Pentax MZ5n + 28–70mm zoom lens, Velvia, tripod.

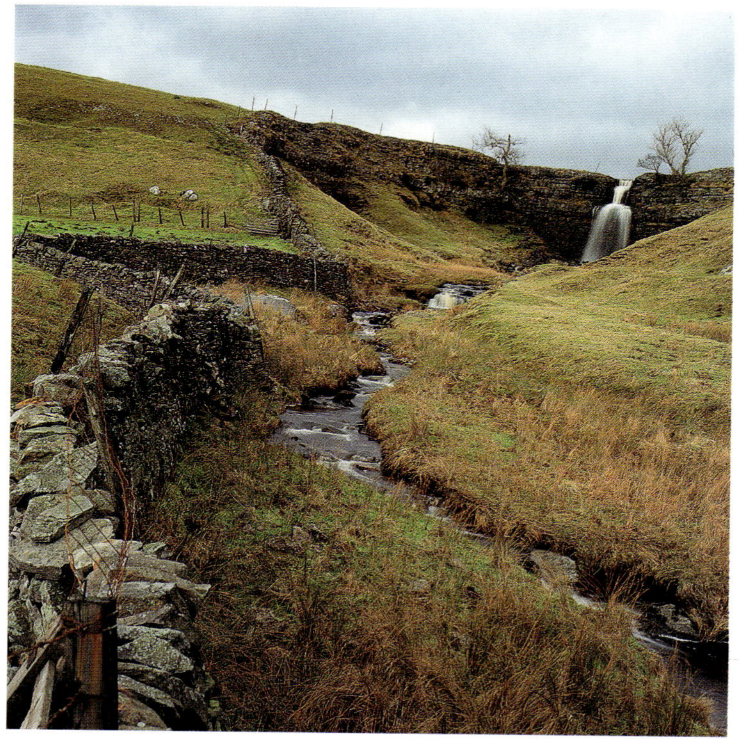

Cray Gill Waterfall in the Yorkshire Dales, England. This picture illustrates perfectly the sinuous water feature in the context of its rather bleak upland environment.
Hasselblad 500CM + 80mm lens, 1/15sec at f/11.5, Velvia, tripod.

water breaking over small twigs and stones. I am particularly fond of shooting such scenes in shady woodland surroundings. However, this necessitates long exposure times and the risk of reciprocity failure. In such cases it is wise to bracket at half stops up to 1.5x the metered EV. My two favourite shots of this type were taken in my local oak woodland at about 5pm in springtime, and required +1 EV compensation at f/16 (see page 68) and in Mossman Gorge, where I waded into the creek and shot eight-second exposures at f/16 (twice the recommended shutter speed). This rainforest scene was shot at around midday (see page 86).

Finally, as I've mentioned elsewhere, if it is possible, I like to remove all obvious evidence of human intervention. At Millaa Millaa Falls, there is a promontory out into the plunge pool that has been reinforced with block paving. When I looked at all the published views of these falls, I was surprised that nearly all pictures showed this utilitarian paving quite clearly. Personally, I would rather not take the picture than include such an incongruous (albeit practical) human element in such a beautiful and pristine natural vista. Much of my time at these falls was therefore dedicated to excluding this annoying anthropogenic element from the view. Sometimes man and nature work together in a view and sometimes, as on this occasion, they do not.

Rocks and mountains

In the United States and the British Isles, landscape photographers probably take more scenic views of rugged mountainous terrain than of any other type of topography. No other scenes conjure up such a sense of wilderness. Potentially, they also provide the viewer with a strong multidimensional image that in many cases allows one to spiritually enter into and travel through the scene. The foreground, mid-ground and distant mountain backdrops all have a critical sense of place, conspiring to provide interest at staggered levels. When these three elements are composed properly, you can almost be transported to the location where the image was taken. Have a look at John Fielder's book *Colorado: Lost Places and Forgotten Words* and you will see what I mean.

Quite often, a fourth element defines the success of a well-composed landscape, and this additional element is light. Light is transient and much harder to find than a good subject with the appropriate fore-, mid- and background components. Indeed, when travelling far from home, it is not always possible to wait around for the light to become harmoniously tuned in to the scene. Sometimes, however, if you are staying overnight in a particularly scenic area, it is much easier to revisit a good mountain landscape at sunset or sunrise than if you are merely passing through. I have missed many potentially perfectly lit scenes because I simply did not have the time to sit and wait. On the other hand, the view from the Nardab lookout at Ubirr in Kakadu, Australia (overleaf), illustrates an example of capturing

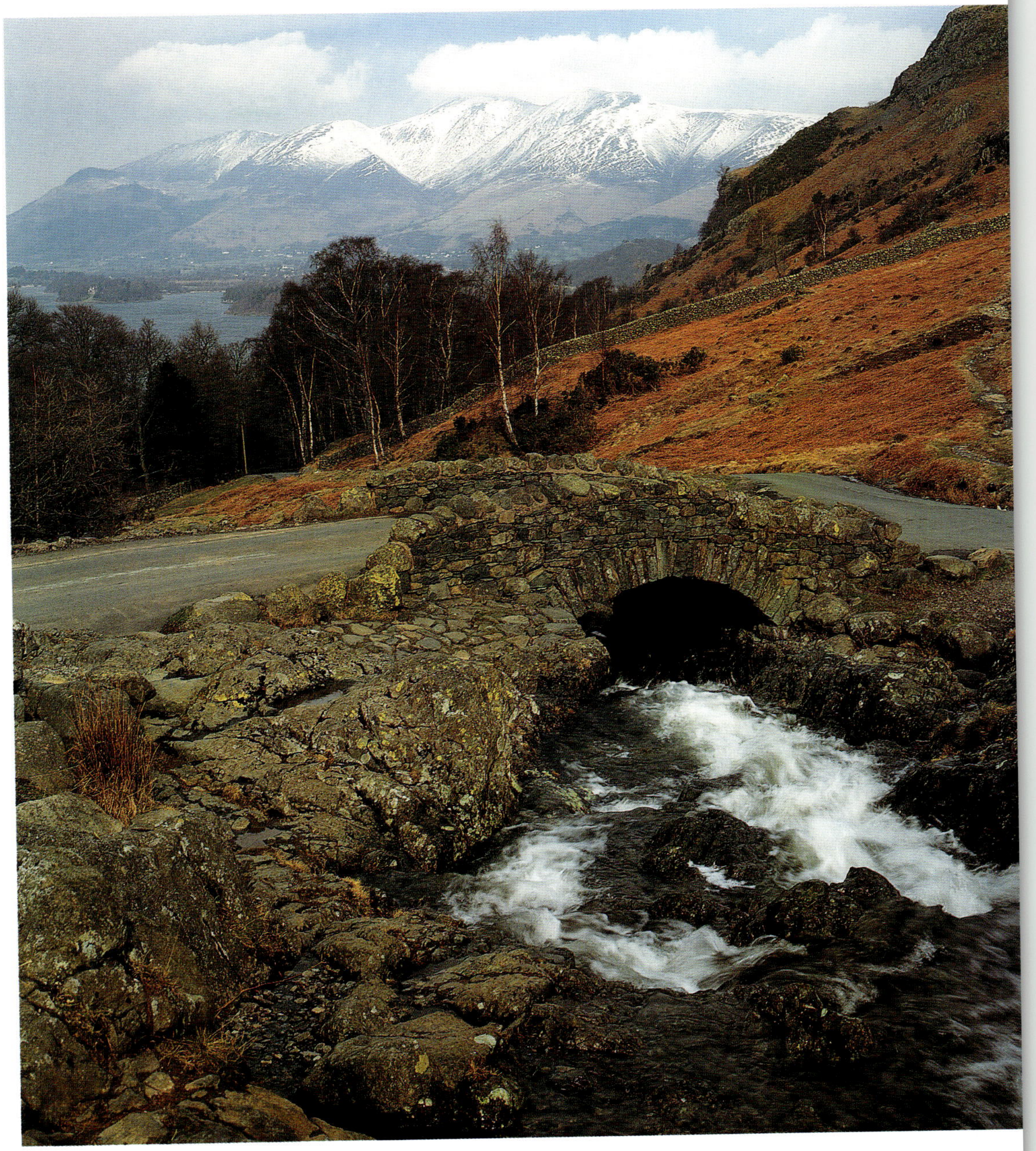

While perhaps not as frequently photographed as Bryce Canyon, Ashness Packhorse Bridge in the English Lake District is an icon for UK photographers. The view over Derwent Water and Skiddaw is simply astounding. ***Hasselblad 500CM + 80mm Carl Zeiss Planar lens, 1/15sec at f/16, Velvia, tripod.***

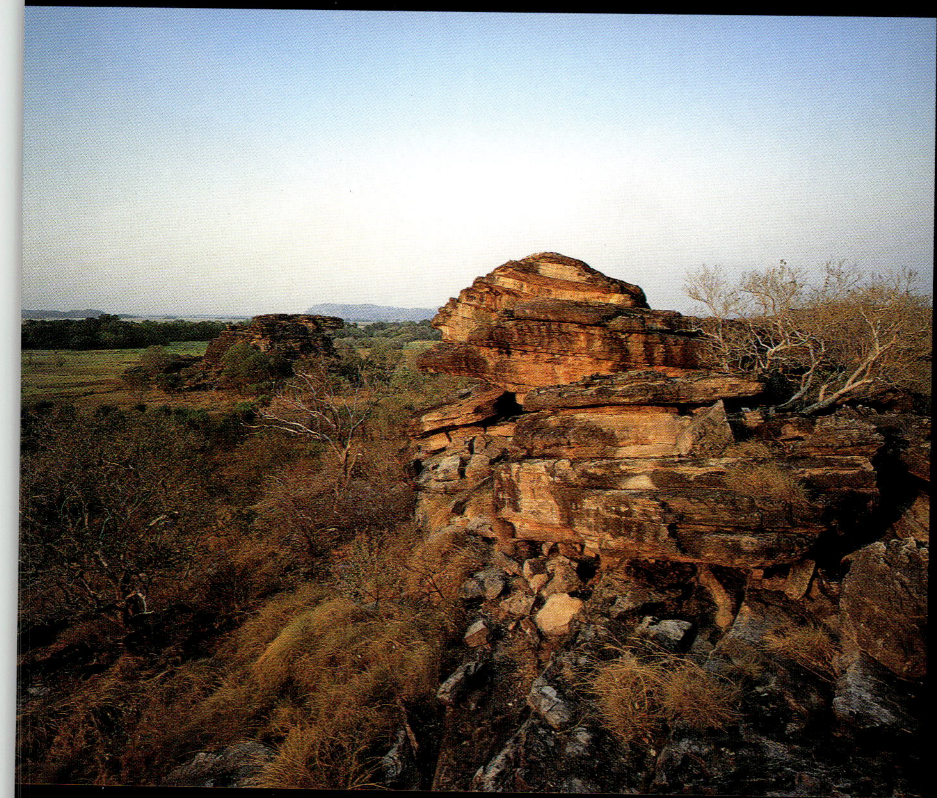

While everyone had their cameras pointed at the setting sun, I had mine aimed at this sandstone outlier of the Arnhem Plateau as it was bathed in warm glowing light from the setting sun. Kakadu National Park, Australia.
Mamiya 7II + 43mm lens, Velvia, tripod.

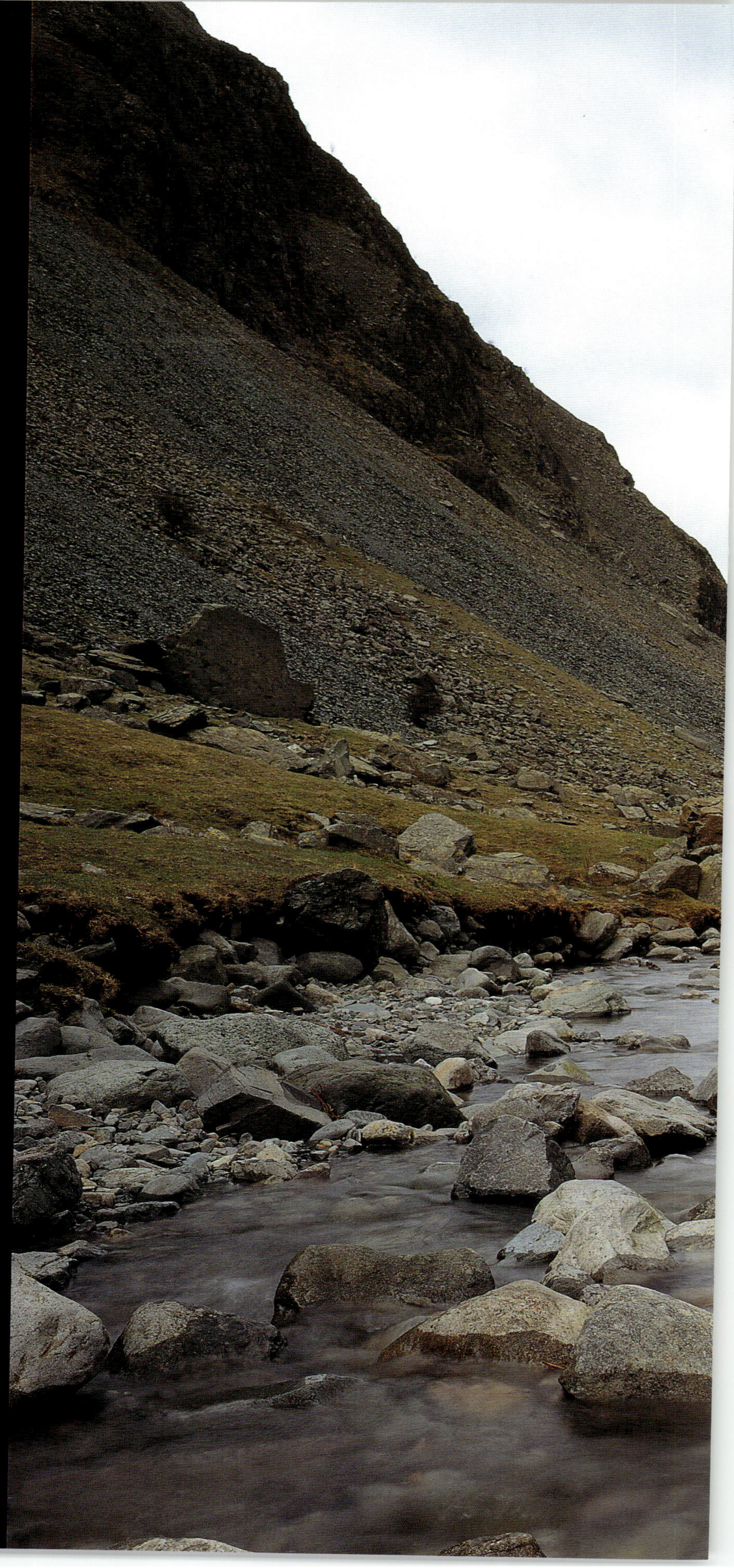

I particularly liked the design of this view, which had Gategarthdale Beck flowing through a fascinating landscape.
Fuji GSW69III, Velvia, tripod.

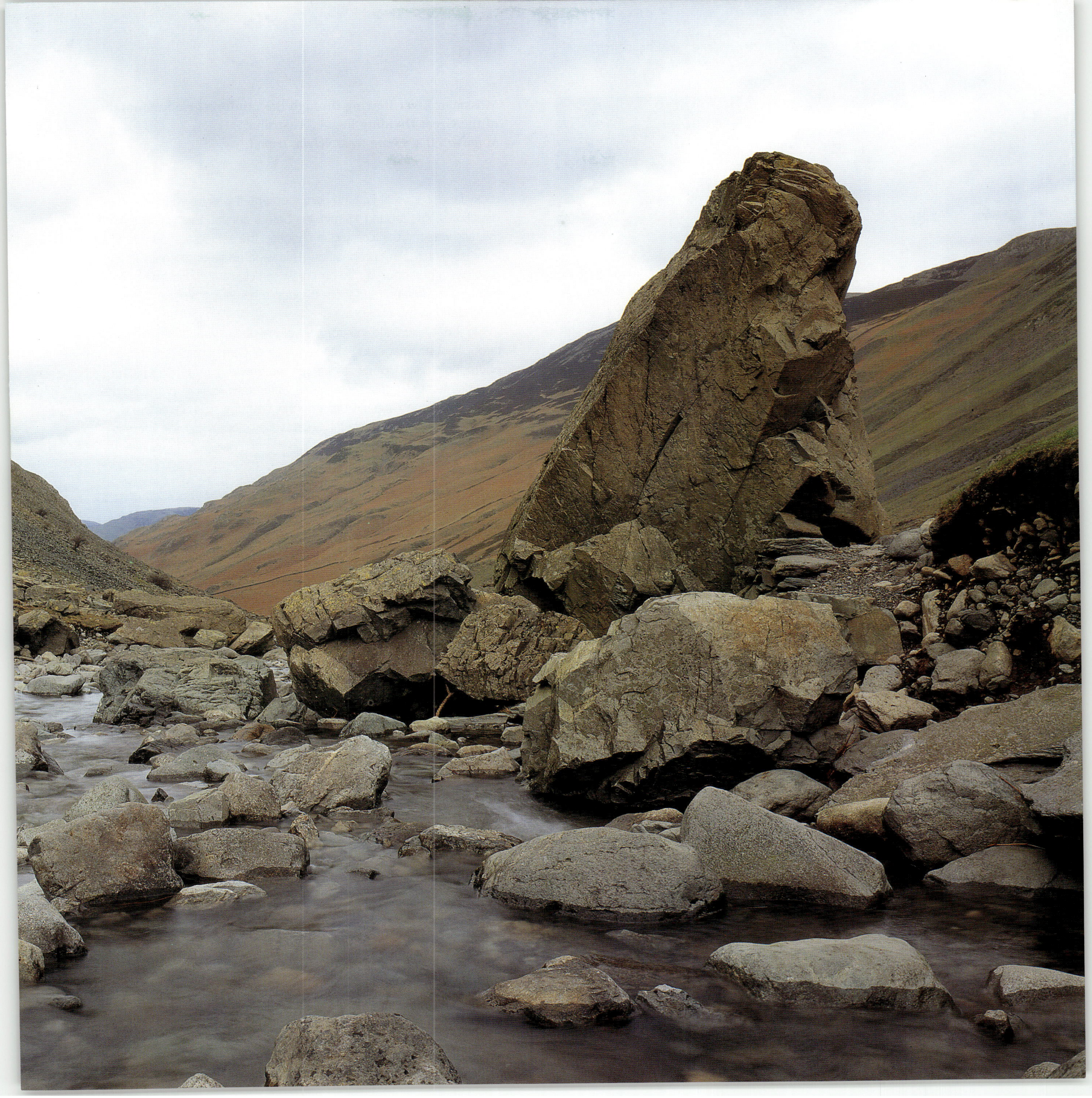

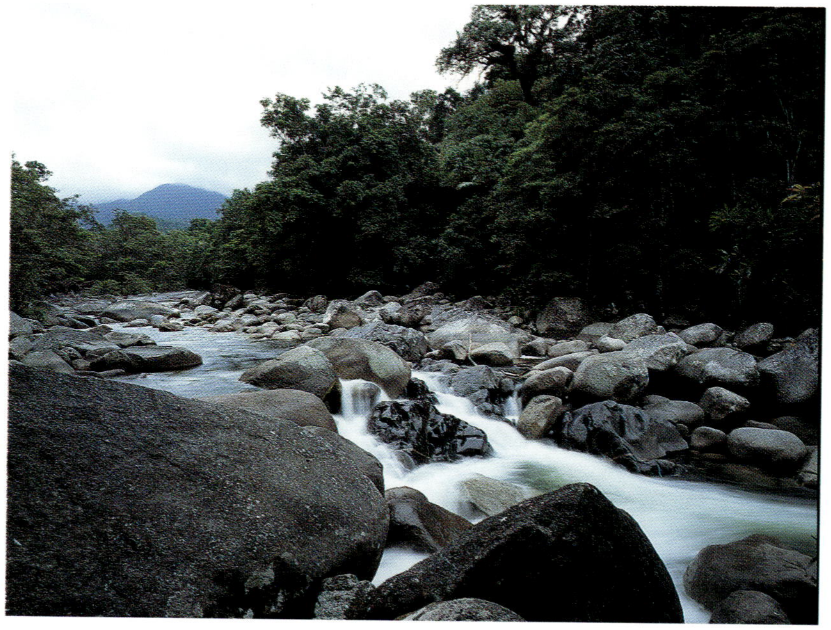

Mossman River flowing through the rainforest-clad mountains of the Great Dividing Range, Australia.
Mamiya 7II + 43mm lens, Velvia, tripod.

rocky landscapes at just the right moment. It was taken in warm, directional light around 15 minutes before sunset. Everybody else at this site was more interested in shooting the setting sun, which was a far less interesting proposition. This wide-angle shot again provides a perspective that can draw the viewer into the image at different levels, and lead them through the scene from the foreground to the background.

To further illustrate the concept of interest at various levels throughout an image, look at the image of Gategarthdale Beck, a photogenic Lake District stream, on the previous page. The picture provides foreground interest as the water flows over and around the rocks and stones, the large slab projecting upwards draws the eye into the mid-ground, while the steep valley slopes provide interest and structure for the backdrop.

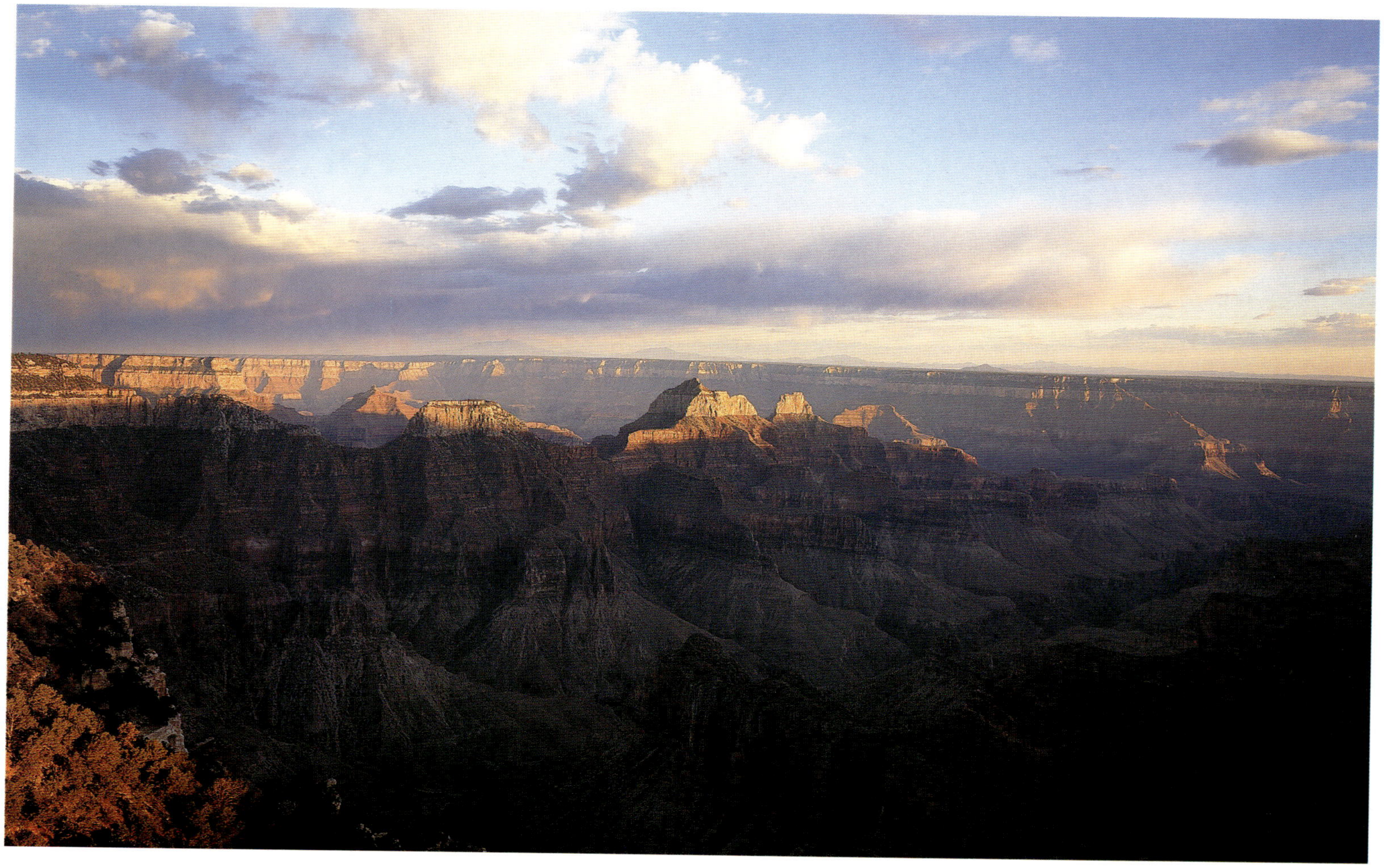

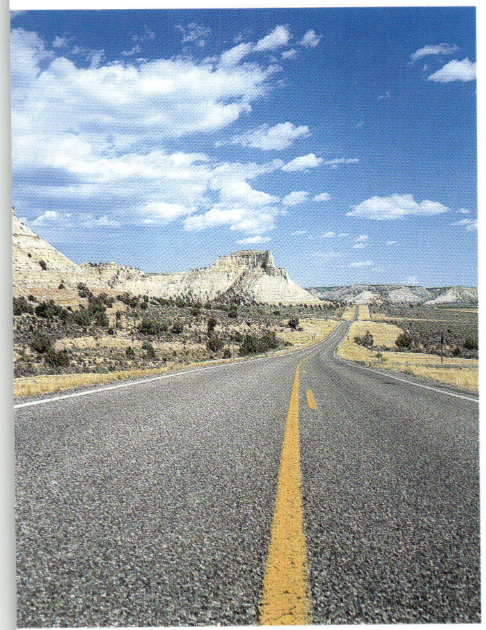

Scenic highway 12 near Henrieville in Utah, USA. I got down low to shoot the road receding into the distance between the rocky mesas.
Mamiya 7II + 65mm lens, Velvia, tripod.

Left: Sunset at the Grand Canyon.
Fuji GSW69III, 1/2sec at f/5.6, Velvia.

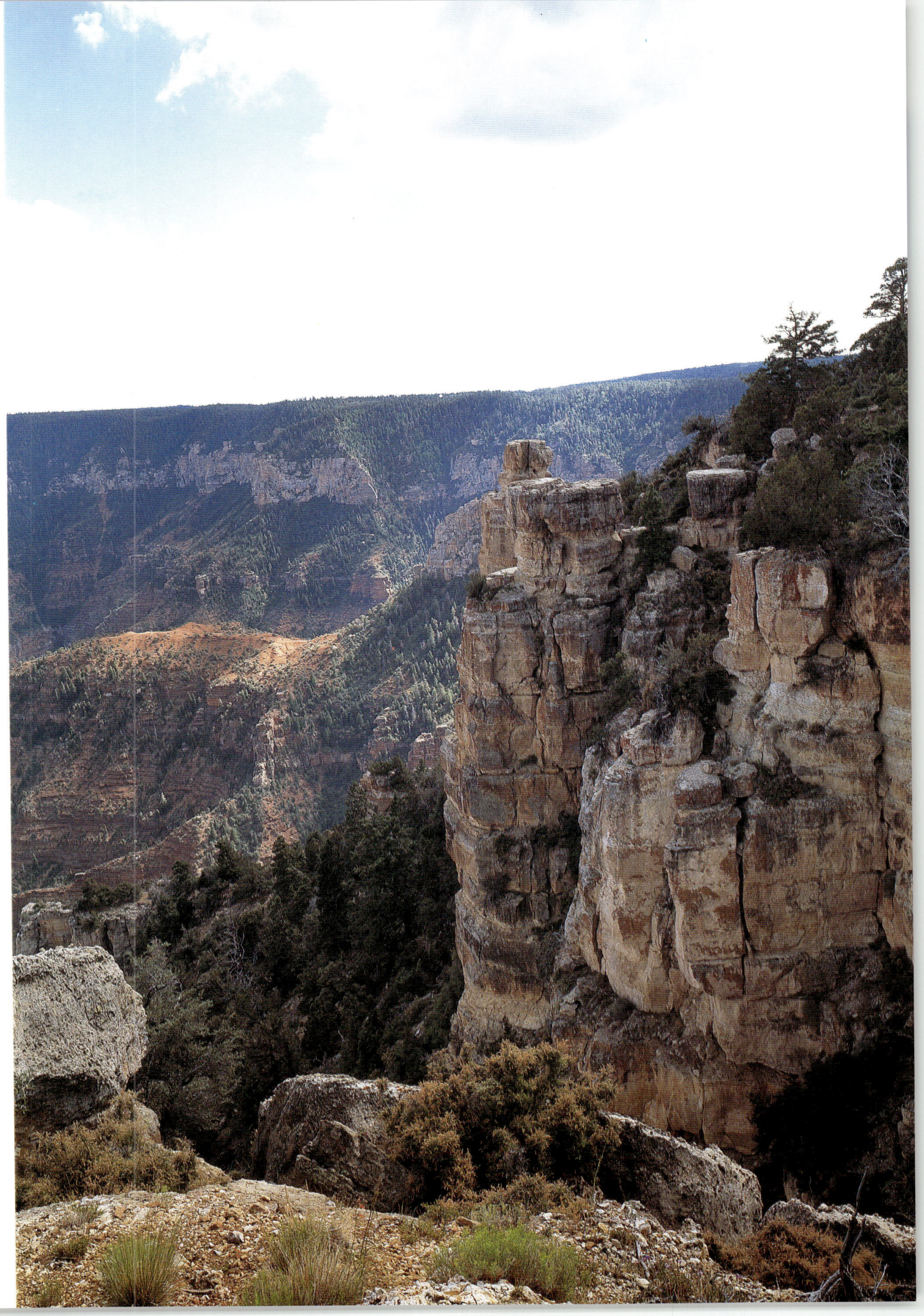

Weathered rocks around the rim of the Grand Canyon at Point Imperial. Here I incorporated significant foreground interest with the rocks nearby, but also incorporated interest in the distance with the forest backdrop.
Fuji GSW69III, 1/60sec at f/6, Velvia, tripod.

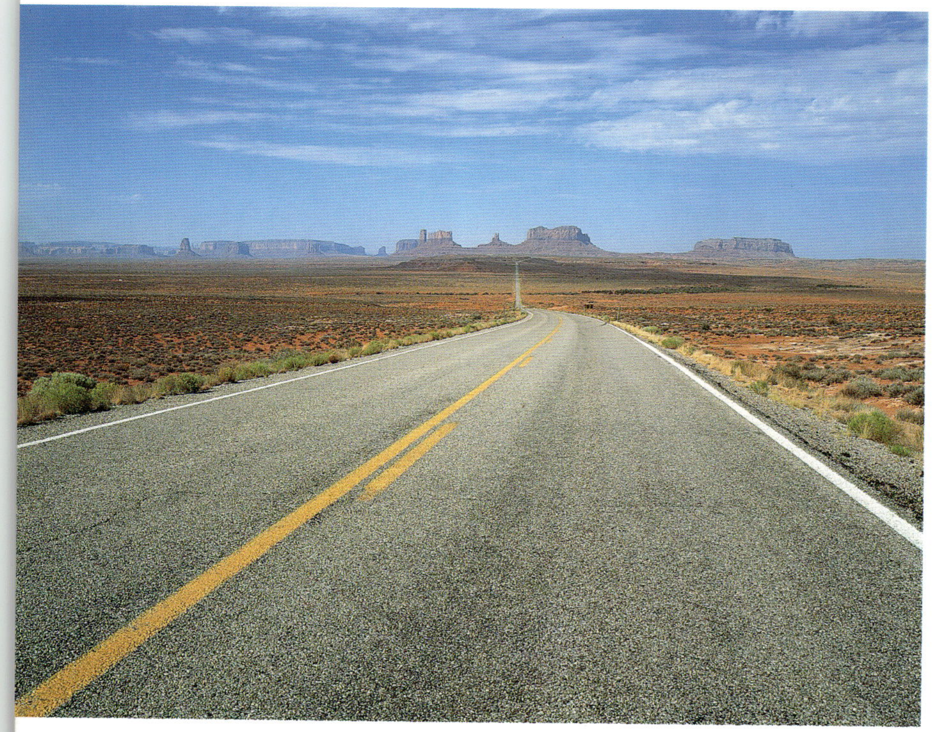

The long straight road into Monument Valley (setting of many a John Ford movie) provides a perfect device for leading the eye into this dramatic view. With hindsight I wish I had also used my 150mm lens to compress the view slightly. I think it would have marginally improved the scene.
Mamiya 7II + 65mm lens, Velvia, tripod.

Rocks always provide a good partner for flowing water. In the image on page 142, I have captured the fast-flowing water of the Mossman River in Queensland as it pounds, polishes and erodes large granite boulders. Like Gategarthdale Beck in the English Lake District, the Mossman River scene shows a multiplane construction: foreground rocks pulling into the mid-ground which is funnelled into the distance by the marginal rainforest vegetation. This picture was made possible thanks to a very wide-angle lens.

Sometimes scenes are so big that it is not easy to add any foreground. For instance, the Grand Canyon in Arizona is almost always at infinity as far as your lens is concerned, with the foreground simply disappearing into the canyon's awesome chasm, even with the widest lens. If you search around however, you can usually find a perspective that puts a mesa or butte into the scene in a way that creates a far more interesting multidimensional view.

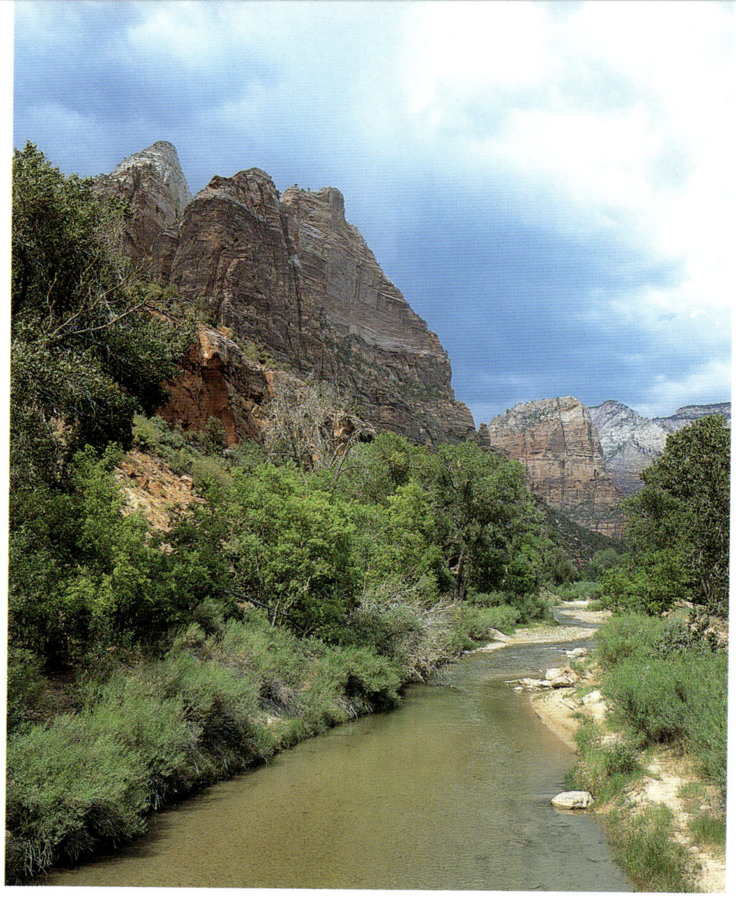

In contrast to creating a three-dimensional image with wide to standard lenses, many people choose to replace their wide-angle lens with a long telephoto (e.g. 200–300mm) in order to compress perspective and yield a more two-dimensional rendering of distant mountains. As I mentioned earlier, I like to see detail at different levels within my images. Personally, I find the compressed perspective in landscapes rather boring, often the detail that can be found in wide-angle views is lost. In my opinion, the latter are far more likely to convey my spirit to the place where the image was taken than telephoto shots.

There are many ways to enliven mountainous terrain without waiting for an elusive rose-coloured sunset. Shoot in winter when there is a covering of snow or add a road that recedes into the distant moutainscape. The latter approach will be immediately intuitive to you in places such as the American West. Here, I have shot the distant road into Monument Valley with its isolated mesas and buttes. Similarly, scenic highway 12 in Utah provides opportunities for shooting classic roadscapes in rugged terrain.

Some rocky landscapes contain highly unusual monolithic structures. In Zion National Park, Checkerboard Mesa provides a fascinating subject, etched with a rectangular network of fissures that cover the entire surface. I shot it with a 65mm lens on the 6 x 7cm format, but this was barely wide enough. It was, however,

Checkerboard Mesa, Zion National Park, Utah.
Mamiya 7II + 65mm lens, Velvia, tripod.

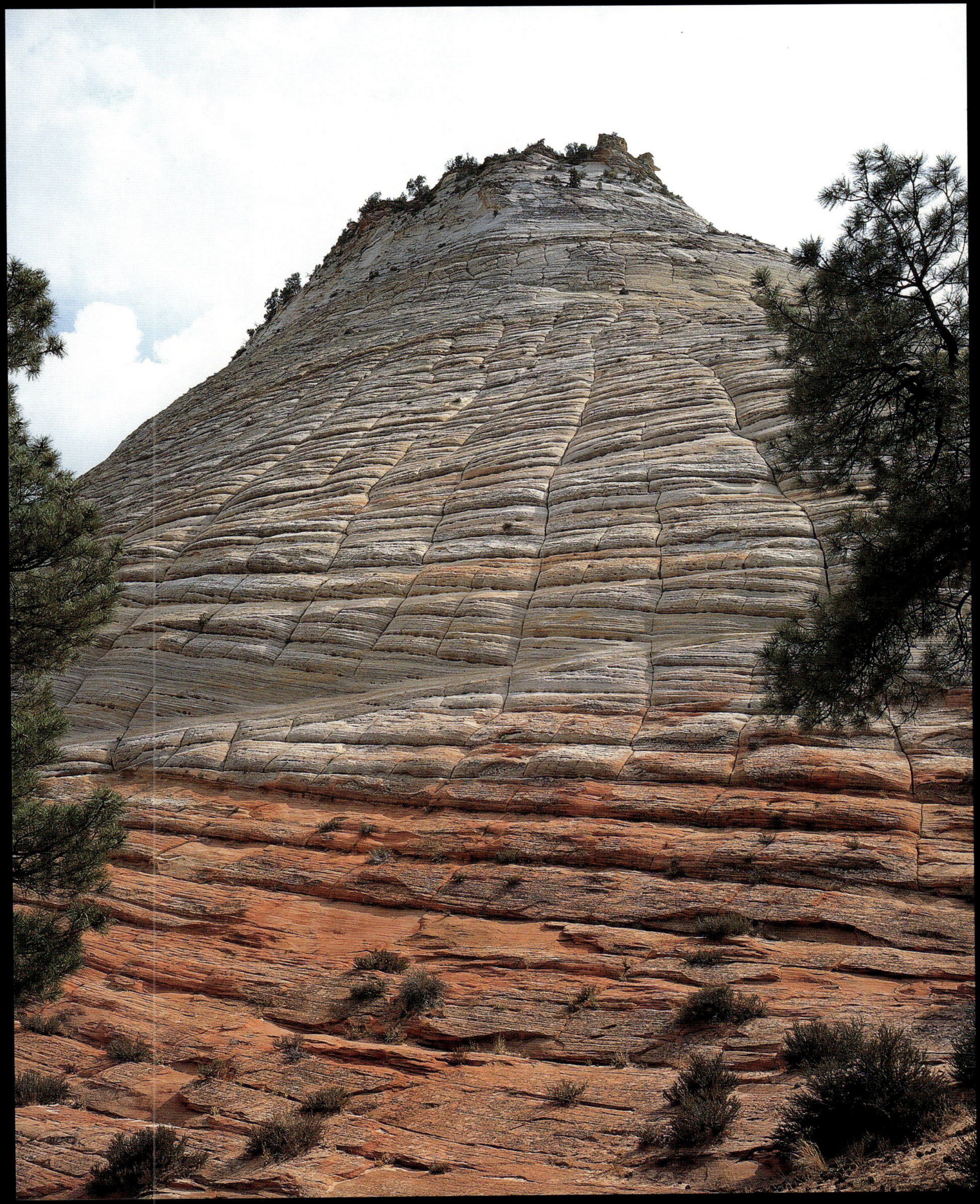

Left: Virgin River, Zion National Park, Utah.
Mamiya 7II + 65mm lens, Velvia, tripod.

perfect for the nearby Zion River and the imposing mountains which line the river and its valley. The river, like the roads, lead the viewer's eye into the image and provides the necessary link between near and far planes, which holds the picture together and gives it a high level of detail and interest.

Grassland, heath and moor

Grassland

Grassland habitats, even garden lawns, are full of marvellous photographic opportunities and a treasure trove for the inquisitive naturalist. Depending on the type of grassland and its location one can expect to find a myriad of mini-beasts, colourful flowers and geological features to shoot.

While my discussion of grasslands is largely confined to Britain, many countries have the same or similar habitats extending over large areas. In Britain, native grasslands have a flora which is largely determined by aspect, soil acidity and whether they are cut for hay or grazed. Undoubtedly, the most impressive grasslands to photograph exist on chalk and limestone soils where a rich flora often includes many rare species. Grazed lands have low-growing plants while hay meadows have an abundance of tall plants that flower through early summer.

Hay meadows

Hay meadows are rare and wonderful. To illustrate the threat they are under, one classic meadow plant, the snake's head fritillary, is now almost entirely (80%) confined to a single Wiltshire meadow. Fifty years ago fritillary meadows existed in nearly 30 counties. Plants act as indicators. In Britain you can identify ancient grassland by the species present: adder's tongue fern, great burnet, yellow rattle, horseshoe vetch and rough hawksbit are restricted to ancient swards. Ploughed and fertilized land destroys the natural balance and can eradicate a delicate meadow ecosystem overnight.

The Yorkshire Dales in the north of England contain beautiful, photogenic hay meadows. Here grassland plants grow without being grazed until their flowers appear. At this point the farmer reaps a maximum yield of tender herbage. The plethora of attractive flowers growing en masse in Britain's various hay meadows includes yarrow, bird's foot trefoil, greater burnet, saxifrage, meadow buttercups and knapweeds. Some species have names with more character – pignut and yellow rattle, for example. However, whatever shape and form they come in, all will have shed their seeds before being cut, thus ensuring the continuation of this colourful and remarkable annual event. Hay meadows in the Dales have an added beauty,

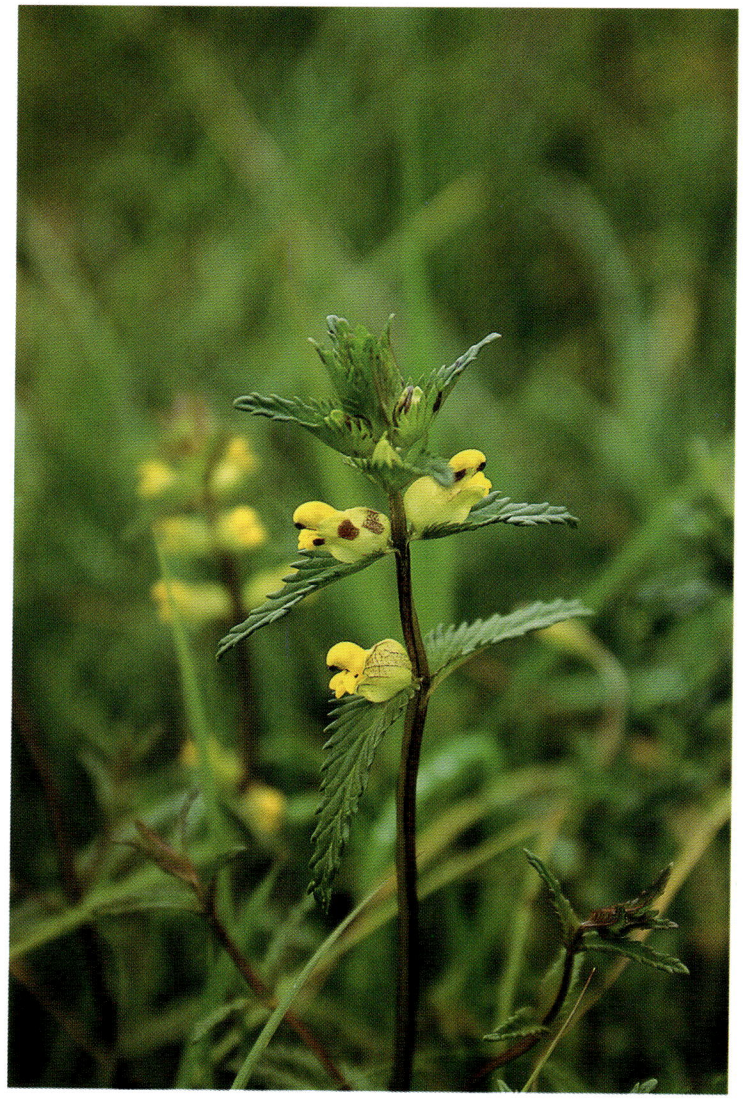

Remember to move in and shoot the elements that make up the landscape. This is a close-up of yellow rattle
Nikon 3T dioptre, 28–70mm zoom lens.

since they are part of a mosaic habitat containing stone barns, dry-stone walling and steep hills which can be ablaze with bluebells as late as June. As mentioned earlier, one of the best places for photographing hay meadows is around Muker in Swaledale. I last visited in early June, shortly before the meadows were mown.

I recommend a solid tripod and 28mm lens (or shorter) to allow a maximum depth of field, and thereby ensure that flowers near and

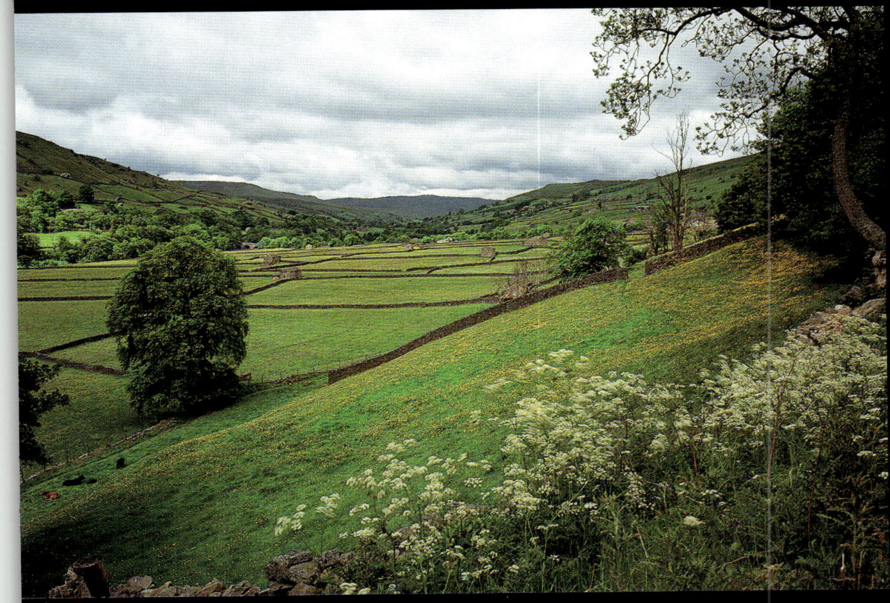

Ancient hay meadows and grassland lie between dry-stone walls in this view from Gunnerside, Yorkshire Dales, England.
Fuji GSW69III, Velvia, tripod.

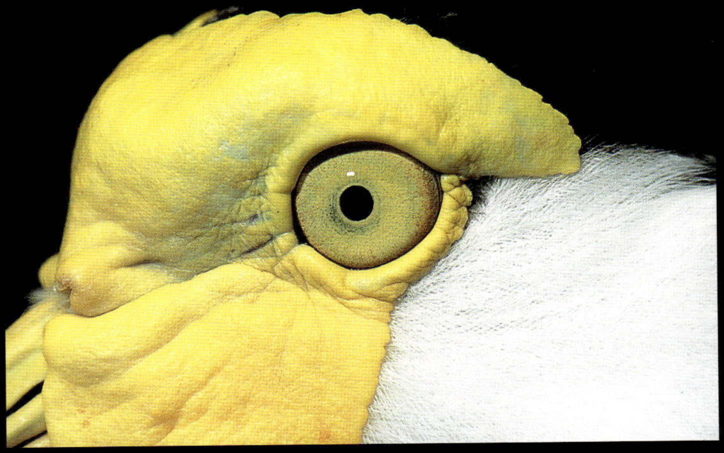

If you were to ask me which bird best exemplifies grassland and pasture in Australia, it has to be the masked lapwing. When I visited, these laughable birds were everywhere on pasture land – not unlike our own lapwing. We were so enamoured by these ridiculous looking birds that we christened them the marigold glove bird, and I vowed to get a shot before we left.

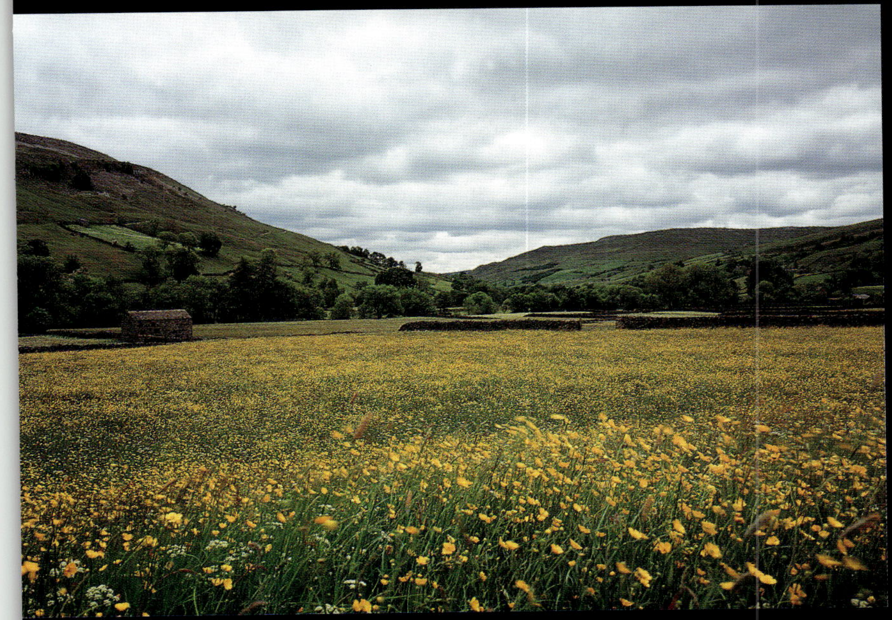

Ancient hay meadow in Swaledale, Yorkshire Dales National Park, England.
Fuji GSW69III, 81B filter, 1/30sec at f/16, Velvia, tripod.

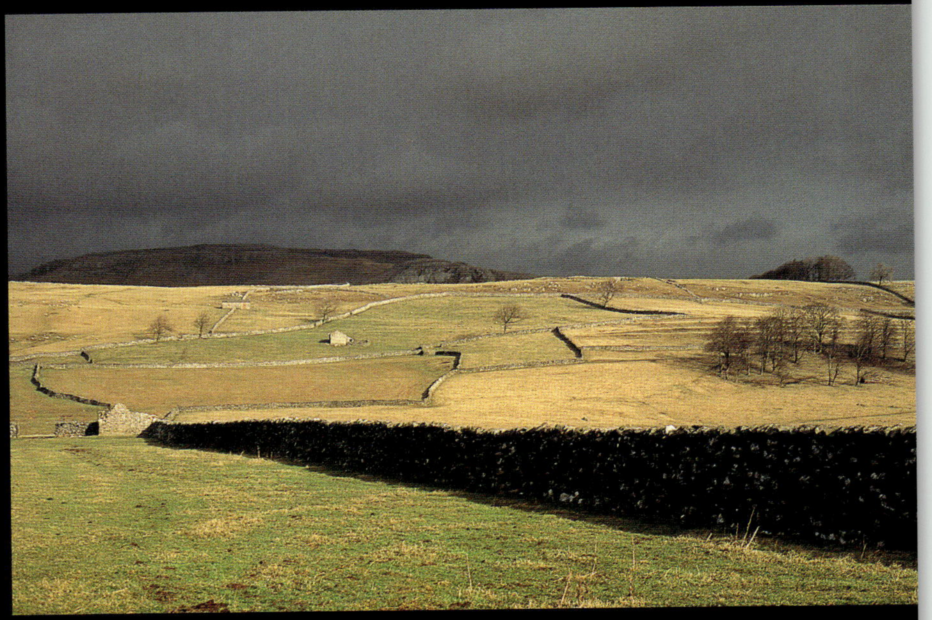

Dull winter days can be enlivened by a dramatic sky. (Camera supported on a stone wall.) Yorkshire Dales, England.
Pentax MZ5 + 28–70mm zoom lens.

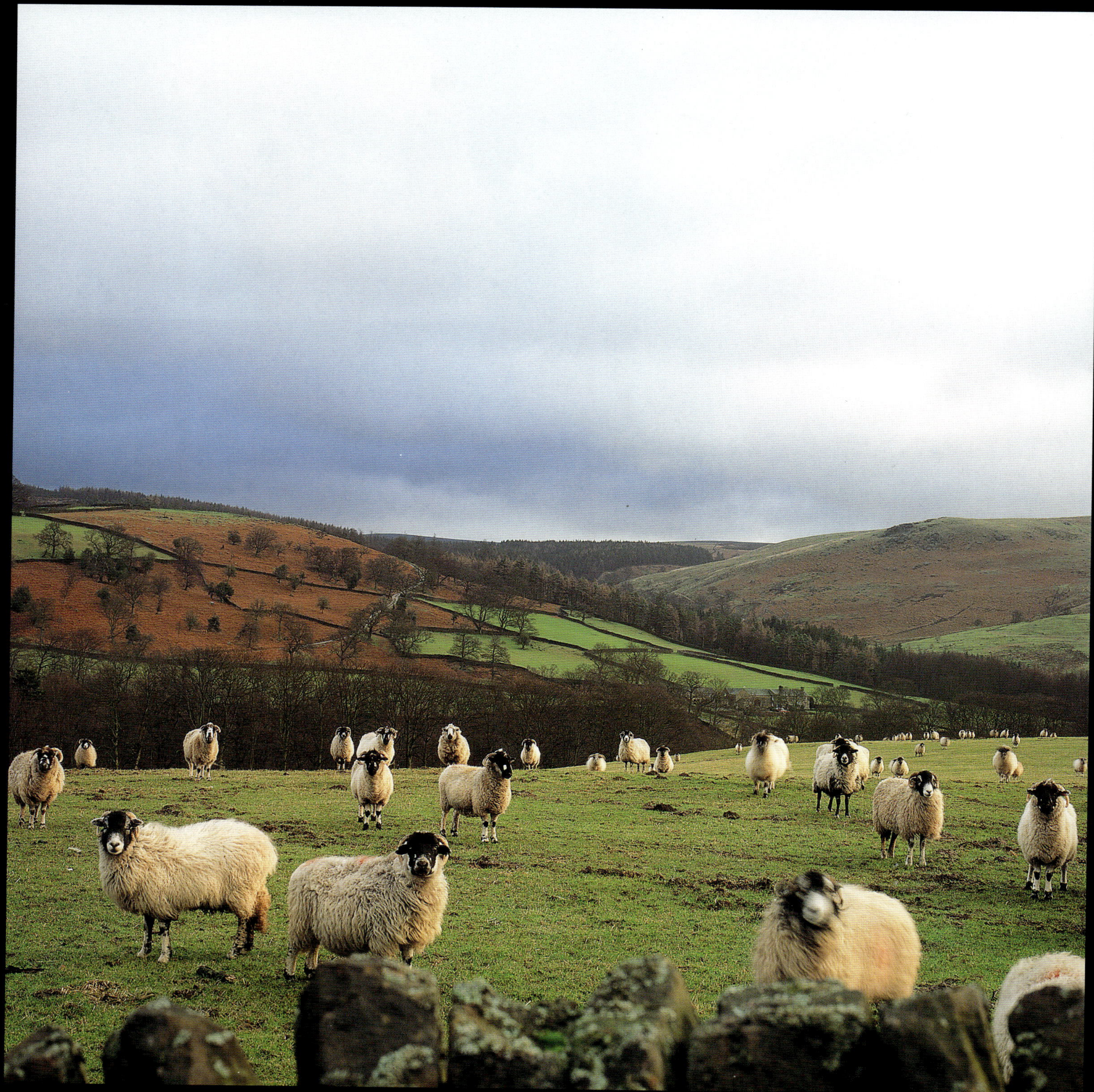

Sheep grazing near Bolton Abbey in North Yorkshire, England. This is a picture from the first roll of film I ever took on medium format.
Hasselblad 500CM + 80mm lens, tripod.

far remain sharply in focus. To achieve good depth of focus use hyperfocal distance on your 35mm kit and an aperture between f/16.5 and f/32. In upland Britain, a breeze is a foregone conclusion and as shutter speeds are in the half-second range at apertures of f/16.5 or less you need patience to wait for that elusive lull which brings the sward to a stand still. Also, I have recently shot the Swaledale hay meadows on my Ebony camera with great success, using front axial tilt and a wide lens on sheet and 6 x 12cm film.

Grazed uplands

On the moors and fells the camera gravitates less to the floral element and more to the geological grandeur of the overall landscape. Sheep trim the greenery between the rich russet bracken, and these two elements come together in winter to create the best in landscape photography, especially when embellishing the steep, precipitous crags. One such example is the Lake District image (see page 140), in which the geometric lines of grassy screes form a symmetry dissected by an icy cold Gategarthdale Beck.

The brown argus butterfly loves open chalk and limestone grassland as do the Essex skipper and other butterflies.
Pentax LX + 100mm macro lens with TTL flash.

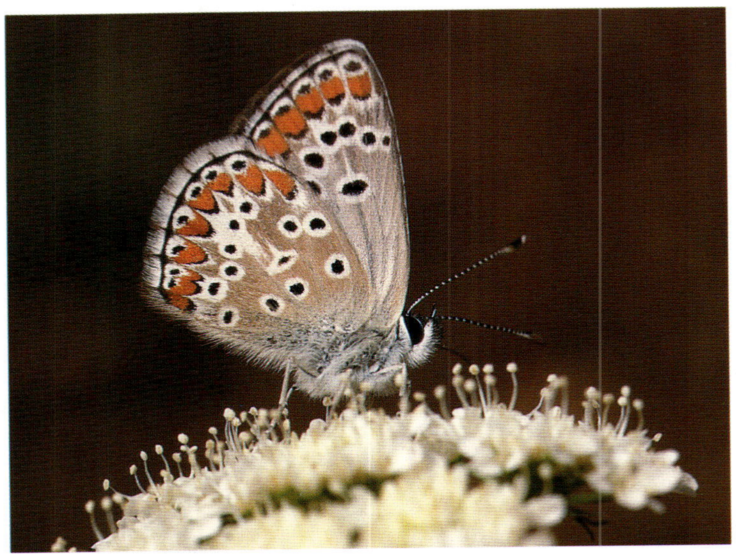

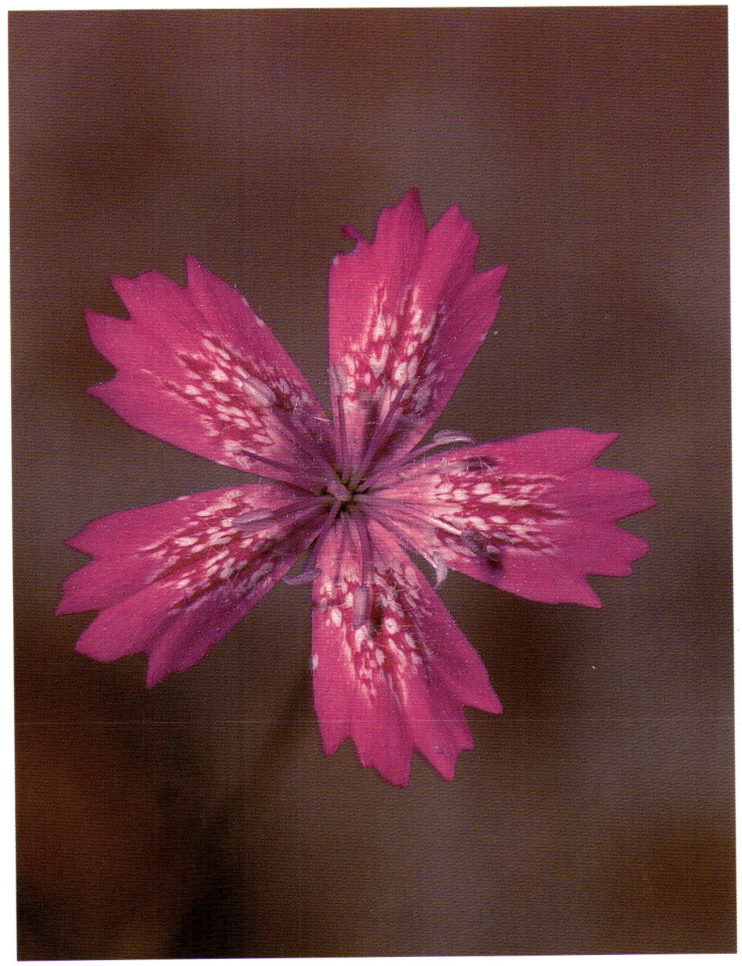

Dianthus species growing in a grassy field. Isolating flowers works well to produce an interesting image with impact.
Pentax LX with 100mm macro lens.

Anthropogenic features also enliven grassy swards. On the outskirts of Keswick in the Lake District is Castlerigg stone circle. Surrounded by mountains these standing stones beckon a few frames of your film. Grassy uplands in alpine Europe are awash with flowery meadows where cutting and grazing are strictly controlled so that only a small part of the vegetation is removed each year, and only animal dung is used to fertilize the ground. Common flowers include eyebright, selfheal and scarlet clovers, and it is hardly surprising that these 'near-natural' meadows – such as the Picos de Europa in Spain – are the richest butterfly fields in Europe.

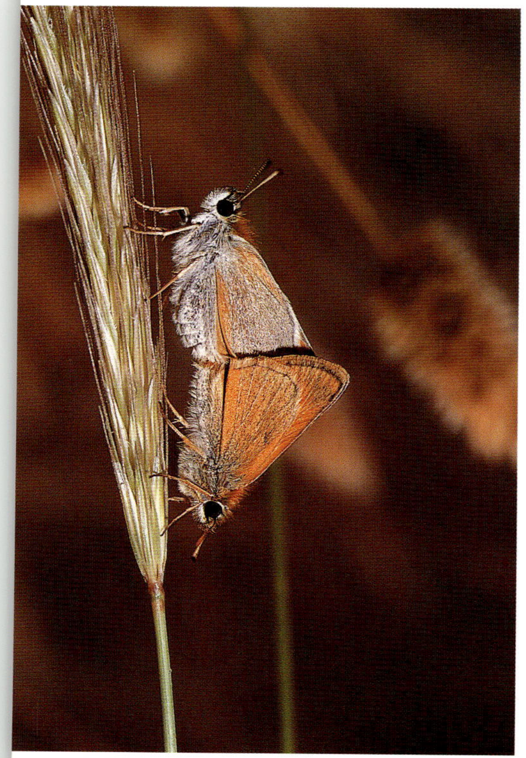

Essex skipper butterflies are common on downland.
Pentax LX + 100mm macro lens with TTL flash.

I shot this scene of heather and gorse on the cliffs between Minsmere and Dunwich in Suffolk, England (a place I often used to visit as a child for Sunday picnics), on consecutive days. On the first occasion an easterly wind made my camera sway a bit – a problem exacerbated by the soft ground on which I was standing – so I used Provia 100F. As the second day was still and bright, I chose Velvia.
Fuji GA645Zi.

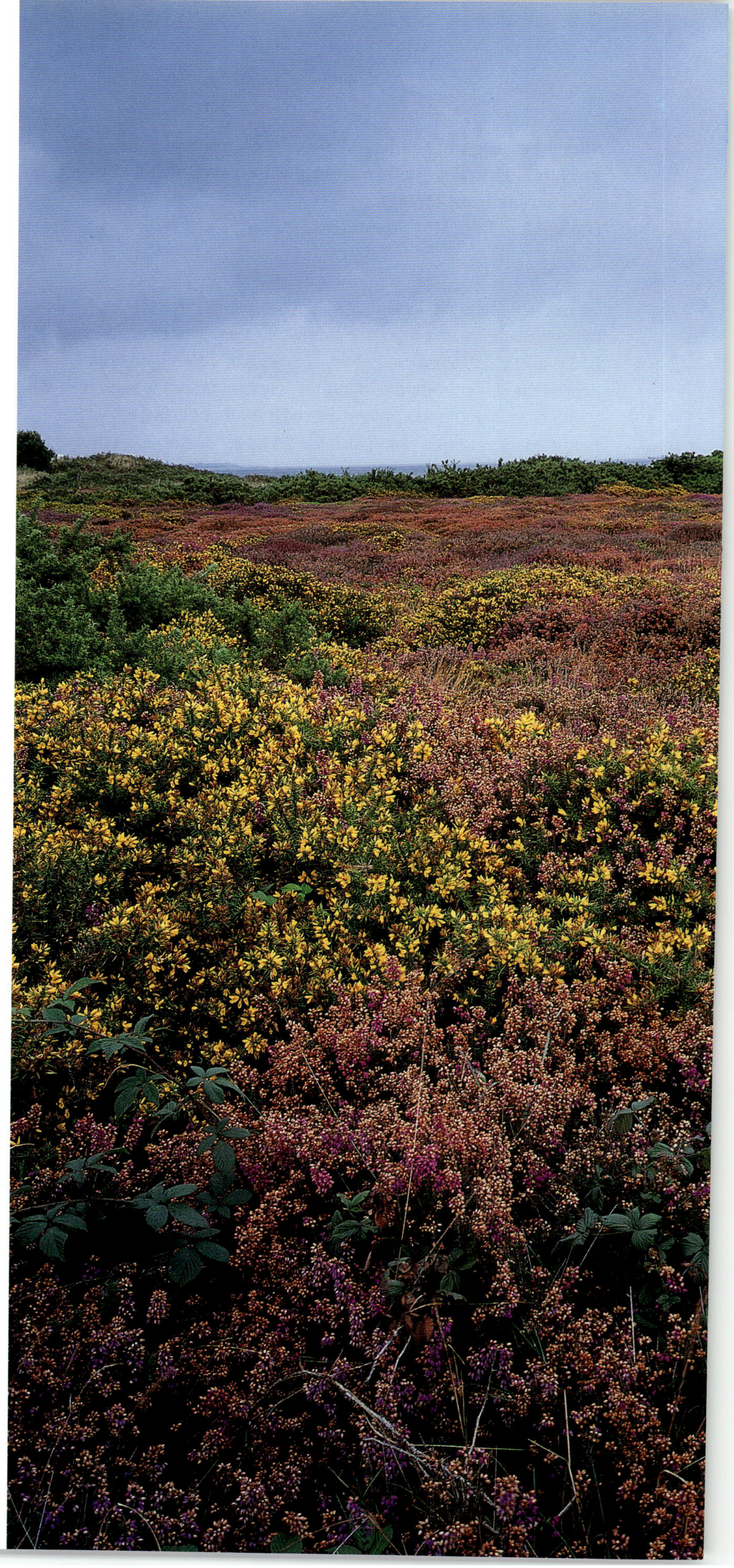

Downland

The close-cropped turf of these gentle southern chalk hills in the south of England, which may contain 30 plant species/m^2, are a repository of jewel-like blue, brown and marbled white butterflies. In the late 1970s as a student on the south coast I can still remember seeing numerous amateur naturalists frenetically chasing butterflies across the sward with their cameras guiding the way. Good exercise, but a poor strategy for shooting butterflies. These creatures should be stalked slowly with a 100mm macro lens and off-camera flash.

Heath and moor

Traditionally considered a poor habitat, this is perhaps my favourite place to photograph. The grassland-heath mosaic is a place to see adders, lizards and spiders, as well as beautiful flowers like the delicate harebell. One of the more 'fun' subjects you can shoot are Grayling butterflies, which tend to continually, but imperceptibly, move out of focus as a result of specific behavioural traits. In hot weather they stand, head facing the sun, to reduce body temperature while, if cold, they orientate laterally to the sun to absorb maximum heat. Cleverly, they move to avoid creating any shadow, which would make them visible to potential predators. Use a flash to arrest movement when photographing this species.

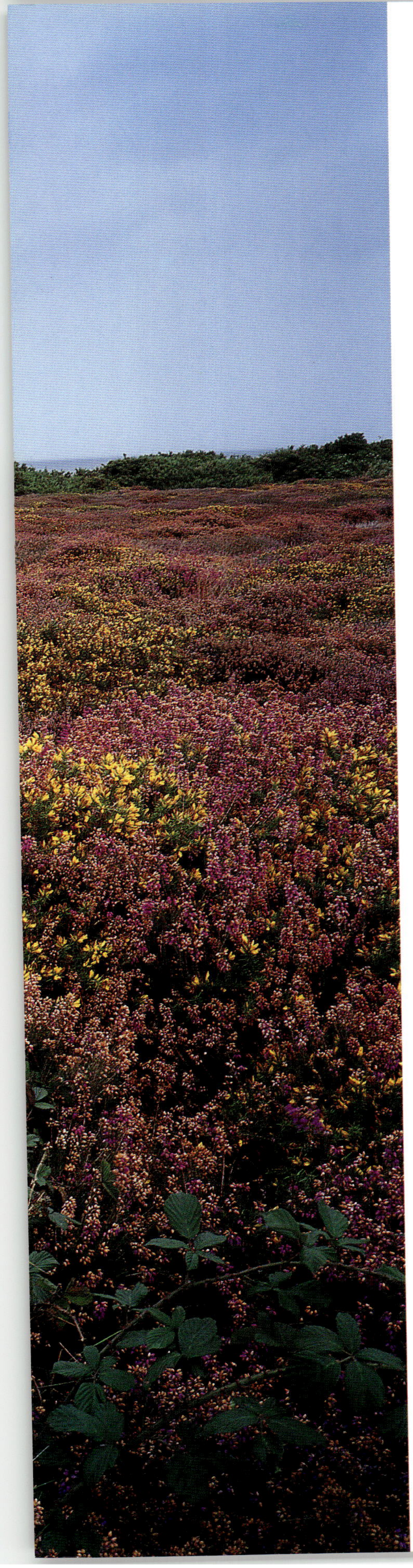

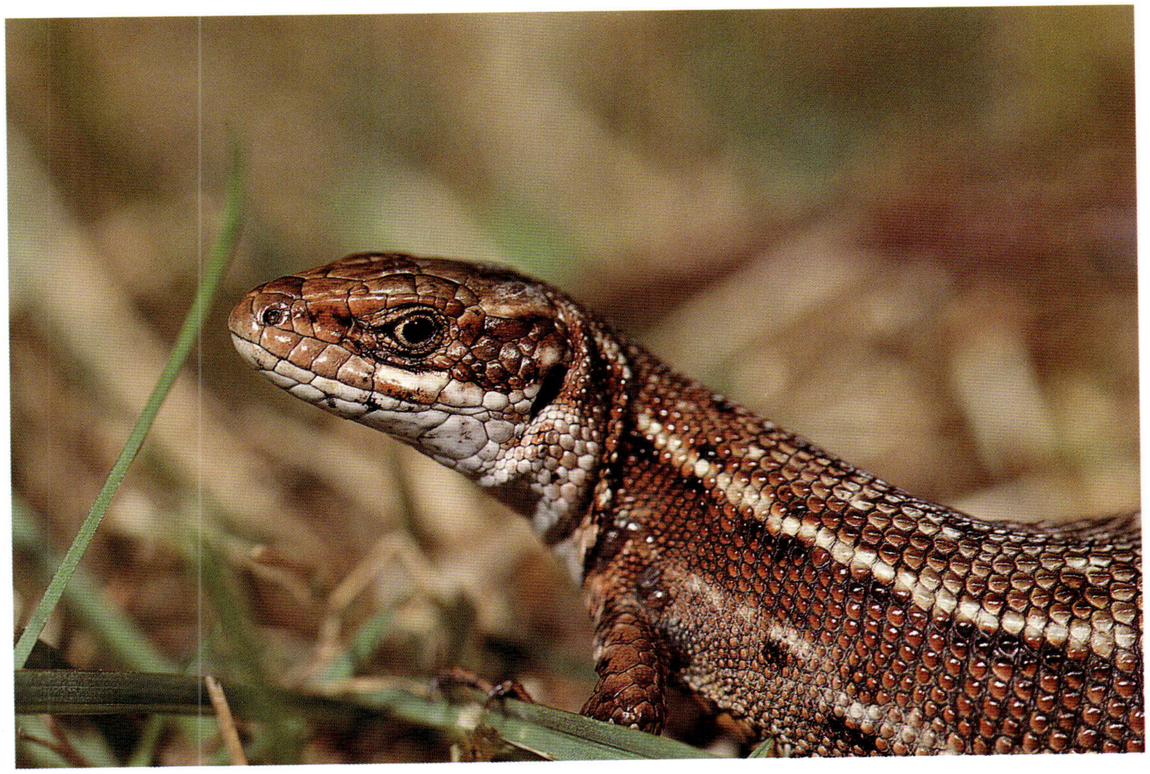

Viviparous lizards are still found on heathlands, but are far less common than they were when I was a young boy. Taken on heathland near Dunwich, Suffolk, England.
Pentax LX + 100mm macro lens.

In Britain, human activity seriously threatens the already fragmented heathland habitat. One area of heath with which I am very familiar was once alive with adders. I never see adders today, but I do see locals walking their dogs far more, and am convinced that this is why the adder population has declined.

One of my favourite locations for photographing the contrasting colours of golden gorse and purple heather is Minsmere in Suffolk on the east coast of England. As a child I spent many Sunday afternoon picnics here. I recently returned with my Fuji rangefinder to take my first photographs of the place that were not family snaps. I ran into two problems: the ground is very springy, which is not ideal for good tripod stability and a real problem when the wind blows; and, secondly, there is high contrast between sky and land. This latter point caused three or four failed images where the bright sky fooled the meter into underexposing the heather. Fortunately, I took several shots that had less of the sky in the frame, and as a result the exposure problem disappeared. With any camera other than a rangefinder, you could correct this problem by using a ND graduate filter (see page 34). Unfortunately, you cannot see the effect of an ND grad on a rangefinder as you do not view the scene through the lens with these types of camara, and the filter assembly might interfere with metering and focusing.

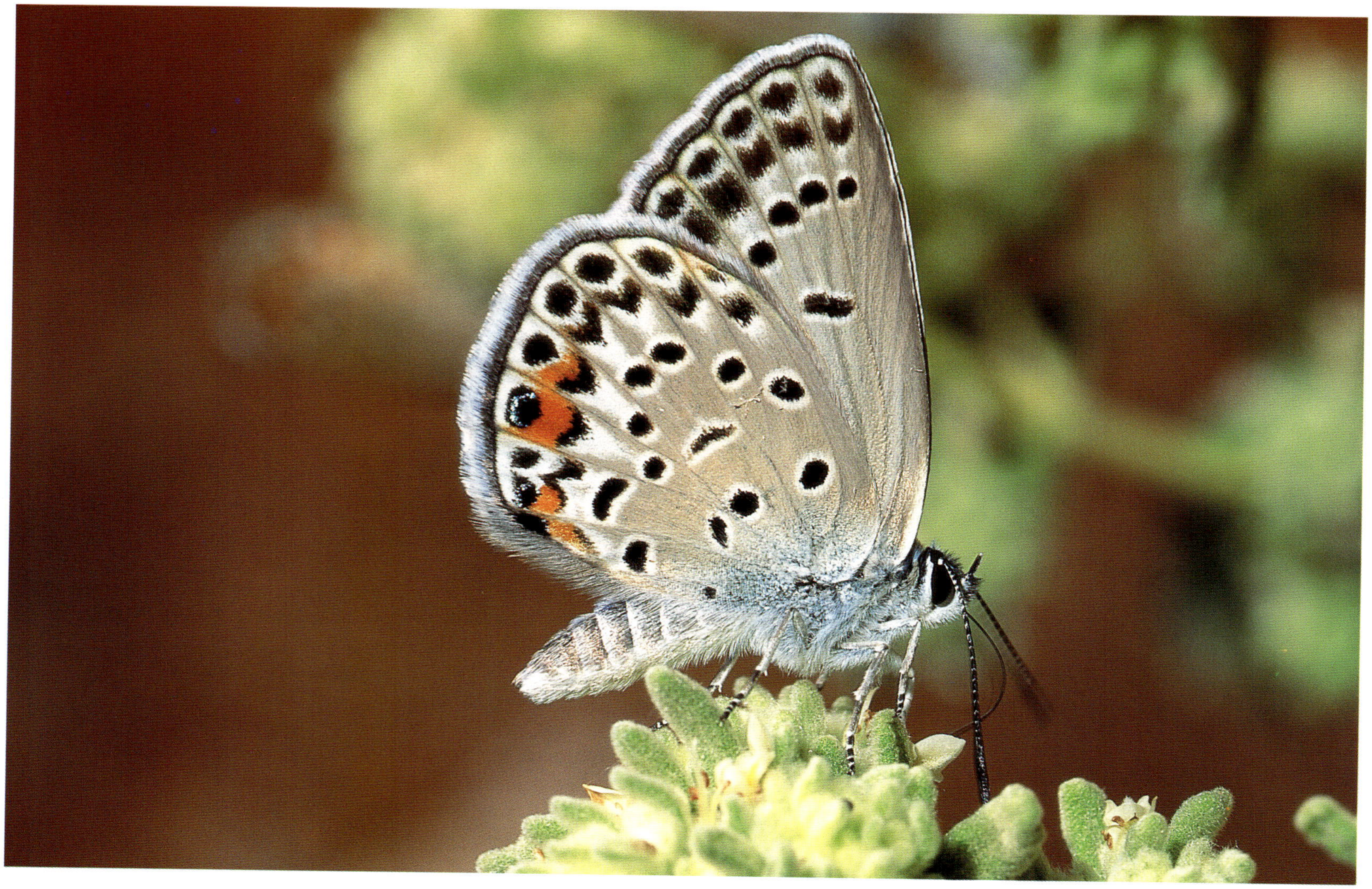

Silver-studded blues are a visual treat that can still be found on heathlands.
Pentax LX + 100mm macro lens, off-camera TTL flash.

The moors of upland Britain are again awash with purple heather in August and, while cooler than the Suffolk Heaths, are none the less interesting. Indeed, one of Britain's finest photographic locations for landscape photography is the high, bleak Rannoch Moor region of Scotland. Just about the first challenge I set myself on entering the world of panoramic photography was to shoot Lochan na h-Achlaise on Rannoch Moor and nearby Glencoe, but I simply hadn't had time to visit. Finally, one autumn (the best season for this part of the world), I drove up for the day, setting off at 2am to get there for sunrise. Well, it rained and rained and, while I failed to get any shots of Glencoe, I got an excellent 6 x 17cm image of Lochan na h-Achlaise shortly after dawn (overleaf), which made the whole trip worthwhile.

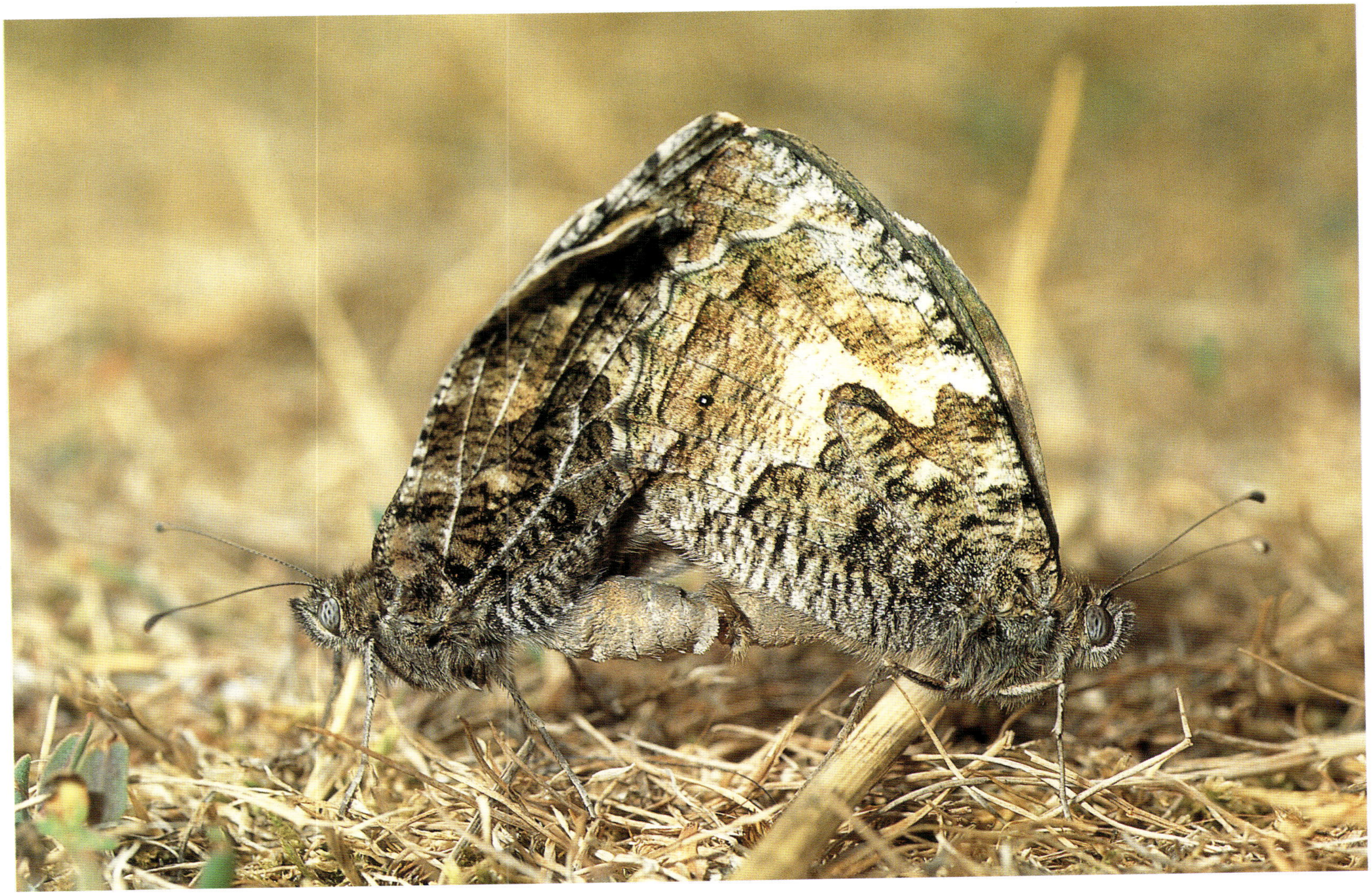

Grayling butterflies are very common on acid grasslands and heath. You need quite good stalking skills to catch them on film – prepare to be frustrated.
Pentax LX.

Cityscapes

If you were to ask any photographer which cities they would like to be transported to for a couple of days of unbridled cityscape photography, my guess is that London, Paris and New York would top the list. This is unsurprising since each of these locations has a plethora of treasures worthy of photographic attention: Tower Bridge, the Eiffel Tower and the twinkle of the Manhattan skyline at dusk. From a sales viewpoint, these urban icons are also highly sought-after by image libraries and other picture buyers. Never mind that they have umpteen shots of the Eiffel Tower on file – if you can find a novel perspective on the same subject they will be interested.

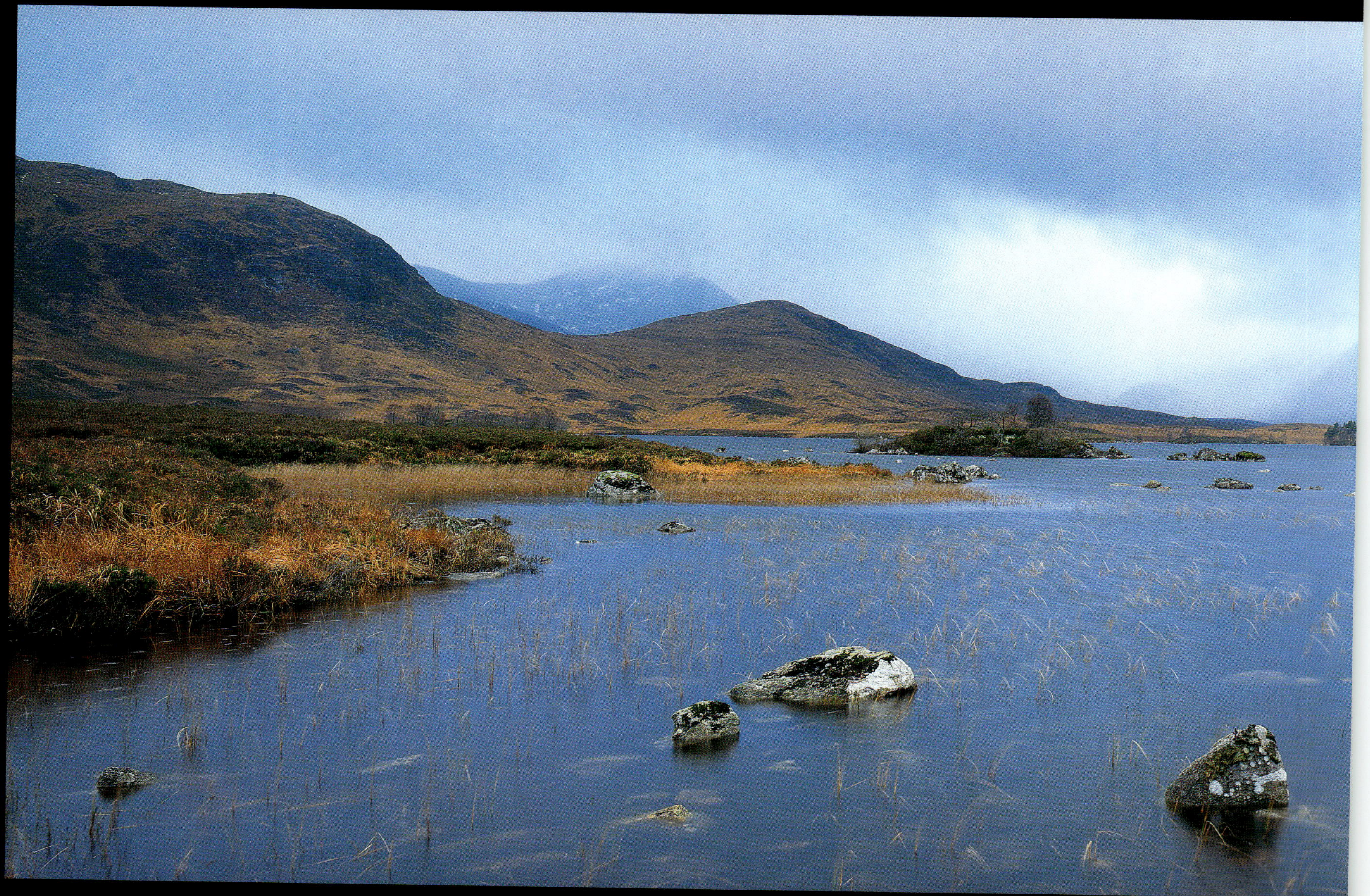

Panoramic view of Lochan na h-Achlaise on Rannoch Moor (near Glencoe, Scotland). This high moor is extremely isolated and bleak, but has a special quality for photographers. I shot this in the middle of November. Initially, while setting up my kit, I fell flat on my face due to the slippery waterlogged ground. I took this picture in driving rain, and between each exposure I had to dry the lens with my hanky.
Fuji GX617 + 90mm lens.

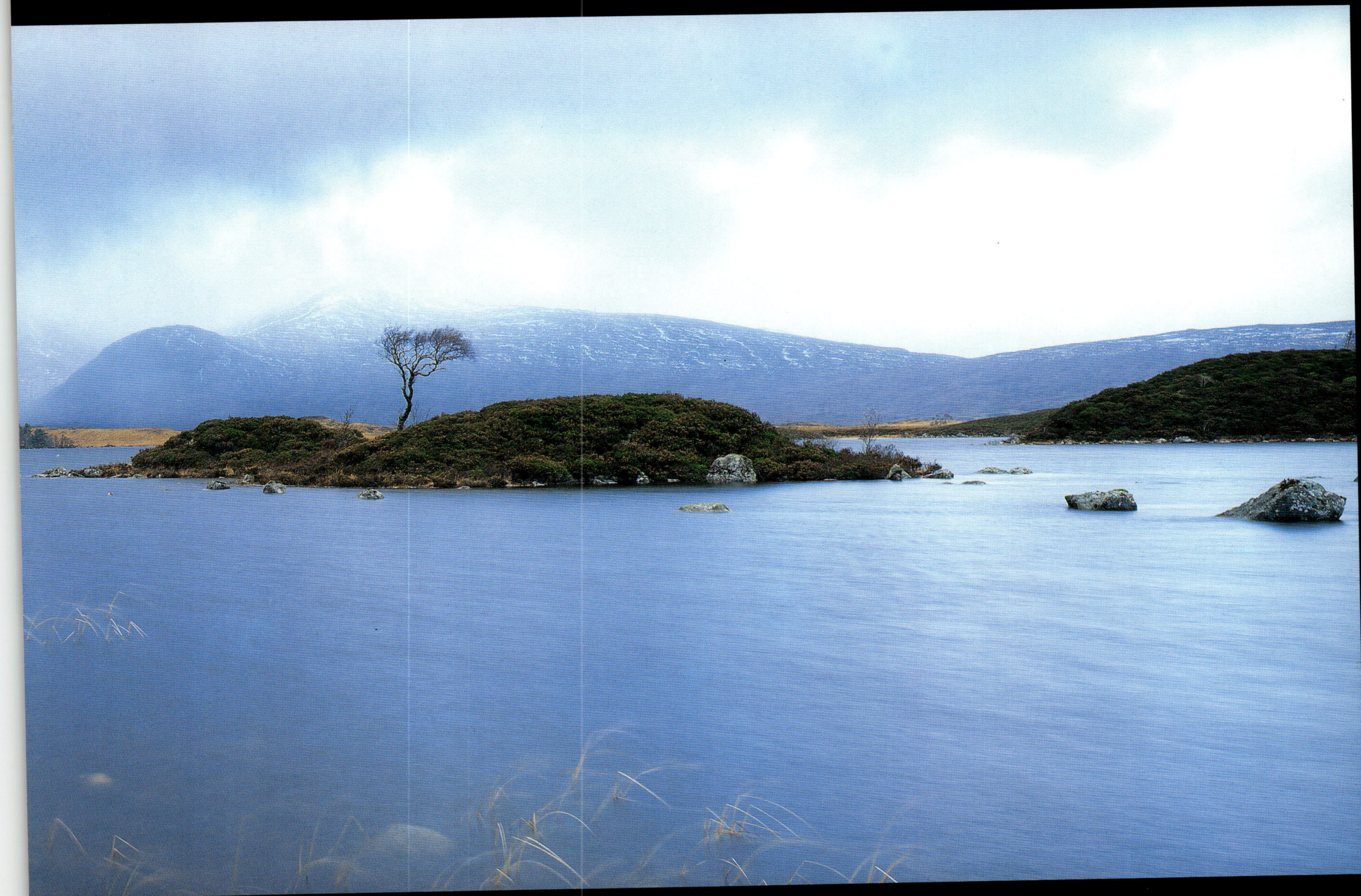

I live in the city and whenever possible I try to get away to the countryside. Nevertheless, I often visit cities on my travels. I am particularly fond of the urban environment in developing countries and, for this reason, I have included examples of my experiences in the Imperial cities of Morocco, and Margao, a typical Indian city. They are fascinating, exotic, sometimes shocking, but always photogenic.

Undoubtedly, one of the most interesting places I have ever visited is Morocco. City slicker, country rambler or beach bum; it really doesn't matter what your travel preference is, the bustling markets and souks of the world mesmerize and enthrall everyone. They invariably provide simmering cauldrons of humanity, constantly overflowing with life that is a cacophony of kaleidoscopic colour. Yet, in a quick hour or two, shuffle-cum-squeeze, they will almost certainly throw up the odd sad and, sometimes, by western standards, shocking sight.

Mediterranean tourists are accustomed to the obligatory morning market excursion, particularly in the Levantine countries of the eastern Med. In Turkey, for instance, age-old wares are sold in profusion alongside less ubiquitous modern tack. Bait is laid for shoppers in the guise of apple or peppermint tea, which is provided gratis and almost *ad libitum*. Despite the visual clash of primary colours amongst a plethora of powdered teas and unusual spices and herbs, these markets have been diluted to accommodate western tastes.

However, indisputably in a class of its own, the best (or worst) market experience is undoubtedly to be had in Morocco, where the colour and magic of Marrakesh's souks contrasts with the more down-to-earth, real-life confusion of Fes' medina. Set on the cusp of northwest Africa, Morocco belongs to the Mahgreb countries, yet maintains an uneasy relationship with its western neighbour, Algeria: a nation undergoing a violent upheaval in Islamic fundamentalism. Further to the south, the Moroccan army exerts control over the Western Sahara: a piece of desiccated land, rich

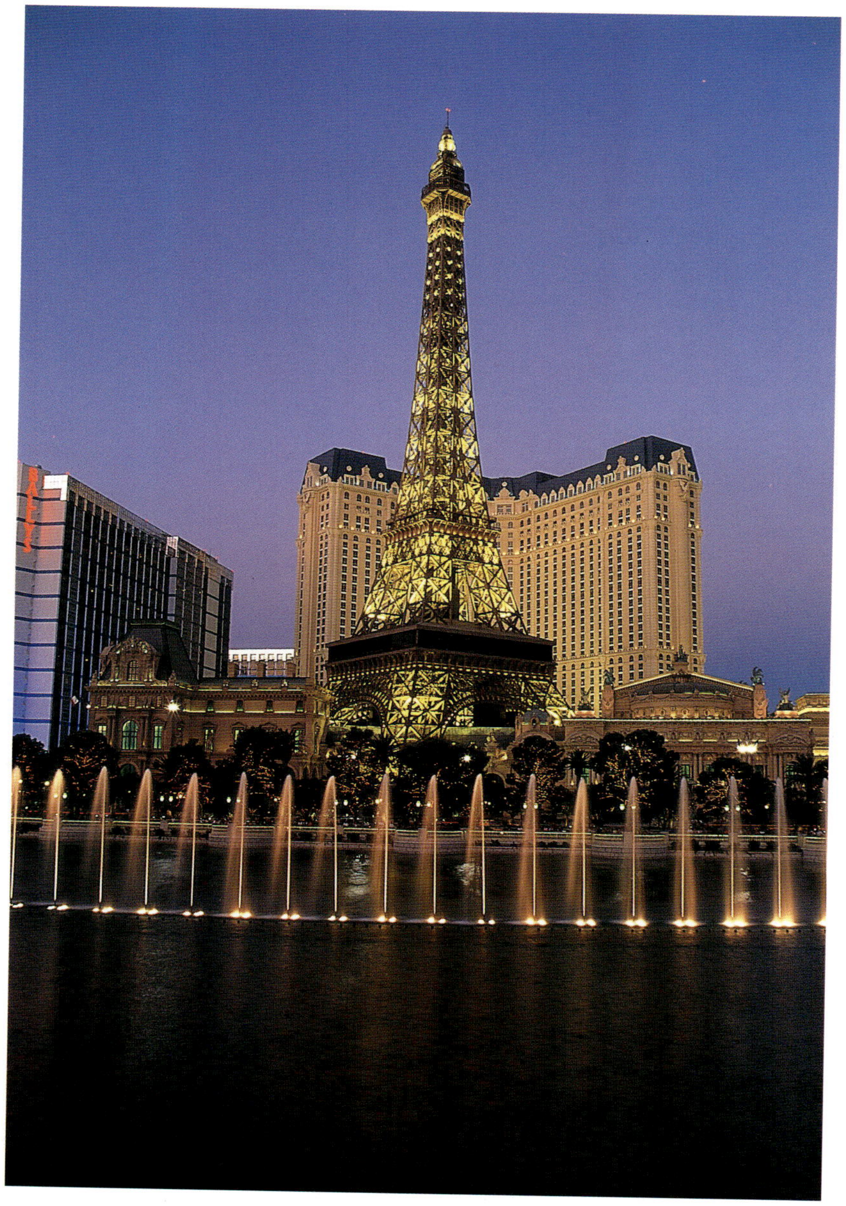

Fountains and mock Eiffel Tower lit up at dusk. Las Vegas, Nevada.
Pentax MZ5 + 28–70mm zoom lens, f/8–11, Velvia, tripod.

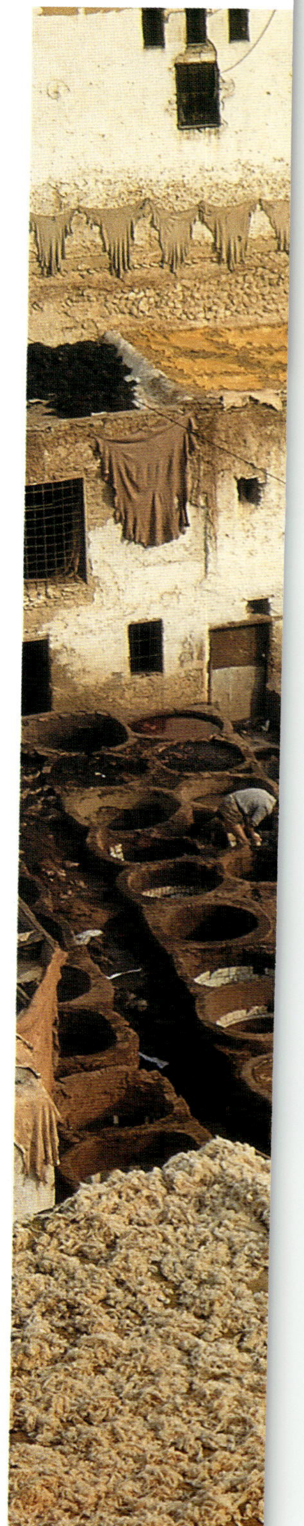

In Morocco, the tanneries and dyeing vats near the Oued Fes River in Fes are a photographer's dream, and beg to be photographed. I rested on a wall to stabilize the camera.
Pentax MZ5 + 28–70mm zoom lens.

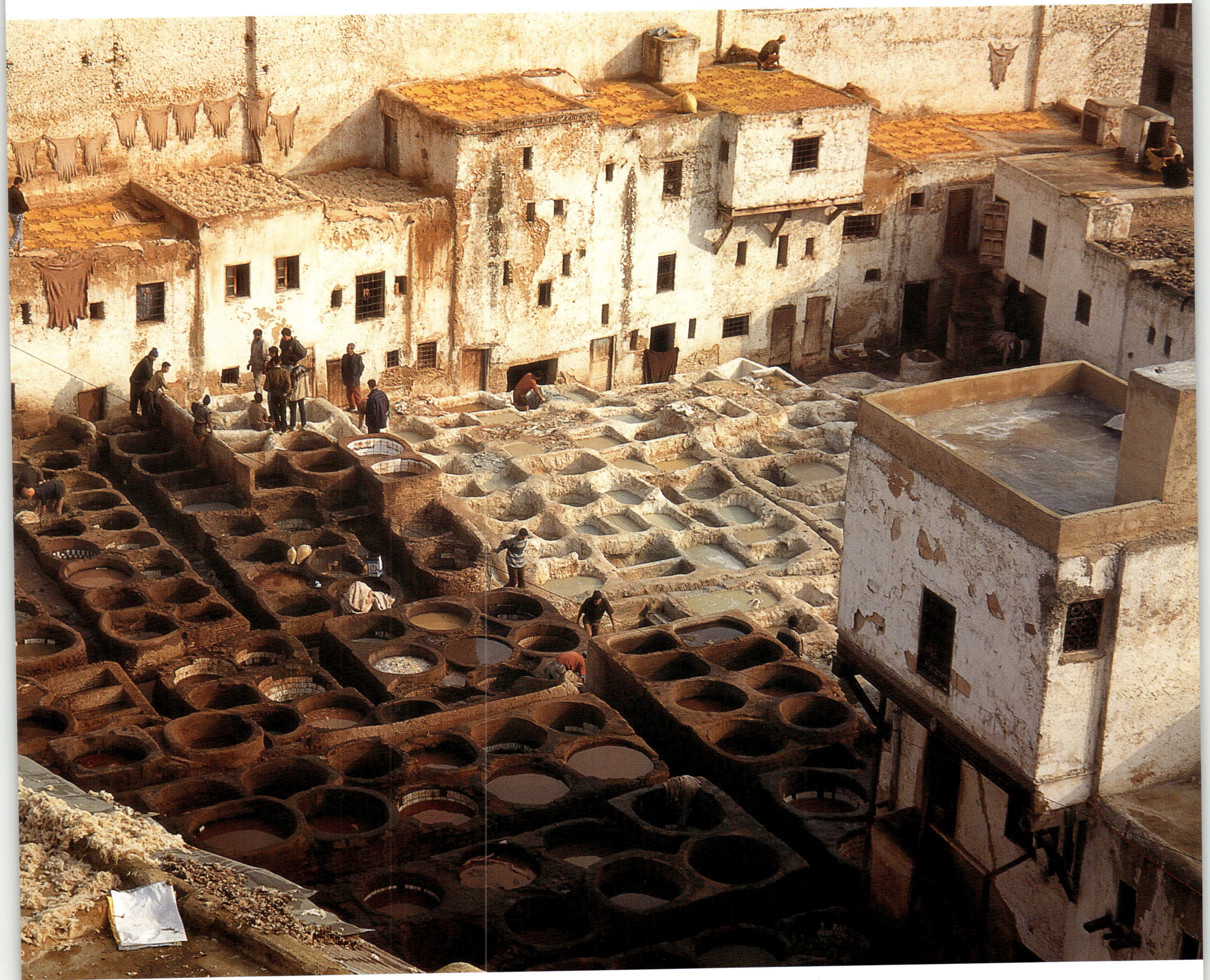

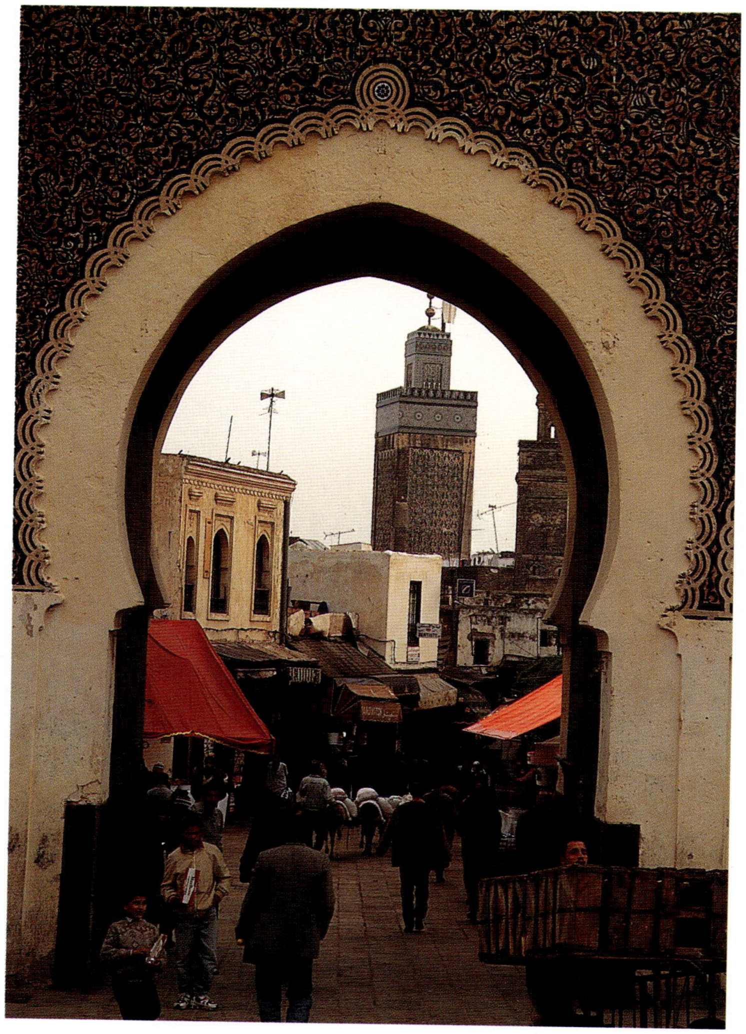

The blue gate leading into the medina in Fes is worth a shot, particularly as it frames the Mosque of Sidi Lezzaz. Morocco is full of photographic opportunity.
Pentax MZ5 + 28–70mm zoom lens.

in phosphates, uranium, fish and potential tourist beaches. To exercise this control, a 1000-mile wall equipped with infrared, self-firing weapons defends a trillion-trillion grains of sand from Sahraouic freedom fighters based in the Algerian town of Tindouf. Unfortunately, it has been equally effective at killing the country's last gazelles.

Fortunately, like the majority of the country, the Imperial cities of Morocco are friendly and trouble-free. Indeed, they rank amongst the worlds most fascinating and beautiful urban centres and were quite simply made for photography. In Fes, the labyrinth of narrow, winding streets within the ancient-walled medina provides a living museum of over a quater-of-a-million people. UNESCO elevated this sector of Fes to world heritage site status in 1976. It is the largest medina in the world and possibly the busiest market (souk) in Africa. You need a guide or you will get lost. You should arm yourself with a short zoom lens (28–70mm); a longer zoom lens is useless in the confined space of the souks. Also, I recommend ISO 100 film. I opted for Provia 100 since light falls off dramatically in the narrow alleyways. Even in the open squares the teeming hordes prevent the use of a tripod. In this respect, ISO 100 wins over Velvia (ISO 50) since the extra stop assists hand-held photography under a variety of potential lighting situations.

Some of the more classic shots of this part of the world depict the huge bronze gates of the Royal Palace (Dar el Makhzen), surrounded by ornate Arabic decor. I was lucky enough to visit while they were

The following route will expose the keen photographer to most of the sights in Fes' medina. Before entering the medina through the blue gate (Bab Boujeloud), shoot the gate as it frames the Mosque of Sidi Lezzaz. Take the main alleyway of Talaa el Kebira or Talaa el Seghira which affords plenty of local colour to shoot en route to the Fondouk Nejjarine and Nejjarine Fountain. These are intricately tiled mosaics, truly Arabic in nature, and well worth a few pictures. A short stroll from here brings you to the enormous 20,000-capacity Kairawine Mosque: the religious centre of Morocco. Photographs are limited to the perimeter as only Muslims may enter. However, close by are preschool Koran classes where for a small donation you can shoot the class encapsulated in an elaborate wooden, cage-like alcove. Undoubtedly, it is the next port of call beside the Oued Fes River which offers up the most fascinating, if olfactorily obnoxious, photo oppotunities. For here are the tanneries and dyeing vats: an evil brewing process reliant upon such ingredients as pigeon poop. In fact, a word of caution is necessary at this point: learn the words 'balek balek'. If you hear this, watch your camera and back, for a donkey heavily laden with dripping hides and filling the entire narrow street, is most likely thundering toward you. Tens of thousands of mules ply the medina in Fes; another good reason for forgetting the tripod. And try to visit on Friday, it is much less busy.

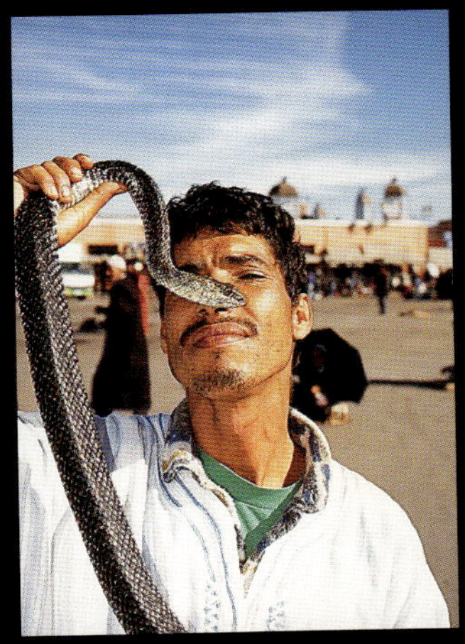

Marrakesh is Morocco's most colourful city and is a dream to shoot (watch out for pickpockets though). This is where you find a kaleidoscope of subjects in the Place Jemaa el Fna, for example this snake charmer. *Pentax MZ5 + 28–70mm zoom lens.*

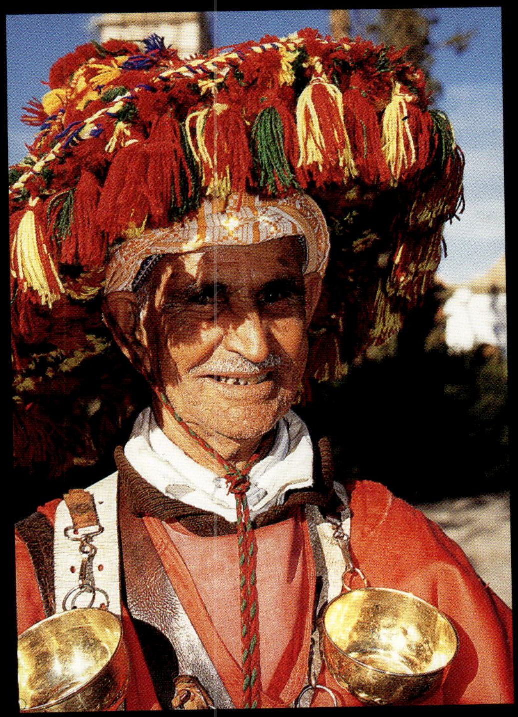

Place Jemaa el Fna: a water seller. *Pentax MZ5 + 28–70mm zoom lens.*

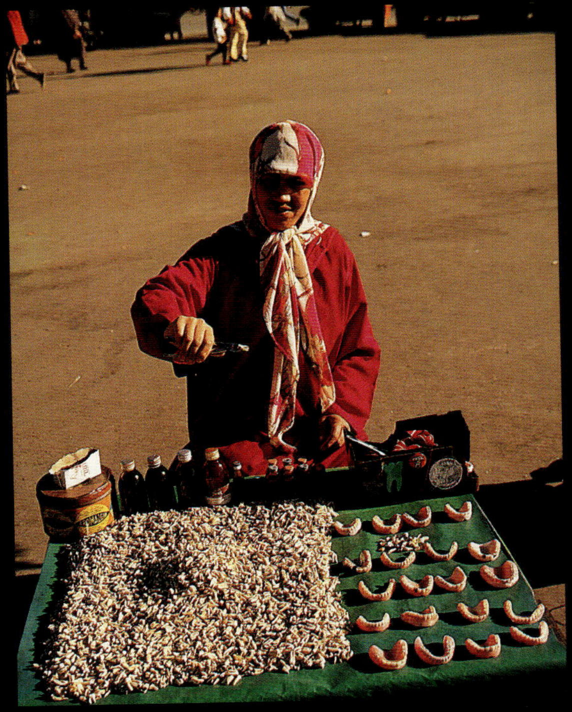

Place Jemaa el Fna: a dentist. *Pentax MZ5 + 28–70mm zoom lens.*

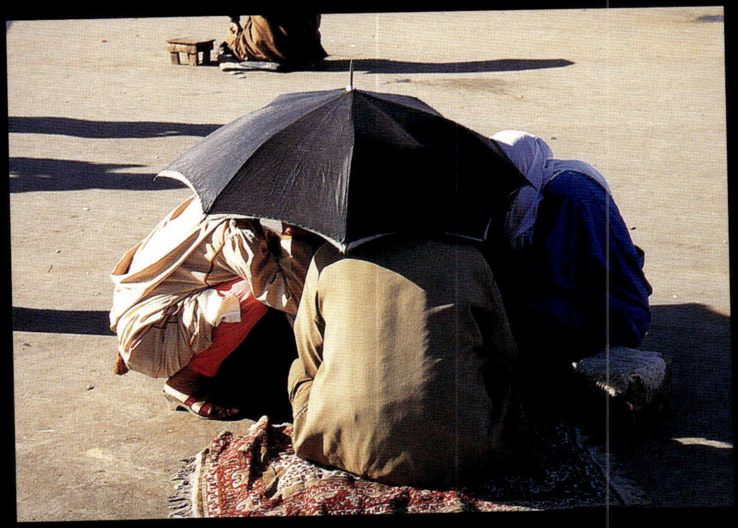

Place Jemaa el Fna: a storyteller. *Pentax MZ5 + 28–70mm zoom lens.*

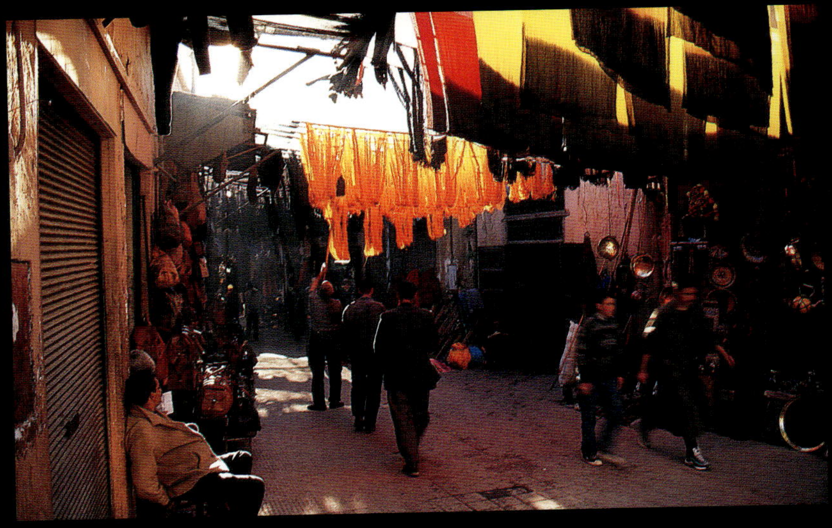

This is the archetypal shot of Marrakesh. This view of colourful silks hanging out to dry in the souk's labyrinthine alleyways was an image I was after even before I left the UK. The souk is a prime location for photogenic subjects. *Pentax MZ5 + 28–70mm zoom lens.*

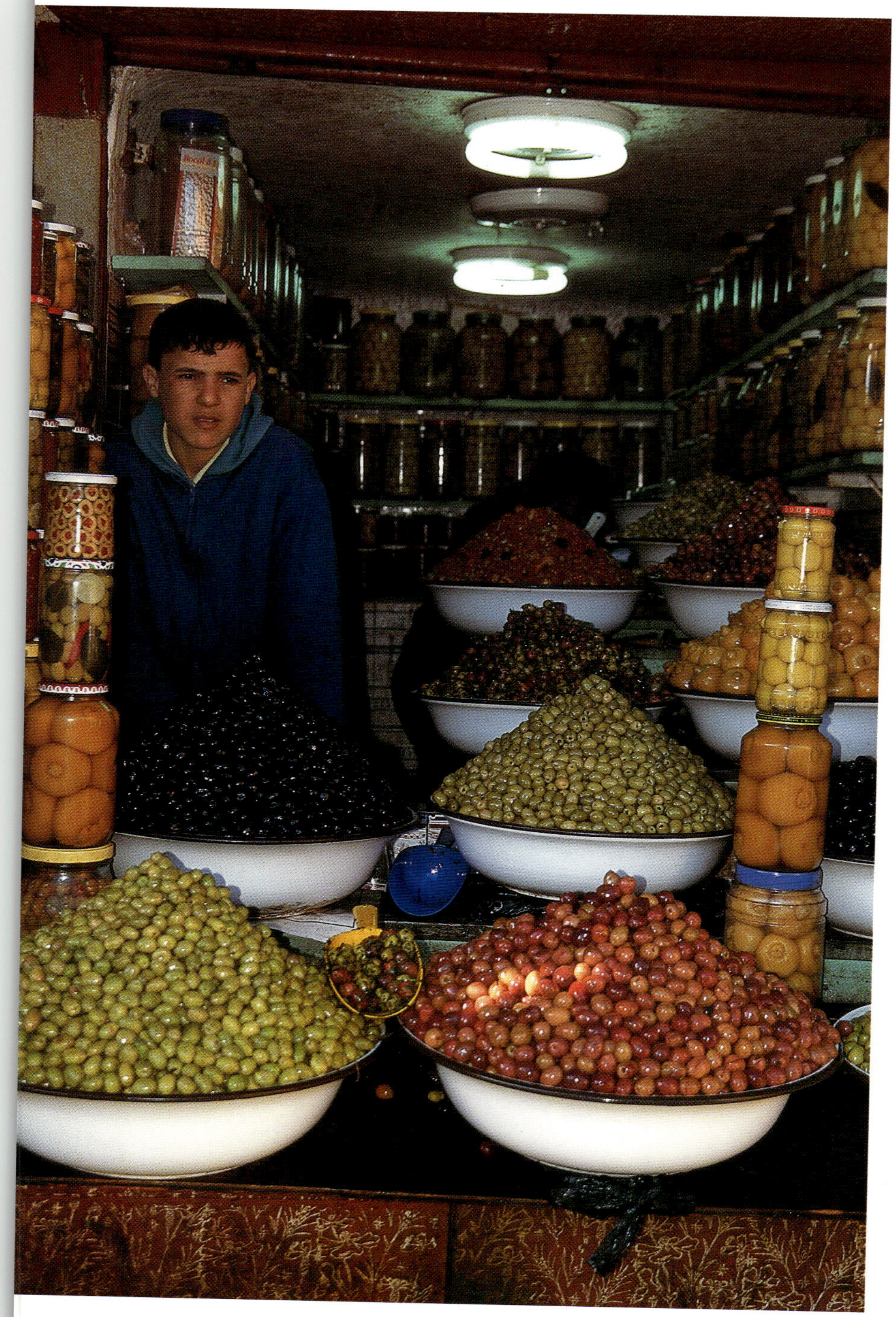

An olive shop just off the Place Jemaa el Fna, Marrakesh, Morocco.
Pentax MZ5 + 28–70mm zoom lens.

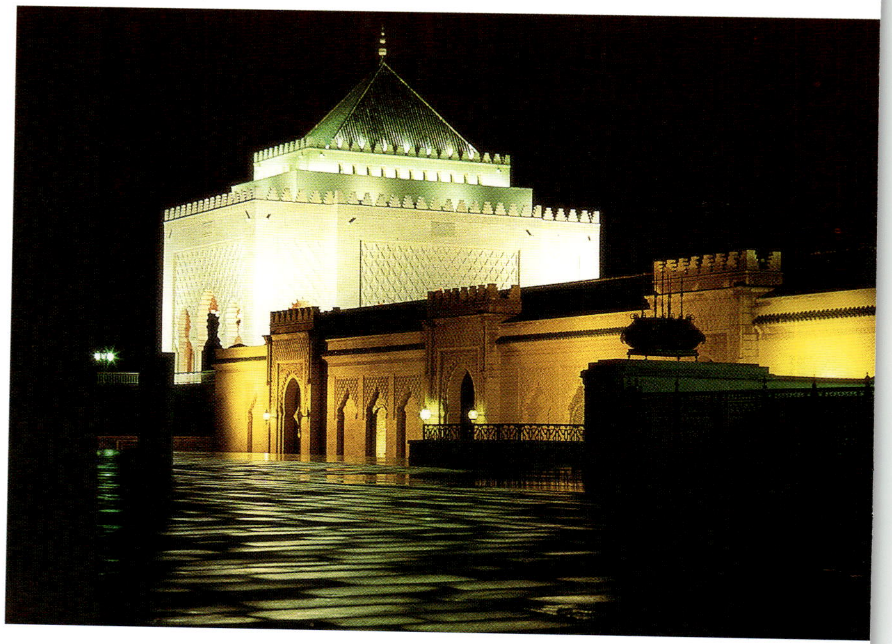

Important buildings are often illuminated at night. This shot was taken in Rabat, Morocco.
Pentax MZ5, about 20 seconds at f/8.

being cleaned, a ritual which only occurs once every two months and involves a gentle massage with several half-lemons. A truly unique and unusual photo opportunity.

As a visitor you should remember it is forbidden by the Koran to produce engraven images of man and animal. The majority of people in Fes do not wish to be photographed and can become aggressive. Do respect their wishes and always seek permission to take a picture. In this way you will be more successful although it may cost you a dirhm or three.

Photography takes on a different dimension in Marrakesh. If Fes is reality, then Marrakesh, on the edge of the Sahara, is colourful exotica. Here all photographs must be paid for. The snake charmers and their cobras and puff adders, the acrobats, blindingly bright watersellers, dentists and freshly extracted teeth (patients in absolute agony are never far away), and storytellers all make a living from the photography of western tourists. All these transactions take place in the amazing Place Jemaa el Fna, a unique gathering place where the most bizarre aspects of humanity come to the fore every day of the year. Snake charmers expect 10 dirhm per picture, but guides suggest 1–2 dirhm per half-dozen shots. Actually it all comes down to whether you are willing to have a cobra used as a bronchoscope. The hassle-factor is

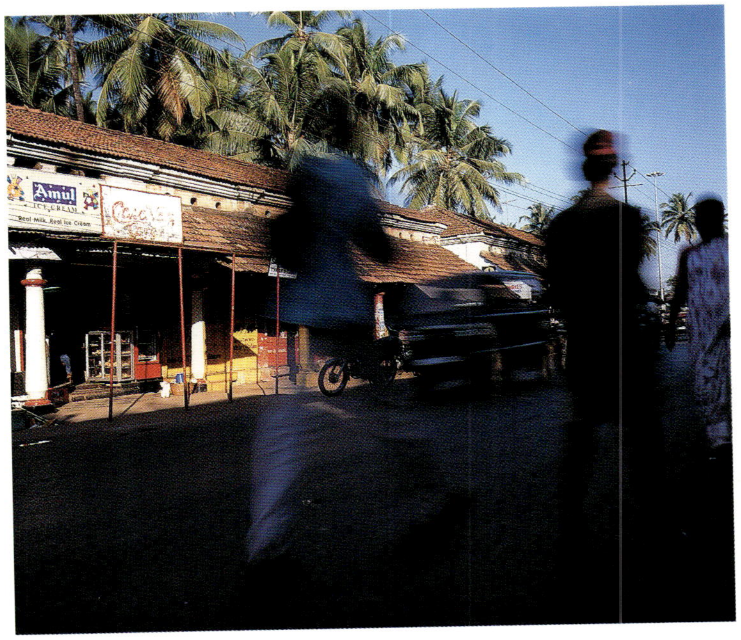

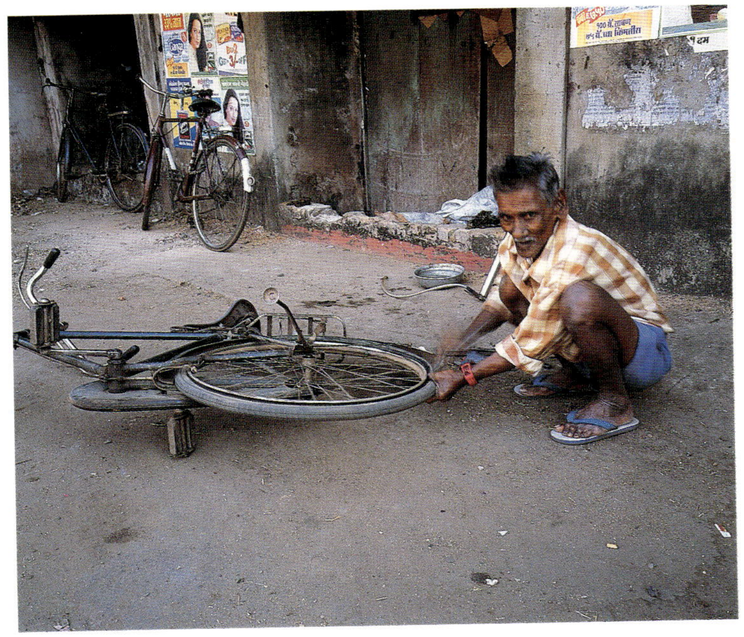

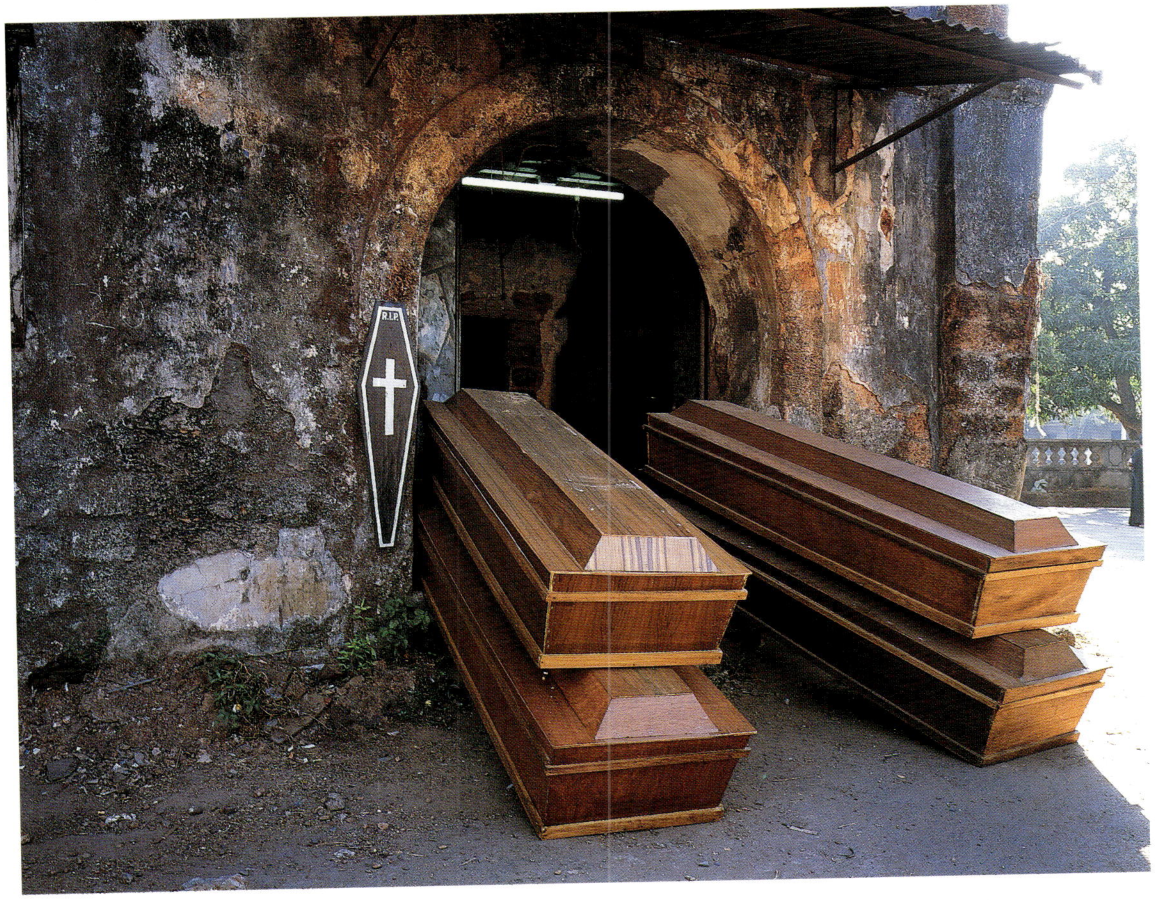

This man was busy fixing bikes on the pavement in Margao, India.
Fuji GA645Wi, Velvia, tripod.

Above left: Margao in India is a busy working town. I used a small aperture and slow shutter speed to catch the ebb and flow of street life on my precariously balanced Fuji GA645Wi, which was on a tripod with its legs tightly pulled in.
Fuji GA645W, Velvia, tripod.

The Margao coffin-makers in India.
Fuji GA645W, Velvia, tripod.

unbelievable – learn to say 'no' with authority and let persistent hassle wash off you like water. However, nowhere on earth is more photogenic and, since these people are far poorer than one can conceptualize in Western Europe or North America, you should pay a fair price for your images and respect those who do not wish to be photographed. Even though it is intensely annoying, you should probably even pay those watersellers who appear out of nowhere when you have photographed a building, claiming that they are the true subject of your photographs.

In the souks of Marrakesh, make for the open alleys where colourful silk hangs out to dry after being dyed with saffron, cochinel or indigo (or so tourists are led to believe). Whatever is used, it provides unparalleled photo opportunities. However, these alleys are not for the faint-hearted. While the pharmacies can be fun – aphrodisiacs and all that (no Viagra yet, the locals still prefer beetle exudate) – the pet shops are no fun at all. They are a lesson in cruelty only tempered by the harsh reality of survival: if it can be sold, sell it or starve. I saw a ragged cage full of newly hatched tortoises afloat in a sea of bird droppings. They where constantly being defacated on by a tethered and sadly tatty falcon on top of the cage. These were pictures which show a much less colourful side to the souk. It is a reminder that this is the third world, where poverty and despair are the flip side of everything which is vibrantly colourful and photogenic about Morocco.

A final word. This part of the world is so rich in historical architecture you should not forget your tripod entirely. Illuminated buildings make excellent night shots, and the daytime landscapes, especially in winter (which is the best time to visit), are verdant and dramatic. In summer, the light is less sympathetic to photographers, as is the Chergui: a dusty hot blast of air from the desert.

Other developing nations offer a similar cocktail of photographic opportunities. Margao, in India, has less in the way of labyrinthine souks and alleyways to photograph, but is equally colourful. Quite apart from the characters in Margao's streets, things are simply different here. Sacred cows wander the roads, coffin-makers work with their grim products in open view, artisans abound in the busy streets and do not rely on any form of technology, including electricity. It is totally absorbing to shoot street artisans as they ply their trades, be it the little man who mends punctures or the fruit seller behind his barrow.

The streets are unbelievably busy with traffic and people. However, the chaos does provide a great opportunity to try shooting crowds with flowing movement, perhaps employing slow-sync flash techniques (flash that is balanced with ambient lighting, but with a slow shutter speed permitting some degree of blur [ghosting] when used on moving subjects). I used speed-efficient 35mm and fully automated 6 x 4.5cm (GA645Wi) cameras for spontaneity and because the ebb and flow of humanity meant tripods could only be erected for a short while as they took up too much space on the heaving kerbs and roads.

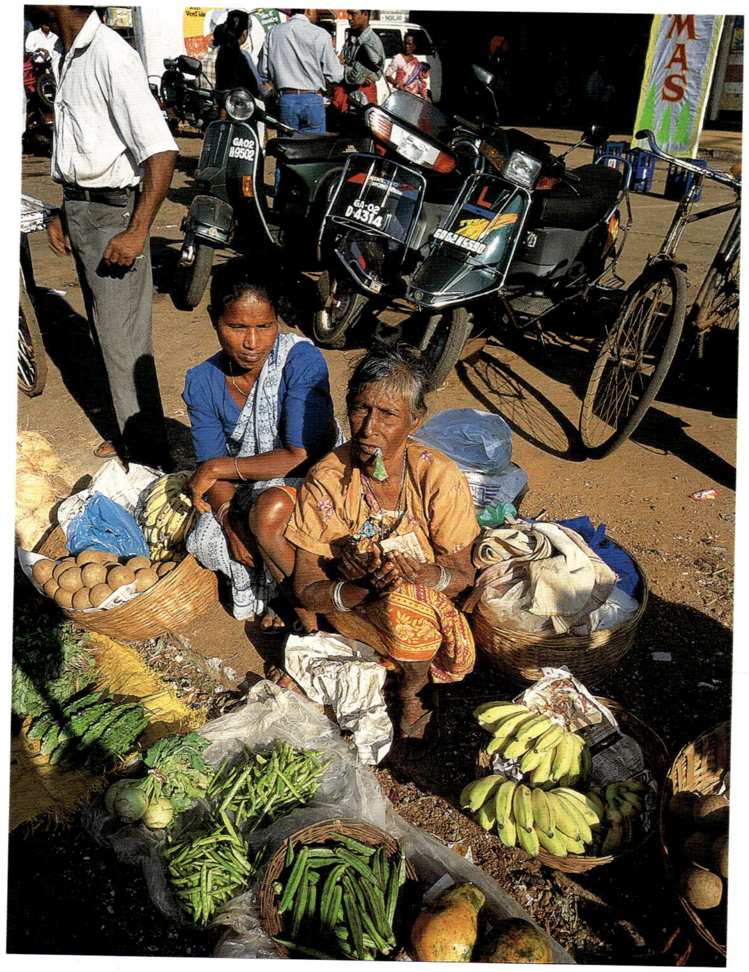

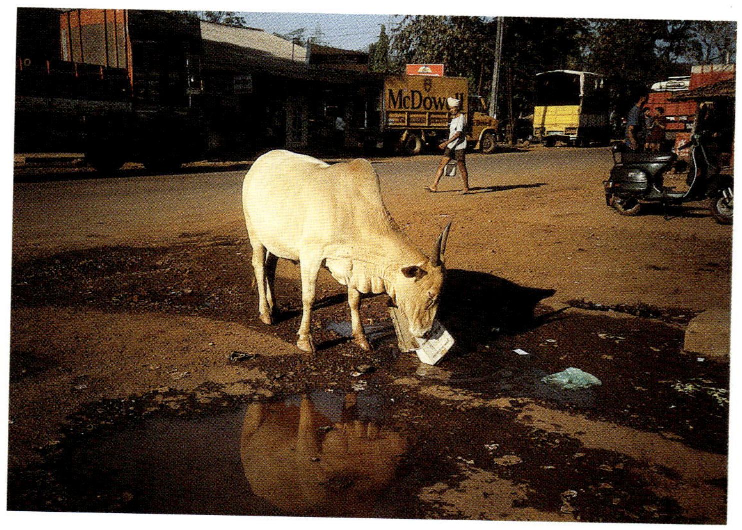

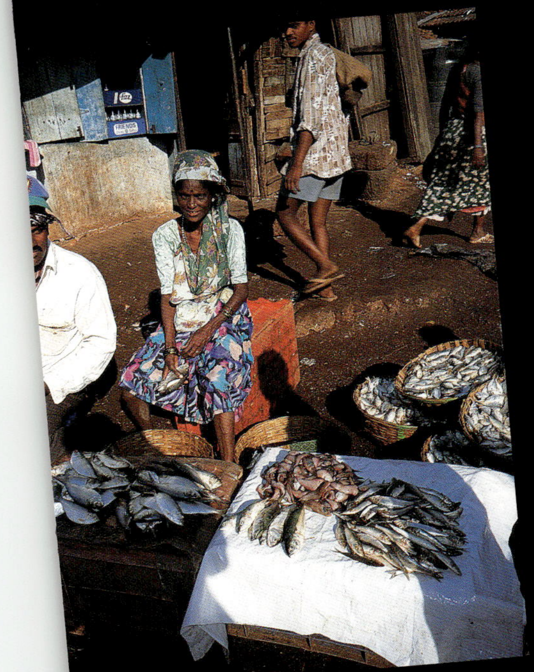

Margao fruitsellers and market traders, India. *Fuji GA645Wi. Velvia, tripod.*

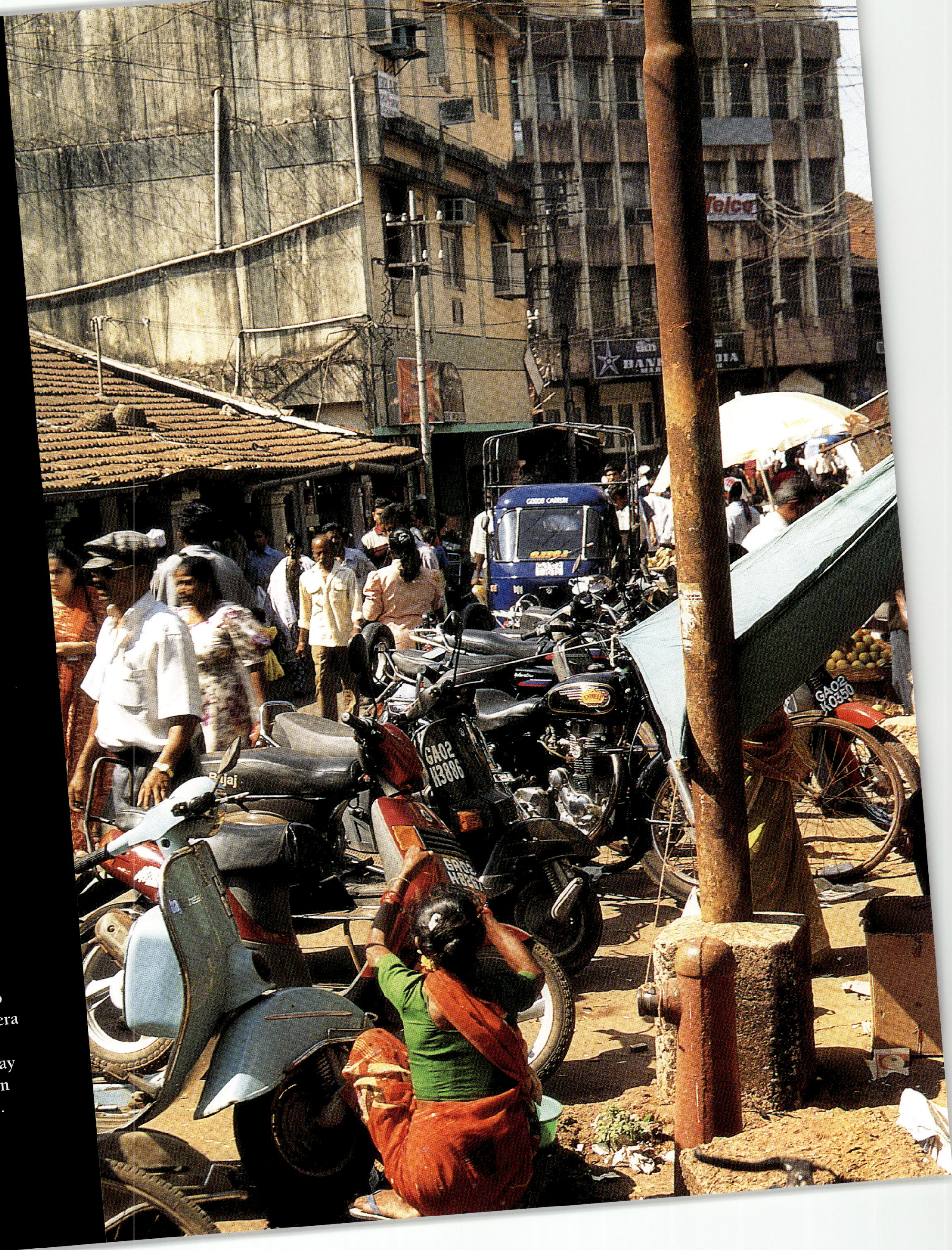

Margao street scene, India. *Pentax MZ5n + 28–70mm zoom lens.*

I took this nonchalant sacred cow using my wife's exceedingly cheap and worn compact camera in an Indian town that was definitely a long way from anywhere. My own camera was out of film.

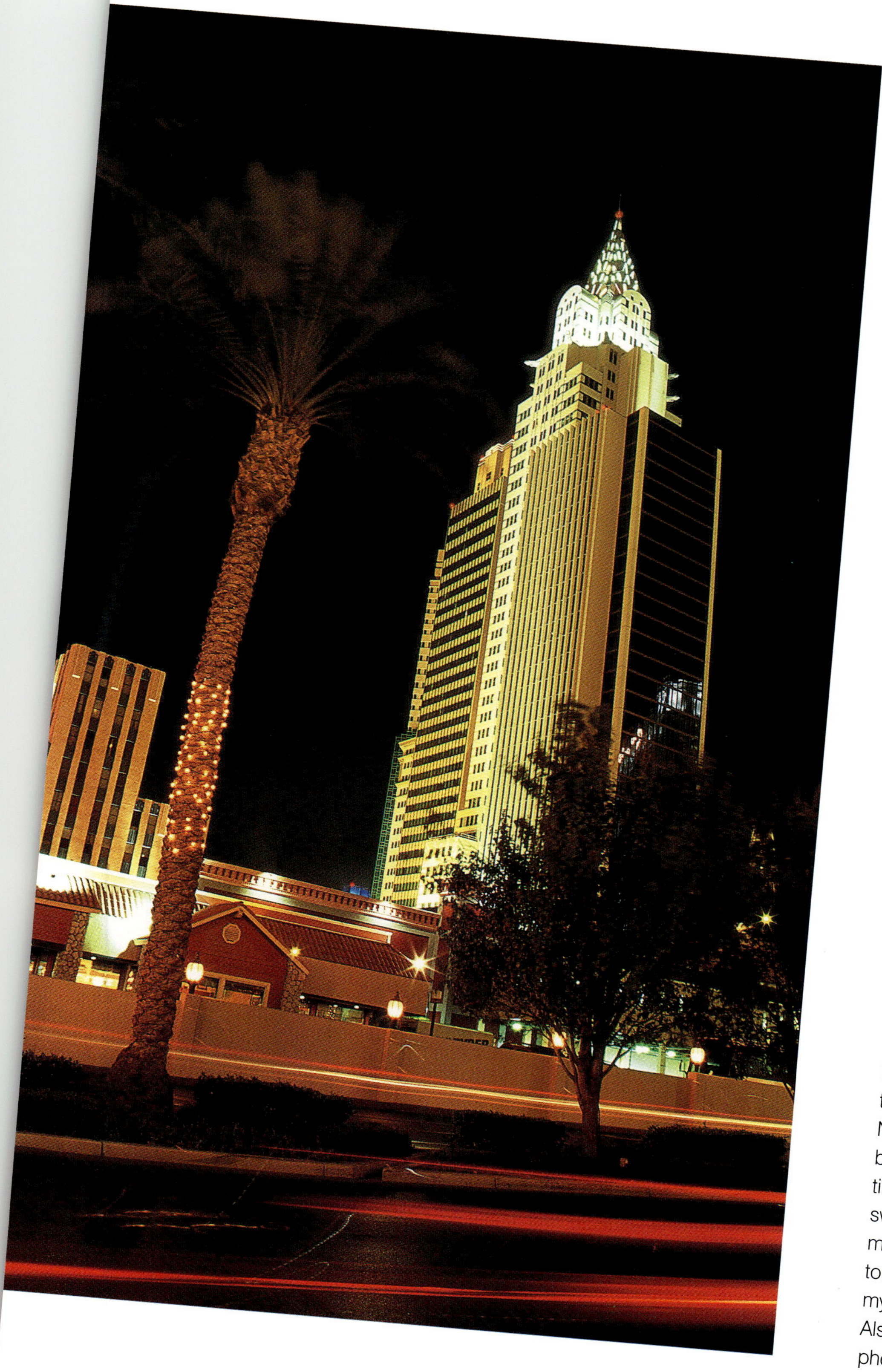

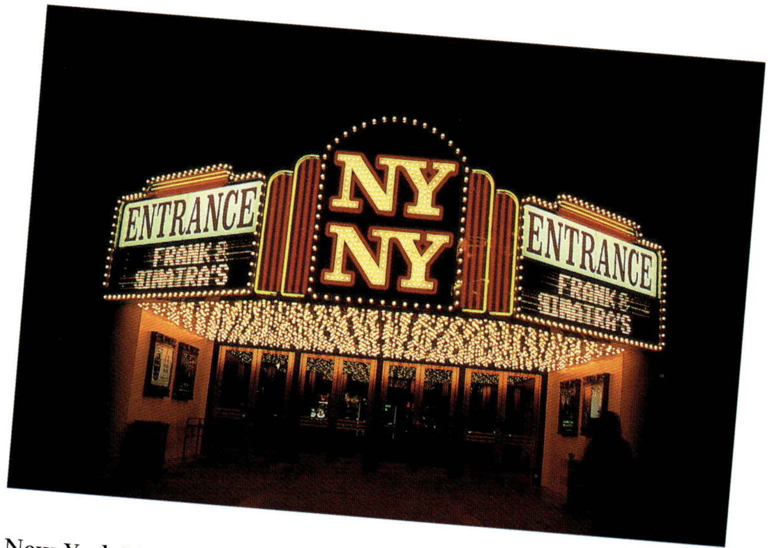

New York-New York sign at night, Las Vegas, Nevada, USA.
Pentax MZ5 + 28–70mm zoom lens on a tripod using Velvia. The aperture was around f/8–11, bracketed up to + 1.5 EV.

New York-New York skyscraper. Taken at night, Las Vegas, Nevada, USA.
Pentax MZ5 + 28–70mm zoom lens, f/8–11, bracketed up to + 1.5 EV, Velvia, tripod.

To contrast with these examples, I end with the one special and quite unique attribute that cities offer photographers: the opportunity to shoot city lights and traffic trails at night. Nowhere is better for this then Las Vegas, a 24-hour, neon-studded gamblers' paradise – and a million miles from India or Morocco. I set off for the 'strip' about 40 minutes before dusk, getting into position with my tripod-borne Pentax MZ5n and cable release. What I really like about this camera is the possibility for 30-second exposure times. The economy of 35mm means that you can bracket extensively and ensure at least one spot-on exposure for each scene. There really are so many possibilities here. I started off outside Bellagio's, shooting Paris and the fountains at twilight, moving down the strip to shoot the Brooklyn Bridge, New York-New York, and numerous traffic scenes. I left the aperture at f/8 and bracketed up to +1.5 stops and down to –1 stop. A typical exposure time would be around 10–15 seconds. To be sure of crisp rendering, I switched off the camera autofocus and composed everything using manual focus. My biggest problem was that dusk is a popular time for tourists to take a stroll along the strip and, on more than one occasion, my tripod was clipped by passing pedestrians, nearly toppling it over. Also, people are generally not sympathetic to nightscape photographers. With ten-second (or longer) exposures, people often take up residence in front of your camera part way through the exposure. With this sort of photography, it is hard to predict the outcome of your endeavours. It is often frustrating in busy streets, but the results, when they work, can be outstanding.

Of course, many people have only infrequent opportunities to travel to exotic cities or places of special interest such as those I have mentioned. Never mind; it is just as easy to shoot your local city. In the UK, double-decker buses and flyovers can provide their own interest. Autumn is a good time to shoot cities in higher latitudes, as the sun sets when people are finishing work at around 5–6pm. The increase in traffic and convenience of the hour makes this an excellent time to practise your traffic-trail shots. All you have to do is find a convenient vantage point such as a footbridge near to a roundabout. And remember to bracket extensively; don't ever rely on the metered value for this kind of photo shoot.

A mock Brooklyn Bridge, lit up at night. Taken in Las Vegas, Nevada, USA.
Pentax MZ5 + 28–70mm zoom lens, f/8–11, bracketed up to + 1.5 EV, Velvia, tripod.

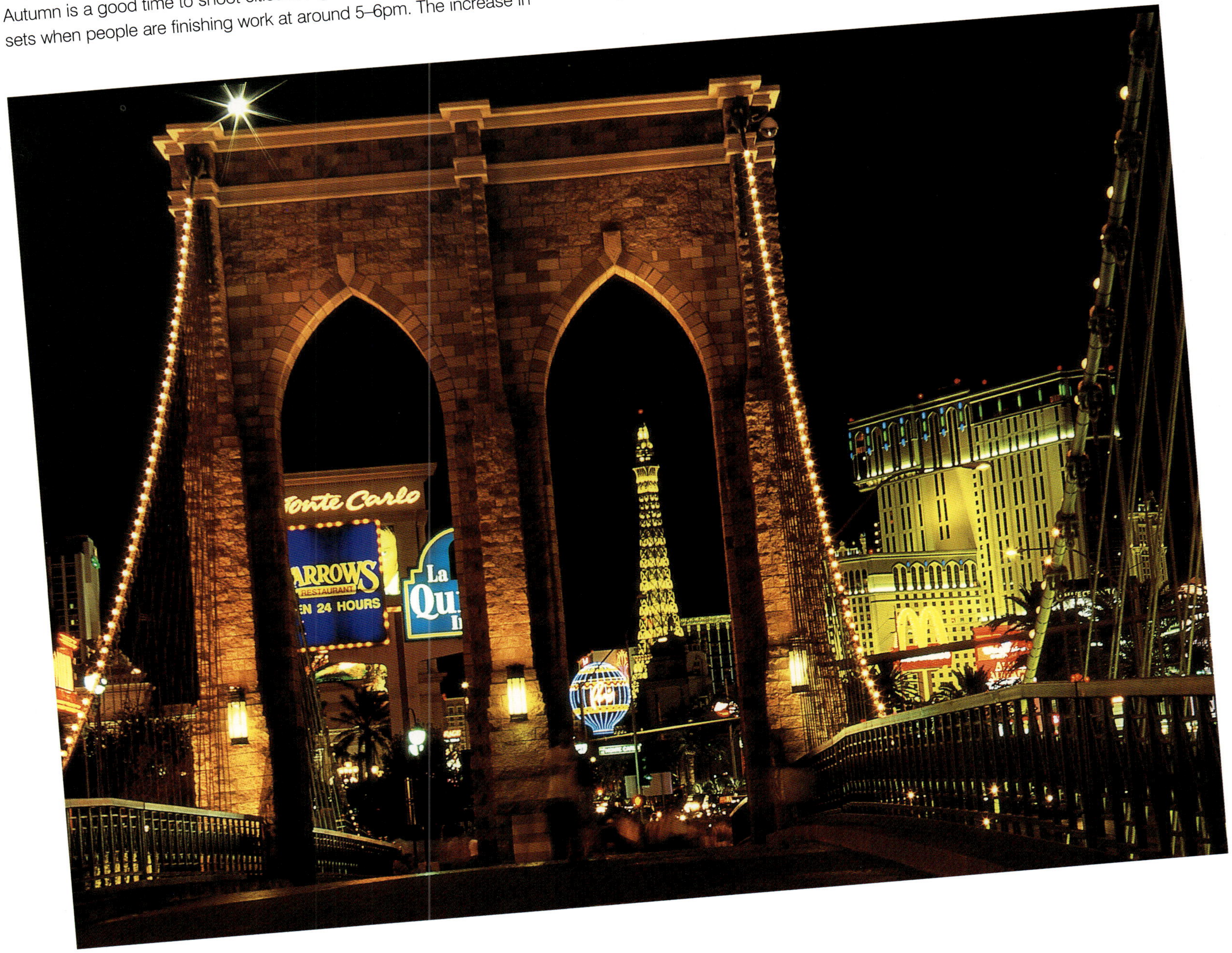

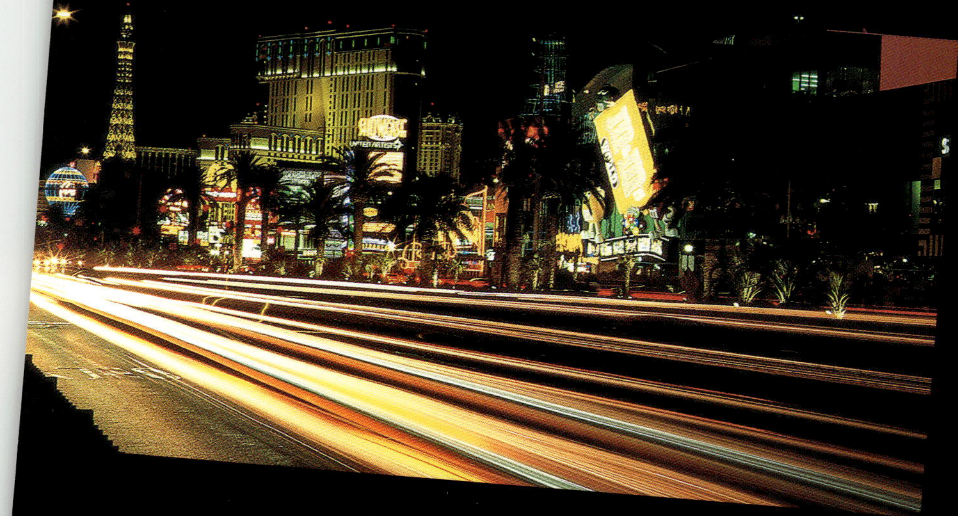

The Strip at night. Las Vegas, Nevada, USA.
Pentax MZ5 + 28–70mm zoom lens,f/8–11, bracketed up to + 1.5 EV, Velvia, tripod.

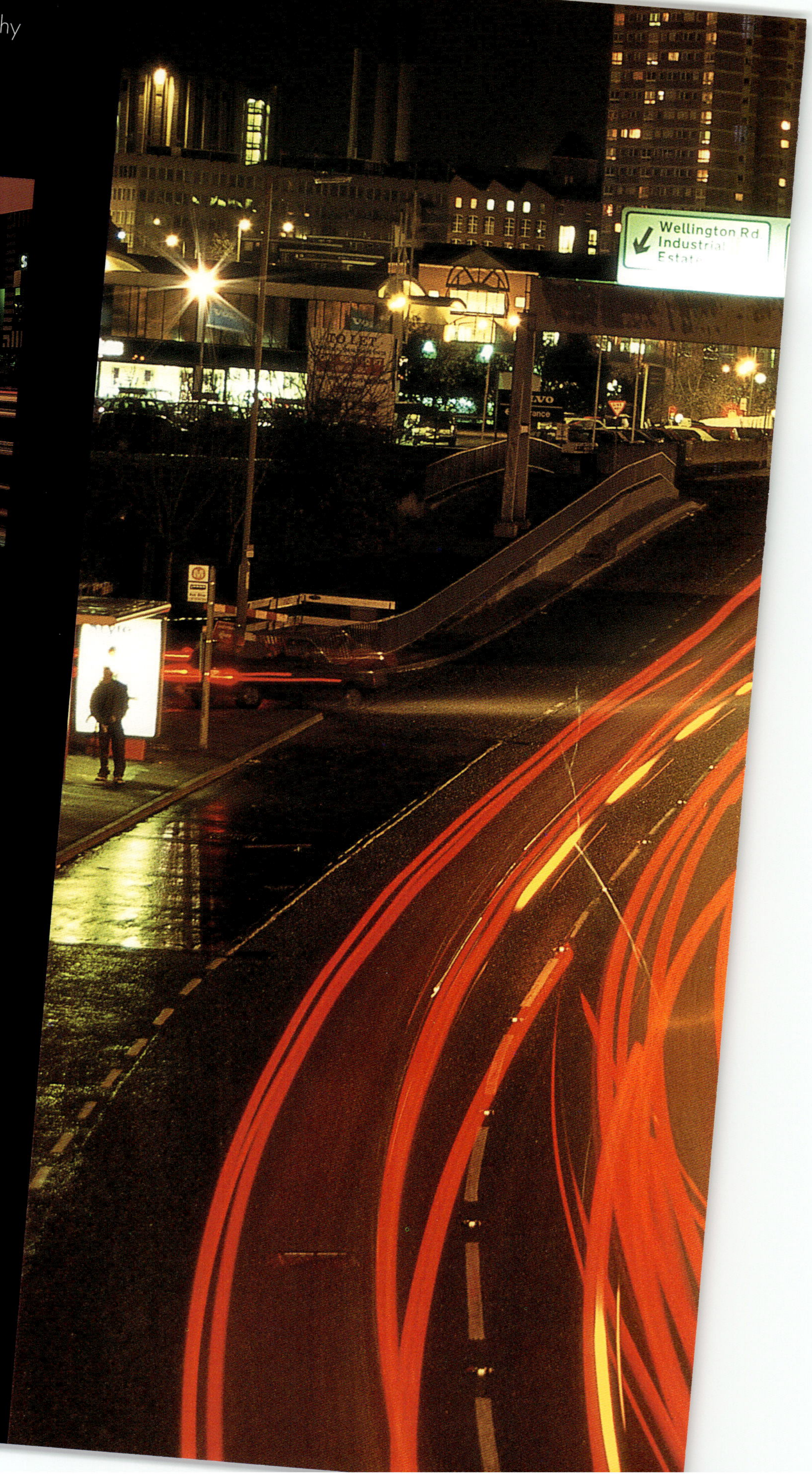

Leeds, England, at night.
Pentax Z1-P + 28–80mm zoom lens. The aperture was around f8–11, bracketed up to + 1.5 EV.

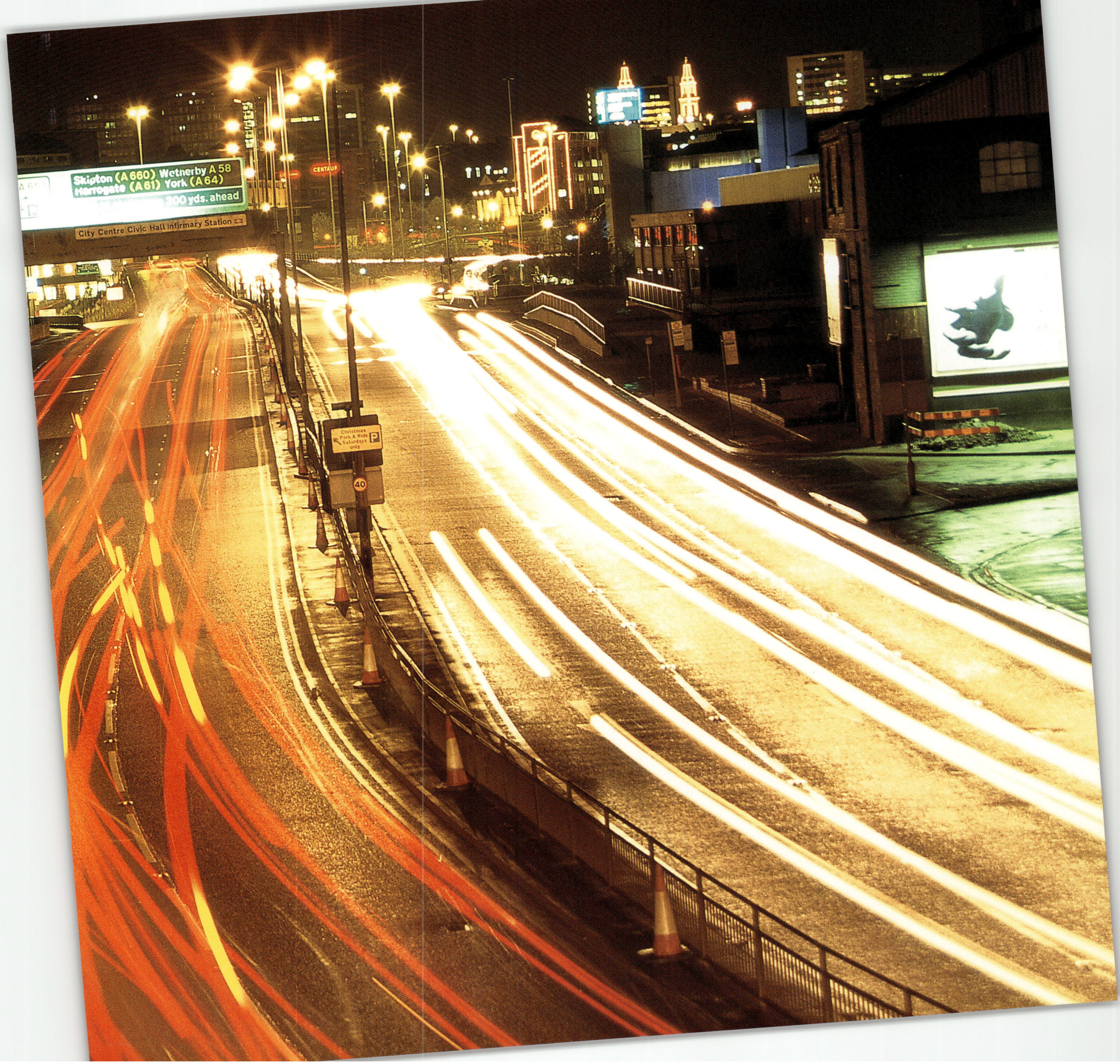
Skipton (A 660) Wetherby A 58
Harrogate (A 61) York (A 64)
200 yds. ahead
City Centre Civic Hall Infirmary Station
40

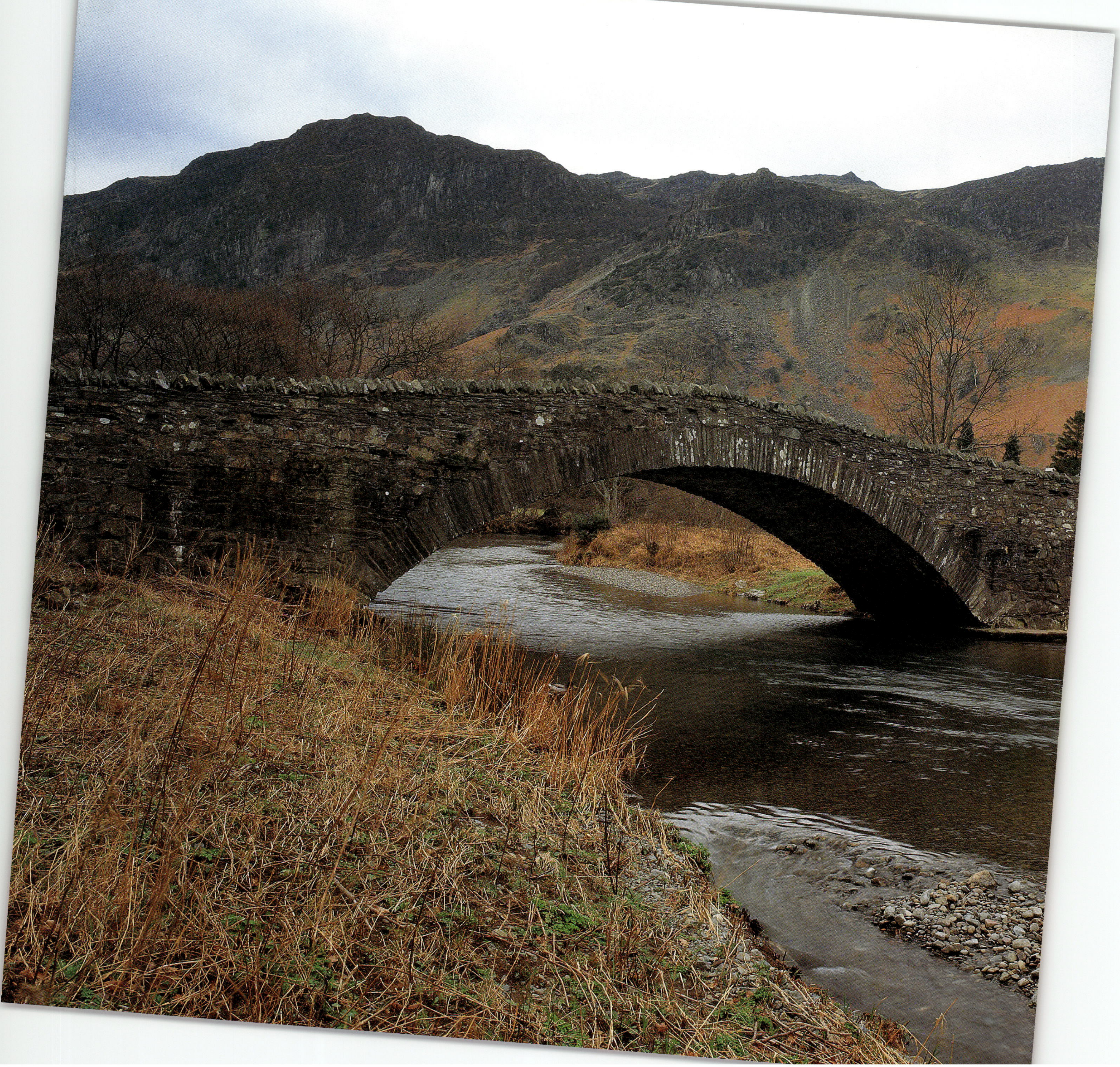

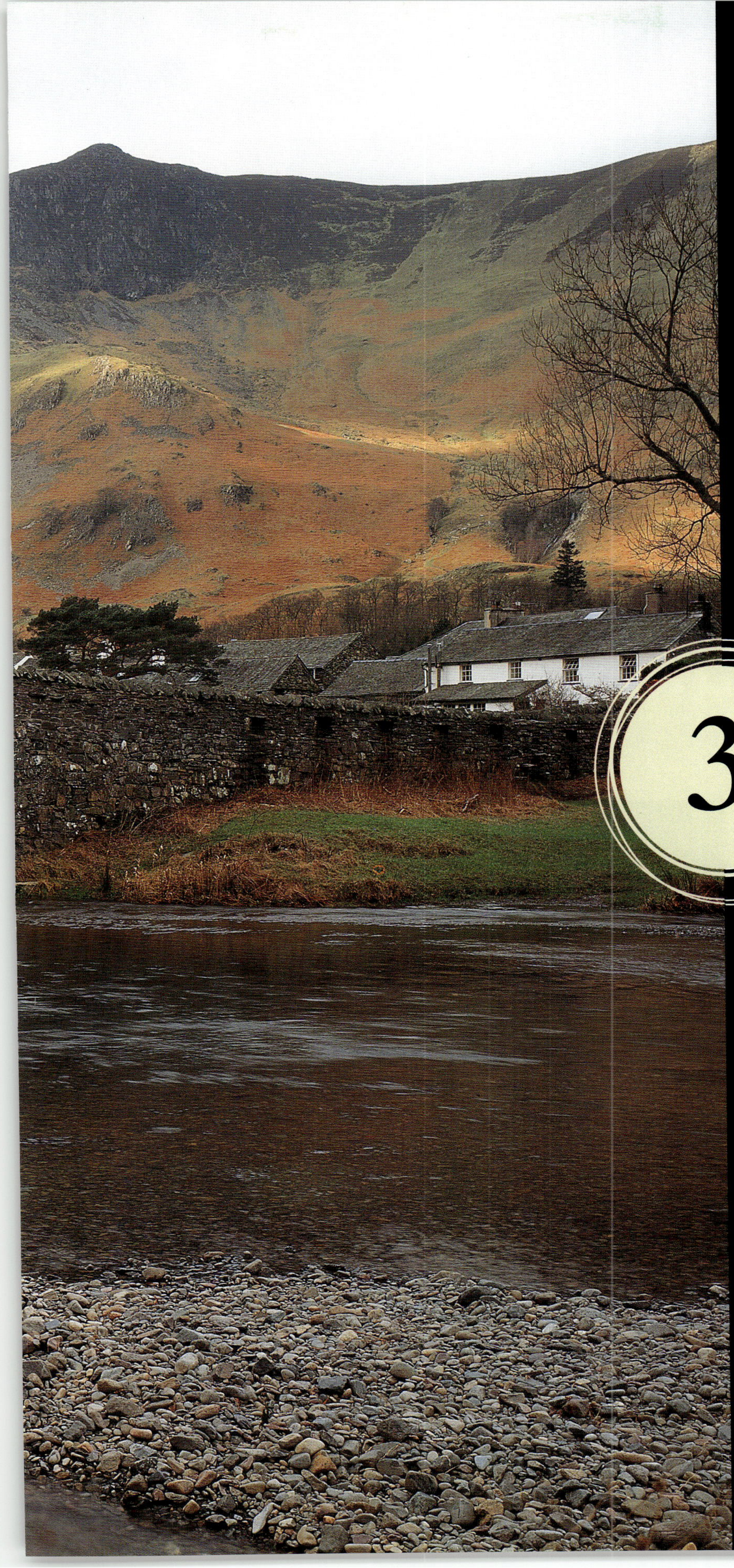

3 Marketing Your Work

Although you may get considerable pleasure from your transparencies when they first drop through your letterbox, the chances are that having viewed them you will want to consign most of them to some kind of storage system and forget them for a period of time. This might be a shoe box under your bed or a small home-filing system.

If you want to increase the pleasure you derive from your pictures, you should think about marketing them for editorial use in magazines and books, on calendars, postcards and, most lucrative of all, for advertising.

Making your transparencies work for you not only helps sponsor your hobby financially (photography is certainly not cheap), but encourages you to move forward with your craft in terms of finding and shooting new subjects as well as returning to old ones and shooting them better than the competition.

Using an agency

You really have two choices when selling your images. Market them yourself or get an agent, such as a picture library, to do it on your behalf. Both approaches have their merits. For instance, if you go it alone, you do not have to pay an agency commission. However, such a fee may be a small price to pay for the additional sales that a good agency with a global presence can offer. This is because successful picture libraries have a far wider client base than you are likely to have access to. On the downside, your work will be viewed alongside that of other photographers contributing to the library, meaning your work must be really good to sell. If you are lucky enough to get your work placed in an image library's catalogue, sales will probably be much better. In addition, with an internationally successful library, you may have to work to a much more commercial remit, producing images that have a generic appeal to picture buyers who are often looking for an image that can sell a concept or an ideal. The result of this may be that your work is forced to become less personalized.

By contrast, if you have a special expertise in an area, and choose to photograph aspects of this interest, you may be in a particularly good position to market your own work without an agency's representation. If few other photographers can supply your specialism you will have a nice little niche that you can exploit. Also, if you go it alone, chances are that you can increase your sales potential by putting together words and pictures that complement one another, perhaps in the form of a photo essay. If you do it right, you could make many a magazine editor's day a happy one. I think it is true to say that words and pictures together sell better than either would do on their own.

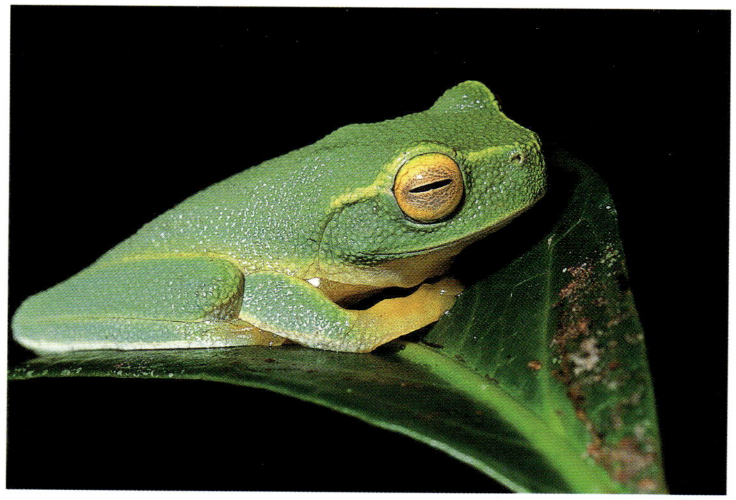

Always be on the lookout for photo opportunities. These minute tree frogs were guests at a small Australian B&B where I stayed. It took but a couple of seconds to take these highly marketable pictures; everyone loves tree frogs. In fact I shot a number of different species.
Both pictures: Pentax Mz5n + 100mm macro lens, off-camera TTL flash.

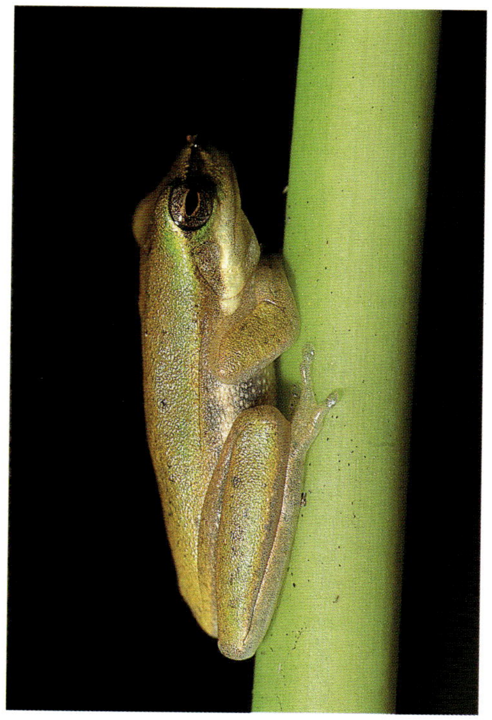

Dos and don'ts

How do you approach the whole issue of speculative submissions? Hopefully, the following tips will be useful in addressing these and other issues facing the budding freelance photographer.

- Only consider submitting slides to magazines. In general, prints are not required (unless you have something very special on offer).
- Research a magazine's picture requirements and style before submitting work.
- Take into account lead times. Most magazines work at least two issues ahead of the current month, so it is best to despatch images that convey a sense of season at the appropriate time of year: for example bluebells in January ready for April, not in April itself, when it will be too late.
- Target the right people within an organization.
- Use the largest film format possible for the subject. For wildlife, 35mm is fine, and is the only truly practical format. However, for certain top-end glossy magazines, medium and large format might well give you the edge, particularly for landscape work.
- Send slides by an insured method of transit. (In the UK, I use Special Delivery.) You should do the same; at the very least send it recorded delivery.
- Never send your slides in glass mounts and never over-pack them. It will only annoy an editor or picture buyer if they impale themselves on a staple or give their finger a palsy removing an excess of sellotape.
- Always include a brief, but lucid cover letter detailing the purpose of the submission.
- Send only your best material. A few good slides are better than many mediocre ones. First impressions are often the ones that count with busy editors. Don't weaken a good portfolio with one or two bad shots.
- Present your slides professionally. Place 35mm slides in transparent A4 wallets. Incorporate medium-format slides in matt black card mounts, which can again be placed in clear A4 wallets that are designed to hold these mounts.
- Don't expect instant results. Your slides can be left on file for up to twelve months – or even longer – before they are used.
- Remember, it is better to have slide submissions back by return post than have them collecting dust in an editor's office for a year, and then have them returned. So, if they come back quickly with a standard rejection slip, don't lose heart – be grateful you can send them off somewhere else tomorrow.
- Keep records of your submissions.
- Label every slide you send out with your name, address and contact number. If you are submitting to a photography magazine include a label with details of the subject and the equipment used to take the picture. If you are submitting to a country, travel or nature magazine, give adequate details on the subject of your picture.
- Send duplicate transparencies only if first rate. If possible, duplicate in camera at the time of the original exposure – the quality will be better, and the cost will likely be less.
- Investigate whether your target publication accepts digital files. More and more publications do. If so, find out how the files must be saved: Mac or PC byte order, file size, colour model (RGB or CMYK), file type (jpeg or tiff), etc.
- Finally, good luck with marketing your work – and have fun!

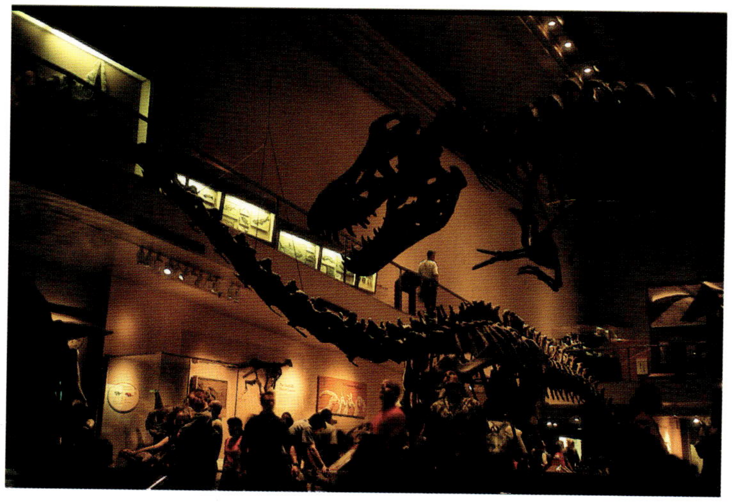

I used a Pentax 90WR compact camera to take this dramatic silhouette of a tyrannosaurus skeleton in the Smithsonian Natural History Museum in Washington DC, USA. The secret was to lean on a rail and switch off the flash. This picture has a 'real life' quality and contains lots of interest.
Pentax 90WR.

Useful publications

When you decide to take your first step into this brave new world, you need to decide who is going to market your work and/or which publications you can speculatively send your pictures to.

- An up-to-date list of all magazine and book publishers along with current photograph libraries and literary agents is published each year by A & C Black entitled *The Writers' and Artists' Year Book*.
- Also useful is a book published by The Bureau of Freelance Photographers entitled *The Freelance Photographer's Market Handbook*. This organization also produces a monthly newsletter which highlights the current needs of many picture buyers.
- In the United States, Writers' Digest produce a parallel tome called *Photographer's Market*.

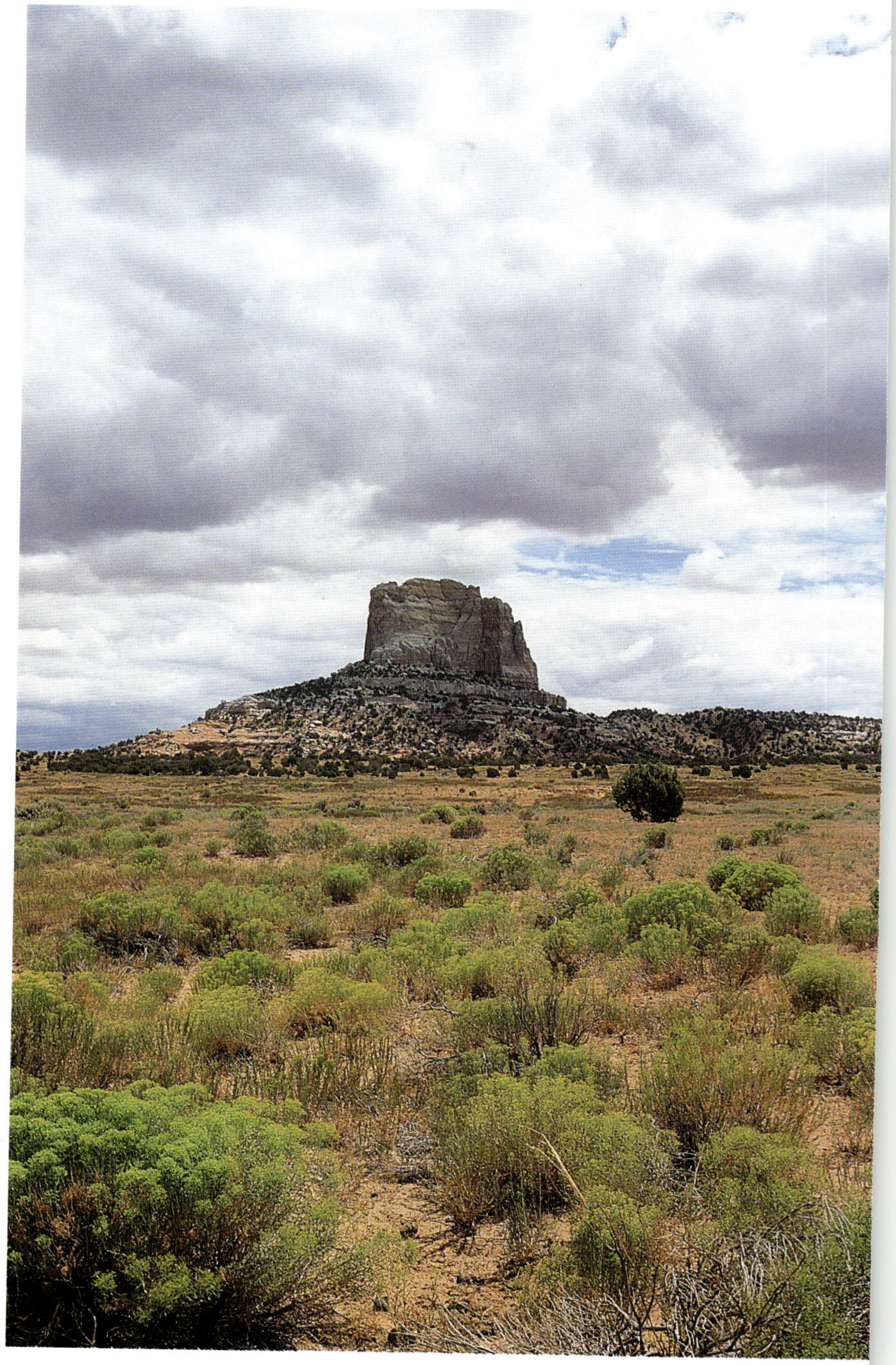

Square Butte, Arizona. I took this shot in portrait as well as landscape format because picture editors prefer to have a choice. This increases my chances of making a sale.
Pentax MZ5n + 28mm lens, Velvia, tripod.

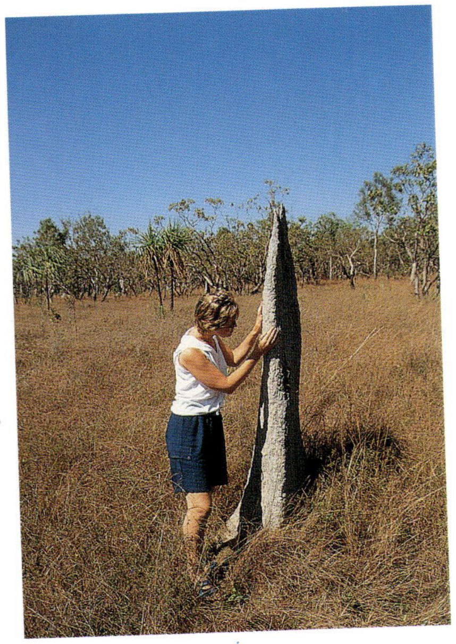

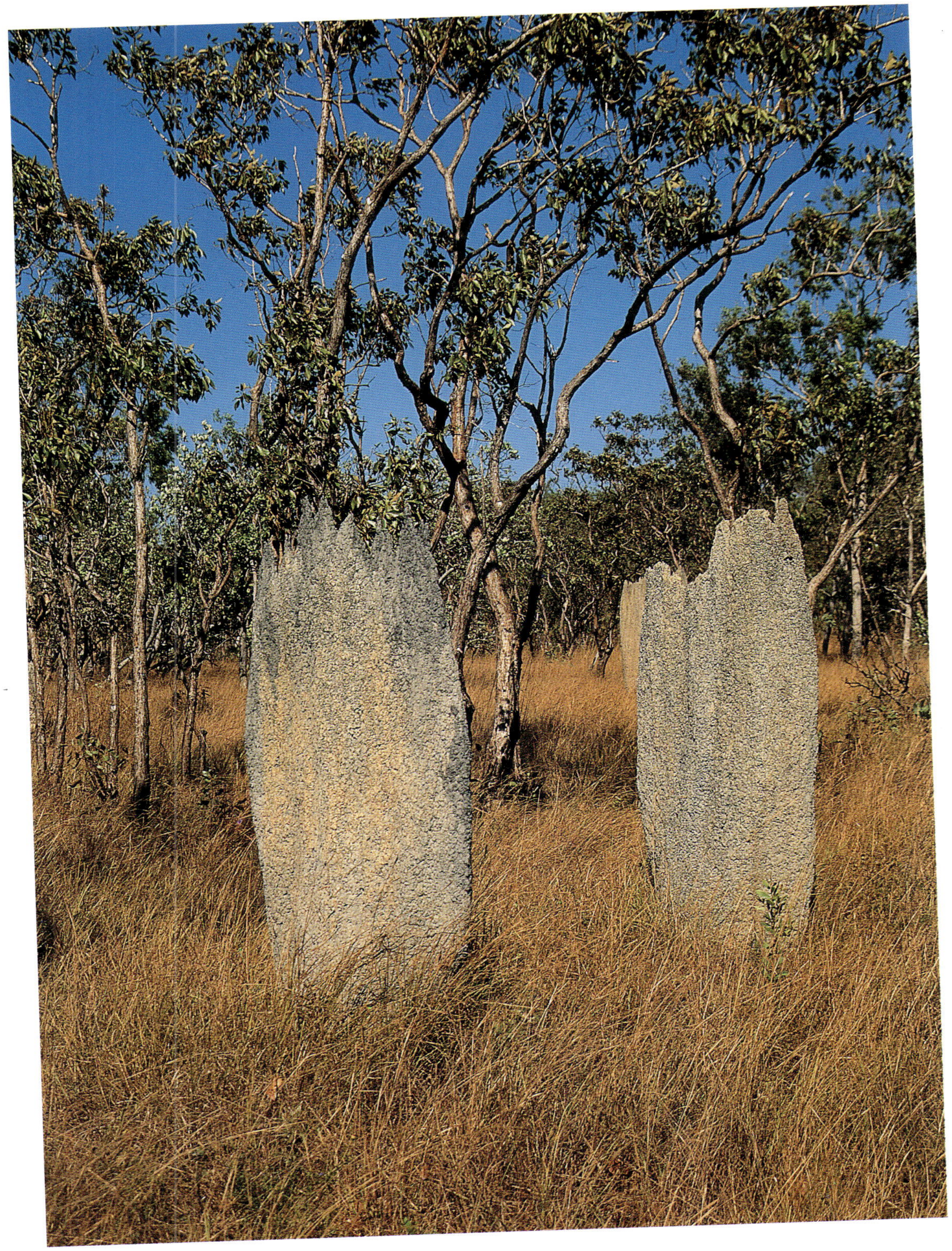

Constantly thinking about potential markets, I shot these two images as both an environmental shot showing rare magnetic termite mounds in their natural setting, and also as a side view to illustrate the principle of how these structures regulate temperature. However, without the human element, it would in itself be an exceptionally boring image because the mounds are, on their own, so thin. The former gives the image both a sense of scale and additional focus, thereby adding to a picture that provides an interesting depiction of termite biology. Litchfield National Park, Northern Territory, Australia. *Pentax MZ5n + 28–70mm zoom lens, Velvia.*

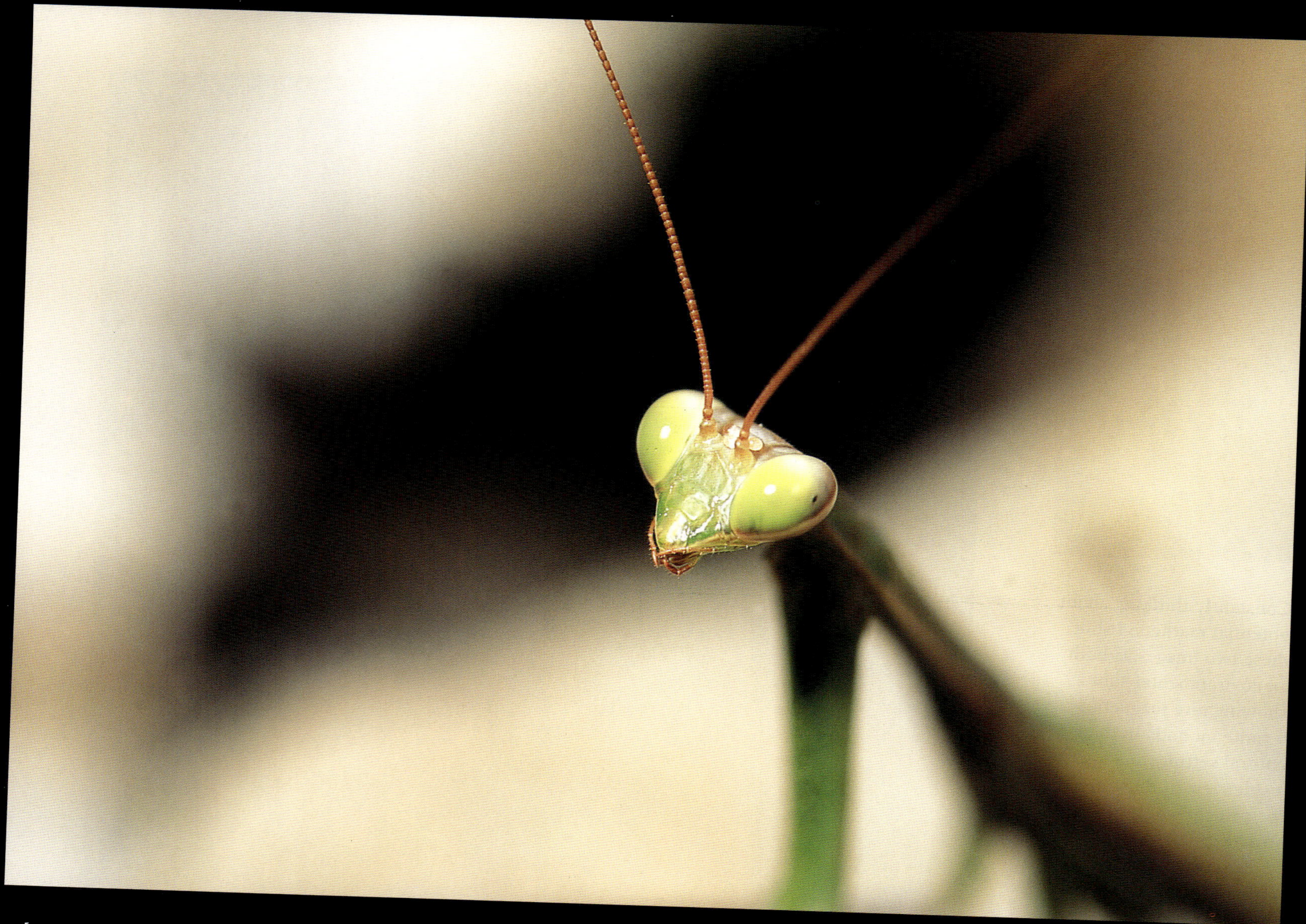

This praying mantis that I took in Turkey is one of my all time favourite images, which, at one time, I used on a card giving my contact details.
Pentax LX + 100mm macro lens, off-camera TTL flash.

Enticing seaside shots that whet the appetite for summer holidays are always in demand. This was taken on Turkey's Mediterranean coast. *Fuji GA645Wi, Velvia, tripod.*

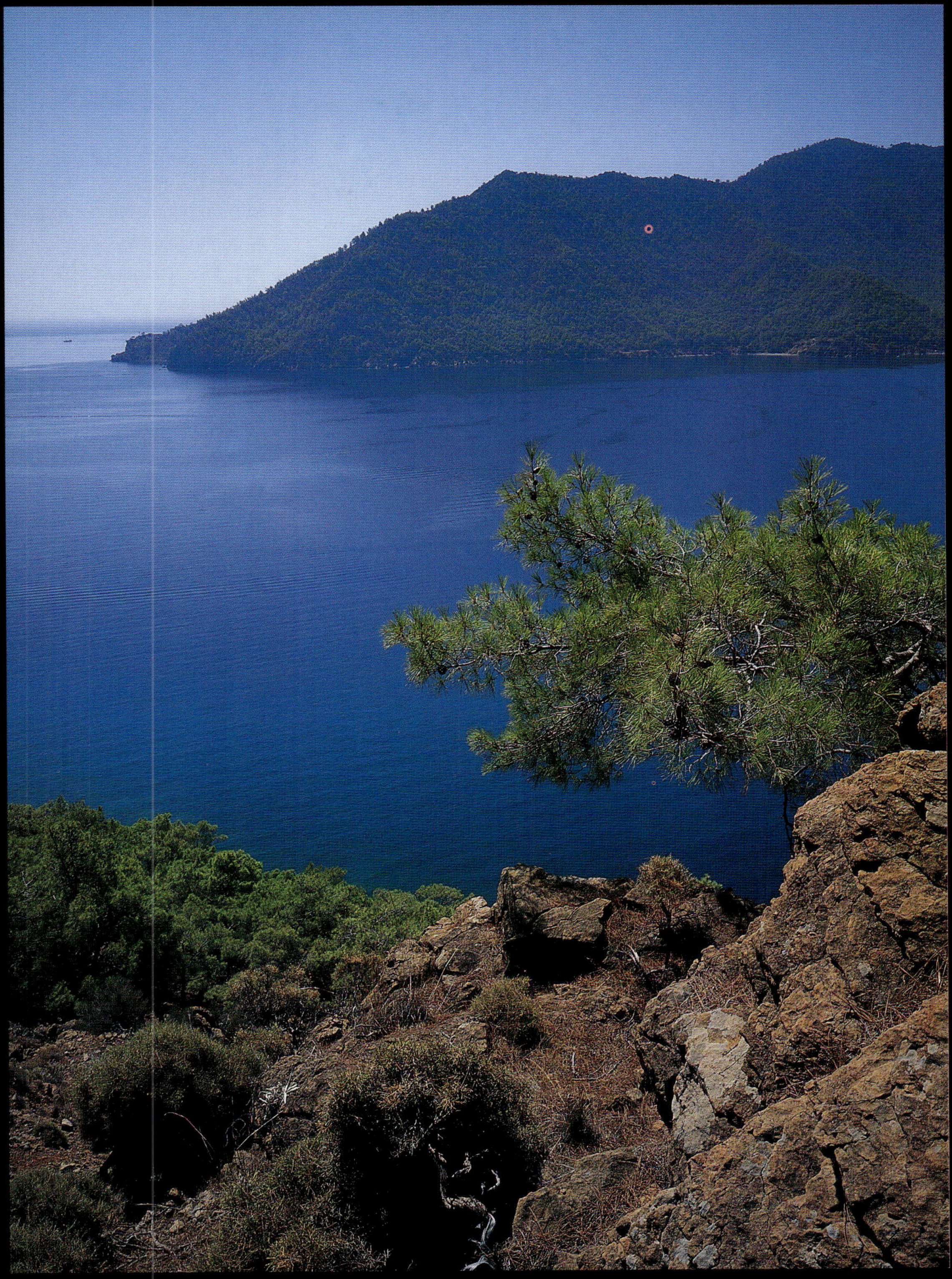

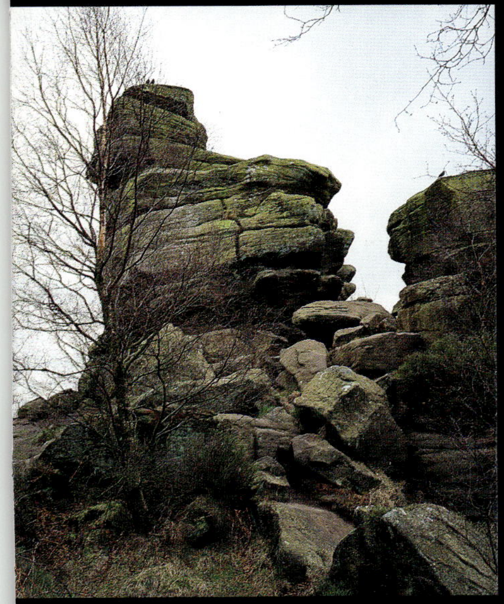

If you have nothing better to do on a cold winter's day, take a drive to local landmarks and shoot a roll of film. You may not have a market in mind at the time, but chances are you will eventually find one as I did for this image of Brimham Rocks near Pately Bridge in North Yorkshire, England. *Mamiya 7II + 65mm lens.*

Sources of useful information

Websites

The Luminous Landscape is a fantastic resource for photographers: http://www.luminous-landscape.com/

Some of my favourite sites by great photographers include:

Peter Adams
http://www.padamsphoto.co.uk

Heather Angel
http://www.naturalvisions.co.uk

Jim Brandenburg
http://www.jimbrandenburg.com/home.html

Laurie Campbell
http://www.lauriecampbell.com

Joe Cornish
http://www.joecornish.com

Peter Dombrovskis
http://www.view.com.au/dombrovskis/index.htm

Jack Dykinga
http://www.dykinga.com/start.html

Michael Fatali
http://www.fatali.com

Jeff Gnass
http://www.jeffgnass.com/jeffgnass/home/home.cfm

Michael Hardeman
http://www.michaelhardeman.com

Peter Jarver
http://www.thunder.com.au

Frans Lanting
http://www.lanting.com

Peter Lik
http://www.peterlik.com

Tom Mackie
http://www.tommackie.com

Joe McDonald
http://www.hoothollow.com

Thomas D Mangelson
http://www.imagesofnature.com

David Muench
http://muenchphotography.com

Edmund Nagele
http://www.nagele.co.uk/index1.htm

William Neill
http://www.WilliamNeill.com

David Noton
http://www.davidnoton.com

Graeme Peacock
http://www.graeme-peacock.com

Galen Rowell
http://www.mountainlight.com

Tom Till
http://www.tomtill.com

Charlie Waite
http://www.charliewaite.com

My apologies to all those great photographers whose sites I have yet to learn of, or which are not yet online.

The best source of information on the most suitable outlets for your photography in the UK is the annual *Freelance Photographer's Market Handbook* (Bureau of Freelance Photographers, Focus House, 497 Green Lanes, London N13 4BP). It cross-references a variety of photographic subjects and their possible markets and gives a comprehensive listing of agents, calendar, card, book and magazine publishers. I can also recommend *The Writers' and Artists' Yearbook* (A&C Black, London) and the *Photographers' Market* (Writers Digest Books, Cincinnati, USA).

There are also regular newsletters to which you can subscribe for making money from your photography. I subscribe to the *Market Newsletter*, which is also produced by the Bureau of Freelance Photographers in London.

The professional lab I use for all my photographic requirements is CC Imaging Ltd, 39 Belle Vue Road, Leeds LS3 1ES, England. Telephone 0113 2330024. Their service is truly excellent.

Finally, there are various computer programmes available for captioning slides. The one I use is Cradoc Caption Writer (Iris Audio Visual, telephone 0208 500 2846), which has proved to be an excellent product.

Bibliography

Identification guides

There are a number of good identification guides available.

Style-led landscape photography books

The following recent publications are guaranteed to inspire:

Rainforest – Ancient Realm of the Pacific Northwest by Graham Osborne (Greystone Books, Douglas & McIntyre Ltd, Vancouver, 1998).

Stone Canyons of the Colorado Plateau by Jack Dykinga (Harry N. Abrams, New York, 2001).

Colorado – Lost Places and Forgotten Words by John Fielder (Westcliffe Publishers Inc., Englewood, 1989).

Scotland: The Wild Places by Colin Prior (Constable Robinson, London, 2001).

Desert by Janice Emily Bowers and Jack W Dykinga (Photographer) (Harry N Abrams, New York, 1999).

The Sonoran Desert by Charles Bowden and Jack W Dykinga (Photographer) (Harry N Abrams, New York, 1992).

The Secret Life of an Oakwood by Stephen Dalton (Photographer) and Jill Bailey (Ebury Press, London, 1991)

Vanishing Paradise by Andrew Mitchell and Stephen Dalton (Ebury Press, London, 1990)

At the Water's Edge by Stephen Dalton (Ebury Press, London, 1989)

Galen Rowell's Inner Game of Outdoor Photography by Galen Rowell (W W Norton, New York, 2001)

Instructional view-camera books

If you want further information on how to use a view camera, I consider the following two books as among the best available:

Large Format Nature Photography by Jack Dykinga (Amphoto Books, New York, 2001)

Using the View Camera by Steve Simmons (Amphoto Books, New York 1992)

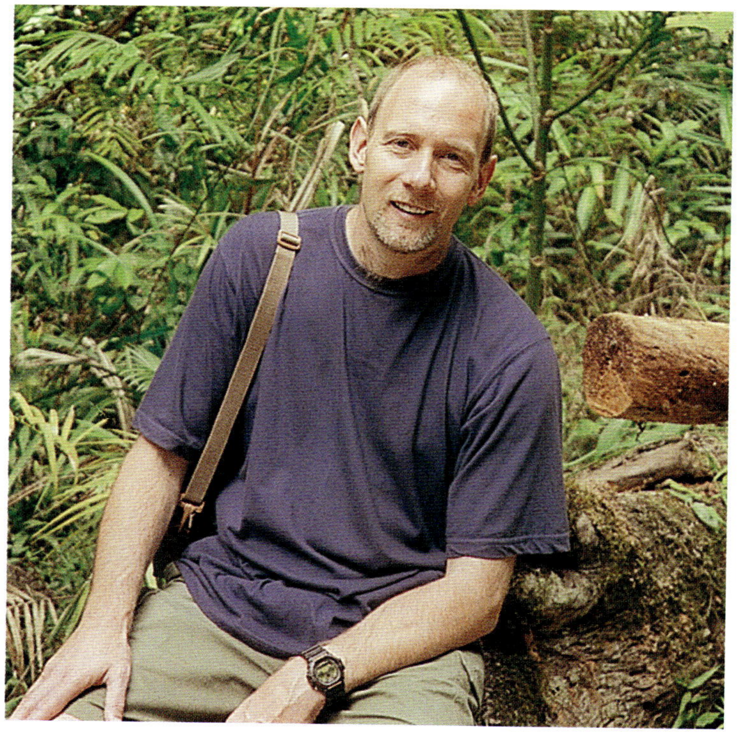

About the author

Mark Lucock is a professional biologist. After graduating from university in 1983 with a degree in Applied Biology, he obtained his PhD in 1991. Today, Mark carries out research at the University of Leeds in England, is a Fellow of the Institute of Biology and a Chartered Biologist. In his spare time he photographs the natural world. His work features a wide range of destinations – including Britain, the United States, India, the Mediterranean and Australia – and reflects the broad spectrum of nature around the world.

Mark has had many publications in the popular press, including illustrated nature articles in both magazines and books. This is his second title with GMC Publications, following *Photography for the Naturalist*. He says he is only truly happy when he has a camera and is in the middle of a remote wilderness, stalking an elusive creature or capturing an ephemeral vista.

A

B

C

D

E

M

N

O

P

R

S